Party Politics
and Elections
in Latin America

About the Book and Authors

Latin America has one of the longest histories of active party politics and elections of any region in the world, yet the experiences there have been very different from those of Western Europe and the United States. In Latin America, party politics has produced governments ranging from democratic to authoritarian, with considerable variations among nations as well as fluctuations within countries over time.

This text provides a comprehensive comparative review of party politics in each Latin American country. The evolution of specific parties is examined, and special emphasis is given to the behavioral aspects of voting patterns and party affiliation. In addition, Drs. McDonald and Ruhl discuss each country's distinctive patterns of organizing and holding elections, including the laws and procedures that regulate them. Finally, the authors identify the general experiences the countries share, especially the long-term impact of sustained modernization on national party politics. The book provides students with a general framework for interpreting party politics in individual countries and for understanding how politics is linked to Latin America's economic development, democracy, and political stability.

Ronald H. McDonald is professor of political science at the Maxwell School of Syracuse University. **J. Mark Ruhl** is professor of political science at Dickinson College.

Party Politics and Elections in Latin America

Ronald H. McDonald
SYRACUSE UNIVERSITY

J. Mark Ruhl
DICKINSON COLLEGE

Westview Press
BOULDER, SAN FRANCISCO, & LONDON

Copyright © 1989 by Westview Press, Inc.

Published in 1989 in the United States of America by Westview Press, Inc., 5500 Central Avenue, Boulder, Colorado 80301, and in the United Kingdom by Westview Press, Inc., 13 Brunswick Centre, London WC1N 1AF, England

Library of Congress Cataloging-in-Publication Data
McDonald, Ronald H., 1935–
  Party politics and elections in Latin America.
  Includes index.
  1. Political parties—Latin America. 2. Elections—
Latin America. 3. Public opinion—Latin America.
I. Ruhl, J. Mark, 1948–   . II. Title.
JL969.A45M37 1989   324.28   87-14278
ISBN 0-8133-0431-8
ISBN 0-8133-0483-0 (pbk.)

Printed and bound in the United States of America

  The paper used in this publication meets the requirements of the American National
  Standard for Permanence of Paper for Printed Library Materials Z39.48-1984.

10   9   8   7   6   5   4   3   2   1

To Shirley
and to Michael and Martin

Contents

Preface

This book is an introduction to party politics, elections, and electoral behavior in Latin America. The subject is vast and the available research on it extensive. Our principal purpose is to summarize and conceptualize the subject, making comparisons where appropriate among nations. We try to point out both the specific, parochial experiences of individual Latin American nations as well as the more universal experiences.

We have explicitly limited our focus to political parties and elections, but there are some subjects pertaining to them that we have intentionally excluded. We are not concerned, for example, with revolutionary organizations or guerrilla movements that have not engaged in electoral activity, even though they may term themselves political parties. Neither do we analyze in depth the development of political ideologies, except as they become important in electoral contexts. These subjects have been thoroughly discussed elsewhere, and we do not feel they are sufficiently relevant to our objectives for inclusion here. We have tried to give weight to political parties and elections with regard to their importance, prominence, and endurance and to countries according to the political significance of their parties and elections: party politics and elections are more complex, part of a longer heritage, and simply more relevant for generally understanding politics in some countries than in others.

We have attempted, in addition, to avoid imposing ideological or political frameworks on our analysis. It is not our intention to pass judgment on the morality or desirability of specific political parties but rather to assess their political evolution, activities, successes, and failures. Our primary tasks are description and explanation. We leave the right and the responsibility for passing judgment on Latin American political parties to those who must live with them.

Neither is this book designed as a "general theory" of Latin American party politics. Our limited objective is to summarize each country's experience with parties and elections, provide what we trust is a reasonable and coherent interpretation of that experience, and summarize some of our recurrent findings. The analytic terms and concepts we employ are discussed either in the first chapter or as they are introduced in the text.

Our book is intended primarily for those with some background either in political science or Latin American studies, although we assume the references and concepts we employ are sufficiently clear to be accessible to the general reader. The book is not an introductory text on Latin American politics. There are many subjects beyond our scope that would be appropriate for a general introduction. Instead, our effort should supplement general texts by providing greater detail and depth on what we consider to be an essential, interesting, and important aspect of Latin American politics. We have tried to include election results through the time of our writing and expect that subsequent elections will be generally consistent with the long-term trends we identify. Party politics is regularly interrupted in some nations by military coups and repression. Such interruptions are inevitable, but they should not alter the fundamental political analysis presented here.

Our country chapters are divided along similar lines, and similar questions are raised in each. The organization of these chapters, however, varies in response to the realities of the different countries, in recognition of the fact that not all the questions we raise are equally important in all nations. McDonald took primary responsibility for the chapters on Paraguay, Uruguay, Venezuela, Argentina, Chile, Bolivia, Brazil, Ecuador, and the Dominican Republic and for the Conclusion; Ruhl was responsible for the Introduction and the chapters on Cuba, Nicaragua, Mexico, Colombia, Honduras, Costa Rica, Peru, Panama, Guatemala, and El Salvador. English names are used for parties throughout the book along with their Spanish or Portuguese acronyms, and a glossary with their Spanish or Portuguese names is provided for those we discuss. We urge those interested in pursuing the subject further to consult the references provided at the end of each chapter.

The quality and quantity of research on Latin American political parties and elections have increased enormously over the past generation, although there are still gaps and inconsistencies in the research and important questions for which there is little evidence or analysis (e.g., the role of women in party politics). Attention to individual countries has been uneven, and research priorities sometimes seem determined by current events. Countries that experience revolutions, political instability, or reformist regimes tend to receive greater attention, and party politics and elections, perhaps more understandably, are studied when civilian governments prevail but are often ignored when military governments replace them. We believe the failures and problems of and impediments to party politics and elections are as important as their successes, and we try to demonstrate this in our analysis.

We have surveyed for this book 19 countries, more than 365 political parties, hundreds of elections (285 have been held since 1946 alone), and countless political leaders. We have reviewed parties, elections, and politicians that, in our view, have been of lasting importance to the countries involved and that illustrate our major analytic themes. Notwithstanding our best efforts and the efforts of those who have kindly read our manuscript, errors will undoubtedly remain. We encourage readers who find errors to write to us so that we can make corrections in future editions.

Many individuals have been of assistance to us in preparing this manuscript. We wish to express our special thanks to John Martz, Robert Dix, William LeoGrande, Enrique Baloyra, John Booth, Steve Ropp, John Peeler, Yaw Akuoko, Vickie Kuhn, Sandra Woy-Hazelton, Gary Hoskin, Kim Fryling, Kristin McCarthy, Shirley Hall, Neale Pearson, June Dumas, Judith Jablonski, and Martha Leggett. Errors of fact or judgment are, of course, our responsibility alone.

Ronald H. McDonald
J. Mark Ruhl

1

INTRODUCTION
Conceptualizing Party Politics in Latin America

In the 1970s, the great majority of Latin Americans lived under military dictatorships. Only in the handful of civilian-ruled countries did political parties and electoral politics receive the attention of academics or journalists. The redemocratization process of the 1980s, however, has dramatically refocused attention on competitive elections and party politics throughout the region. With the reestablishment of civilian governments in Argentina, Brazil, Uruguay, and many other countries, parties have reemerged as subjects of central concern to analysts of Latin American politics (O'Donnell and Schmitter, 1986:57; Drake and Silva, 1986). Accordingly, academic research on Latin American parties and elections, which had stagnated after a promising beginning, now shows healthy signs of renewed activity.[1]

The Significance of Party Politics in Latin America

Although the importance of party politics has increased during the 1980s, the recent proliferation of elections should not lead us to exaggerate the role of political parties. The significance of parties in the political process varies widely in Latin America, and in only a few countries such as Venezuela or Costa Rica have these institutions become as politically influential as their counterparts in Western Europe or the United States. In the majority of Latin American nations, the armed forces, not the parties, remain the most powerful political actors. In addition, many key foreign and domestic private-sector groups continue to bypass party politics in favor of more direct governmental contacts. In fact, in some parts of the region, parties

1

TABLE 1.1
Political Significance of Party Politics in Latin America:
Country Comparisons, 1968-1988

Category one: Parties as dominant actors

    Costa Rica   Venezuela
    Colombia   Mexico

Category two: Parties as primary but non-dominant actors

    Argentina   Cuba
    Brazil   Nicaragua
    Chile   Dominican Republic
    Uruguay

Category three: Parties as secondary actors

    Peru   Honduras
    Ecuador   Guatemala
    El Salvador   Bolivia

Category four: Parties as marginal actors

    Paraguay   Haiti
    Panama

still are relegated to peripheral roles even during periods when elections are permitted.

Nonetheless, the current redemocratization underscores some of the reasons that political parties remain important in Latin America in spite of the military's power. Parties are an indispensable element of competitive electoral politics, and the popular enthusiasm that has greeted redemocratization reaffirms that political legitimacy is inextricably bound to democratic elections in the Americas (Rouquie, 1986:120). Because they lack legitimacy, military regimes generally are viewed as "temporary," regardless of how long they endure or how many plebiscites they stage. Sooner or later, when the armed forces restore free elections, parties invariably reemerge even in countries in which they have been persecuted. Indeed, their durability and lasting popular appeal suggest that parties are a more salient feature of the Latin American political landscape then many observers have previously recognized.

Over time, the importance of party politics has fluctuated within Latin America as a whole and within each nation in the region. Table 1.1 offers a subjective ranking of Latin American party systems in terms of their political significance from 1968 to 1988. During this period, parties have been consistently dominant political actors in Costa Rica, Colombia, Venezuela, and Mexico. In each of these four countries in category one, national politics has clearly revolved around the civilian parties. In four of the seven nations in the next and largest category (Argentina, Brazil, Chile, Uruguay), parties also traditionally have played central roles; however, in each of these countries, the military has frequently suspended party activities. In the Dominican Republic, too, where parties have become politically relevant only since the late 1960s, the army remains powerful. Cuba and Nicaragua also fall in category two (not the first one, where they belong today) because (1) the Cuban Communist party has only lately assumed a major role after many years of less-institutionalized revolutionary politics, and (2) parties did not figure prominently in Nicaragua until the Sandinista National Liberation Front (FSLN) came to power in 1979.

Six Latin American countries (Peru, Ecuador, El Salvador, Honduras, Guatemala, Bolivia) are in the third category—nations in which parties generally have been actors of secondary importance even when the government has not been under formal military control. At present, political parties are cautiously attempting to enlarge their influence in nearly all of these nations, but the armed forces remain dominant. Finally, the fourth category encompasses the three nations in which parties have been of least consequence since the late 1960s: Paraguay, the area's last personalist dictatorship, military-controlled Panama, and traditionally partyless Haiti.[2]

The tentative rankings in Table 1.1 indicate that parties are more significant political actors in nations where democratic elections have become entrenched (Costa Rica, Colombia, Venezuela) than in countries where authoritarian military rule has always been the norm (El Salvador, Guatemala, Bolivia). As Huntington (1968:408–409) has observed, the significance of the party system is closely associated with the subordination of the military to civil authority. But, as we can see in Table 1.1, the association is an imperfect one. Authoritarian Mexico falls in category one because of the centrality of the ruling Institutional Revolutionary party (PRI), and Communist Cuba merits a similar ranking now that its vanguard party has gained ascendancy. Political parties can obviously play dominant roles in democratic and nondemocratic contexts.[3]

The Functions of Latin American Political Parties

The best way to evaluate the significance of parties is to examine their specific functions. Political parties, defined simply as groups that seek to elect officeholders under a given label (Epstein, 1967:9), vary radically in function depending on the political system they inhabit and their relative strength within it. Only a few of the more than 125 parties active in Latin America today play all of the roles attributed to them in the general theoretical literature—literature that is based on Western European and Anglo-American systems in which military obedience and legislative power are taken for granted (Duverger, 1954; Key, 1964; Epstein, 1967; Lipset and Rokkan, 1967; Sartori, 1976; Sorauf, 1984).[4] Nevertheless, parties are an essential component of Latin America's electoral process and perform a variety of other functions, the most important of which include political recruitment, political communications, social control, and government organization/policymaking.

Political Recruitment

Parties have always played a major part in integrating potential leaders, political activists, and newly relevant social groups into Latin American politics (Chalmers, 1972:123–124). Most of Latin America's contemporary leaders, such as Alan García (Peru), José Sarney (Brazil), and Raúl Alfonsín (Argentina), entered political life through partisan channels. Ambitious individuals who seek government positions and the benefits of having influence in the public sector are attracted to parties because these organizations usually control patronage and nominations to public office. Other citizens with strong political opinions join parties in hopes of affecting policy outcomes.

Political Communication

Parties are valuable intermediaries between elites and mass publics in Latin America. In electoral campaigns, competing party elites present their views to the mass electorate and mobilize voter support. Even though the typical Latin American election campaign involves more slander than policy analysis, some political education and political socialization do occur. Campaigns can also produce increased social mobilization[5] and popular demands for government action.

Party leaders try to manipulate public opinion and to channel political participation to suit their own designs. But in their drive to capture votes, they also adapt party platforms to reflect popular attitudes. To the degree that democratic practices are present, elites are compelled to respond at least rhetorically to the concerns of the public. In addition, for citizens unalterably opposed to the existing government, parties provide an outlet for expressing their dissatisfaction with elite policies.

Social Control

Parties have regularly been employed as instruments of social control. Today this function is most evident in Communist Cuba where the ruling party is responsible for indoctrinating and regimenting the mass population. To a lesser extent, the official parties of conservative authoritarian governments have also sought to enforce mass compliance with the directives of the regime. Of course, official parties of whatever stripe rely on co-optation as well as coercion. Mexico's centrist Institutional Revolutionary party (PRI) has long been recognized for its success in aggregating diverse interests through co-optation. In addition, O'Donnell and Schmitter (1986:58) point out that parties also act as instruments of social control in many of the nations now experiencing redemocratization because party leaders restrain their followers' demands in order to prevent renewed military intervention.

Government Organization and Policymaking

Under military governments, parties generally have little to do with policy formation unless they are explicit allies of those who have seized control. Civil-military cabinets are quite common, but in recent years civilian officials have tended to be nonpartisan technocrats drawn from the private sector or the state bureaucracy. Conversely, when formal governmental authority rests with elected civilians, the armed forces tend to retain substantial influence over policy.

Except in a handful of Latin American nations, parties do not dominate the policymaking process as they do in Western Europe. Latin American parties do not represent all of the powerful groups in society, and party resources for influencing government decisions (votes, mass demonstrations) are limited compared with those of their rivals (Chalmers, 1972:120–121). Still, democratic elections do increase the role of parties in policymaking because they place partisan politicians in the presidency, the legislature, and in much of the bureaucracy.

Only a few Latin American parties have developed the coherent programs and organizational strength necessary for party government on a Western European model. Yet, when in power, most Latin American parties do play important roles in enhancing the chief executives' ability to implement their policies. In contrast, opposition parties play only a marginal role in policy formation because of the enduring tradition of executive dominance in most of Latin America.

Origins and Common Characteristics

It is difficult to offer generalizations about Latin American political parties because they vary so widely in origins, ideology, organization, and mass support. According to Charles Anderson (1967), Latin America is a "living museum" that contains exhibits of nearly every type of party that has ever emerged there.

Once Latin American countries became independent, rival aristocratic elites in different countries created informal political groups that gradually evolved into competing Liberal and Conservative parties by the mid-nineteenth century. Influenced by political thought in France, Britain, and the United States, Liberals often adopted these more modern nations as models. Liberal intellectuals commonly promoted the separation of church and state, the federalism, and the free-trade economics that they admired abroad. In contrast, Conservatives remained loyal to Spanish authoritarian traditions and fought to preserve the Catholic church's privileged status as well as a centralized state with strong economic controls. Most of the Liberal and Conservative parties of the past century have disappeared, along with the issues that divided them. A few of these old parties, however, have maintained their influence. They continue to dominate electoral politics in both Colombia and Honduras, and vestiges of Liberal or Conservative parties still compete in Nicaraguan politics.

In the late nineteenth and early twentieth centuries, a modernized, urban middle class began to enter politics. It formed the principal base of support for new reformist parties that drew on European liberalism. Advocating universal male suffrage, educational reform, and liberal democracy against military rule, these parties became significant actors first in the Southern Cone and later in other parts of Latin America. The Chilean Radical party was the first of such parties, but the Argentine Radical Civic Union and Uruguayan Colorados became the most influential. Having extended their appeal to some working-class elements, these latter two parties remain key political players to this day.

By World War I, parties based on Marxist revolutionary principles were active in Argentina, Cuba, Brazil, and Mexico (sometimes in competition with anarcho-syndicalists). But Latin American socialism was soon disrupted by the factionalization of the world socialist movement that followed the Bolshevik Revolution in 1917. Although severely repressed, the Communist parties that emerged in the 1920s became the most important of the hemisphere's Marxist parties for many decades. Notwithstanding the fact that orthodox, pro-Soviet parties acquired influence over organized labor and even won some legislative seats, Communists never attained government control except as junior partners in a small number of multiparty coalitions (Chile, Costa Rica). Although the Communists eclipsed the few right-wing parties that adopted European fascism (e.g., Brazil's Integralistas) in the 1930s, the small size of the industrial proletariat and internal divisions caused by further international Communist schisms (e.g., Trotskyism) proved to be permanent obstacles to party expansion.

After 1945 many revolutionaries who were attracted to Marxism organized new political groups outside of the staid and dogmatic Communist parties. The triumph of Marxist guerrilla leader Fidel Castro in Cuba in 1959 convinced many other radicals to follow his independent example, but the movements they formed were fraught with ideological and personalist divisions. By the late 1980s, Latin American Marxism had spawned a bewildering variety of parties, factions, and guerrilla organizations. Marxist parties are in power in Cuba and Nicaragua, and a Marxist coalition constitutes a major electoral force in Peru. Elsewhere, Marxist political groups play only minor roles in electoral politics because they (1) enjoy only modest popular support (Argentina); (2) are suppressed (Chile); or (3) are involved in guerrilla movements seeking the violent overthrow of the existing government (El Salvador).

As Latin American electorates swelled to include new social strata, a great many indigenous nationalist/populist parties appeared between the 1920s and 1950s,[6] inhibiting the growth of Marxist parties. Beginning with Victor Haya de la Torre's American Popular Revolutionary Alliance (APRA) in 1927, these homegrown parties used platforms combining nationalism with state-directed socioeconomic reform to draw multiclass followings. Social democratic parties inspired by Peru's Apristas arose in many countries, too (Cuba's Auténticos, Guatemala's Revolutionary party, Paraguay's Febreristas), and have persisted as dominant parties in such democracies as Venezuela (Democratic Action) and Costa Rica (Liberación). Other indigenous parties less committed to liberal democratic principles, such as the authoritarian PRI, which emerged from the Mexican Revolution, have also employed the dual appeal of nationalism and populism to mobilize voters. Similar in some respects (authoritarianism, nationalism, populism) were the urban, popular-sector-based personalist parties founded by Getúlio Vargas in Brazil and Juan Perón in Argentina, although these parties showed less interest in the peasantry than the Aprista party or the PRI. Nearly all of the nationalist/popular parties have since diluted their once fiery political platforms, yet they retain substantial support.

Finally, many party systems also encompass the reformist Christian Democrats, which draw their inspiration from progressive Catholic social doctrines. Like the Apristas, these Social Christian parties have tried to attract both middle- and lower-class voters with moderate reform programs promising benefits to urban and rural sectors alike. Since the 1960s, Christian Democracy has become particularly influential in Chile, Venezuela, El Salvador, and Guatemala. Radical Christians, however, have rejected these mainstream parties and formed alliances with Marxists.

In spite of their many historical and ideological differences, Latin American parties do seem to share some important characteristics. Like most electoral organizations everywhere, Latin American parties tend to be highly elitist and plagued by factionalism. Unlike Western European parties, though, most of the parties of South and Central America are also characterized by personalism, organizational weakness, and heterogeneous, as opposed to class-based, mass support (Martz, 1980:147). Moreover, these five basic characteristics do not appear to be linked to any particular level of socioeconomic development; they are as common in modern Argentina as in backward Honduras (Chalmers, 1972:103).

Elitism

Latin American parties, whether purely personalist or fairly institutionalized, tend to be elitist with respect to internal decisionmaking. Party policy and candidate selection are usually decided by a small group of party chieftains. Whatever the party's location on the ideological spectrum, most of its leaders are drawn from the middle and upper-middle classes. Some parties give the appearance of greater rank-and-file participation in decisionmaking by providing for internal party primaries, but these contests are frequently manipulated.

Factionalism

Factionalism is an endemic problem. Unless a single leader is strong enough to eliminate potential rivals, parties become divided by competing ambitions and personalist cliques. APRA was a unified political force for as long as the charismatic Haya de la Torre lived, but after his death, the party split into warring factions. Factions also arise over ideological or policy disputes. For example, within the Colombian Liberal party, progressives have frequently led reformist factions against factions sponsored by the party hierarchy. In many cases, personalist and policy-based factions overlap, and generational divisions within a party can sometimes complicate matters even further. Under these circumstances, it is not surprising that party discipline has proved elusive in Latin America and that dissident factions often break away to form new parties.

Personalism

Latin American parties tend to be organized around personalities rather than ideologies.[7] Indeed, many important parties are little more than electoral vehicles for ambitious politicians who have no scruples about changing their party's stances on short notice. The list of such parties is endless. Some of the more famous examples include Perón's Peronistas (Argentina), Arnulfo Arias's Panameñistas (Panama), and José María Velasco Ibarra's Velasquistas (Ecuador). The roots of personalism lie deep in Latin American political culture and stretch back into the caudillo politics of the postindependence period and beyond. Mass identification has always been more easily achieved with powerful individuals than with abstract party symbols and doctrines. Most Latin American parties, in fact—even those as highly institutionalized as Mexico's PRI—are composed of competing personalist networks.

Organizational Weakness

A number of parties in Latin America possess elaborate organizational structures; strong, multifunctional grass-roots organizations; and large numbers of permanent members. Peru's APRA, Mexico's PRI, Venezuela's AD, and both of the major Uruguayan parties, for example, are all highly institutionalized mass parties, each of which maintains an extensive, permanent party apparatus.[8]

Notwithstanding this, most Latin American parties are weakly organized institutions that come alive only at election time. Many of these groups approximate what Duverger (1954) has called "cadre parties," loose aggregations of notables with only skeletal organizations, no real ties to interest groups or the grass roots, and few card-carrying members. Although they, too, lack the strong organizational structures that characterize genuine mass parties, the traditional parties of Colombia and Honduras, like U.S. parties, appear to fall into a category between mass and cadre parties because of the broad, hereditary mass-party identification that sustains them. Such strong party identification, however, is unusual in Latin America.

Heterogeneous Mass Support

The majority of Western European parties have traditionally had fairly clear class characteristics. However, in Latin America, where labor unions and other class-based organizations have been slow to develop, most parties have multiclass support. Mexico's PRI, the traditional parties of Colombia and Honduras, and the Uruguayan Colorado party are some of the most obvious examples of parties with heterogeneous mass support. Even in Chile, which is known for class-based politics, the Christian Democrats have attracted a socially diverse following. Chile's Communists, in contrast—like Peru's United Left (IU) and Brazil's Worker's party (PT)—are exceptions to the Latin American norm because of their base of support in the lower classes. Chalmers (1972:126) argues that the heterogeneous character of Latin American parties makes them especially adept at absorbing new social groups.

It is sometimes easier to describe the mass bases of Latin American parties in terms of region rather than class. In many countries during the nineteenth century, warring Liberal and Conservative parties developed definite regional strongholds. Today, a number of parties in the Americas are tied to particular geographical regions, and regional voting patterns are pronounced in such nations as Colombia, Uruguay, Honduras, and Peru. Regionalism in voting, however, is not common in all of Latin America; Chilean voting returns, for example, do not reveal strong ties between parties and regions.

Party Systems

Political party systems have traditionally been classified as one-party, two-party, or multiparty. A larger number of parties indicates a wider dispersion of power as well as greater complexity in interparty relationships, party tactics, and coalition behavior (Sartori, 1976:120–121; Martz, 1980:150). Many theorists (Blondel, 1968; Sartori, 1976) have developed variations on this simple ordinal classification scheme by dividing one or more of the basic categories into subtypes, but there is no generally accepted typology. In light of the difficulty of making clear distinctions among categories, other scholars (Powell, 1981:865) have preferred to use statistical indices that assess the degree of party-system fragmentation on a more precise interval scale and that account for both the number of parties in a system and their relative sizes.[9] Douglas Rae's (1967) index of party fractionalization (ranging from .000 for the least-fragmented system [i.e., one party only] to a maximum of 1.00) is the indicator most commonly used for this purpose. In order to distinguish among Latin American party systems, it is helpful to use both simple numerical categories and Rae's quantitative index. The basic categories employed here are discussed below.

The Single-Party System. This is a system in which a single party consistently monopolizes government power. It has three major subtypes:[10] (1) an exclusive single-party system in which only one party is legal (e.g., USSR), (2) a hegemonic single-party system in which peripheral minor parties may exist but only as permitted by the official party (e.g., Poland, Somoza's Nicaragua), and (3) a predominant single-party system in which one party dominates

TABLE 1.2
Latin American Party Systems

Country	Rae Fractionalization Index		1968–1988 Category
Cuba	.000	(1986)	Single party
Mexico	.452	(1985)	Single party
Paraguay	.495	(1988)	Single party
Colombia	.538	(1986)	Two party
Honduras	.538	(1985)	Two party
Costa Rica	.545	(1986)	Emerging two
Nicaragua	.555	(1984)	Single party
Peru	.571	(1985)	Multiparty
Venezuela	.586	(1983)	Emerging two
El Salvador	.591	(1988)	Emerging multi
Argentina	.602	(1987)	Emerging two
Brazil	.635	(1986)	Emerging multi
Guatemala	.664	(1985)	Emerging multi
Uruguay	.665	(1984)	Two party
Dominican Republic	.679	(1986)	Emerging multi
Panama	.683	(1984)	Multiparty
Bolivia	.765	(1985)	Multiparty
Chile	.772	(1973)	Multiparty
Ecuador	.853	(1988)	Emerging multi

Note: Rae Index calculated by author.

the system simply by winning legislative majorities in democratic elections on a consistent basis (e.g., Ulster).

The Two-Party System. This is a competitive party system in which the government always is controlled by one or the other (or a coalition) of two major parties. Although minor parties may also compete, one of the two principal parties normally wins a legislative majority (United States).

The Multiparty System. This competitive system has no consistent pattern of one-party or two-party dominance. None of the several parties in the multiparty system is capable of maintaining a legislative majority and exercising full control of the government for an extended period (Italy).

An application of these categories to Latin America (1968–1988) reveals the great diversity of party systems (see Table 1.2). Cuba is an exclusive single-party system because no parties other than the Cuban Communist party are tolerated. Mexico, Paraguay, and Nicaragua are hegemonic rather than predominant single-party systems because the official party in each of these countries completely controls the rules under which minor parties participate and refuses to share power (although some offices and influence may be permitted to the opposition). In contrast, politics and government in Colombia, Honduras, and Uruguay have traditionally been dominated by two competing parties. It should be noted, however, that the institutionalized factionalism that has characterized parties in Uruguay and, to a lesser extent, in Colombia has led some observers to consider them multiparty systems in disguise (Martz, 1964:517; Sartori, 1976:107). More classic multiparty systems in which several parties compete for power with none able to maintain dominance include Chile, Panama, Bolivia, and Peru. The multiparty system is the most common one in Latin America, as it is in Western Europe.

Most of the nations discussed above have had the same type of party system for many years, but in other countries the number of important parties has fluctuated. Long periods of military rule, for example, interrupt normal party competition and can cause the party system to change.[11] Party systems that had no consistent pattern during the past two decades or are changing from one type of system to another are referred to in this volume as "emerging" systems of one kind or another based on indications from recent electoral results and speculation about long-term trends. Countries that appear to be moving, for example, from a multiparty system to a two-party mode include Argentina, Venezuela, and Costa Rica. At the same time, multiparty systems seem to be more likely to develop in Ecuador, Guatemala, the Dominican Republic, El Salvador, and Brazil. But one should not discount the possibility that one or more of these countries could produce a predominant single-party system in which one party consistently wins legislative majorities, e.g., Brazil.

Latin American party systems are also ranked on Table 1.2 by degree of current (ca. 1986) party-system fragmentation as measured by Rae's fractionalization index, calculated using the most recent distribution of lower house legislative seats in each country.[12] Fractionalization coefficients vary widely from the .000 minimum in Communist Cuba to a high of .853 in Ecuador's highly fragmented multiparty context. As expected, single-party Cuba and Mexico constitute the most concentrated party systems in the Americas with fractionalization levels well below .500 (a coefficient equivalent to a legislature divided exactly evenly between two parties). Colombia, Honduras, Costa Rica, Venezuela, and Argentina, on the other hand, have fractionalization coefficients ranging from .500 to about .600, levels generally representative of two-party systems. Data from the last elections in Paraguay, Nicaragua, Peru, and El Salvador, however, produce misleadingly similar index scores. The apparent fractionalization of the Paraguayan and Nicaraguan systems is artificial given the actual dominance of the ruling parties in those two countries, and the latest electoral results from Peru were very atypical (APRA won its largest vote percentage ever in 1985 but seems unlikely to be able to sustain it). The fractionalization score for El Salvador does not reflect the existence of some important leftist parties that did not participate in elections. All of the other party systems in the region score well over .600 on the fractionalization index, as one would expect of multiparty systems. This last group of countries somewhat surprisingly includes Uruguay because a radical electoral front challenged the dominance of the two traditional parties in the last election.

Students of comparative politics once believed that two-party systems promoted democratic political order, while more fragmented systems encouraged instability. But most scholars have come to reject this hypothesis, noting, for example, the obvious compatibility of multiparty politics and democratic stability in Switzerland, the Netherlands, and elsewhere (Lijphart, 1984:107–114). The Latin American experience with party politics also fails to reveal any clear relationship between the type of party system (or degree of internal party system fragmentation) and democratic political stability. The intensity of interparty hatreds in two-party Colombia, for instance, led to extreme violence during the 1948–1958 era, and the military has ruled two-party Honduras for most of the last three decades. In contrast, multiparty politics coexisted quite comfortably with democracy in Costa Rica and Venezuela for many years. The degree of political polarization in a system, not the number of parties, is a better predictor of instability.[13]

Electoral Systems

Three basic types of electoral systems are employed in Latin America: the plurality system, the runoff-majority system, and proportional representation (PR). In the version of the plurality system most commonly used in Latin America and the United States, the candidate who receives the most votes in a single-member district wins the seat. A plurality system also can be adapted to multimember districts and structured to provide consolation seats to losing parties. A runoff-majority system works much like a single-member-district plurality system, except that a candidate must capture an absolute majority of the votes cast in order to win in the first round. Otherwise, a runoff election is held between the top two finishers in the first round. Proportional representation systems are based on the principle of distributing legislative seats in direct proportion to the shares of the vote won by contending parties.

All Latin American countries have presidential rather than parliamentary systems, and all but the six Central American nations, Ecuador, and Cuba have bicameral legislatures. Most use a plurality or runoff-majority system to elect their president and a PR system to select their national legislature. Simple plurality systems are utilized to choose the presidents in ten countries, the senates of the Dominican Republic and Mexico, and the largest segment of Mexico's Chamber of Deputies. Variations on the basic plurality system, which give two-thirds of the seats in a multimember district to the winning party and one-third to other parties, have been instituted in Bolivia (Senate) and Paraguay. Runoff-majority electoral systems, however, are relatively new to Latin America and are used only in presidential contests. Thus far, six countries (Brazil, Chile, Ecuador, El Salvador, Guatemala, Peru) have adopted runoffs. In Bolivia, the national legislature chooses the president if no candidate secures an absolute majority. Argentina has created an electoral college for presidential elections.

Except for the relatively few exceptions mentioned above and Communist Cuba, all Latin American legislatures are chosen by proportional representation (PR) using some form of "party list" PR system in which voters choose from competing slates of legislative candidates offered by the different parties. The "open party list" format traditionally employed in Chile, which allows voters to indicate their preferences for individual candidates within a party's slate, is not very common elsewhere. Instead, most countries use "closed party list" PR systems, in which voters must accept the hierarchical order of candidates as defined by the party they select. In this system the higher the candidate's placement on the party slate, the more likely he is of election because seats won by the party are distributed from the top down.

The most common mathematical formulas used to translate votes into seats in Latin American PR systems are the d'Hondt system (Ecuador, Costa Rica) and the largest-remainder, or electoral quotient, system (Honduras). Under the d'Hondt system, a party's total vote in each multimember constituency is divided by consecutive divisors (1, 2, 3, etc.), and each party's resulting quotients are arranged in numerically descending order, with seats awarded successively to the party with the highest quotient. Under the largest-remainder system, the total votes cast in a multimember constituency are divided by the total number of seats to be distributed, which produces the electoral quotient, or quota. Seats are then awarded to each party for every multiple of the quota in its total vote. At the end of this process, the seats that remain available are allocated to the parties with the largest remainders of votes after one quota has been subtracted from each party's vote for each seat it has been given.

Duverger (1954) argues that plurality systems based on single-member districts favor the development of two-party politics because of the winner-take-all character of these elections and because voters are naturally reluctant to waste their ballots on small, third parties. Conversely, he reasons that runoff-majority electoral systems, and especially PR systems, facilitate multiparty systems because votes for minor parties still "count" in these contexts. Proportional representation gives small parties a fair share of legislative seats, and a two-step electoral process allows minor parties to demonstrate, in the first round, their value as second-round coalition partners. Riker's (1982) thorough review of the literature finds substantial support for Duverger's views.[14] Unfortunately, it is difficult to evaluate the utility of Duverger's propositions in Latin America because (1) many of the nations in the region use both plurality and PR electoral systems, (2) almost every Latin American nation with competitive elections employs PR to elect at least a portion of its national legislature, and (3) military intervention often disrupts electoral politics.

Even if Duverger's propositions cannot be properly tested, it is obvious that electoral frameworks can affect the structure of party systems in Latin America. One need only consider what would occur in existing party systems if current electoral rules were altered. The full-scale introduction of a PR system in Mexico, for instance, would undermine the dominance of the ruling party. Electoral systems clearly can act as "accelerators or breaks" on party proliferation (Duverger, 1972:19–23), although the actual number of parties in a system is the product of many factors, e.g., tradition, number, and intensity of political cleavages.

Concepts of Voting

According to classic democratic theory, a citizen's ballot should reflect a considered personal choice based on issues and candidate preferences. In Latin America, however, several additional interpretations of voting are also relevant. Characteristic voting patterns include affirmative voting, patron-client voting, protest voting, and ritualistic voting.

Affirmative Voting

Political inertia and a desire not to alienate the powerful lead many Latin Americans to vote for the existing government without really considering the alternatives. Affirmative voting is particularly characteristic of rural areas and undereducated, impoverished sectors of the population. Regimes can also induce affirmative voting through intimidation—perhaps the most common form of electoral manipulation in Latin America. Few political systems in the area are entirely free of affirmative voting, but this type of voting behavior is especially prevalent in dictatorial regimes where elections take on the symbolic function of ratifying the existing authority.

Patron-Client Voting

Voters in most of nineteenth-century Latin America simply followed the dicates of their local rural *patron* without examining the issues or the relative merits of competing candidates. In return, the local boss would dispense favors. Patron-client voting is still quite common in a somewhat modernized form and is not restricted to rural areas. Clientelistic voting, for example, underlies the durability of the traditional parties that continue to dominate the party systems of Colombia and Honduras. The widespread mass partisan identification that characterizes both of these countries originally grew out of patron-client ties.

Protest Voting

Some Latin American voters regularly reject all of the candidates who have a reasonable chance to win in order to cast a ballot in protest against the political system. Protest voters sometimes mark their ballots for parties that represent their views but have no prospects of winning. On other occasions, alienated voters express their opposition by depositing blank or spoiled ballots. This form of protest is most likely to occur when a major party has been banned from electoral competition, as the Peronistas were in the late 1950s. Some citizens, of course, choose to protest by refusing to vote, but it is always difficult to isolate the protest-voting element within any nonvoting population. Studies of nonvoting in countries such as Colombia, which have experienced fairly high abstention rates, have found that most citizens who fail to vote have not abstained out of a sense of alienation. Inconvenience and disinterest appear to explain most nonvoting.

Ritualistic Voting

Finally, some voting is largely ritualistic because elections have become a major national holiday in many Latin American countries, a day to celebrate with friends and family, to drink, to wave flags, to get into fights, and in a rather vague sense exercise one's obligations to the national community. That election day is recognized as a day of national obligation is indicated by the fact that voting is compulsory in most of the region, even though penalties for abstention are seldom imposed.

A more thorough discussion of Latin American voting behavior is not really possible as yet. Elections have been suspended too often in too many countries, and the voting data that are available do not always lend themselves to comparative analysis. Moreover, without a more substantial body of reliable survey-research results, it is not possible to analyze Latin American public opinion or voting behavior in sufficient depth. In some countries, public-opinion polling for academic purposes is still in its infancy, and the political climate in many nations has often made the collection of reliable survey information impossible. To date, only a few Latin American nations, such as Argentina and Venezuela, have produced enough survey data for scholars to be able to define voting behavior as carefully as has been done in the United States or Western Europe.

The Future of Party Politics in Latin America

The redemocratization process of the 1980s has once again focused attention on party politics and elections in Latin America. But are parties likely to remain important enough to sustain this renewed interest? In nations where social revolutions have created single-party regimes (Cuba, Mexico, Nicaragua), ruling parties can be expected to continue to be pivotal political actors well worth analysis. But the significance of party politics and elections elsewhere in the region will largely depend on the survival of liberal democracy. Unfortunately, there is no guarantee that the present resurgence of democratic politics will not be followed by renewed military intervention and "de-democratization" (Drake and Silva, 1986:7).

Students of Latin American politics have learned that modernization does not necessarily ensure democracy or competitive party politics. The increased social mobilization of the twentieth century helped to create mass electorates and made the capacity of civilian politicians to win votes a valuable political resource. Yet, these important social and political developments have not fundamentally reduced the power of the Latin American military. The armed forces have demonstrated an unflagging ability to suspend democratic party politics whenever and wherever their interests are threatened. In fact, because advanced social mobilization tends to create popular demands that pose wholly unacceptable costs for the army and its private-sector allies, many of the most modernized nations in the region have endured highly repressive military regimes (e.g., Chile, Argentina, Brazil, Uruguay) (O'Donnell, 1973).

Increased economic growth also cannot assure the survival of competitive party politics. Greatly improved economic conditions could enhance chances for democracy by providing the resources to permit civilian politicians to encourage investment and to implement needed social programs at the same time. But the medium-term prognosis for the dependent and debt-ridden Latin American economy is poor. Renewed economic expansion apparently will require years of unpopular economic austerity and readjustment.

In light of persisting military power and economic weakness, the survival of democracy in Latin America is likely to require civilian politicians to resist redistributive pressures. It is well to remember that with the exception of Costa Rica, which has no real army, democracy has become entrenched only in countries where the principal parties have acted to limit popular-sector demands (Venezuela, Colombia) (O'Donnell, 1986:9). Where the interests of the military and private sector (foreign and domestic) are thus protected, armed forces intervention becomes unnecessary and, over time, the military can evolve into a less significant actor. Conversely, political leaders who have refused to acknowledge that democracy must be self-limiting to survive in Latin America have found themselves replaced by the army.

Latin American party leaders who follow the example of Venezuela's Rómulo Betancourt, pursuing reformist policies that recognize the constraints imposed by the military's power, will have the best chance of institutionalizing democratic practices. In large part, the success of these politicians will depend on the mass public's willingness to defer socioeconomic demands in the interest of building liberal democratic institutions. One hopeful sign is that, in reaction to the gross excesses of recent military regimes, the consolidation of democratic institutions appears to have assumed a higher priority for Latin Americans today than ever before (O'Donnell, 1986:15).

Notes

1. Mary J.R. Martz (1980) provides a valuable survey of the literature on Latin American political parties. In particular, the early studies I refer to are Fitzgibbon, 1957; Martz, 1964; Angell, 1966; Scott, 1966; Martz, 1966; Williams, 1967; McDonald, 1971; and Alexander, 1973. The later studies are Alexander, 1982; Dix, 1984; Remmer, 1985; Drake and Silva, 1986; Nohlen, 1987; and Booth and Seligson, 1988.

2. There is so little to say about party politics in Haiti that this volume contains no chapter on the country.

3. A policy is defined as procedurally democratic to the extent that its most powerful public policymakers are selected through free elections in which virtually all adults may vote.

4. Martz (1980:147) points out the problems of assuming anything about Latin American political parties on the basis of the general theoretical literature on parties.

Theorists such as Duverger (1954) and Sartori (1976) have little to say about Latin American parties. See Sartori (1976) for an overview of the general literature and Sorauf (1984) for works specific to U.S. parties. Janda (1980) offers a detailed conceptual framework.

5. Social mobilization is a process whereby individuals are changed from traditional to modern in their perspectives, identifications, values, and expectations as they experience modernization.

6. For interesting case studies of Latin American party politics in the 1920s and 1930s, see Duff (1985). Populist movements are discussed in a useful volume edited by Conniff (1982).

7. With the exception of the indigenous ideology of the Peruvian Aprista party and a few other parties, most Latin American parties have adopted or modified foreign ideologies.

8. The terms "mass party" and "cadre party" originated with Duverger (1954), who has since noted many intermediate variations (1972:6–18). The five parties listed seem generally to fall into Duverger's mass party classification. Each would also appear to fit Huntington's (1968:412) definition of a strong party as one with high levels of both political institutionalization and mass support.

9. Alternative, nonnumerical ways to classify party systems have been suggested. See Kaufman (1977) and Powell (1981).

10. These subtypes are based on, although they modify, distinctions made by Sartori (1976:127–128, 192–193) in his more complex typology.

11. In a study of Latin American redemocratization (1940–1983), Remmer (1985:269–270) discusses the circumstances under which authoritarian rule can induce major changes in party systems. She observes that two-party systems seem to be more resistant to change than systems characterized by many parties.

12. It is assumed that legislative representation is a meaningful reflection of party influence even though the legislature itself may not be powerful. This measure, however, ignores parties that are legally denied representation or that choose to boycott elections.

13. Weiner and Ozbudun (1987:32) observe that the potential for democratic stability in developing countries is greater in party systems where (1) party system divisions do not mirror class, ethnic, religious, or regional cleavages and (2) extreme fragmentation or centralization is avoided.

14. See Grofman and Lijphart (1986) and Rae (1967) on the political consequences of electoral laws.

References

Alexander, Robert J. 1973. *Latin American Political Parties*. New York: Praeger.
———, ed. 1982. *Political Parties of the Americas*. Westport, CT: Greenwood.
Anderson, Charles W. 1967. *Politics and Economic Change in Latin America*. Princeton, NJ: Van Nostrand.
Angell, Alan. 1966. Party Systems in Latin America. *Political Quarterly* 37:309–323.
Blondel, J. 1968. Party Systems and Patterns of Government in Western Democracies. *Canadian Journal of Political Science* 1:180–203.
Booth, John A., and Mitchell A. Seligson, eds. 1988. *Elections and Democracy in Central America*. Chapel Hill: Univ. of North Carolina Press.
Chalmers, Douglas A. 1972. Parties and Society in Latin America. *Studies in Comparative International Development* 7:102–128.

Conniff, Michael L., ed. 1982. *Latin American Populism in Comparative Perspective*. Albuquerque: Univ. of New Mexico Press.

Dix, Robert H. 1984. Incumbency and Electoral Turnover in Latin America. *Journal of Interamerican Studies and World Affairs* 26:435–448.

Drake, Paul, W., and Eduardo Silva, eds. 1986. *Elections and Democratization in Latin America, 1980–85*. San Diego: The Center for Iberian and Latin American Studies of the Univ. of California, San Diego.

Duff, Ernest A. 1985. *Leader and Mass Party in Latin America*. Boulder, CO: Westview.

Duverger, Maurice. 1954. *Political Parties*. New York: John Wiley.

_____. 1972. *Party Politics and Pressure Groups: A Comparative Introduction*. New York: Thomas Crowell.

Epstein, Leon D. 1967. *Political Parties in Western Democracies*. New York: Praeger.

Fitzgibbon, Russell H. 1957. The Party Potpourri in Latin America. *Western Political Quarterly* 10:3–22.

Grofman, Bernard, and Arend Lijphart, eds. 1986. *Electoral Laws and Their Political Consequences*. New York: Agathon.

Huntington, Samuel P. 1968. *Political Order in Changing Societies*. New Haven, CT: Yale Univ. Press.

Janda, Kenneth. 1980. *Political Parties: A Cross-National Survey*. New York: Free Press.

Kaufman, Robert R. 1977. Corporatism, Clientelism, and Partisan Conflict: A Study of Seven Latin American Countries. In James M. Malloy, ed., *Authoritarianism and Corporatism in Latin America*. Pittsburgh: Univ. of Pittsburgh Press.

Key, V. O., Jr. 1964. *Politics, Parties, and Pressure Groups*. 5th ed. New York: Thomas Crowell.

Lijphart, Arend. 1984. *Democracies: Patterns of Majoritarian and Consensus Government in Twenty-One Countries*. New Haven, CT: Yale Univ. Press.

Lipset, Seymour M., and Stein Rokkan, eds. 1967. *Party Systems and Voter Alignments: Cross-National Perspectives*. New York: Free Press.

McDonald, Ronald H. 1971. *Party Systems and Elections in Latin America*. Chicago, IL: Markham.

Martz, John D. 1964. Dilemmas in the Study of Latin American Political Parties. *Journal of Politics* 26:509–531.

_____. 1966. *Acción Democrática: Evolution of a Modern Political Party in Venezuela*. Princeton, NJ: Princeton Univ. Press.

Martz, Mary J.R. 1980. Studying Latin American Political Parties: Dimensions Past and Present. *Journal of Latin American Studies* 12:139–167.

Nohlen, Dieter. 1987. *La Reforma Electoral en América Latina: Seis Contribuciones al Debate*. San José, Costa Rica: Instituto Interamericano de Derechos Humanos.

O'Donnell, Guillermo. 1973. *Modernization and Bureaucratic-Authoritarianism: Studies in South American Politics*. Berkeley, CA: Institute of International Studies, Univ. of California.

_____. 1986. Introduction to the Latin American Cases. In Guillermo O'Donnell, Philippe C. Schmitter, and Laurence Whitehead, eds., *Transitions from Authoritarian Rule: Latin America*, Baltimore: Johns Hopkins Univ. Press.

O'Donnell, Guillermo, and Philippe C. Schmitter. 1986. *Transitions from Authoritarian Rule: Tentative Conclusions about Uncertain Democracies*. Baltimore: Johns Hopkins Univ. Press.

Powell, G. Bingham, Jr. 1981. Party Systems and Political System Performance: Voting Participation, Government Stability, and Mass Violence in Contemporary Democracies. *American Political Science Review* 75:861–879.

Rae, Douglas W. 1967. *The Political Consequences of Electoral Laws.* New Haven, CT: Yale Univ. Press.

Remmer, Karen L. 1985. Redemocratization and the Impact of Authoritarian Rule in Latin America. *Comparative Politics* 17:253–275.

Riker, William H. 1982. The Two-party System and Duverger's Law: An Essay on the History of Political Science. *American Political Science Review* 76:753–766.

Rouquie, Alain. 1986. Demilitarization and the Institutionalization of Military-Dominated Polities in Latin America. In Guillermo O'Donnell, Philippe C. Schmitter, and Laurence Whitehead, eds., *Transitions from Authoritarian Rule: Comparative Perspectives.* Baltimore: Johns Hopkins Univ. Press.

Sartori, Giovanni. 1976. *Parties and Party Systems: A Framework for Analysis.* Cambridge: Cambridge Univ. Press.

Scott, Robert E. 1966. Political Parties and Policy-Making in Latin America. In Joseph LaPalombara and Myron Weiner, eds., *Political Parties and Political Development.* Princeton, NJ: Princeton Univ. Press.

Sorauf, Frank J. 1984. *Party Politics in America.* 5th ed. Boston: Little, Brown.

Weiner, Myron, and Ergun Ozbudun. 1987. *Competitive Elections in Developing Countries.* Durham, NC: Duke Univ. Press.

Williams, Edward J. 1967. *Latin American Christian Democratic Parties.* Knoxville: Univ. of Tennessee Press.

PART ONE

Single-Party Systems

2

CUBA

Cuba is the only Latin American nation that has adopted Marxism-Leninism as its official ideology and has declared itself to be a proletarian dictatorship led by the Communist party. Cuba also constitutes the sole exclusive single-party system in the Americas because it is the only country that tolerates no other political parties or organized opposition groups of any kind.

During the exuberant and sometimes erratic early years of the revolution, the party grew slowly and failed to play the leading role ascribed to it in Communist doctrine. However, as a result of the political institutionalization drives of the 1970s and 1980s, the expanded party has become a central political actor in Fidel Castro's regime. Under the Communist party's careful supervision, more Cubans participate in political activities today than ever before. The significance of their participation is open, however, to conflicting interpretations.

The Evolution and Context of
Cuban Party Politics

Cuba's political parties were first organized in 1865 while the island was still a Spanish colony. The Reformist party represented Cuban Creoles, who demanded fairer treatment by colonial authorities, while the Spanish Unconditional party defended the imperial order (Roca, 1982:326, 343). After losing the first war for independence (1868–1878), reformist elements coalesced into the Autonomist party, which pressed for a measure of self-government and ran against the pro-Spanish Constitutional Union party. In 1879 both of these political organizations began to elect representatives to the Spanish Cortes. Eventually, the failure of the Autonomist party to win concessions contributed to the development of a new and ultimately successful independence movement led by José Martí's Cuban Revolutionary party (PRC).

In the decade following independence, won in 1898, two new but essentially indistinguishable parties, the Conservatives and Liberals, dominated Cuban party politics. Neither offered a coherent governmental program and both were divided into competing, personalist factions. In search of the best route to power, Cuban politicians often switched back and forth between the two parties (Aguilar, 1972:33). In a notoriously corrupt and sometimes violent political context, the only policy-oriented party to emerge was the short-lived (1908–1912) Independent Colored party (PIC), an Afro-Cuban party that lobbied for agrarian reform, labor rights, and racial equality until it was repressed by the government (Roca, 1982:336). Interparty conflict frequently precipitated U.S. intervention.

In 1924 Gerardo Machado, a Liberal, was elected president on promises of nationalism and clean government and proceeded to govern with a coalition of Liberals, Conservatives, and the small Popular party (PP). Formal party cooperation persisted throughout the Machado era in spite of the regime's degeneration into a venal and repressive dictatorship carefully protective of American interests. When Machado became unpopular in the economically troubled 1930s, several party leaders defected to the opposition but gained little influence with the new middle-class, student, and labor forces that eventually overthrew the dictatorship. Important groups within the anti-Machado uprising of 1933 included the radical Student Directorate, the middle-class ABC party, and the Cuban Communist party, founded in 1925. These organizations fought among themselves in the months after Machado's downfall, making it easier for U.S.-supported Fulgencio Batista and his sergeants' faction of the military to take power in 1934.

Batista ruled Cuba until 1944 but exercised power through Liberal party figureheads until 1940. During this period, many political parties were also co-opted by the regime—including the Communists, who exchanged their assistance for legalization and a free hand in the labor movement. Changing its name to the Popular Socialist party (PSP) in order to broaden its appeal, the Communist party continued to endorse Batista candidates until 1944.

Opposition to the unsavory Batista regime centered in the Authentic Cuban Revolutionary party (PRCA). When reasonably open elections resumed in 1939, these Auténticos (led by 1933 revolutionaries such as Ramón Grau San Martín) campaigned on an appealing platform of nationalism, social democracy, and honest government. In coalition with the small, conservative Republican party (PR), the Auténticos temporarily ended Batista's reign in 1944 by electing Grau to the presidency. The Auténticos and their Republican allies also went on to win the 1948 elections behind presidential candidate Carlos Prío Socarrás. Unfortunately, the eight years of Auténtico government were bitterly disillusioning to Cubans. The party instituted no significant reforms and engaged freely in the graft, corruption, and electoral manipulation typical of Cuban politics. In disgust, many Auténtico supporters joined the new Orthodox Cuban People's party (PPCO), founded in 1947 by puritanical

Eduardo Chibás. In the 1948 elections growing public discontent with the established parties gave these fledgling Ortodoxos a surprising 17 percent of the vote, compared to 46 percent for the Auténticos, 7 percent for the Communist PSP, and 30 percent for the Liberals and other traditional forces (Domínguez, 1978:107).

Batista, returning to the political arena from his retirement in the United States, organized his followers into the United Action party (PAU) in order to run for president in 1952, but polls indicated that he had little chance of winning. Trailing both the Auténtico and Ortodoxo candidates, the former sergeant returned to power by military coup and thereafter allowed only rigged elections to take place. With most Auténtico leaders discredited and democratic electoral channels closed to the Ortodoxos (a party fragmented since Chibás's suicide in 1951), opponents of the dictatorship began to form more radical, armed anti-Batista groups outside of the party system. In this context, Fidel Castro, an Ortodoxo candidate for the Cuban congress in 1952, assaulted the Moncada Barracks with a group of followers on July 26, 1953, and three years later launched the July 26th Movement (M-26-7). This guerrilla movement, in collaboration with other groups such as the Revolutionary Student Directorate (DER) successfully deposed Batista in January 1959. After having first ridiculed Castro as an adventurist, the pro-Soviet PSP joined his revolutionary coalition belatedly in the summer of 1958.

The Cuban multiparty system disappeared later in 1959 when all parties except the PSP were banned. Yet, a strong single-party system was not constructed immediately in its place. Instead, as he moved to the left, Castro relied on the guerrilla-led Revolutionary Armed Forces as his vanguard institution and principal administrative apparatus. The new Communist party, in contrast, grew slowly and acquired little power.

In 1961 the three main groups in the revolutionary coalition—Castro's M-26-7 purged of its right wing, the student-based DER, and the Communist PSP—were merged into the Integrated Revolutionary Organizations (ORI). Primary responsibility for building the new party structure was entrusted to Aníbal Escalante, formerly the PSP's executive secretary. But after Escalante used his position to flood the new party and government with PSP militants, he was dismissed by Castro and exiled to Czechoslovakia. By 1963 ORI had been dismantled and reorganized into the United Party of the Socialist Revolution (PURS), with Fidel himself in place as secretary-general. Suspicious of a powerful party that might limit his freedom of action and bureaucratize the revolutionary process, Castro made certain that PURS gained no significant influence. PURS was also weakened by internal dissension, particularly between its DER and PSP components.

In 1965 PURS was officially renamed the Cuban Communist party (PCC) but throughout the rest of the decade still failed to assume an important role. Castro's control of the PCC was assured by placing loyal M-26-7 veterans and military officers in top leadership positions; otherwise, the organization was poorly staffed. The party's executive organs, the Politburo and Secretariat, as well as its Central Committee, met infrequently, and no party congress ever took place. By 1969 the PCC had only 55,000 members, which made it the smallest Communist party relative to population in any Marxist state (LeoGrande, 1979a:466).

In the late 1960s the party's role largely involved the supervision of production, but the PCC had enough cadres to oversee only about half of Cuban production workers (LeoGrande, 1979a:463). The party also participated in the general antibureaucracy campaign of the era directed against inefficiency and corruption, but its involvement with administrative detail caused frictions with the state bureaucracy and led the PCC to neglect political mobilization tasks. During this most radical period of the revolution, marked by serious strains in Soviet-Cuban and Fidelista-PSP relations, Castro resisted Soviet advice to rely more heavily on the party. In 1968 Castro imprisoned forty-three party and state officials (including the repatriated Aníbal Escalante) who had held meetings with USSR representatives on the need for more orthodox policies in Cuba.

The Cuban Communist party did not assume its current role as the revolution's vanguard institution until the 1970s. After the traumatic failure in 1970 of the "ten million tons" sugar-harvest campaign, the Cuban revolution dramatically changed direction. Unorthodoxy and informality gave way to an institutionalization drive that produced a new set of political, administrative, and economic institutions modeled on those of the Soviet bloc. The strengthening of the party became a high priority, and the PCC quadrupled in size in just six years (1969–1975). In addition, the quality of party cadres was upgraded, institutional roles were clarified, and internal party-coordination mechanisms were improved. The process of party institutionalization culminated in 1975 when Cuba finally held its first Communist party congress.

In the early years of the revolution, Cuba was ruled by the charismatic authority of Fidel Castro, his loyal inner circle, and the revolutionary armed forces (González, 1974). Since the mid-1970s, however, the strengthened PCC has moved into the forefront of Cuban politics. Although Castro's personal power is still unquestioned, he has begun to emphasize the party as his primary political instrument. Consistent with orthodox Communist theory, the 1976 Cuban constitution formally subordinates all other institutions to the party, and power has become centered in the PCC's Politburo. The Politburo controls all of Cuba's representative bodies through the party's right to nominate candidates to the executive committees of the People's Power Assemblies, especially the critically important Council of State of the National Assembly. The Council of Ministers, whose executive committee coordinates the work of the state bureaucracy, is, in practice, subordinate to the Council of State (del Aguila, 1984:143–146).

Nevertheless, in spite of the fact that Cuba, since 1970, has formally modeled its political system after that of the Soviet Union, the character of the Cuban polity still reflects its peculiar revolutionary history. Castro was the author of the Cuban revolution, and he won his struggle against Batista with a small core of guerrilla followers. Moreover, in order to rule the country, he relied on the revolutionary army more than on any other institution for many years. Thus, it should come as no surprise that despite the dramatic growth in the role of the PCC, the authority of Castro and his inner circle has not been diminished and the military has remained a major political actor (Thomas et al., 1984:13–17).

Fidel, his brother, Raúl, and their loyal inner circle (many of whom were members of M-26-7), have delegated important responsibilities to the increasingly institutionalized PCC as it has grown up around them, but they have retained ultimate control. The Cuban constitution may carefully specify the legal boundaries between the country's decision-making institutions, but, in reality, because of overlapping memberships, the Castros and a group of no more than twenty individuals maintain a secure hold over the entire political system (del Aguila, 1984:16–17). Fidel himself, for example, is first secretary of the party, a member of the Politburo, president of the Council of State, president of the Council of Ministers, and commander-in-chief of the armed forces. Raúl, now highly visible and officially designated as his brother's successor, is second secretary of the party, a member of the Politburo, first vice-president of the Council of State and the Council of Ministers, and second-in-command of the military. Furthermore, loyal allies of the Castro brothers sit with them on the three high regime councils.

Although the party now has supreme authority and cannot be challenged by other institutions, the PCC, the state bureaucracy, and the military still bargain and compete with one another to protect their own interests and to advance their own visions of the nation's priorities. In this policy process, the armed forces have continued to prosper in the 1980s (Domínguez, 1982:65). The army is no longer involved in directing the domestic economy, as it was in the 1960s, and has become more of a regular professional force concentrating on national defense and security. But this change of institutional focus does not appear to have reduced the armed forces' significance, particularly in light of the importance of the Cuban military role in Africa. Top officers sit on the Politburo, and the armed forces continue to absorb much of Cuba's best talent and a large share of its national budget.

Although Cuban politics have become more orderly and institutionalized under the Communist party's direction since 1970, important continuities with the revolution's past persist. Castro appears to be building the PCC and other formal institutions that he feels the country will need when he is gone. As the 1986 party congress suggests, he is also encouraging the entry of younger, better-educated technocrats into positions of power, sometimes at the expense of old Fidelistas. In the late 1980s, however, Fidel himself remains the Cuban revolution's undisputed Maximum Leader.

The Cuban Communist Party in the 1980s

The Cuban Communist party is highly centralized and rigidly hierarchical in accordance with orthodox Leninism. Castro and the party elite dominate the organization through their control of the party's three principal ruling bodies: the Politburo, the Secretariat, and the Central Committee. The Politburo has twenty-two members, including alternates, and makes all major national decisions. Personal loyalty to the Castro brothers has always been a key criterion for appointment. Traditionally, the body has had a majority of former M-26-7 activists, but in 1986 three well-known Sierra Maestra veterans were demoted and the representation of women, blacks, and younger Cubans was increased. The Secretariat functions as the second executive branch of the PCC; it oversees staff operations for the Politburo, Central Committee, and regional party apparatus, and ensures that all party levels comply with Politburo directives.

The Central Committee formally chooses the party's executive leadership, but actually the relationship is reversed. The 225-member Central Committee is selected by the Politburo and Secretariat and serves as the key forum through which senior party officials disseminate policy to lower party organs. The Central Committee staff is organized in specialized departments that oversee specific issue areas, monitor internal affairs, and provide liaison to other political institutions. The composition of the Central Committee was altered considerably at the 1986 party congress. Fully one-third of its full members and one-half of its alternates were replaced, lowering its average member's age to forty-seven while increasing the representation of blacks, mulattoes, and women (Domínguez, 1986:120). Patterns of institutional representation on the Central Committee remained stable during the early 1980s, with the large majority of seats divided fairly equally among the party apparatus, the state bureaucracy, and the armed forces (Domínguez, 1982:24). However, at the 1986 party congress, the number of military officers on the Central Committee fell to an all-time low (Domínguez, 1986:120), although this may have been offset to some extent by the addition of senior officers to the Politburo.

All lower party bodies, from the fourteen provincial organizations to the thousands of individual party cells, are subject to the three top PCC national institutions. The party elite controls internal elections and regularly intervenes in subordinate units. The rule of democratic centralism permits criticism by party militants but strictly forbids both dissent once decisions are made and the formation of party factions. In fact, the only really serious public critic of the party is Castro himself, who castigates the PCC regularly for its shortcomings.

The PCC now has within its ranks more than 480,000 members, or just under 5 percent of the Cuban population (del Aguila, 1985:124). Although these figures represent a doubling of the party's size in the past decade, recruitment has remained highly selective. Cells in workplaces and in residential areas identify potential recruits, who must receive the support of two-thirds of a cell's membership and obtain the approval of the party administration to be admitted. About half of the party's new members enter directly from the Communist Youth Union (UJC).

The great majority of party members have urban working-class or peasant origins, but more than half are not directly involved in production. A persistent shortage of cadres has regularly led the PCC to promote to leadership positions many individuals who join as workers. Today, a high proportion of party members are administrative officials, full-time party functionaries, and military men. The party still underrepresents women and blacks, although their numbers have grown in recent years.

Public Opinion, Political Participation, and Elections

In Communist Cuba, Castro and the party elite claim the right to rule because they are the most committed and most able revolutionaries, not because their decisions are in accord with Cuban public opinion. In any event, it is impossible for outside analysts to obtain a trustworthy reading of Cuban mass attitudes. No independent survey research is permitted, and, if it were, no firm conclusions could be drawn from its results because of the understandable reluctance to voice discontent while living under an all-encompassing dictatorship. Public opposition and dissent are suppressed more completely in Cuba than in the pre-Gorbachev USSR; no Sakharovs are permitted to attract foreign attention (Montaner, 1981:163). Indeed, Castro has been critical of recent political liberalization measures (glasnost) in the Soviet Union.

Hugh Thomas and his colleagues (1984:51–52) speculate that there are three general sectors of Cuban opinion regarding the Communist regime: a small core of strong supporters, a small collection of real opponents, and a large, resigned majority who feel neither strongly supportive nor strongly opposed to the new Cuba. Whatever the absolute level of genuine mass support for the revolution may be in the 1980s, many observers (del Aguila, 1984:155) agree that popular enthusiasm has declined markedly since the 1960s, evidenced, for example, in the exodus of 125,000 Cubans from Mariel in 1980.

Those who stay in Cuba must participate, and for the vast majority, participation means involvement in one or more of the party-directed mass organizations, especially the Committees for the Defense of the Revolution (CDR). The CDRs claim more than 6,100,000 members, meaning that they encompass nearly the entire adult population (del Aguila, 1985:124). Organized into neighborhood groups of about one hundred people, the CDRs have monthly meetings to discuss party directives and local affairs and engage in a wide range of other activities. Because CDR membership has become a requirement for normal life in Cuba, the party is able to use these organizations both to monitor behavior and to assess public reactions to policy. Most women (80 percent) also belong to the 2.7-million-member Federation of Cuban Women (FMC), headed by Raúl Castro's wife and new Politburo member, Vilma Espín (del Aguila, 1984:156–157), while 2.6 million workers are organized in the Confederation of Cuban Workers (CTC). These large membership figures do not indicate either power for the mass organizations or popularity for the regime. The CDRs, FMC, and CTC are all weak players in Cuban politics, and mass participation is exceptionally high largely because the costs of nonparticipation are prohibitive (del Aguila, 1984:154).

Since 1976 all Cubans over the age of sixteen have also been allowed to participate in the election of representatives to the Assemblies of Peoples' Power. Every two-and-one-half years (most recently in 1986), 169 municipal assemblies, charged with local affairs, are elected by secret ballot. According to the PCC the purpose of the elections is not to reflect Cuban public opinion but, rather, to identify the best revolutionaries. The establishment of the municipal assemblies, Cuba's only directly elected governing bodies, also has helped to promote citizen contact with lower officials and to improve local services.

In the Cuban electoral system, all municipalities are divided into electoral zones called circumscriptions, each of which sends one delegate to the municipal assembly. Every circumscription is further split into neighborhoods, where candidates are nominated at mass meetings of all eligible voters. Nominees are discussed and then voted on by show of hands, with the majority winner becoming the neighborhood's candidate for municipal delegate. The PCC does not offer nominees officially at this level, but party members intervene conspicuously to assure the selection of acceptable individuals (LeoGrande, 1979b:55; Domínguez, 1978:289). Because each circumscription contains several neighborhoods, the Cuban voter has a choice of candidates when he goes to the polls. The significance of this choice is reduced, however, because campaigning is illegal. The PCC simply prepares lists of candidate biographies, distributes them to registered voters, and promotes turnout through the mass organizations and mass media. There is no public discussion of issues and the party-issued biographies do not provide information about candidates' views.

Shortly after their election, the municipal assemblies convene to elect their executive committees and their delegates to the fourteen provincial assemblies and the 510-member National Assembly in Havana (if its five-year term has concluded). However, all candidates for these higher level posts are formally proposed by special PCC-dominated nominating commissions.

The results of recent Cuban elections demonstrate the Communist party's monopoly over the electoral process. Heavy party pressure to vote regularly has produced turnout rates of 95 percent to 97 percent of registered voters. Moreover, in 1984, when 10,963 municipal delegates were elected from a total of 23,099 candidates, about three-quarters of those elected were party (or UJC) members (del Aguila, 1985:125). Of the 1,377 indirectly elected provincial assembly delegates, the percentage of PCC militants was still higher, and virtually all of the National Assembly delegates held PCC cards.

Long-Term Trends

In the early years of the revolution Castro ruled without a genuine Communist party, but in the 1970s and 1980s he constructed Latin America's only exclusive single-party system modeled on that of the Soviet Union. The Cuban Communist party's power has grown strikingly in the course of the nation's institutionalization process, although Castro remains the regime's unquestioned leader and the military retains influence. One can expect the party's role to continue to expand, especially with the passing of the revolution's first generation of leaders.

In addition to becoming the key locus of Cuban decisionmaking, the PCC has also demonstrated its ability to mobilize political participation in the mass organizations and in the electoral process. Unfortunately, the impressive participation statistics that result from the party's efforts cannot reveal anything about the opinions of the Cuban mass public. The public's level of allegiance to the party and to the revolution in the late 1980s is an unknown about which external supporters and opponents of the Cuban regime can only speculate.

References

Aguilar, Luis E. 1972. *Cuba 1933: Prologue to Revolution*. New York: Norton.

del Aguila, Juan M. 1984. *Cuba: Dilemmas of a Revolution*. Boulder, CO: Westview.

_____ . 1985. Cuba's Revolution After Twenty-five Years. *Current History* 84:122–126, 133–134.

Domínguez, Jorge I. 1978. *Cuba: Order and Revolution*. Cambridge: Harvard Univ. Press.

_____ . 1982. Revolutionary Politics: New Demands for Orderliness. In *Cuba: Internal and International Affairs*, ed. Jorge I. Domínguez. Beverly Hills, CA: Sage.

_____ . 1986. Cuba in the 1980s. *Foreign Affairs* 65:118–135.

González, Edward. 1974. *Cuba Under Castro: The Limits of Charisma*. Boston: Houghton-Mifflin.

LeoGrande, William M. 1979a. Party Development in Revolutionary Cuba. *Journal of Interamerican Studies and World Affairs* 21:457–480.

_____ . 1979b. The Theory and Practice of Socialist Democracy in Cuba: Mechanisms of Elite Accountability. *Studies in Comparative Communism* 12:39–62.

_____ . 1980. The Communist Party Since the First Congress. *Journal of Latin American Studies* 12:397–419.

Montaner, Carlos A. 1981. *Secret Report on the Cuban Revolution*. New Brunswick, NJ: Transaction.

Roca, Sergio. 1982. Cuba. In Robert J. Alexander, ed., *Political Parties of the Americas*. Westport, CT: Greenwood.

Thomas, Hugh S., et al. 1984. *The Cuban Revolution 25 Years Later*. Boulder, CO: Westview.

3

NICARAGUA

Since deposing the corrupt Somoza dictatorship in 1979, the Sandinista National Liberation Front (FSLN) has begun a revolutionary transformation of Nicaraguan society. However, the Sandinistas have not embraced Marxism-Leninism formally as their official ideology nor established a Cuban-styled, exclusive single-party system. A variety of non-Sandinista political parties participate in the system, and competitive elections were held in 1984.

Nevertheless, the dominant FSLN makes the rules that govern political activity in this hegemonic single-party system, and the ruling party, at times, has narrowed the political space allowed to the opposition. As the activities of the U.S.-sponsored *contra* guerrillas expanded in the 1980s and the country became more polarized, the Sandinistas showed decreasing willingness to tolerate dissent. Yet, in 1987–1988, in compliance with the Central American Peace Accord (Esquipulas II), the Nicaraguan government reversed itself and removed many political controls over the opposition parties and mass media in hopes of bringing an end to the economically catastrophic war.

The Evolution and Context of
Nicaraguan Party Politics

Nineteenth-century Nicaragua was dominated by two parties. The anticlerical Liberals represented the elite families of León in western Nicaragua, while the pro-church Conservatives protected the interests of Granada in the east. Relations between the two groups became so hostile that each willingly collaborated with foreign powers in efforts to defeat the other. The Conservatives cooperated with the British, and the Liberals recruited the notorious U.S. mercenary, William Walker. Walker's attempt to rule Nicaragua in the 1850s both discredited his Liberal allies and helped to ensure a long period of Conservative ascendancy (1857–1893). During these four decades, Liberals sometimes accepted their subordinate status in return for a share of local offices, but more often they rebelled against Conservative authority.

In 1891 the election of a Conservative from the traditionally Liberal León served to divide the ruling party. This division enabled the Liberals, led by Gen. José Santos Zelaya, to ally with Conservative dissidents and to assume power in 1893. Zelaya soon purged his Conservative partners and proceeded to persecute opponents in both parties throughout his sixteen-year dictatorship. In addition, his strong nationalism aroused great resistance from the United States and identified his party as anti-American. American opposition to Zelaya helped bring about the Liberals' downfall in 1909 when the United States assisted a Conservative rebellion.

Aided by frequent U.S. interventions on its behalf, the Conservative party remained dominant well into the 1920s, although it was riven by feuding, personalist factions. Liberals, in spite of their own divisions, took advantage of this situation by forming a coalition with a minority wing of the Conservative party to create the hybrid Conservative Republican party in 1924 (Millett, 1982:21). This new party, running a Conservative for president and a Liberal for vice-president, won the elections that year by a large majority. The Conservatives refused to abide by the results, and again the country was plunged into a period of violence that ended only after a U.S. reoccupation forced a negotiated truce in 1927.

Under the terms of the 1927 agreement, the Liberals and Conservatives pledged to disarm and to share governmental posts. The United States agreed to supervise the 1928 elections and to train a neutral National Guard to replace partisan armies. Gen. José María Moncada, a Liberal, won the closely monitored contest, but not all Liberals were satisfied with U.S.-imposed political arrangements. A populist Liberal general, Augusto César Sandino, condemned the recurring U.S. military presence in Nicaragua and waged a guerrilla war against the National Guard and U.S. Marine units throughout Moncada's term.

Liberal Juan Bautista Sacasa was elected president in the U.S.-supervised 1932 elections and, with U.S. approval, appointed his nephew-by-marriage, Anastasio ("Tacho") Somoza García, to head the National Guard. In 1934 Somoza García solidified his position within the Guard by arranging the assassination of General Sandino, against the wishes of the president with whom the guerrilla leader had negotiated a truce. By 1936 Somoza had acquired enough strength within the Guard and the Liberal party to oust Sacasa and initiate the long reign of the Somoza family.

During the next four decades Nicaragua was ruled by Somoza García and his two sons, Luis Somoza Debayle and Anastasio Somoza Debayle. The National Guard and the Liberal party were their principal instruments of control. The Liberal party was renamed Nationalist Liberal party (PLN) and became the family's personal vehicle, invariably nominating one of the Somozas or an adherent for the presidency. In return, party members received government jobs, contracts, and other tangible favors.

The PLN was organized throughout Nicaragua and capitalized on the traditional Liberal party identification of many voters to mobilize votes for the Somozas. When mass support was lacking, electoral victories were assured by intimidating and defrauding the opposition. The Liberal party adopted whatever program the Somozas dictated, whether it was a mild anticlericalism consistent with Liberal principles or a slavishly pro-U.S. foreign policy that reversed a traditional Liberal stance (Woodward, 1976:220). Liberals who could not tolerate the party's subservience to the Somozas formed the Independent Liberal party (PLI) in 1944 and mounted several unsuccessful electoral challenges, often in coalition with Conservatives.

The Somozas were almost as adept at manipulating the Conservatives as they were at controlling their own party. Although a number of Conservative revolts had to be subdued by the Guard, most Conservative leaders eventually collaborated with the Somozas, at least to the extent of providing a facade of electoral opposition. In return, cooperative Conservative politicians received a share of public offices. Conservative collaboration was made easier by the fact that policy differences between the two parties eventually disappeared. The traditional oligarchical families that dominated the Conservative party had no more interest in social reform than the Somozas. The willingness of politicians in both parties to collaborate with the regime disillusioned many younger Nicaraguans, who turned to new reformist and radical anti-Somoza groups.

Luis Somoza fostered a modest liberalization of the dictatorship after his father's assassination in 1956, but his West Point–educated brother, Anastasio ("Tachito"), saw no need to continue this process when he gained sole power after Luis's death in 1967. Formally elected president in 1967 with 71 percent of the vote over Conservative Fernando Agüero Rocha—the candidate sponsored by the Conservatives, PLI, and small Nicaraguan Social Christian party (PSCN)—the youngest Somoza surrounded himself with a particularly greedy and unsavory group of associates. In fact, Anastasio II proved to be both the most corrupt and the least politically adept of the Somozas. Opposition to the regime expanded even among Nicaraguan elites who had prospered from the economic growth of the Somoza era.

Demoralized Liberals defected to the PLI or to the newly formed Constitutionalist Liberal party (PLC), headed by Ramiro Sacasa Guerrero, a moderate former cabinet minister. Although Conservative collaboration was briefly won by Somoza in exchange for a promise of a 40 percent share of public offices (Booth, 1982:89), the agreement unraveled, forcing Somoza to run without credible opposition in 1974. Nonvoting was made a crime, but less than half of the electorate turned out to participate in Tachito's "landslide."

During the middle and late 1970s, many new political groups and coalitions formed to oppose the Somoza dynasty. Leaders of traditional party elements (PLC, PLI, and Conservatives led by *La Prensa* publisher Pedro Joaquín Chamorro), as well as business leaders unwilling to collaborate further with Somoza, joined forces with minor parties and unions to create the reformist Democratic Liberation Union (UDEL) in 1974. By 1978 UDEL had merged into the Broad Opposition Front (FAO), which added the PSCN; the middle-class Nicaraguan Democratic movement (MDN) led by Alfonso Robelo; and the Group of Twelve, a collection of progressive intellectuals; and businessmen.

These groups, however, were unable to negotiate the end of the Somoza regime, which became progressively more repressive. The FSLN and its allies in the United People's movement (MPU) were thus able to broaden their support in a drive to depose Somoza by force. The FAO became paralyzed, and some of its elements, such as the PLI and the Group of Twelve (which was always closely linked to the FSLN), defected to join a new, broader pro-FSLN coalition termed the National Patriotic Front (FPN), which also included a leftist PSCN splinter, the Popular Social Christian party (PPSC).

The FSLN had been waging a small-scale guerrilla war against the regime since 1961, when it was founded by Carlos Fonseca, Tomás Borge, and Silvio Mayorga, three Marxist student activists who had withdrawn from the pro-Soviet Nicaraguan Socialist party (PSN) because of its opposition to armed struggle. Although Sandino himself had not been a Marxist, his name was incorporated into the organization's title because of the Liberal general's persistent popularity and his association with the nationalist struggle against U.S. imperialism. After years of fruitless combat, the FSLN had grown little and had become divided over tactics into three factions: The Proletarian Tendency favored a gradual mobilization of the urban working class as the best route to revolution, while the Prolonged People's War faction advocated slowly building up a rural peasant following. A third, or Tercerista, segment promoted a plan of mass insurrection designed to incorporate non-Marxist elements.

This division, however, was overtaken by events in 1978 when the broad cross-class rejection of the Somoza regime following the assassination of Chamorro sparked a spontaneous mass uprising. The FSLN seized this opportunity by reconciling its three factions (with Cuban assistance), moderating its program to embrace political pluralism, and opening its ranks to non-Marxists. The FSLN guerrilla army grew quickly and, with wide popular support, defeated the disintegrating National Guard. By the time the Somoza regime collapsed in 1979, the FSLN had acquired both broad popular legitimacy and sufficient military strength to construct a new, hegemonic single-party system. The FSLN gained control of the interim Governing Junta of National Reconstruction and of the quasi-legislative Council of State by early 1980, although other anti-Somocista parties and groups continued to be represented in both institutions.

The FSLN's long guerrilla struggle had made it into a much more formidable organization upon its assumption of power than Castro's amorphous July 26th Movement had been. The FSLN began the revolutionary period united under its National Directorate (DN), a collective leadership organ that made all major party decisions and instructed the FSLN's government representatives. After his election as president in 1984 Daniel Ortega, a former Tercerista, was recognized as the DN's most influential member. The 1987

Nicaraguan constitution gave the chief executive substantial independence in policymaking, and when government measures have required legislative approval, Ortega has been able to rely on the support of the highly disciplined FSLN legislative majority elected in 1984.

Governmental decisions are implemented through the FSLN-dominated state bureaucracy, and many key ministries are administered by National Directorate members. For example, DN member Tomás Borge, the FSLN's only surviving founder, is minister of interior, and Humberto Ortega, the president's brother, is minister of defense. Compliance with the regime's revolutionary program is enforced by the Sandinista Popular Army, the Sandinista Popular Militia, and the Sandinista Police—all of which grew out of the FSLN guerrilla army (purged of unreliable elements). By the late 1980s, largely as a consequence of the *contra* insurgency, these security forces consumed well over half of all government expenditure.

The FSLN has constructed a hegemonic, rather than exclusive, single-party system and has tolerated vastly more internal opposition and personal freedom than is permitted in Cuba. As in Mexico (prior to the 1988 Mexican political upheaval discussed in Chapter 4), the opposition parties have little hope of wresting power from the dominant party, but they are represented in the national legislature and can lobby the government and influence public opinion (Colburn, 1987:405). The Nicaraguan economy also is far less socialized than the Cuban, and anti-Sandinista unions and business groups such as the Superior Council of Private Enterprise (COSEP) are allowed, within limits, to oppose government policies. Although Marxist-Leninist ideology is deeply ingrained in the DN's membership, many observers (Booth, 1986:405) argue that most of the Sandinistas are pragmatic Marxists who believe that the country's proximity to the United States and economic dependence on the West requires them to maintain a substantial measure of pluralism and private enterprise. The FSLN recognizes the unwillingness of the USSR to take on a second major financial burden in the Americas in addition to Cuba.

The amount of political space allowed to the opposition has varied over the course of the Nicaraguan revolution. At first, the FSLN made many concessions to other political and economic actors. Parties such as the PLI, PPSC, and PSN, which had opposed Somoza, were invited to share power as junior partners of the FSLN within a broad political front, and cooperative members of the private sector were treated favorably by new state financial institutions. Parties and interest groups clearly opposed to the Sandinista program, however, such as the independent unions and the Catholic church hierarchy led by Cardinal Miguel Obando y Bravo, were attacked in the government-controlled mass media and hindered in their activities.

After the beginning, in 1982, of a concerted U.S. effort to topple the Nicaraguan government through support for counterrevolutionary forces led by former National Guard officers, the political space given opposition groups began to contract. The *contras'* activities contributed to increased FSLN suspicion of the opposition, to the economy's decline, and to greater dependency on the Soviet Union and other Communist countries. In addition, the tighter political controls and military draft (imposed in response to the *contra* threat) diminished the regime's popularity. Although many restrictions on the stridently antiregime newspaper *La Prensa*, the church, and the opposition parties and interest groups were rescinded for the 1984 elections, they soon were renewed and expanded. In October 1985 many basic civil rights, including habeas corpus, the right of assembly, the right of judicial appeal, and freedom from arbitrary searches, were suspended. The Catholic church's radio station, Radio Católica, was closed in late 1985 and *La Prensa* was shut down in June 1986. As polarization increased, the government's previously laudable performance on human rights (particularly in comparison with its Central American neighbors other than Costa Rica) began to deteriorate.

In 1987–1988 the political climate dramatically changed once again. In hopes of negotiating an end to the devastating civil war (45,000 dead), the Sandinistas embraced Esquipulas II and began an extensive program of political liberalization that convinced the U.S. Congress to deny further military aid to the *contras*. More than one thousand political prisoners were released, both *La Prensa* and Radio Católica were permitted to resume operations, and in 1988, the state of emergency that had restricted political demonstrations, press freedoms, and labor activities since 1982 was lifted (LASA, 1988). Opposition parties and interest groups responded to the new, more open political context by pressing the Sandinistas for further concessions, including a depoliticization of the security forces and the creation of an independent electoral commission. As the hyperinflationary, war-torn economy neared collapse, labor unrest also widened in the freer political environment. With continued U.S. support uncertain, the *contras* became more interested in Sandinista peace proposals, and direct negotiations produced a temporary cease-fire in March 1988. However, with the U.S. government clearly opposed, a permanent peace settlement proved elusive and in July 1988 the FSLN regime showed the limits of liberalization when it broke up a major opposition protest rally in Nandaime, south of the capital, and closed *La Prensa* for two weeks for misreporting the event.

Contemporary Political Parties

The FSLN has not adopted Marxism-Leninism as its official doctrine. Instead, the party professes to follow *Sandinismo*, a hybrid ideology that blends Marxism with liberation theology and elements of Nicaraguan nationalism and populism. Although the Sandinista leadership regularly employs Marxist analysis and is closely associated with Cuba and the USSR, the party recognizes the need for an undogmatic application of Marxism, particularly in light of the nation's strong Catholic tradition, its desperate need for Western economic assistance, and its proximity to the United States. The FSLN's intent to carry out a thorough Socialist transformation of the country has not altered since the movement's foundation, but many different forms of socialism are compatible with Sandinista principles.

The party's leadership is composed of a small group of revolutionaries who were members of the FSLN when it was a tiny guerrilla force. FSLN leaders have sometimes disagreed over how much political pluralism to allow in Nicaragua (and over other policies), but, in general, they have maintained a remarkably united front against both internal and external threats.

The FSLN is by far the largest and best-organized political party in Nicaragua. It is highly centralized and hierarchical, with the DN and its three commissions at the top. Since its restructuring in 1985 the five-member Executive Commission, headed by its coordinator Daniel Ortega, has become the most important power center in the party. This commission acts for the entire DN when the larger body is not in session and oversees the work of the other two commissions. The State Commission is entrusted with implementing the FSLN's economic and social programs, while the Defense and Security Commission is responsible for protecting the regime and maintaining public order. The DN also has seven auxiliary departments (general affairs, organization, propaganda, political education, international organization, finance, and Sandinista studies) (Valenta and Valenta, 1985:28) and has created the FSLN Secretariat and the Sandinista Assembly.

The FSLN also has built up a nationwide party infrastructure. Regional committees staffed by full-time party professionals direct thousands of community-organizing committees that conduct the FSLN's electoral campaigns and other mobilizing activities (LASA, 1984:7). Official party membership is earned only after a six- to twelve-month probationary period, and, since 1984, the FSLN has trimmed its ranks of party members who show insufficient commitment. To become a candidate member, one must have participated in and be nominated by one of the FSLN mass organizations (LASA, 1984:8).

The Sandinista mass organizations, to which about half of all Nicaraguan adults belong, play a major role in mobilizing support for the regime (LASA, 1984:5) and also provide a way for group members to petition the government (Colburn, 1987:406). The Sandinista Youth, with more than thirty thousand members, organizes students and prepares young people for party membership (CIERA, 1985:58). The Luisa Amanda Espinosa Nicaraguan Women's Association (AMNLAE) promotes the FSLN program among women and provides some social services. In addition, about 80 percent of all organized urban and rural workers are members of one of the various Sandinista unions, such as the Sandinista Workers' Central (CST). Finally, the largest mass organization is composed of the fifteen thousand neighborhood Sandinista Defense Committees (CDS). These groups conduct political discussions and organize community projects, but the CDSs mobilize only one-third of Nicaraguan adults, a much lower percentage than in Cuba, and have declined in importance since the early days of the revolution. Support for the FSLN and its mass organization appears to be greatest among the popular-sector beneficiaries of the revolution and among younger Nicaraguans generally. Although the party's leadership is composed mainly of middle-class intellectuals, its followers come predominantly from the urban working class and peasantry, which have gained access to education, health care, and land. Government employees are also a mainstay of the party.

At the time of the 1984 elections, two additional parties, the Popular Social Christian party (PPSC) and the Nicaraguan Socialist party (PSN), were allied with the FSLN in the form of the Revolutionary Patriotic Front (FPR), although both have since broken with the regime. The PPSC was founded in 1976 by young intellectuals, professionals, and unionists who left the Social Christian party (PSCN) because of its overly timid anti-Somoza strategy. The PPSC favors a socialist society inspired by progressive Christian ideals but criticizes the FSLN for its pro-Soviet foreign policy, hostility to the church, and opposition to independent labor unions. Small-scale entrepreneurs, artisans, and peasants provided most of the PPSC's modest following in 1984 (5.6 percent of valid votes), which was concentrated in Granada and Boaco.

The FSLN's other ally in 1984 was Nicaragua's orthodox Communist party, the Nicaraguan Socialist party (PSN), founded in 1944. Like the Cuban PSP, the PSN cooperated with the prerevolutionary dictatorship in the 1940s in order to gain labor influence and was late to join the revolutionary coalition. Unlike the PSP, however, the PSN has not been integrated into the revolution's vanguard party. Indeed, since the 1984 election the PSN has become a severe critic of the FSLN's monopoly of power. The PSN is structured along standard Communist organizational lines and encompasses affiliated groups for youth, women, and trade unionists. Its support comes almost entirely from urban manual workers, who gave the party an un-impressive 1.3 percent of the vote in 1984.

Several Nicaraguan parties were not affiliated either with the FSLN or with the 1984 opposition coalition, the Nicaraguan Democratic Coordinating Committee (CDN). These independent groups included two parties to the right of the FSLN, the Independent Liberal party (PLI) and the Democratic Conservative party (PCD), and two parties to the Sandinistas' left, the Communist Party of Nicaragua (PC de N), and the Marxist-Leninist Popular Action movement (MAP-ML).

The center-left Independent Liberal party favors social democracy and until early 1984 was a member of the FSLN's Revolutionary Front. However, its leader, Virgilio Godoy, formerly labor minister in the Sandinista government, took his party out of the front and, at the last minute, withdrew from the 1984 elections in protest against the radicalization of the revolution. A minority faction of the party (including PLI vice-presidential candidate Constantino Pereira and many of the party's legislative candidates) nevertheless refused to give up the campaign. The PLI has substantial support throughout Nicaragua and despite a boycott by many of its members garnered nearly 10 percent of the national vote. Drawing from both the popular sector and middle class, the PLI ran best in León, Rivas, and southern Zelaya.

The Democratic Conservative party (PCD) was founded in 1979 as an anti-Somoza splinter of the Conservative party. Its platform favors liberal democracy and a mixed economy. Conservative Democrat leaders, such as former junta member Rafael Córdova Rivas, long supported the Sandinistas, but many PCD members became critical enough of the government to urge withdrawal from the 1984 elections. Presidential candidate Clemente Guido dissolved the party's convention before a vote on participation could be taken, and the party finished second in the election. Its 14 percent of the vote was drawn particularly from the urban and rural popular sectors (LASA, 1984:8); its strongest showings were in Boaco, Masaya, and Granada.

No more than 3 percent of the electorate is represented by the two Marxist parties, which did not participate in the FSLN's Revolutionary Front in 1984. The Communist Party of Nicaragua (PC de N) left the PSN in 1970 following an internal dispute. The Marxist-Leninist PC de N criticizes the Sandinistas as petit bourgeois reformers and opposes elections despite its own participation in 1984 (1.5 percent of vote). Its major organizational base is in the textile workers' union. The Marxist-Leninist Popular Action movement (MAP-ML) was another PSN splinter. Established in 1972, it managed to attract only 1 percent of the vote in 1984. The Maoist-inspired MAP-ML is the most radical of the Marxist parties and, like the PCN, faults the Sandinistas for their moderation. Several members of these parties and their union affiliates have been arrested by the Sandinistas for overzealous labor agitation.

The Coordinadora coalition, which boycotted the 1984 election, was composed of two political parties (Social Christians and Social Democrats); two tiny Liberal and Conservative factions; the principal private-sector group, COSEP; and two small unions, the Social Christian Nicaraguan Confederation of Workers (CTN) and the Confederation of Trade Union Unification (CUS). The Coordinadora, with the endorsement of the church hierarchy, attacked the FSLN's radicalization of the revolution, demanded the establishment of a genuine liberal democracy, and favored the reintegration of the *contras* into the political system.

The oldest and strongest of the Coordinadora parties is the Social Christian Party of Nicaragua (PSCN), founded in 1956. The party had been a leader in the electoral struggle against the Somozas. The well-organized PSCN advocates centrist Christian Democratic principles and is supported by a social cross section of Nicaraguans. The Social Christians, who receive financial assistance from the Venezuelan and West German Christian Democratic parties, are outspoken critics of Sandinista attacks on the church and on political pluralism. In 1988 the party split into three rival factions.

The Social Democratic party (PSD), created in 1979, is led by businessmen and professionals, most of whom are former Conservatives or Nicaraguan Democratic movement (MDN) members (CIERA, 1985:40). Its party platform endorses liberal democracy and private enterprise. A strong Sandinista critic, the PSD collects its support from the remaining private sector, the middle class, and CUS-linked unions, yet its total size is estimated to be small. Smaller still are the Liberal Constitutionalist party (PLC) and Nicaraguan Conservative party (PCN), two remnants of the traditional parties that also reject the Sandinista's revolutionary program.

The armed *contra* opposition to the FSLN is led by the Nicaraguan Democratic Force (FDN), a 9,000-man guerrilla army financed by the United States and directed by right-wing former National Guard officers such as its chief Enrique Bermúdez. In mid-1987 the FDN and most other *contra* elements formally united in the Nicaraguan Resistance (RN), but the movement still was riven by personal, tactical, and ideological differences as direct negotiations with the Sandinistas began in 1988.

Public Opinion, Political Participation, and Elections

Few doubt that the Sandinistas enjoyed great public acclaim in 1979 or that their following declined in later years because of the costs of civil war and the radicalization of the regime. Unfortunately, there is no consensus regarding the mass support that remains for the FSLN in the late 1980s nor any reliable survey research data to analyze. Critics of the regime claim that only a minority of Nicaraguans still back the FSLN (Leiken, 1985; Valenta and Valenta, 1985; Christian, 1985). In contrast, those more friendly to the Sandinistas, often citing the FSLN's 1984 electoral victory, assert that the majority of Nicaraguans still are allied with the regime against both legal and illegal opposition forces (Walker, 1985; LASA, 1984:16–18). Most analysts (Colburn, 1987:406) agree, at least, that the Sandinistas are much more popular than the armed resistance. The Sandinistas have shown an undeniable concern for the poor majority of Nicaraguans and have mobilized (and politically educated) large segments of the population through the mass organizations. In contrast, the *contras* are tainted by the Somocista past and have failed to articulate a coherent political program and to gain any significant territorial control in their battle with the larger and highly motivated Sandinista army.

Contrasts between Cuba's single-party exclusive system and Nicaragua's single-party hegemonic system are quite apparent with respect to political participation. Although the Sandinistas have constructed mass organizations on the Cuban model, these institutions do not regiment the country's mass population as completely as they do in Cuba. About half of Nicaraguan adults choose not to involve themselves in the FSLN organizations, which suggests that the costs of nonparticipation in less coercive Nicaragua are much lower than in Cuba. In addition, electoral participation is more meaningful in Nicaragua than in Cuba because voters can choose from a number of competing party candidates, many of whom oppose the FSLN.

Faced with intense anti-Sandinista U.S. propaganda, the FSLN held general elections in 1984 in order to demonstrate its legitimacy. In February 1984 the Governing Junta created the Supreme Electoral Council (CSE), to organize and oversee the contest. Three CSE members were appointed by the FSLN-controlled Supreme Court and two additional members were chosen by the National Council of Political Parties, on which all registered parties had a representative. The CSE operated relatively impartially as it carried out its many functions: registration drive, distribution of public campaign subsidies (U.S. $1.5 million to each party), vote tallying, investigation of campaign law violations (LASA, 1984:13–15; Booth, 1986a:45). During a four-day drive in July 1984, the CSE registered 1,560,580 Nicaraguans, or an estimated 93.7 percent of those over the voting age of sixteen (LASA, 1984:14). Registration was mandatory, but no real sanctions were imposed. As a concession to opposition criticism of the FSLN's unfair media advantages, the CSE was also directed to distribute free television (twenty-two hours) and radio (forty-four hours) time to each of the opposition parties (Booth, 1986a:45). Existing censorship controls were loosened for the campaign but parties were expected not to criticize the draft or to promote abstention.

In 1984 voters cast two ballots: one for president and vice-president, to be chosen by plurality, and a second for a closed party list of National Assembly candidates to be selected by proportional representation. Both the president and the National Assembly serve for six years. The six losing presidential candidates each were guaranteed a National Assembly seat, but the other ninety delegates were chosen in nine territorial districts with varying numbers of seats allotted to each according to population size. The use of the PR system resulted in a much larger number of non-FSLN National Assembly delegates than would have won office under a single-member-district plurality system.

Voters used a ballot printed on a heavy opaque white paper with dark stripes on the back to protect its secrecy (LASA, 1984:14). Although the FSLN had control of the electoral machinery, the small number of complaints lodged by other parties with the CSE indicates that the Sandinistas did not engage in significant electoral irregularities and fully expected to win without having to do so.

The major problem with the 1984 elections was the Sandinistas' inability to convince the Coordinadora to participate. Coordinadora candidate Arturo Cruz, a former member of the Governing Junta and Group of Twelve, did campaign in Nicaragua, drawing both good crowds and some FSLN interference, while at the same time negotiating for better electoral terms. Ultimately, however, with COSEP and other Coordinadora groups unalterably opposed to participation, Cruz quit the contest, claiming that complete Sandinista control of the country made a free election impossible (although he has since admitted that his withdrawal was a mistake). Later, Virgilio Godoy, the PLI candidate, also withdrew citing similar reasons. U.S. pressure on both groups not to participate and thereby legitimize a FSLN victory was intense and is suspected of having been decisive (LASA, 1984:19–20). Hence, the FSLN faced no strong opposition parties when the election finally took place. Of the other six parties on the ballot, three (PC de N, PSN, MAP-ML) were tiny Marxist-Leninist parties backing the revolution; two (PPSC, PCD) were collaborating closely with the FSLN at the time; and one, the PLI, formally withdrew.

In the weeks before the election, there was heavy pressure to vote (Colburn, 1985:106), but observers reported that there was no pervasive

TABLE 3.1
Nicaraguan Election Results by Party, 1984

Party	Pres. Votes	Vote (%)	Seats
FSLN	735,967	67.0	61
PCD	154,327	14.0	14
PLI	105,560	9.6	9
PPSC	61,199	5.6	6
PC de N	16,034	1.5	2
PSN	14,494	1.3	2
MAP-ML	11,352	1.0	2
Null votes	71,209		
Total	1,170,142	100.0	96

Source: Adapted from Latin American Studies Association, The Electoral Process in Nicaragua: Domestic and International Influences (Austin, TX: 1984), p. 17.

climate of fear, as was evident in El Salvador in 1982 or Guatemala in 1984. Three-quarters (1,170,142) of those registered to vote cast ballots; turnout was highest in Estelí and Managua and lowest in northern war-zone areas (Jinoteca) despite FDN promises of an electoral cease-fire (The Elections, 1985:7b). The FSLN won the election handily, collecting two-thirds of the valid votes cast (Table 3.1). Daniel Ortega was elected president, and the FSLN captured sixty-one of the ninety contested National Assembly seats. Of the other participating parties, only the Democratic Conservative (14 percent) and the Independent Liberals (9.6 percent) attracted a significant number of votes. The FSLN won in all eighteen departments but ran best in the northwestern Estelí, Chinandega, and León, and in southern Río San Juan and northern Zelaya (The Elections, 1985:7b). The ruling party was most seriously challenged in Boaco, Granada, and Masaya. In urban Managua the FSLN won its largest share of the vote in poorer areas, and in rural Nicaragua the party did better among rural wage laborers than among peasant smallholders (Booth, 1986a:46).

Naturally, interpretations of the 1984 elections vary widely. Most analyses of the election (LASA, 1984:17–18; Booth, 1986a) assert that the results demonstrate strong, enduring support for the Sandinistas, particularly among the lower classes, in spite of the deteriorating economy and the unpopular draft. In contrast, opponents of the Sandinistas reason that the FSLN actually did fairly poorly against only token opposition despite complete control of the electoral machinery and security forces (Christian, 1985:297–299; Valenta and Valenta, 1985:17).

Long-Term Trends

The existence of a large number of non-Sandinista parties as well as the competitive character of the 1984 Nicaraguan elections demonstrate obvious contrasts between Communist Cuba's single-party exclusive system and Nicaragua's single-party hegemonic system. Nonetheless, although the more flexible FSLN tolerates dissent and even organized opposition that would be violently suppressed in Cuba, the Sandinistas retain a secure hold on all instruments of state power and the policymaking process. Moreover, convinced of its revolutionary legitimacy, the regime is unlikely to relinquish its hard-won control of the country no matter how popular the opposition might become. The FSLN has also shown that its tolerance of criticism has limits. Other parties are permitted (indeed encouraged) to participate in elections in hegemonic single-party systems like that in Nicaragua but they are not allowed to win power by electoral means.

The role of opposition parties and elections in a consolidated Nicaraguan revolutionary regime no longer threatened by a U.S.-backed insurgency is unknown. At this writing, direct negotiations between the FSLN and the *contras* have been suspended, although the war has not resumed. But if municipal elections postponed since 1987 are held in the near future, they will offer an important clue about government intentions. The ruling party failed to win a majority in 24 of the 139 municipalities in 1984 (The Elections, 1985:11b), and the opposition parties have announced plans to field joint candidates in municipal contests. The holding of municipal elections, therefore, would indicate that the FSLN is prepared to expand political space significantly by sharing control of local government with its opponents.

References

Booth, John A. 1982. *The End and the Beginning: The Nicaraguan Revolution*. Boulder, CO: Westview.

———. 1986a. Election Amid War and Revolution: Toward Evaluating the 1984 Nicaraguan National Elections. In Paul W. Drake and Eduardo Silva, eds., *Elections and Democratization in Latin America, 1980–85*. San Diego: The Center for Iberian and Latin American Studies of the Univ. of California, San Diego.

———. 1986b. War and the Nicaraguan Revolution. *Current History* 85:405–408, 432–434.

Centro de Investigaciones y Estudios de la Reforma Agraria (CIERA). 1985. *La Democracia Participativa en Nicaragua*. Managua: CIERA.

Christian, Shirley. 1985. *Nicaragua: Revolution in the Family*. New York: Random House.

Colborn, Forrest D. 1985. Nicaragua Under Siege. *Current History* 84:105–108, 132–133.

———. 1987. Embattled Nicaragua. *Current History* 86:405–408, 431.

The Elections Reagan Would Like to Forget. 1985. *Envío* (Managua) 4:1b–29b.

Latin American Studies Association (LASA). 1984. *The Electoral Process in Nicaragua: Domestic and International Influences*. Austin, TX.

_____ . 1988. *Extraordinary Opportunities and New Risks: Final Report of the LASA Commission on Compliance with the Central American Peace Accord.* Pittsburgh, PA.

Leiken, Robert S. 1985. The Nicaraguan Triangle. *New York Review of Books,* December 5.

Millett, Richard L. 1982. Historical Setting. In James D. Rudolph, ed., *Nicaragua: A Country Study.* Washington, DC: U.S. Government Printing Office.

Valenta, Jiri, and Virginia Valenta. 1985. Sandinistas in Power. *Problems of Communism* 34:1–28.

Walker, Thomas W. 1970. *The Christian Democratic Movement in Nicaragua.* Tucson: Univ. of Arizona Press.

_____ . 1985. Nicaragua: From Dynastic Dictatorship to Social Revolution. In Howard J. Wiarda and Harvey F. Kline, eds., *Latin American Politics and Development.* Boulder, CO: Westview.

Woodward, Ralph L. 1976. *Central America: A Nation Divided.* New York: Oxford Univ. Press.

4

MEXICO

For more than half a century the Institutional Revolutionary party (PRI) thoroughly dominated Mexican politics and won every important electoral contest. The highly institutionalized hegemonic party permitted a variety of opposition groups to compete in elections but never allowed any of them to capture a significant share of power. As long as economic growth continued to promise opportunity, most Mexicans passively accepted this authoritarian system despite high levels of government corruption. But when the end of the country's oil boom brought economic collapse in the 1980s, public disenchantment with the anachronistic and increasingly conservative official party became widespread, and demands for a genuinely competitive electoral process expanded. The economic crisis also aggravated the PRI's internal divisions and ultimately led to the defection of a major left-wing faction.

Rising discontent with the ruling party culminated in 1988 when both the leftist National Democratic Front (FDN) coalition led by PRI dissidents and the conservative National Action party (PAN) mounted strong electoral challenges. Although the PRI still claimed to have won the election, its margin of victory was the smallest in its history, and the party was forced to concede an unprecedented number of congressional seats to the opposition. Moreover, opposition forces alleged that they had been defrauded of millions of additional votes and refused to accept the electoral returns compiled by the government. Carlos Salinas de Gortari thus entered office with both an uncertain mandate and a demoralized ruling party.

The Evolution and Context of
Mexican Party Politics

Until the late nineteenth century, Mexico's postindependence politics was convulsed by a violent struggle between the anticlerical Liberals and the pro-church Conservatives. The Conservatives were defeated in the War of

47

the Reforma in 1861 but remained influential by aligning themselves with French occupation forces. After the departure of the French in 1866–1867, however, the Conservative party disintegrated. The victorious Liberal party later atrophied during the long dictatorship of Gen. Porfirio Díaz (1876–1911), a Liberal.

Political parties played little part in the revolutionary upheaval that followed the *Porfiriato*, but the military *jefes* and regional bosses who competed for power did collect civilian supporters. Some of the fragile political aggregates that resulted called themselves parties and sought ties to labor or agrarian groups. After the 1917 constitutional convention, head of state Venustiano Carranza, for instance, formed his followers into the Constitutionalist party. But the triumvirate of generals who deposed Carranza—Alvaro Obregón, Plutarco Calles, and Adolfo de la Huerta—declared this organization illegal. The 1920 elections were orchestrated so as to permit Obregón to win the presidency under a Liberal Constitutionalist party label, but after taking office Obregón distanced himself from this vehicle, and it too disappeared.

While Obregón was president (1920–1924), two new, more substantial parties emerged to vie for his favor: the National Labor party (PNL), led by trade unionist Luis Morones, and the National Cooperatist party (PNC), based in the agricultural cooperative movement. The PNL emerged temporarily as the stronger of the two parties after the Cooperatists made the mistake of backing an abortive attempt by de la Huerta to oust Obregón. Unfortunately for the PNL, Obregón also distrusted Morones and, in the last months of his presidency, turned to another group that had supported him against de la Huerta, the National Agrarian party (PNA).

When General Calles, Obregón's hand-picked successor, took office in 1924, he continued to favor the PNA but demonstrated his independence by reinstating the PNL. Relations between Calles and Obregón cooled, and Calles agreed only very reluctantly to support the latter's return to the presidency in 1928. But Obregón was assassinated before he was able to assume office, and Calles saw an opportunity to extend his reign. Obregón's Agrarista supporters were suspicious of his plans, however, and the constitution prohibited him from a second term in any event.

Calles therefore negotiated with the nation's most important generals and political bosses and agreed to have Emilio Portes Gil, affiliated with the Agraristas, installed as provisional president. Then, in his last congressional message, Calles called for the formation of a new party that would embrace all of the conflicting elements in the revolution so as to end the violence surrounding the competition for office. In 1929 the National Revolutionary party (PNR) was formally established at a convention in Querétaro. Precursor of today's PRI, the PNR initially was a loose coalition of local political machines, agrarian and labor groups, and military leaders. Everyone employed by the government was required to join the new organization, and most existing political parties were cajoled or bribed into merging with it. The PNR won its first presidential election in 1929 behind Calles's personal choice, Pascual Ortiz Rubio, against conservative José Vasconcelos of the Anti-Reelectionist party (PA).

Calles's strategy worked well. The former general was able to dominate Mexican politics through the PNR, sanctioning the selection of candidates and formulating policy for puppet presidents. As Calles dispensed patronage and favors through the PNR, the party grew stronger. The organization also prospered on contributions from government employees and businessmen. By 1933, when the PNR held its second convention, the party had developed a centralized network of formal party structures and affiliated organizations. The fragmented party system of 1929 with its fifty-one registered parties had thus been consolidated into the hegemonic PNR. Only three other legal parties still existed, and none of them posed a credible challenge (Levy and Székely, 1983:38).

The conservative policies Calles promoted, however, disillusioned Mexicans, who had expected the PNR to bring social justice. With popular unrest mounting, Calles acquiesced in 1934 to the party's selection of reformer Lázaro Cárdenas, a man he expected to control, as its standard-bearer. Once elected, Cárdenas purged Calles loyalists from the government and replaced them with individuals committed to revitalizing the revolution. When Calles conspired against the new president, the former strongman was arrested and sent into exile.

During his term, Cárdenas instituted a broad land reform, promoted wage increases for urban unions, and nationalized foreign oil interests, policies that made him immensely popular with the nation's hitherto neglected mass population. In order to protect lower-class gains, Cárdenas organized the beneficiaries of his programs into strong interest groups and formally incorporated them into the ruling party as its mass base. Agrarian-reform participants formed the National Confederation of Peasants (CNC), while urban workers were encouraged to join the Confederation of Mexican Workers (CTM), a new labor federation headed by leftist Vicente Lombardo Toledano.

Cárdenas renamed the PNR the Party of the Mexican Revolution (PRM) in 1938 and imbued it with his socialist ideology. The party was restructured along corporatist lines into four sectors directed by a national executive committee. The CTM formed the basis of the labor sector, while the CNC provided most of the members of the agrarian segment. The continued importance of the armed forces was recognized with the designation of a military sector. A popular sector was created as a catch-all to absorb federal employee unions, middle-class elements, and other groups. Sectoral interests were carefully balanced; at election time, each sector was allocated a number of nominees on the PRM ticket commensurate with its strength. Because all patronage and influence flowed through the party, unaffiliated groups or politicians were soon frozen out of Mexican politics.

Cárdenas's successors, Manuel Avila Camacho (1940–1946) and Miguel Alemán (1946–1952), completed the construction of the ruling party. Avila Camacho, the last of the revolutionary generals, dissolved the military sector of the PRM and organized the popular sector more coherently around a

TABLE 4.1
Mexican Presidential Elections, 1934-1988 (in percentages)

Year	Winner	PRI	PAN	Others
1934	Lázaro Cardenas	98		2
1940	Manuel Avila Camacho	94		6
1946	Miguel Alemán	78		22[a]
1952	Adolfo Ruíz Cortines	74	8	18[b]
1958	Adolfo López Mateos	90	9	
1964	Gustavo Díaz Ordaz	89	11	
1970	Luis Echeverría	86	14	
1976	José López Portillo	99		1
1982	Miguel de la Madrid	72	16	12
1988	Carlos Salinas de Gortari	51	17	32[c]

[a]Ezequiel Padilla's Democratic party won 19 percent.
[b]General Miguel Henríquez's Federation of Mexican People's parties won 16 percent.
[c]Cuauhtémoc Cárdenas's National Democratic Front (FDN) won 31 percent.

Sources: Leopoldo Gómez and Joseph L. Klesner, "Mexico's 1988 Elections: The Beginning of a New Era of Mexican Politics?" LASA Forum 19 (Fall 1988), p. 4, and Daniel Levy and Gabriel Székely, Mexico: Paradoxes of Stability and Change (Boulder, CO: Westview, 1983), p. 69.

National Confederation of Popular Organizations (CNOP), a group dominated by the government employees' unions. In addition, Avila Camacho and especially Alemán moved the party to the right, diluting its revolutionary ideology and changing its principal goals from social justice and nationalism to economic growth and political order. Both presidents attempted to build a consensus party capable of attracting Mexicans from all across the political spectrum. In 1946 Alemán christened the restructured party the Institutional Revolutionary party (PRI).

The creation of the hegemonic party was instrumental in producing one of Latin America's most stable polities. Every president from Avila Camacho to Miguel de la Madrid (1982–1988) won election by a huge margin (Table 4.1), completed his six-year term on schedule, and transferred power to his legally elected successor. Throughout this period, the Mexican system operated on two key principles: complete but temporary presidential authority and a comprehensive turnover of political offices every six years.

The Mexican president has nearly unlimited power while he is in office. He can pass whatever legislation he likes in the compliant PRI-dominated legislature and can freely spend the government's financial resources. The president also commands all internal security institutions, including the obedient armed forces. In implementing his policies, the chief executive is assisted by an army of administrators and elected officials who owe their positions to the PRI patronage system he oversees. Mexican presidents choose cabinet members and other high officials principally from within their personal political network (camarilla) of loyal followers, but they also reserve places for the supporters of other influential leaders.

The president is extremely powerful during his six-year term, but he is prohibited from seeking reelection and is expected to pass into political obscurity when he leaves office. Before he steps down, however, he has the privilege of naming his own successor. In 1987, in an attempt to placate reformers' demands for a more open selection process, President Miguel de la Madrid had the PRI leadership formally go through the motions of considering precandidates (six) for the first time, but the final decision remained his alone. Normally, after the president's candidate is unveiled, the party closes ranks around him in an impressive display of discipline. But in 1987 an important party faction, the leftist Democratic Current (CD), refused to accept the designation of minister of planning and budget, Carlos Salinas de Gortari, and formed the National Democratic Front (FDN) with several smaller parties in an effort to contest his election.

The arrival of a new president signals the wholesale sexennial turnover of administrative and elective positions. Typically, about 80 percent of the important posts in the new administration are filled by individuals who were not members of the previous government (Levy and Székely, 1983:108–109). Once appointed, top officials redistribute lower-level appointments to their followers and friends in the next echelon, who in turn hand out subordinate jobs to their networks. The institutionalized turnover every six years prevents a single clique from monopolizing power and facilitates both the co-optation of new talent and the redefinition of policy.

Although dominant in the party system, the Institutional Revolutionary party neither makes major policy decisions nor constitutes the preferred route to power in contemporary Mexico. In recent years the nation has been ruled less by PRI politicians than by a class of career administrators who combine technical and political skills. Roderic Camp (1985:98) has dubbed these individuals "political technocrats" and has shown that their careers are built in public administration or academia rather than in the PRI organization. Currently, most members of the regime's elite are recruited because of personal connections and/or academic success at the national university (UNAM) or abroad and are promoted on the basis of bureaucratic performance and membership in the right political network. The three most recent Mexican presidents—José López Portillo (1976–1982), Miguel de la Madrid (1982–1988), and Carlos Salinas de Gortari (1988–)—for example, had never held elective office before their selection as chief of state. All three gained prominence in administrative positions involving economic management and planning. With policy made elsewhere, the party's primary functions are to organize electoral campaigns and mobilize public opinion. Additionally, the PRI distributes some social services and other material benefits directly to lower-class followers and acts as a channel through which public grievances can reach administrators.

Nationally, the PRI kept its hegemonic position for decades by maintaining its unity and its mass support, but in some areas it sustained its dominance only through electoral fraud. The PRI is ideologically heterogeneous and divided into hundreds of competing camarillas. Yet, until the damaging defection of the CD in 1987, the party had remained very cohesive (less-troublesome dissident factions ran presidential candidates in 1940, 1946, and 1952). Party cohesion persisted because (1) the camarilla competition, rather than a more divisive ideological conflict, was paramount; (2) the six-year cycle of turnovers spread the material benefits of power widely; and (3) party groups that carried their demands too far found themselves isolated.

The PRI still enjoys the support of more Mexicans than any other party. Affiliated organizations of urban workers (CTM) and peasants (CNC), which are favored by the government, and federal employees' unions, whose members owe the party their jobs, represent a co-opted mass base. In addition, many other Mexicans associate the PRI with the country's post-1940 stability and fear change. Nonetheless, in many areas where malad-ministration, corruption, and recession have weakened the PRI's appeal, local party functionaries stuff enough ballot boxes to ensure victory.

In single-party Cuba, private enterprise is almost nonexistent, but in Mexico the private business sector is a major political force that is independent of the PRI, and the government must negotiate with it. Since 1940 the state has encouraged private capital in the interest of economic growth. The industrialists and the political technocrats still distrust one another, however, and their tacit alliance is an uneasy one. Frictions between the government and the private sector increased in the 1970s and 1980s in reaction to the populist programs of Luis Echeverría (1970–1976) and the policy of bank nationalization ordered by José López Portillo in 1982. The selection of Carlos Salinas, architect of the economic austerity program of the de la Madrid government, as the PRI's presidential candidate in 1987 seemed intended to reassure domestic and international business.

The Mexican government also permits more press criticism and freer opposition activity than is tolerated in many single-party systems. The mass media operate without direct government censorship and often find fault with the regime; but the vast majority of editors still endorse the regime and accept its financial assistance or oppose it with restraint, recognizing the state's latent power to disrupt their activities.

After decades of political success, the PRI's ability to maintain its hegemony is now very uncertain. With money scarce because of the aborted oil boom and the nation's massive debt, the regime lacks the material rewards and the growth expectations that have typically sustained it. The PRI's component sectors have grown restive because of austerity measures, while many other Mexicans in both the urban, educated middle class and the unorganized lower classes have lost faith in the government. Rising dissatisfaction with the system and a growing sense of indignation over PRI corruption and electoral fraud was clearly expressed at the polls in 1988 when a strikingly large segment of the population voted for opposition parties.

Contemporary Political Parties

The Institutional Revolutionary party continues to pay lip service to many aspects of its once-radical ideology, and some members of the party still retain a fierce nationalism and a suspicion of private capital. However, inasmuch as the PRI is the permanent governing party, it attracts opportunists of all kinds. The PRI may claim to be a party of the left, but it is more accurately described as centrist because of its diluted ideology, its poly-class composition, and its post-1940 policy emphases on stability and growth over equality. Nonetheless, the PRI continues to collect its electoral support disproportionately from the nation's lower classes.

The president of Mexico chooses the PRI's president, who directs the National Executive Committee (CEN)—the most powerful organ in the centralized, hierarchical party structure. The CEN also includes a party secretary-general, secretaries for the three formal sectors, and secretaries for political action, finance, media, and public relations (Alisky, 1984:679). Directors of the party's youth and women's organizations also attend CEN meetings. Subordinate to the CEN is the National Council, composed of all state committee chairmen and additional representatives from the labor, agrarian, and popular sectors. The council guides the PRI's extensive state and municipal organizations and oversees nominating conventions. Theoretically supreme, the 1,500-member PRI National Assembly actually meets only once every three or four years to confirm CEN decisions.

In drawing up its lists of candidates for office, the regime's inner circle consults with sectoral representatives and attempts to balance demands. The popular sector is reputed to be the most influential of the party's three functional segments (Story, 1986:94) and regularly receives as many PRI legislative seats as the other two sectors combined (Gómez and Klesner, 1988:7). This sector is composed largely of the CNOP, which is in turn dominated by the million-member Federation of Unions of State Workers (FSTSE). In addition to bureaucrats, the popular sector includes professionals, proprietors of small businesses, teachers, and even slum dwellers. The civil servants form an especially disciplined group of PRI stalwarts who pay regular dues and turn out for campaign rallies.

The leaders of the unionized minority of the industrial working class also are a force within the PRI. The 2.5-million-member CTM is the labor sector's most important component, but several other union federations are integrated into the party as well under the umbrella of the Congress of Labor (CT). The weakest of the three party sectors is the agrarian section, which is made up of a number of peasant groups, the largest being the CNC.

In addition to these formal party sectors, the PRI is divided into competing personalist networks that expand or contract depending on individual leaders' fortunes. In the past the party always managed to remain cohesive in spite of the constant jockeying for position among camarillas. However, in the 1980s, a split between the newer "political technocrats" and more traditional PRI politicians factionalized the party. In late 1986 the PRI was also split by the creation of the leftist Democratic Current (CD) led by Porfirio Muñoz Ledo, PRI president under populist Luis Echeverría, and Cuauhtémoc Cárdenas, ex-governor of Michoacán and son of former president Lázaro Cárdenas.

The Democratic Current advocated internal party reforms and a return to the nationalist and populist policies of earlier years. It encountered resistance, though, from the political *técnicos*, who favored conservative economic policies, and from the old-line *políticos* of the labor and peasant sectors, who opposed democratization measures that might threaten their own power (Reding, 1988a:324). Although labor politicians such as the aged CTM boss, Fidel Velásquez, made clear their disapproval of Carlos Salinas's background and economic ideas, most of them reluctantly agreed to support him in 1988 (the powerful pro-FDN oil workers' union was a major exception). The Democratic Current defected from the PRI, as mentioned earlier, and joined with several minor parties in the National Democratic Front (FDN) behind the dissident presidential candidacy of Cuauhtémoc Cárdenas.

The Popular Socialist party (PPS), the Authentic Party of the Mexican Revolution (PARM), and the Socialist Workers' party (PST)—three minor political parties that have traditionally aligned with the PRI—formed the FDN. The nationalist and rhetorically Marxist PPS was founded in 1948 by earlier PRI defector Vicente Lombardo Toledano. Composed primarily of urban intellectuals and trade unionists, the PPS long criticized the ruling party for its failure to fulfill its revolutionary promise. But before backing Cárdenas in 1988, the party had endorsed the PRI's presidential candidate in every election since 1958 and had been a reliable ally in the legislature. In spite of financial assistance from the PRI, the PPS's membership had been shrinking, and the small party had won less than 3 percent of the vote in recent elections. In 1988, however, PPS ballots accounted for more than 10 percent of the presidential vote.

The PARM is another former PRI collaborator that regularly embraced the hegemonic party's presidential nominee. Organized in 1952 by a group of retired generals who favored cleaner government, the largely middle-class PARM maintains only a rudimentary organization. Although in danger of disappearing after garnering less than 2 percent of the vote in post-1976 elections, the PARM rebounded somewhat in 1988 by contributing more than 6 percent of the presidential vote to FDN candidate Cárdenas.

The third FDN party that had generally cooperated with the PRI in the past (although it ran its own presidential candidate in 1982) is the PST, a well-organized group founded in 1973. It changed its name to the Cardenist Front for National Reconstruction (PFCRN) for the 1988 elections. Although the PST/PFCRN subscribes to a Marxist ideology and favors expropriation of most private industry, it has modest support among urban workers. Its activists tend to be students and intellectuals, and many of its followers are peasants. After obtaining less than 3 percent of the vote in 1985, the PST/PFCRN attracted more than 10 percent of the presidential electorate to Cárdenas in 1988.

Five other political parties have provided determined opposition to the PRI for a much longer period: the National Action party (PAN) and the Mexican Democratic party (PDM) on the right, and the Unified Socialist party of Mexico (PSUM), the Mexican Workers party (PMT), and the Workers

Revolutionary party (PRT) on the left. In 1987 the PSUM and PMT merged into the Mexican Socialist party (PMS).

PAN emerged in 1939 in reaction to Lázaro Cárdenas's socialist policies and the anticlerical bias of the official party. A pro-Catholic party favoring religious education, free enterprise, and honest government, PAN attacks the PRI for its statist stranglehold on the economy and for its abuse of power. A party president and secretary-general direct the PAN's national executive committee, which guides subordinate state and municipal organizations and ancillary associations for women and youth. Nearly everyone in the PAN organization is a volunteer, and the party's nomination procedures are open and competitive. The PAN is financed by dues from its half-million members, donations from businessmen and Catholic interest groups, and monies generated by fund-raising events (Alisky, 1984:682).

As a pro-Catholic party and the PRI's most credible electoral opposition for many years, PAN attracts everyone from right-wing zealots to reformist Christian Democrats. This diversity, as well as personalist power struggles, has caused internal frictions, but a common hatred of the PRI has held the party together. The selection of agricultural entrepreneur Manuel Clouthier as the party's 1988 presidential nominee reflected the ascendance of the more aggressive, pro–free market "neo-panista" faction within the PAN. The PAN draws its roughly 15 percent to 17 percent of the electorate mostly from more devout Catholics and from the urban middle and lower-middle classes. Traditionally, the PAN has had greater appeal for small businessmen than for large corporations because the latter have been able to negotiate directly with the government.

To the right of PAN is the Mexican Democratic party. With origins in the Fascist National Union Against Anarchy (UNS), PDM was started in 1971 by conservatives who found PAN too tame. The party is violently anti-Socialist, favors a union of church and state, and competes with PAN for many of the same voters (religious, middle class, and owners of small businesses) (Alisky, 1984:681). In 1988 PDM presidential candidate Gumersindo Magaña won only 1 percent of the vote and the party lost its legal status, but it has pockets of strength in traditionally conservative Jalisco, Querétero, Guanajuato, and San Luis Potosí.

In the 1982 and 1985 elections, leftist opposition to the PRI was led by the Unified Socialist party of Mexico, which was created in 1982 by a merger of the Mexican Communist party (PCM), active since 1919, with several other Marxist groups. The PSUM was a revolutionary party intent on transforming Mexico into a nonaligned, Socialist state free of U.S. imperialism. Its members, however, differed widely over the pace and nature of this transformation. The PSUM was organized according to the usual Communist format, with a politburo, secretariat, central committee, and national assembly.

Neither the PSUM, its long-illegal PCM precursor, nor its PMS successor ever has been able to gain a strong foothold in the PRI-controlled industrial working class. With the exception of a few dissident unions, all three parties have been composed mostly of students and intellectuals living in Mexico's biggest cities. With such a narrow social base, it is not surprising that the Marxist left has done poorly at the polls, never winning as much as 5 percent of the nationwide vote in recent elections.

To broaden its appeal, the PSUM merged in 1987 with the small Mexican Workers party (PMT), which had grown out of a coalition of extra-official labor and student groups. The PMT was led by its founder, Heberto Castillo. A respected Marxist journalist and university professor, Castillo was selected in an open primary to be the first presidential candidate of the new Mexican Socialist party (PMS) in 1988. However, a month before the end of the presidential campaign, Castillo withdrew from the race and endorsed National Democratic Front (FDN) candidate Cárdenas. In contrast, the Workers Revolutionary party (PRT), a tiny Trotskyist group, refused to back the FDN candidate and continued to solicit support for human-rights activist Rosario Ibarra de Piedra, who won less than 1 percent of the vote. Consequently, the PRT, like the conservative PDM, lost its legal registration.

Public Opinion and Political Participation

In the Cuban and Nicaraguan single-party systems, the ruling party attempts to convince the masses to become fervent believers in the regime's ideology. The Cuban Communist party and the FSLN also strive for a high level of participation in revolutionary mass organizations. The PRI, in contrast, has traditionally been content as long as Mexican public opinion did not become opposed to the regime and as long as political participation was restricted to a respectable turnout at the polls.

Only a limited amount of survey research has been carried out in Mexico, and much of the published data are unreliable, out-of-date, or based on unrepresentative samples. Yet, the data available do suggest that Mexican patterns of public opinion and political participation met regime requirements in the past (Booth and Seligson, 1984; Fagen and Tuohy, 1972; Almond and Verba, 1965). Major survey research studies found, for example, that Mexicans accepted their political system regardless of their cynicism about governmental corruption. Citizens also associated the government positively with the revolution and recognized the state's constructive role in Mexico's economic expansion. In addition, there appeared to be no widespread sense of repression; the mass public perceived a climate of free expression in which public officials were willing to listen to their grievances. Actual expectations for government performance were minimal; Mexicans largely accepted the country's unequal class structure as a given and relied on individual initiative for mobility.

Not surprisingly, political participation was low in this context. The average Mexican was uninformed, uninvolved, and politically apathetic. Most political participation simply involved petitioning the local bureaucracy for basic services. Although the government claimed that the majority of Mexicans also regularly voted in presidential elections, most analysts suspected heavy padding of final turnout figures. Voting is compulsory for everyone over eighteen years of age, but there are no penalties for abstention. Nonvoters, however, abstained more out of disinterest than protest (Middlebrook, 1986:97).

The benign character of Mexican public opinion and political participation was obviously a great asset to the regime. Yet, these patterns were based on a more rural and less educated population than Mexico now has and on expectations of an economic growth that can no longer be sustained. In the midst of the protracted economic crisis of the 1980s, more Mexicans than ever before began to participate actively in politics and to oppose the PRI. The dramatic events surrounding the 1988 elections indicate that traditional patterns of public opinion and participation can no longer be relied upon to preserve the hegemonic single-party system.

Elections and Voting

In the past, elections were important in Mexico not because they determined who would rule but because they helped the regime keep its democratic facade intact and forced the official party to maintain its ability to mobilize the electorate. Even before the hotly contested 1988 race, the PRI party apparatus devoted enormous resources to electoral campaigns, behaving as if victory were not certain. Every PRI presidential candidate since Lázaro Cárdenas made a ritual of campaigning across the entire nation, and in every election year, PRI advertising covered just about every available wall space in the country. The 1982 elections are reported to have cost the PRI U.S. $100 million (Riding, 1986:142).

Through 1988 the Mexican president and the sixty-four-member Senate were chosen concurrently once every six years. But, in future, only half of the senators will be selected at the time of the presidential election. The remaining thirty-two senators will be chosen at a midterm election to be held three years later (thirty-two of the senators who won office in 1988 were elected for three-year terms to accommodate this change). The entire five-hundred-seat (four hundred before 1988) Chamber of Deputies is renewed every three years. Governors' six-year terms are staggered so that some are selected each year. With the exception of two hundred federal deputies' seats (one hundred before 1988) distributed by proportional representation, all officials are elected by plurality in single-member districts. No elected officeholder may immediately succeed himself, and governors, like the president, may never hold their office a second time.

In the elections for the Chamber of Deputies, each voter actually votes twice, once for a candidate in his or her winner-take-all district (one of three hundred uninominal districts), and a second time for a closed party list of candidates running at large in his or her electoral region (one hundred seats distributed among five plurinominal regions in 1985). Each party obtaining a minimum of 1.5 percent of the national vote is entitled automatically to one deputy from each of the five regions; the remainder of the plurinominal seats are allocated to qualifying parties in proportion to their relative vote totals in each of the regions. Before 1986 no party winning sixty or more of the single-member-district contests could share in the plurinominal seats. Because only the PRI fell into this category, all one hundred deputies selected regionally were allotted to the minor parties. Under a 1986 electoral reform the PRI became eligible to receive a small number of the now two hundred plurinominal seats.

The Interior Ministry controls the nation's electoral machinery. The minister of the interior heads the Federal Election Commission, a body that has an assured PRI majority. The commission has the responsibility for compiling the official election results and for investigating charges of electoral irregularities. Formal confirmation of election outcomes is reserved by the PRI-dominated national legislature. Obviously, the ruling party is in an ideal position to "adjust" election results when necessary and to dismiss charges of fraud.

The appearance of electoral competition is crucial to the regime's claims of democratic legitimacy. One hundred regionally selected federal deputies were guaranteed to the minor parties in the 1977 electoral reform, which had created the plurinominal seats for precisely this reason. The 1977 reform also provided increased opposition access to the media. The Federal Election Commission now requires radio and television networks to donate free air time to all registered parties. The electoral authorities aid parties with postage expenses and other campaign materials, too. The PRI, however, encourages the opposition to fragment by requiring only a low vote percentage for parties to qualify for government assistance and for Chamber seats.

A brief overview of Mexican election results before 1988 demonstrates the PRI's traditional dominance over the party system. From the 1930s to 1987 the ruling party won every single presidential, gubernatorial, and senatorial election ever held, with the sole exception of a 1976 Senate race, from which it withdrew in favor of its PPS ally. The PRI also prevailed in about 98 percent of all other elections. The PRI boasts of an extended string of lopsided presidential victories (see Table 4.1), and the ruling party has rarely admitted to losing even a plurality election for federal deputy (col. I, Table 4.2). The PRI claimed to have won 887 out of 900 uninominal races (98.6 percent) contested between 1979 and 1985. After the 1977 electoral reform the PRI enticed more parties into the electoral process, and the opposition at least increased its share of the vote. De la Madrid's winning percentage in 1982 (72 percent) was the lowest achieved by the PRI in thirty years, and the total PRI vote for uninominal Chamber of Deputies seats declined from 80 percent to 65 percent between 1976 and 1985 (Table 4.3).

Before 1988 the conservative National Action party was the most successful long-term opposition party, winning an average of 15 percent of the vote and holding between thirty-eight and fifty-seven seats in the Chamber. PAN support was strongest in Mexico City and other urban areas, in the northern border states (Sonora, Chihuahua, Coahuila, Nuevo León, Baja Norte), and in traditionally conservative regions such as Guanajuato and Jalisco. The

TABLE 4.2
Party Composition of the Mexican Chamber of Deputies by Mode of Election, 1979-1988

	1979			1982			1985			1988		
	I	II	III	I	II	III	I	II	III	I	II	III
PRI	296	0	296	299	0	299	292	0	292	233	27	260
PPS	0	12	12	0	10	10	0	11	11	4	32	36
PARM	0	12	12	0	0	0	2	9	11	5	25	30
PST/PFCRN	0	11	11	0	9	9	0	12	12	7	34	41
PAN	4	38	42	1	56	57	6	32	38	38	63	101
PDM	0	9	9	0	9	9	0	12	12	0	0	0
PSUM[a]	0	18	18	0	16	16	0	12	12	0	19	19
PMT							0	6	6			
PRT				0	0	0	0	6	6	0	0	0
CD										13	0	13
Total	300	100	400	300	100	400	300	100	400	300	200	500

[a]PCM in 1979; PMS merged PSUM and PMT for 1988.

Note: I = Uninominal Seats; II = Plurinominal Seats; III = Total Seats. All Mexican Senate seats were won by the PRI except for four garnered by the FDN coalition in 1988.

Sources: Adapted from Uno Más Uno (August 31, 1988), p. 1, Delal Baer and John Bailey, "Mexico's 1985 Midterm Elections: A Preliminary Assessment," LASA Forum 16 (Fall 1985), p. 7, and Marvin Alisky, "United Mexican States," in George E. Delury, ed., World Encyclopedia of Political Systems and Parties (New York: Facts on File, 1984), p. 674.

TABLE 4.3
Vote by Party for the Mexican Chamber of Deputies, 1961-1985 (Single-Member Districts; in percentages)

	PAN	PRI	PPS	PARM	PDM	PSUM	PST	PRT	PMT	Annulled	Abstention
1961	7.6	90.2	1.0	.5							31.7
1964	11.5	86.3	1.4	.7							33.4
1967	12.4	83.3	2.8	1.3							37.7
1970	13.9	80.1	1.4	.8						3.90	35.8
1973	14.7	69.7	3.6	1.9						10.00	39.7
1976	8.5	80.1	3.0	2.5						5.70	38.0
1979	10.8	69.7	2.6	1.8	2.1	4.9	2.7			5.90	50.7
1982	17.5	69.3	1.9	1.4	2.2	4.4	1.8	1.3		.04	34.3
1985	15.5	65.0	2.0	1.7	2.7	3.2	2.5	1.3	1.5	4.60	49.5

Note: Excludes the PNM, which won .28 percent of the vote in 1961, and the PSD, which won .19 percent in 1962.

Source: Adapted from Delal Baer and John Bailey, "Mexico's 1985 Midterm Elections: A Preliminary Assessment," LASA Forum 16 (Fall 1985), p. 5.

PSUM (formerly the Mexican Communist party and now the core of the Mexican Socialist party) was Mexico's third-ranking party during this period with a mean 4.2 percent of the electorate and from twelve to eighteen deputies. Its votes came disproportionately from Mexico City and other major urban centers. In 1985 the opposition parties' combined vote already exceeded that of the ruling party in the Federal District. Neither the PAN nor the parties of the left, however, seemed able to crack the PRI's traditional strongholds in rural Mexico. Economically backward states such as Chiapas, Tabasco, and Campeche regularly cast up to 85 percent of their votes for the PRI.

Despite their limitations, the electoral reforms of the late 1970s did raise voter interest and led many citizens to hope that the political process would become more open. In the 1982 election, many voters found de la Madrid's promise of moral renewal attractive, and no one doubted that his triumph over the PAN's colorless Pablo Emilio Madero was genuine. Few charges of fraud arose either in the 1982 contest or in the following year's state and local elections. The PRI even conceded defeat in several important mayoral races in 1983.

Unfortunately, expectations of further political liberalization proved to be short-lived. Between 1985 and 1987, in several northern states, the ruling party resurrected heavy-handed forms of electoral fraud characteristic of the 1950s. Popular outrage against stolen elections was most evident in Chihuahua, where citizens staged mass protests. Some analysts argued that although many of the nation's administrative elite favored more honest elections, PRI politicians at local levels were not willing to risk the career damage and loss of spoils entailed in recognizing opposition victories. Others suspected that many of the political technocrats themselves feared to give freer rein to the opposition during the economic crisis. In any event, these electoral frauds infuriated the opposition and began to unify it. In 1988, despite their intense ideological disagreements, leaders of PAN, PMS, and FDN joined together in the Democratic Assembly for Effective Suffrage to organize a nationwide opposition poll-watcher system.

Initially, four major candidates competed in the 1988 presidential election, which because of the unusual split in the PRI emerged as the most competitive and significant electoral contest in Mexico since 1929. The PRI's candidate was the young, Harvard-educated Carlos Salinas de Gortari, former minister of planning and budget and former director of the PRI's Institute of Political, Economic, and Social Studies. With the economy deteriorating and real wages down 40 percent over the past five years, Salinas tried rather unconvincingly to distance himself from the policies of the outgoing administration and promised to restore economic growth and to modernize the country's political institutions. His campaign was very well financed and benefited from the efforts of the vast PRI party apparatus and a strongly supportive mass media. Salinas was opposed principally by popular Sinaloan businessman Manuel Clouthier of the conservative PAN, who focused his criticisms on PRI's corruption, electoral fraud, and economic mismanagement, and by PRI dissident Cuauhtémoc Cárdenas of the National Democratic Front (FDN) coalition, who offered a nationalist, populist alternative to government policies. The fifty-three-year-old civil engineer and son of revered leftist President Lázaro Cárdenas advocated, among other measures, a debt-repayment moratorium, reduced oil exports, larger food subsidies, and increased government assistance to the peasantry. Marxist academic Heberto Castillo also campaigned actively on the Mexican Socialist party's (PMS) revolutionary platform but gained little support and, as we noted earlier, ultimately withdrew from the race in favor of Cárdenas.

The official results recorded by the Federal Election Commission gave Salinas only a bare majority (50.7 percent) of the vote, which represented the poorest performance ever by a PRI presidential candidate and a 21 percent vote decline since 1982. Cárdenas placed second with an impressive 31.1 percent of the electorate, the largest vote won by an opposition presidential candidate since the revolution. Clouthier finished a disappointing third, credited with 16.8 percent of the vote—only a marginal increase over PAN's showing in the previous presidential contest. Profiting both from mass discontent with the nation's economic situation and from the power of his father's revolutionary name, Cárdenas gained his greatest success in his family's home state of Michoacán (64.2 percent) and in the Federal District (49.2 percent) and its neighboring states of Morelos (57.7 percent) and Mexico (51.6 percent) while conservative Clouthier did best in his native state of Sinaloa (32.1 percent) and in Chihuahua (38.2 percent), Jalisco (30.8 percent), and Guanajuato (29.9 percent), where the PAN had attracted substantial support in the past. Salinas, in contrast, ran particularly well in the poor rural states of Chiapas (89.9 percent), Tabasco (74.3 percent), and Campeche (70.9 percent), although the PRI also gained a strong following in more developed Puebla (71.6 percent) and Nuevo León (72.1 percent).

In the legislative elections, the PRI was greatly aided by the fragmentation of the opposition and by the plurality electoral system but still captured a smaller share of seats than in any previous election. Although the PRI claimed 60 senate seats for itself, the ruling party admitted the loss of contested senatorial races for the first time in its history by acknowledging 4 FDN victories (2 in the Federal District, 2 in Michoacán). While winning in 233 of the 300 single-member (uninominal) congressional districts, the PRI also conceded more opposition victories in these contests than ever before with the PAN (38 seats) being the principal beneficiary (see Table 4.2). Leftist coalitions, which varied from district to district, collected 29 more uninominal seats, and the left and right opposition forces together stood to receive 173 additional plurinominal seats in the chamber (PAN, 63; FDN, 110). Because of these results, Salinas faced an unexpectedly strong opposition in Congress (PRI, 260 seats including 27 plurinominal ones, versus 240 opposition deputies) and became the first PRI president to lack an assured two-thirds congressional majority necessary for constitutional changes.

In spite of the opposition parties' unprecedented success in the official results, both the FDN and the PAN alleged that they had been defrauded of millions of other votes, especially in rural areas where the opposition had not been able to monitor the voting process as carefully as in the cities. Cárdenas asserted that by a narrow margin he, rather than Salinas, had actually won the presidential election, and Clouthier called on President de la Madrid to annul the results entirely. Both right and left opposition forces staged large protest demonstrations in the weeks following the election. Opposition suspicions of vote fraud were based on many factors, including the government's long delay in making electoral returns public (reportedly while the PRI party leadership fought over how much electoral damage to admit) and a seemingly inexplicable decline in official voter turnout (51.5 percent) compared with 1982 (74.8 percent)—this despite enormous interest in the 1988 contest and long lines at the polls (Reding, 1988b:624). The FDN claimed that government officials had both grossly inflated the PRI presidential vote in the past and destroyed great numbers of Cárdenas's ballots in 1988. Most independent observers believed at the very least that Salinas's margin of victory over Cárdenas was much smaller than recorded and that the PRI lost more legislative seats than it admitted.

Long-Term Trends

Since the 1930s the Institutional Revolutionary party has exercised hegemony over the Mexican party system. Although the official party has allowed more and more latitude to the opposition in recent years, the PRI and its administrative elite have consistently refused to share real power. While Mexico was a rural, undereducated country enjoying an impressive rate of economic expansion, the ruling party's highly institutionalized and authoritarian brand of machine politics functioned extremely well. Indeed, few nations have been as politically stable or as economically successful as Mexico has been over the past half-century.

But the striking results of the 1988 elections demonstrate that the PRI's old-fashioned methods are no longer adequate to the demands of the urban, educated, and economically troubled nation that Mexico has become in the late 1980s. Although the PRI remained strong enough to have Salinas elected as president in 1988, the official party was more seriously challenged than in any previous election largely because its prized, traditional unity was ruptured by the defection in 1987 of the leftist Democratic Current. President Salinas thus took power weakened by the PRI's declining popular appeal and confronted with both a poor economic prognosis and unrelenting demands for full political liberalization. The future of Mexico's once-invincible PRI had suddenly become very uncertain.

References

Alisky, Marvin. 1984. United Mexican States. In George E. Delury, ed., *World Encyclopedia of Political Systems and Parties*. New York: Facts on File.
Almond, Gabriel, and Sidney Verba. 1965. *The Civic Culture*. Boston: Little, Brown.

Baer, Delal, and John Bailey. 1985. Mexico's 1985 Midterm Elections: A Preliminary Assessment. *LASA Forum* 16:4–10.

Booth, John A., and Mitchell A. Seligson. 1984. The Political Culture of Authoritarianism in Mexico: A Reexamination. *Latin American Research Review* 19:106–124.

Camp, Roderic A. 1985. The Political Technocrat in Mexico and the Survival of the Political System. *Latin American Research Review* 20:97–118.

Cornelius, Wayne A. 1986. Political Liberalization in the 1985 Elections in Mexico. In Paul W. Drake and Eduardo Silva, eds., *Elections and Democratization in Latin America, 1980–85*. San Diego: Univ. of California, San Diego.

Fagen, Richard R., and William F. Tuohy. 1972. *Politics and Privilege in a Mexican City*. Stanford, CA: Stanford Univ. Press.

Gómez, Leopoldo, and Joseph L. Klesner. 1988. Mexico's 1988 Elections: The Beginning of a New Era of Mexican Politics? *LASA Forum* 19:1–8.

Johnson, Kenneth F. 1984. *Mexican Democracy: A Critical View*. New York: Praeger.

Levy, Daniel, and Gabriel Székely. 1983. *Mexico: Paradoxes of Stability and Change*. Boulder, CO: Westview.

Middlebrook, Kevin J. 1986. Political Liberalization in an Authoritarian Regime: The Case of Mexico. In Drake and Silva, eds.

Needler, Martin C. 1982. *Mexican Politics*. New York: Praeger.

Reding, Andrew. 1988a. The Democratic Current: A New Era in Mexican Politics. *World Policy Journal* 5:323–366.

———. 1988b. Mexico at a Crossroads: The 1988 Election and Beyond. *World Policy Journal* 5:615–649.

Riding, Alan. 1986. *Distant Neighbors: A Portrait of the Mexicans*. New York: Vintage.

Story, Dale. 1986. *The Mexican Ruling Party: Stability and Adaptability*. New York: Praeger.

5

PARAGUAY

Party politics in Paraguay exists within an authoritarian tradition; from 1954 to 1989 the country was controlled and manipulated by the hemisphere's longest-surviving dictator, Gen. Alfredo Stroessner. The country has never experienced democratic politics or for that matter mass parties that openly and freely compete with each other for power. The Stroessner regime was a distinctive one, at times brutal and self-serving but also at times more benign than its counterparts elsewhere. The kind of old-fashioned, personal dictatorship exemplified by the Stroessner regime had become outmoded and implausible, and on February 3, 1989, Stroessner was removed from power by Gen. Andrés Rodríguez, a high-ranking military officer whom Stroessner had earlier been trying to force to retire. It was a family coup; Stroessner's son is married to Rodríguez's daughter, and they share grandchildren. Rodríguez proclaimed that free elections would be held within 90 days, but it is premature to speculate on just what implications, if any, the coup or any subsequent changes or elections will have on Paraguayan politics. Party politics in Paraguay has been defined by the 35-year dictatorship of Stroessner; its legacy suggests a sustained period of change and instability.

The Context of Paraguayan Party Politics

The two major political parties in the country, the Colorado party (PC) and the Liberal party (PL), have existed for more than a century. Overshadowed by regimes, they have been antagonistic and competitive, but factionalized, lacking clear ideological or programmatic differences and cohesive, motivated followings. Within the framework of the Stroessner dictatorship, Paraguayans were largely alienated and indifferent to the traditional political parties. There were many economic, social, and political problems in Paraguay, but the overwhelming issue was Stroessner himself— what, if any, alternatives there were, and what the consequences of those alternatives might be. Indifference to and alienation from politics generally and parties specifically have been fundamental realities in Paraguay for generations. Yet these realities exist within a culture where party affiliations are clearly defined, though they may be passive and limited in their consequences.

Elections in Paraguay have even less institutional basis than do parties. Held periodically, elections rarely if ever decided anything—neither who would rule the country nor what the policies of the rulers would be. They were chronically fraudulent, controlled by the regime through intimidation and coercion. They were no more than a national ritual, from Stroessner's perspective a "patriotic" one, in which the masses were prodded into celebrating Stroessner's benevolence and the joy of being Paraguayan. For the loyal opposition, which was permitted to participate, elections were an opportunity for carefully attacking the government, focusing international attention on its policies and leaders, and calling for change, while simultaneously acquiring a small bit of political influence and patronage for itself. Elections provided an opportunity for the regime to try to legitimate its rule and to build a facade of democracy around it, a useful function domestically and internationally but one of rapidly declining credibility.

Traditionalism and the politics of patrimony are common in Latin American politics, but in Paraguay they have been a way of life. Stroessner tried to present himself as the great benefactor, a godfather to almost four million Paraguayans, in ways not dissimilar to those of Rafael Trujillo in the Dominican Republic, Somoza in Nicaragua, Díaz in Mexico, and countless others. This traditionalism was based on a network of informal relationships rather than on bureaucratic, legalistic, or institutional politics. It was a network of friends, patrons and clients, and personal allegiances, and was characterized by mutual protection and support. The regime's well-worn slogan, "Peace, Jobs, and Well-being with Stroessner," summed it up.

Historically, Paraguayan politics has been affected by international influence and intrigue, particularly that initiated by Brazil and Argentina, whose governments have often viewed Paraguay as a fertile land for their own economic exploitation and political hegemony. These influences have grown even more significant in recent years, affecting Paraguayan political parties and leaders at home and in exile and encouraging the regime to play off one foreign interest against another.

Although an unabashed dictatorship, the Paraguayan regime differed somewhat from others in the region. It used force, coercion, and fraud to maintain control, especially in recent years, but somewhat irregularly. Stroessner was less conspicuously self-serving and less ostentatious in his manner than his counterparts elsewhere, although many of his friends and close associates, those benefiting from the regime, were both. A myth circulating in Paraguay and abroad suggested that Stroessner could probably have won a national election even if it were honest and included capable opposition. Like many myths, there was probably some truth in it, which may account for the sense of resignation about Paraguay's electoral experiences. Stroessner seemed to understand the principle that informal controls and potential sanctions work better in the long run than overt repression and conspicuous sanctions, which are used only when all else fails. Increasingly, however, the regime relied on repression to maintain control as its viability corroded.

The Evolution of Contemporary Party Politics

The two traditional parties, the Colorado party and the Liberal party, emerged about 1876 and have dominated party politics ever since. They have primarily been elites of like-minded politicians since their inception, without significant programmatic or ideological differences, held together by personalities, mutual self-interests, and expediency. Their national posture has been one of the "ins" and the "outs," and they have played their roles accordingly.

The Colorado party was founded by Gen. Bernardino Caballero, who ruled the country from 1874 to 1904 following Paraguay's disastrous defeat in the Tripartite War with Argentina, Brazil, and Uruguay. Caballero and his party were tacitly supported by Brazil as a means of perpetuating Brazil's influence in the country. The Liberal party, organized in opposition to Caballero, took power in 1904; it held control until the revolution of 1936. The Liberals had tacit support from Argentina. In principle they advocated free elections, limited constitutional government, and private property, at least while in opposition to the Caballero regime. The Colorados presented themselves as the natural heirs to Solano López, a strong-armed dictator of earlier times who nonetheless serves, perhaps, as Paraguay's only national hero. While in power, the Colorados criticized the Liberals for being too privileged, too educated, too "liberal," and for collaborating with Argentina—in other words, they were traitors. The backwash of the Tripartite War helped to establish the direction of Paraguayan party politics for years to come (Lewis, 1980:19–20).

The Liberals found their regime at war in the 1930s with Bolivia, which was seeking an outlet to the sea—having lost its only one to Chile in the War of the Pacific. The outlet Bolivia sought was through Paraguayan territory and rivers, and the resulting conflict was known as the "Chaco War." Paraguay largely prevailed, but the experience cut loose new political forces in the country, specifically a reform movement called the Febreristas. This group of younger, disillusioned Paraguayan liberals tried to impose a series of major changes on their country, including land reform, broad social reforms, labor unions, and controls over private enterprise, by a popularly based but severely authoritarian regime. The Febreristas were overthrown in August 1937; their leaders and eventually many of their supporters fled into exile in Argentina. They formed a political party of exiles, which opposed subsequent Paraguayan regimes, including Stroessner's (Lewis, 1968:65–68). From 1937 to 1954 Paraguay underwent a period of military control, repression, and extended civil conflict, culminating in the ascendancy of

Alfredo Stroessner, an army officer whose regime would redefine Paraguayan politics.

Contemporary Political Parties

Stroessner came to power in a political vacuum. He had the support of many army officers and of a substantial portion of the Colorado party leadership eager to extend and renew its political control over the country. In the vicissitudes of the previous decade, the Liberal party had been declared illegal. This injunction was not lifted until a faction of the party's leadership was legalized in 1962 to serve as a loyal opposition to the regime. In effect, Stroessner co-opted the Colorado party, converting it into his personal vehicle as the "government party," and he relied on the army to guarantee the survival of his regime. (The example of Anastasio Somoza comes to mind, for he used Nicaragua's Liberal party in much the same way—employing the party as a personal vehicle for his regime while tolerating the opposition faction of the Nicaraguan Conservative party.)

By 1962 Stroessner's control over the country was firmly established. But during the Kennedy administration Latin American dictators were suddenly out of vogue in Washington. Stroessner therefore legalized an opposition party in an effort to provide a nicer international image for his regime. That party, a splinter of the Liberal party, became known as the Liberal Renovation Movement (MLR) and eventually gained representation in the nation's unicameral legislature. A new constitution was instituted in 1967 and with it another party, the United Liberal party (PLU), was legalized. The PLU constituted most of what remained of the Liberal party leadership. The PLU leaders accepted Stroessner's invitation to return to Paraguay and to compete in the 1968 national elections. But there were terms: they had to accept the political system, change the name of their organization, and avoid electoral alliances with other groups. Eventually Stroessner recognized yet another faction of the former Liberal party, a group that came to be known as the Radical Liberal party (PLR). The dictator's recognition of this party was an effort to divide the Liberals, specifically the PLU. The PLR is often regarded as the furthest left of the Liberal groups because it advocates a form of socialism and opposes foreign investments. By using the power of the state to recognize and legalize some of the Liberal party factions but requiring them to be recognized as separate parties, Stroessner both denied them a political martyrdom of exile while preventing them from becoming a serious challenge to the powerful, well-financed, and state-protected Colorado party.

Following the 1937 coup, most of the Febrerista leaders went into exile in Argentina, where they continued to oppose and criticize the Paraguayan governments that replaced them. In 1951 they formed a political party in exile, the Febrerista revolutionary party (PFR). During the years that followed, many Paraguayans chose to live in Argentina—perhaps as many as 1.5 million—and they came to identify with the Febrerista party as an exile organization. In an effort to lend credence to his democratization process, Stroessner allowed the Febreristas to return to Paraguay in 1965 to compete in the forthcoming national elections. But the group was by then becoming smaller and was divided and without substantial popular support inside Paraguay. They were no longer a viable alternative to Stroessner, as he unquestionably understood. But he also understood that their presence in the country would help deflect some of the criticism of his dictatorial regime. The party's support has been mostly from the urban middle class in the capital city, a small, alienated part of Paraguay's electorate.

Other groups have tried to form political parties since the 1960s but have failed to achieve legal status. These have included the Authentic Radical Liberal party (PLRA), yet another faction of the PLR, and the Christian Democratic party (PDC), which was organized in 1965. Similar to other Christian Democratic parties in Latin America, the PDC perhaps most resembles those in Guatemala and El Salvador, whose struggles against military regimes parallel in part the PDC's difficulties. The party's leadership is largely middle class and is centered in the capital city, although it also tried to organize peasant leagues—promptly crushed by the regime. Like other opposition groups in Paraguay, the PDC has tried to establish itself as the antiregime party but has had to do so without legal recognition.

Like most Latin American nations, Paraguay has a small Communist party, which enjoyed legal status only for about a year in 1946. Its leaders are also in exile, its following small, and its influence virtually nonexistent. Given the regime's obsessive anticommunism, there is no possibility that the organization will be tolerated or, under present circumstances, find many adherents willing to risk the wrath of the government security forces. From Stroessner's viewpoint, a more serious threat came from another illegal organization, the Colorado Popular movement (MOPOCO), which is a splinter faction of the Colorado party opposed to Stroessner's leadership. Its principal leaders, again exiled by the dictator, operate from Argentina, calling for sweeping reforms, a "democracy" of workers and peasants, anti-imperialism, and, of course, an end to the Stroessner dictatorship. Although the organization has no legal status, its leadership contains some respected individuals whose opposition was often troublesome to Stroessner and who could play a role in a post-Stroessner Paraguay.

In recent years two of the illegal parties (MOPOCO and the PDC) have joined in a loose, informal coalition with the legalized Febrerista party, forming an alliance known as National Accord (AN). The association began as an act of futility, held together by a shared hatred of the Stroessner regime. But by the time of the 1988 elections, the organization began to take on new relevance and focus as the principal legitimate opposition to the Stroessner dictatorship.

Elections and Public Opinion

Elections were a highly controlled process in Paraguay having little or no governmental significance. Nonetheless, they were of some political importance to the regime. The outcome of the elections held under Stroessner was never in doubt. He and his candidates always won, either unopposed or by wide margins. Electoral fraud was common and often gross, but the principal mechanisms for control were applied long before the actual voting took place: electoral laws virtually precluded an opposition victory, and agreements on the outcome of the vote count were made with the "loyal" opposition groups that were allowed to participate.

Nevertheless, Stroessner and the Colorado party waged vigorous campaigns. The president used campaigns as an opportunity to be seen throughout the country, as he came into personal contact with tens of thousands of Paraguayans. The Colorado organizations and officials prepared rallies, turned out supporters, and blanketed the country with campaign propaganda. To an outsider it might appear as though Stroessner were campaigning on the assumption he could be defeated, which of course he could not be. The opposition's access to the media was strictly controlled and limited, either directly by the regime or indirectly by the media themselves. Even the loyal opposition leaders were often harassed and detained, their rallies controlled by Stroessner's troops. Campaigning was personalistic, with Stroessner presenting himself as the benefactor of modern Paraguay—sensitive, caring, irreproachable, and utterly committed to the welfare and progress of his people. His lack of charisma was carefully balanced by a sense of the dignity of his office as he mingled with the voters. An ineffective public speaker, Stroessner could almost turn his lack of charisma into an asset of humility as he tried to persuade Paraguayans to identify themselves and their country with him. He characterized his political opposition as unpatriotic, self-serving, and often as "Communists," a broadly defined term in the regime's lexicon.

Local Colorado organizations and party headquarters came alive during a campaign, but they also functioned at other times as social and community clubs, integrating and sometimes assisting local residents under the banner of the Colorado party and the protection of its leader. Health and educational services were commonly exchanged for intelligence information on political dissidents (Lewis, 1980:150).

For the legal opposition, campaigns were at most an opportunity to score a few points against the regime and to maintain a degree of public visibility; campaigns were an investment in the future. The Colorados had virtually unlimited access to campaign funds; anyone Paraguayan with privilege or wealth could hardly avoid seeing the logic of contributing to the Colorado party. Moreover, the party functioned within the general financial structure of the state itself, an endless source of financial assets and campaign workers. With elections constituting, at most, a ritualistic approbation of the Stroessner years, the regime could point with some accuracy to Paraguay's gradual modernization and its extended period of political stability—not unvalued experiences given the country's turbulent history. Ironically, the regime charged that opposition leaders, virtually all of whom spent time exiled in Argentina, collaborated with "international interests" (by implication Argentina) against the welfare of the nation. This accusation struck a responsive chord in many Paraguayans but belies the fact that Stroessner himself had generally warm relations with Argentine dictators over the years and willingly accepted their assistance and investment.

Election results since 1965 display a monotonous uniformity. The Colorado party consistently achieved between 69 percent and 90 percent of the reported vote. The Radical Liberal party normally came in second, with between 6 percent and 21 percent of the vote.

Studies of public opinion and survey research were not easily conducted or readily tolerated in Stroessner's Paraguay. However, one such study was conducted during the brief political thaw of the 1960s and was published in 1968 (Nichols, 1968). The results generally confirm what might be expected in attitudes toward Paraguayan party politics. Party affiliations appear quite stable. About 75 percent of the respondents said they had never considered changing party affiliation, and only 10 percent reported that they had. The most common reason given for joining a party was its ideological orientation, with about 75 percent believing that a comprehensive ideology was the best way for a party to increase its strength. This may represent less a commitment to ideology than a rejection of personalism as a basis for party leadership. Interest in ideology was positively related to educational levels: the higher the educational level, the greater the ideological concern. Educational levels also affected expectations about desired consequences of party affiliation.

Stroessner used a distinctive formula for determining party representation, which is modeled after one once used in Argentina and named after the former Argentine president, Roque Sáenz Peña. The formula awarded two-thirds of the party representation in the legislature to the party that received a plurality of the popular vote, while the remaining one-third was divided proportionally to the opposition. Because the Colorado party always received more votes than any of the opposition parties, it was assured of a two-thirds majority in the legislature, while the loyal opposition was assured of one-third of the legislative representation.

From 1940 to 1968 Paraguay had a single-chamber (unicameral) national legislature. The Constitution of 1967, however, established a bicameral legislature, with sixty deputies and thirty senators. The Colorado party consistently elected forty deputies and twenty senators, enough to control voting in the legislature, irrespective of the electoral margin. Given the overwhelming strength of the Stroessner and the Colorado party, the results of any national election were certain even before the voting occurred, regardless of how large the Colorado majority might be.

Besides providing a legal means for ensuring control over the legislature, the electoral formula had another advantage for the regime. It created the illusion of opposition in the legislature, a loyal opposition that accepted the political system and in effect Stroessner's control of it. As I suggest above, the same electoral system was used in Nicaragua by the Somoza family for exactly the same reasons: to create a domestic and international image of a legislature with opposition representation.

Political organizations that were not legally granted party status had been able to urge a blank vote as a protest to the regime—potentially an embarrassment to the regime. Stroessner countered with the infamous Law 600, which declared that blank votes were improper and illegal and were therefore not counted in the final tally. The same regulation outlawed party coalitions as well as parties with ties to political organizations in other countries, an unsubtle way to exclude Marxist parties (Codas, 1981:1).

With extensive electoral controls, fraud was less critical than it might otherwise have been had the opposition been provided a realistic opportunity to compete. Yet, reports of voting irregularities persisted—double voting, denial of registration to supporters of opposition groups, irregularities in the counting and reporting of the vote. Voting was compulsory in Paraguay, and penalties existed for those who did not vote, although the penalties were relatively mild and largely unenforced. But the idea of compulsory voting was politically important: it allowed the government—should it have been necessary—to report a very high voter turnout (and consequently a large government vote) whether or not it occurred. There is no evidence to prove the point, but it is likely and reasonable, given the realities of elections and voting in Paraguay, that far fewer people bothered to vote than the final tallies imply.

In February 1988 Paraguay once again held national elections, and Stroessner was elected for the fifth time, receiving 89 percent of the vote, according to the official report. The PL received only 3 percent, the PLR 7 percent. Many believe the outcome of the election was settled beforehand by Stroessner and the leaders of his two "opposition" parties. Reports of government intimidation, fraud, and the detention of party leaders and journalists were widespread. Parties that directly opposed the Stroessner dictatorship did not participate in the election.

Long-Term Trends

Paraguay was both the oldest dictatorship and the last of the traditional ones in Latin America. Its durability rested on the personality of a single leader and his control over the military, the economy, and the opposition. The dictator was in poor health, although he gave no indication that he was about to retire from office. No assassination attempts were reported, and there were no revolutionary organizations within Paraguay strong enough to challenge his regime. Such organizations had been formed in Argentina and Brazil, but neither country encouraged them. They would probably not have appreciated any instability that a violent attack on Stroessner or his regime might have produced given their economic interests in Paraguay. What plans, if any, Stroessner had for succession were unknown, but it is difficult to imagine any Paraguayan leader who could have easily replaced him. Most of his longtime associates were old, and many had been purged from the regime or had died. Now that Stroessner finally has passed from the scene, the potential for instability is substantial, and the future of the country's political parties is uncertain.

Beyond the question of Stroessner, long-term patterns of change have been occurring in the country. The patrimonial relations embodied in the Colorado party that held the country together politically were becoming anachronistic, perhaps even dysfunctional, and they are unlikely to survive Stroessner despite strong pressures to preserve them from those with a vested interest in the status quo (McDonald, 1981).

New wealth is complicating the country's politics, especially the wealth generated by the hydroelectric projects built or planned with Brazil and Argentina. The multibillion dollar Itaipú project with Brazil is already partially operational, and that project alone makes Paraguay one of the world's largest exporters of energy. New revenues to the government from the project are substantial (Reisner and McDonald, 1986:270–307). The new wealth has created a consumer mentality in the capital city among the rich, among a more affluent middle class, and among the military. And with this new mentality has come a greater distinction between those groups and the poor. An underground economy, beyond the control of the government, is flourishing as never before. Thousands of Paraguayan workers, recruited from rural areas to work on Itaipú, are unemployed now that the project is completed. Unwilling to return to their former life, these workers constitute an alienated, frustrated, and potentially hostile group. Despite the long-term economic advantages to Paraguay from the hydroelectric projects, in the short run they have created a backlash against the country's traditional politics. Political meddling or intervention by Argentina, Brazil, or the United States could further complicate the situation.

It was once thought that Stroessner might try to impose a family dynasty on the country, passing control to his son, but the widespread opposition that arose in Nicaragua when that was done made it seem an inadvisable alternative in Paraguay. A transitional clique has emerged, only postponing the inevitable political realignments and confrontations.

The political climate for Stroessner deteriorated rapidly over the past few years. International attention was focused on the fraudulent 1988 elections, and the church began to take a hostile attitude toward the regime, a position that was dramatized during the papal visit to Paraguay in 1988. The United States charged some of Stroessner's cronies with drug trafficking as they scrambled to turn their political influence into personal gain. An era in Paraguayan politics has come to an end. In the resulting political vacuum, new political pressures and realignments will undoubtedly emerge; an extended period of political instability is also quite likely. The last of Latin America's traditional, patrimonial dictatorships outlasted its credibility and was overtaken both by its protracted abuse of power and by some of the very changes it instituted.

There is a possibility that the political system will be renovated to allow for freer party participation. This could be partially achieved by revising the electoral laws that regulate party registration and representation and by promulgating more reputable electoral procedures. Conversely, of course, Paraguay could find itself in yet another civil war or in a period of increasing instability. The roles that political parties, elections, public opinion, or representative government might play in Paraguay's new political scene are as yet unanswerable questions. What is certain is that change is imminent.

References

Codas, Roberto. 1981. Structural Change in Paraguay Threatens Old Order. *Washington Report on the Hemisphere* 1 (10):1–2, 6.

Lewis, Paul H. 1968. *The Politics of Exile: Paraguay's Febrerista Party.* Chapel Hill: Univ. of North Carolina Press.

_____ . 1980. *Paraguay Under Stroessner.* Chapel Hill: Univ. of North Carolina Press.

McDonald, Ronald H. 1981. The Emerging New Politics in Paraguay. *Inter-American Economic Affairs* 35:25–44.

Nichols, Brian A. 1968. Las Espectativas de los Partidos Políticos en el Paraguay. *Revista Paraguaya de Sociología* 5:22–61.

Reisner, Marc, and Ronald H. McDonald. 1986. The High Costs of High Dams. In A. McGuire and J. W. Brown, eds., *Bordering on Trouble: Resources and Politics in Latin America.* Bethesda, MD: Adler and Alder.

PART TWO

Two-Party Systems

6

COLOMBIA

Colombian political life has been dominated by the Liberal and Conservative parties since the middle of the nineteenth century. From their inception, both parties have been led by members of the nation's socioeconomic elite, yet mass partisan loyalties have been unusually widespread and deeply rooted. In addition, more than a century of intense interparty conflict has produced a distinctive pattern of strong, hereditary party identification that has frustrated prospective third parties.

The Liberal and Conservative parties have been the central actors in Colombian politics, but the party system has not always closely resembled a classic two-party model. Although military rule has seldom interrupted party competition, there have been long periods when one party has achieved clear supremacy. On other occasions, factionalism has fostered a de facto multiparty system. Moreover, during crises, particularly when the socioeconomic elite has perceived its interests to be threatened, Liberal and Conservative leaders have governed together. In the 1950s when the interparty bloodshed of *la Violencia* led to Colombia's only experience with military government in the twentieth century, party elites set aside their differences to form the National Front (1958–1974), a framework for institutionalized coalition government.

In the four major elections that have been held since the end of the National Front in 1974, voters have continued to favor the multiclass Liberals and Conservatives by a wide margin. Populist and Marxist parties have acquired few adherents even though neither of the traditional parties has addressed the nation's glaring socioeconomic inequalities or developed an effective strategy for confronting the growing power of the Colombian drug cartel. Declining party identification in the urban areas, however, indicates that the traditional parties' hold on voters is becoming weaker. Colombians still identify more with the Liberal party than with the Conservative party, yet the increasing size of the uncommitted electorate and the Liberals' intraparty divisions have enabled the Conservatives to remain competitive.

Although the two traditional parties continue to command the party system in the late 1980s, they have been unable to stem the violence associated with the narcotics traffic or to prevent the guerrilla opposition from endangering the country's stability.

The Evolution and Context of Colombian Party Politics

The Conservative party (PC) and the Liberal party (PL) both grew out of the political controversies of mid-nineteenth century Colombia. The Liberals, influenced by the Enlightenment, sought to strip the church of its economic and political power and often advocated other foreign ideas such as federalism and free trade. In contrast, Conservatives defended the established church and preferred centralized political and economic arrangements inherited from Spain. These disputes became interwoven with personal, familial, and regional rivalries.

Political conflicts among Liberals and Conservatives caused intense electoral competition and frequently degenerated into violence. Rural landlords regularly rallied their peasants to vote or to fight for one of the parties and, as a result, families, villages, and even entire regions began to develop unshakable allegiances. Governments were forced to rely on such irregular party forces to defend them because the country lacked a sizable regular army until well after the turn of the century (Ruhl, 1981:133).

Policy differences and competing ambitions caused factional divisions within each of the parties, and dissident party elites sometimes aligned with their party's enemies. In 1880, after having controlled the country's politics since 1863, the Liberal party lost its preeminent position when party moderates allied with Conservatives to form a National party coalition. Backing Rafael Nuñez for the presidency (Sharpless, 1982:288), they catapulted to power. Nuñez, a former Liberal, ushered in a lengthy period of Conservative leadership as Colombia adopted a centralist constitution and reestablished the Catholic church. Liberal attempts to depose the Conservatives by force ended with the War of the Thousand Days (1899–1902), the longest and most destructive of Colombia's many nineteenth-century civil wars.

Ideological contrasts between Liberal and Conservative elites gradually eroded and interparty enmities lessened during the first decades of the twentieth century. The hegemonic Conservative party manipulated elections and controlled policymaking, but it usually granted minority shares of legislative seats and patronage to the Liberals. The Liberals boycotted most presidential contests between 1902 and 1930 but were otherwise a well-behaved opposition. When President Rafael Reyes appeared to amass inordinate personal power, Liberals joined forces with many Conservatives in the Republican Union coalition (1909–1914) to resist him.

A split in the Conservative party produced two presidential candidates in 1930 and allowed a moderate Liberal, Enrique Olaya Herrera, to recapture the presidency for the Liberal party for the first time in fifty years. Conservatives preserved their congressional majority and participated in Olaya Herrera's bipartisan cabinet, but they lost control of local electoral machinery because the right to select departmental governors (who in turn appointed mayors) rested with the executive branch. Liberal vote totals in the countryside thus increased in the subsequent election, and the party also attracted strong support in the cities by promising reforms to the urban popular sector. In 1933 the Liberals easily wrested control of the Congress from the Conservatives by winning more than 60 percent of the vote.

President Alfonso López Pumarejo (1934–1938), a Liberal, expanded the state's economic role and its value as a source of patronage. He also launched the ambitious "Revolution on the March," which entailed reforms in union rights, land tenure, education, and taxation. López's populist program was never fully implemented, but its promise attracted leftists such as Jorge Gaitán, a magnetic orator who ceased organizing the Socialist party. But López's policies and the Liberal monopoly over patronage incensed Conservatives, especially those associated with reactionary Laureano Gómez. The president's populism also disturbed moderate, probusiness Liberals who managed to slow the pace of reform by electing one of their own to the presidency in 1938.

A fierce intraparty struggle preceded López's return to office in 1942, and by 1946 the Liberal party was too divided to agree on a presidential candidate. The Conservatives seized this opportunity and for the first time since 1930 vied for the presidency. With only 41 percent of the vote, moderate Conservative Mariano Ospina Pérez was able to defeat both of his Liberal opponents: mestizo populist Jorge Gaitán (26 percent) and moderate Gabriel Turbay (32 percent). Ospina invited Liberals to join a bipartisan cabinet, yet after control of local government changed hands, his rural followers tried to reduce the Liberal vote through intimidation. The Liberals still succeeded in maintaining their electoral majority in the 1947 congressional elections behind new party chief Gaitán, whose leftist faction had gained ascendancy.

This volatile situation polarized further in 1948 when Gaitán's assassination provoked widespread rioting in the capital. Liberal party guerrilla bands, which had begun to resist local rural authorities, became more active. When the Liberal Congress threatened impeachment in 1949, Ospina, with the military's cooperation, dissolved the legislative body and supervised the unopposed election of Laureano Gómez to the presidency. Gómez proceeded to institute an autocratic dictatorship that alienated many moderates within his own party as the nation drifted further into la Violencia. This period of interparty warfare ultimately cost the lives of more than 200,000 Colombians and precipitated a military coup (thus far, the only one for Colombia in the twentieth century) in 1953 by Gen. Gustavo Rojas Pinilla, an officer linked to the moderate Ospinista faction of the Conservatives.

General Rojas's government was initially welcomed by nearly all major factions in both parties, with the exception of the Laureanistas, whom he had ousted. Nevertheless, the feuding politicians united against the military ruler when he started to expound his own brand of authoritarian populism and began to organize a Peronist-inspired political movement. The threat posed by Rojas as well as the potential for social revolution represented by the armed peasantry convinced party elites of the need to reduce partisan hostilities. By the time Rojas was toppled in an internal military coup in 1957, representatives of the traditional parties had negotiated an institutionalized system of coalition government.

During the National Front period (1958–1974), the Liberals and Conservatives agreed to share all ministerial, legislative, and bureaucratic positions equally and to alternate control of the presidency. Relations between the two parties improved dramatically under this power-sharing arrangement, and interparty violence came to an end. But the Front encouraged intraparty factionalization (and voter apathy) because the only legally permitted electoral competition took place within each party to determine how its half of government positions would be allocated. At the national level, the Liberal party split into two factions: the Officialistas were headed by Alberto Lleras Camargo (president, 1945–1946 and 1958–1962) and Carlos Lleras Restrepo (president, 1966–1970); the Liberal Revolutionary movement (MRL), a left-of-center group, was founded by Alfonso López Michelsen, son of the populist former president. The two most important Conservative factions continued to be the Ospinistas and Laureanistas. In addition, General Rojas had founded the National Popular Alliance (ANAPO), a populist group that ran candidates under Conservative and Liberal labels. ANAPO seemed to represent a viable third-party alternative when, in 1970, it drew on strong lower-class urban support to capture 36 percent of the congressional vote and almost elected its leader to the presidency (39 percent). Indeed, many observers believe ANAPO was defrauded of victory in this contest. Nonetheless, when normal interparty electoral competition was restored in 1974 and ANAPO competed under its own label with a more radical posture, most Anapistas returned to their traditional parties. By this time the MRL had also rejoined the Liberal party; López Michelsen became the Liberal standard-bearer in 1974.

The National Front formally disbanded in 1974, but the traditional parties agreed to continue to divide all appointed government positions equally until 1978 and thereafter to distribute an "adequate and equitable" share to the minority party. This accord, formalized as Article 120 of the Colombian constitution, has helped to sustain the pattern of Liberal-Conservative cooperation that developed during the National Front era. Conservatives have benefited more from the post–National Front power-sharing arrangement: the four major elections held since 1974 have confirmed the Liberals' majority status.

The minority Conservatives did manage to capture the presidency in 1982 (and nearly won in 1978) in part because the party has maintained its cohesiveness better than the Liberals have. The two major Conservative factions of the 1980s (the Ospino-Pastranistas, led by former president

Ospina's wife, Berta Hernández de Ospina, and former president Misael Pastrana Borrera (1970–1974); and the Alvaristas, headed by former president Gómez's son, Alvaro Gómez Hurtado) have collaborated closely. In contrast, the Liberals have become seriously divided since 1973. A moderate majority faction is controlled by past presidents Turbay (1978–1982) and López Michelsen (1974–1978), and a dissident reformist faction is associated with the ambitions of former president Lleras Restrepo and the young Luis Carlos Galán, a former cabinet minister. Leaders of the minority faction have refused to endorse the Liberal party presidential candidate in the last three elections, and, in 1982, Galán ran independently as presidential candidate of the New Liberalism movement.

Throughout the post–National Front period, the traditional parties' dominance of the Colombian party system has not been challenged. Populist ANAPO received less than 10 percent of the vote in 1974 and then disintegrated as a political force after the death of its founder in 1975. Thereafter, traditional party candidates have won more than 90 percent of the ballots cast in every election. The Marxist left remained splintered and unpopular, although several guerrilla groups have demonstrated an increasing ability to disrupt political order in the 1980s.

The principal competitors for power thus remain the Liberal and Conservative party factions, each of which is subdivided into a number of loose, patronage-based networks, or *roscas*, organized around individual politicians (Kline, 1983:76, 93). The presidency constitutes the greatest prize of their rivalry because it is the most important dispenser of patronage as well as the foremost policymaking institution. Unlike most other Latin American legislatures, the Colombian Congress can block legislation, and the Supreme Court enjoys powers of judicial review. But the executive is still the most powerful branch of government and has extensive decree and emergency prerogatives. In addition, since the 1960s a large state bureaucracy has coalesced around the president, although many politicians complain that the new *técnicos* have acquired too much autonomy.

The president has broad powers of appointment with which to reward his loyalists and allies or to placate opponents. The chief executive is required by law to offer a share of these appointments to the opposing party commensurate with its electoral support, but the constitution does not require that the distribution of offices accurately reflect existing factional balances within the parties. For example, a Conservative faction might decide not to participate in a particular Liberal president's government, or a president might choose to reward more heavily those factions in either party that will be most supportive of his programs. Interestingly, President Virgilio Barco Vargas, a Liberal, began his term in 1986 with an entirely Liberal cabinet because Conservatives resolved not to accept any portfolios in order to develop a clearer opposition identity.

The socioeconomic elite that makes up the leadership of both parties is also directly connected to the nation's major private-sector interests (Sharpless, 1982:288). Large corporations and business associations such as the National

Association of Industrialists (ANDI) and the National Federation of Coffee Growers (FEDECAFE) have privileged access to government officials and attempt to develop close ties with both parties. In recent years many observers have become deeply concerned about the political influence of Colombia's illegal narcotics enterprises—but reliable information on this subject is scarce. Medellín drug lords assassinate or intimidate their political opponents but also reputedly offer generous financial support to compliant politicians.

Other political actors are of secondary importance. The church still carries weight on education, social welfare, and traditional church/state issues, but it has suffered from political divisions. The labor movement, which is small by Latin American standards, is also divided into several competing union federations, some of which are linked to the traditional parties, e.g., pro-Liberal Confederation of Colombian Workers (CTC).

The Colombian military is less powerful than most other Latin American armed forces, but it still plays an important political role. The army has stepped up internal security operations in response to the expansion of guerrilla activity and has acquired a major voice in public-order matters. Notwithstanding the military's power, Colombian presidents have stayed firmly in control of the armed forces and have dismissed generals who have carried public criticism of government policies too far. Essentially, military intervention has been avoided for the past thirty years because (1) the civilian political elite has prevented its interparty competition from becoming unmanageable, as it was in the 1940s; (2) the Liberal/Conservative coalitions since 1958 have pursued orthodox economic programs that have been agreeable to the army and the private sector; and (3) the traditional parties have managed to retain substantial mass support, which has inhibited the rise of radical parties (Ruhl, 1981:142).

Contemporary Political Parties

Policy differences between the Liberal and Conservative parties are minimal. The Conservatives (who adopted the name Social Conservatives in 1987) continue to advocate church doctrine on traditional church/state matters (e.g., divorce) against the more secular Liberals, but such controversies no longer figure prominently in Colombian politics. On more central issues such as economic and social policy or internal security, Liberals and Conservatives take similar centrist positions. Both parties preach social reform during electoral campaigns, yet emphasize probusiness economic policies when in office.

The traditional parties are decentralized and organizationally weak institutions and come to life only during electoral campaigns. Each party is a loose confederation of politicians from all levels of government who are bound to one another in clientelistic relationships. The parties' national leaders bargain for support from the influential regional powerbrokers, or *caciques*, who in turn negotiate with the local party bosses, or *gamonales*, who are most responsible for getting out the vote. Politicians' loyalties to the specific factions and *roscas* are based chiefly on personal connections and pragmatic calculations regarding material gain. In addition to these patron-client networks, organized ancillary groups (e.g., youth, women, students) are attached to each party, but these small organizations are not especially active.

National party conventions formally select national directorates and presidential candidates. Most convention delegates are incumbent congressmen, but all former presidents, cabinet ministers, and governors also have a right to seats (Dix, 1987:89). In spite of the convention format, a handful of top party leaders, often called "natural chiefs" (*jefes naturales*), actually make most important national party decisions. These *jefes*, many of whom are former presidents, also exercise influence in departmental party conventions, although the lower levels of the party enjoy substantial autonomy. Once elected, legislators display independence from the party organization because they have built personal bases of regional support and raised campaign expenses without the party's assistance.

The majority Liberal party is the less well organized and disciplined of the two major parties because its factional conflicts have been more serious. During the late 1960s and early 1970s, supporters of former president Lleras Restrepo and ex-MRL leader López Michelsen formed a reform faction against Turbay's followers, who controlled the party apparatus. In 1973, however, López switched factions after he and Turbay agreed to endorse one other, in turn, for the presidency. Since then, the larger and more broadly based Turbay-López faction has held sway. Dissident forces have recently been involved in the New Liberalism movement led by Galán, a former cabinet minister and protégé of Lleras Restrepo. Activists who adhere to New Liberalism's more nationalist and progressive platform tend to be political amateurs and *técnicos* from the urban middle class (Hoskin, 1983:11–13). The reform faction is not particularly well organized, but it does have a sizable following in Bogotá. After achieving little electoral success on its own, Galán's movement formally reintegrated with the regular Liberal party in 1988.

Relations among the personalist Conservative factions are less acrimonious. The Alvaristas, with longtime ties to agriculture, and the Ospino-Pastranistas, based especially in industrial, coffee-rich Antioquia (Dix, 1987:99), have cooperated effectively with each other since the end of the National Front. The Alvaristas are somewhat more rightist than the Ospino-Pastranistas, with whom populist Belisario Betancur has been more closely associated, but policy differences have not been serious. The Conservative party's minority status has encouraged internal party cohesion.

The foregoing discussion shows that the traditional parties resemble classic, weakly organized cadre parties in many ways. Yet, because of widespread hereditary party identification felt by most Colombians, both parties have mass mobilizational capabilities that are more characteristic of European mass parties (Dix, 1987:89). Most Colombians still develop an emotional attachment to one of the two traditional parties (but not to any particular faction) as part of their early political socialization. Recent polls, however, have revealed an erosion in the degree and intensity of partisan attachment. By 1982, 38 percent of the Bogotá electorate claimed to have no party identification (Dix, 1987:121), and a great number of the capital's nominal Liberals did not vote for the party's presidential nominee either in 1978 or 1982. The new urban, independent vote is concentrated among the young (under age twenty-five), the better-educated, and the middle class (Hoskin, 1983:26–27). Kline (1983:78) speculates that party identification has declined because the existence of coalition governments since 1958 has reduced the importance of partisanship and because the country's growing cities have proved more difficult to control with traditional political techniques.

Both parties attract a multiclass following but still retain distinct geographical strongholds; e.g., Liberals on the Atlantic coast and in departments such as Tolima and Cundinamarca (Bogotá), Conservatives in Antioquia (Medellín) and other departments where the church is strong (Dix, 1987:96–97, 116). Urban areas and more industrialized departments (other than proclerical Antioquia) are more likely to be Liberal, but the minority party has begun to narrow the Liberal's vote advantage in the cities.

None of the other parties that participate in Colombian elections is a significant political force. Nearly all of the minor parties offer left-of-center programs highly critical of existing socioeconomic and political conditions, but none of these organizations has succeeded in attracting more than a token share of the electorate, usually concentrated in Bogotá and other large cities. The most important opposition party on the left is the pro-Soviet Colombian Communist party (PCC), founded in 1930. This small but well-disciplined party is organized along standard Communist lines and includes an assortment of affiliated bodies, e.g., Communist Youth, and the Labor Confederation of Colombian Workers (CSTC), which has been the party's most important affiliate. The PCC frequently provides the institutional core around which smaller Marxist splinter parties unite in electoral coalitions, although its pro-Moscow stance and its desire to dominate the left have inhibited wholehearted cooperation. The Communist party is also connected with Colombia's largest guerrilla force, the Revolutionary Armed Forces of Colombia (FARC). In 1986 the two groups allied formally in the Patriotic Union (UP), a radical electoral front. Other guerrilla organizations, including the April 19 Movement (M-19), which originated in the ANAPO movement and the National Liberation Army (ELN), refused to participate in the 1986 campaign, a contest disrupted by the assassinations of many UP figures. Violence against UP officeholders and supporters by right-wing paramilitary groups continued after the election, and in 1986 claimed the life of the UP's presidential candidate, Jaime Pardo Leal.

Electoral Politics

Colombian elections are held in a climate of free expression and are conducted without notable irregularities. Electoral participation is not com-

TABLE 6.1
Colombian House of Representatives: Election Returns by Party and Rates of
Participation, 1958-1986 (in percentages)

	Liberals	Conservatives	ANAPO[a]	Other[b]	Voting
1958	57.7	42.2			68.9
1960	58.1	41.7			57.8
1962	54.5	45.4	(3.7)		57.9
1964	51.2	48.5	(13.7)		36.9
1966	55.4	44.2	(17.8)		44.5
1968	53.2	46.5	(16.1)		37.3
1970	51.1	48.6	(35.5)		51.9
1974	55.6	32.0	9.5	3.1	57.1
1978	55.1	39.4	--	4.3	33.4
1982	56.3[c]	40.3	--	2.5	40.7
1986	56.2	37.0	--	6.8	47.3

[a]From 1962 through 1970, ANAPO candidates ran as Conservatives or Liberals,
hence ANAPO votes are included in traditional party totals.
[b]Primarily the Colombian Communist party and other leftist groups.
[c]Lists associated with the New Liberalism movement won 10.2 percent of the
1982 vote and 6.6 percent of the 1986 vote.

Sources: Adapted from Robert A. Dix, The Politics of Colombia (New York:
Praeger, 1987), p. 112, and Gary Hoskin, "The Colombian Party System: The
1982 Reaffirmation and Reorientation," paper presented at the 1983 Latin
American Studies Association meeting, Mexico City, p. 34.

pulsory, and turnout fluctuates considerably depending on the type of election
(presidential elections generate a great deal more interest) and on the
candidates themselves. Official electoral turnout levels (congressional) have
ranged from 68.9 percent in 1958 in the optimistic climate of the National
Front's initiation to 33.4 percent in the dull 1978 contest; they have averaged
48.5 percent for the entire 1958–1986 period (Table 6.1). The actual proportion
of eligible citizens (over eighteen) who vote, however, may be as much as
10 percent higher than indicated (Hoskin, 1983:3), because Electoral Registry
turnout statistics assume incorrectly that every national identity card (cédula)
represents a potential voter. This error inflates the eligible electorate by
including soldiers, who are ineligible; deceased citizens whose card numbers
have not been deleted; Colombians abroad; and many people who have
moved (reregistration is slow). From this perspective, Colombian abstention
rates do not seem unusually high. Survey researchers also have confirmed
that lack of interest or inconvenience rather than discontent are the reasons
most often cited for staying away from the polls (Dix, 1987:111–112).
Abstention is highest in the large cities and among younger and less-educated
citizens.

   The Colombian president is elected every four years by plurality and is
prohibited from immediately succeeding himself. The Senate and House of
Representatives are chosen in a separate election that occurs two or three
months earlier. Members of Congress are elected by proportional representation using closed lists and an electoral quotient system. Each of the nation's

twenty-four departments is allotted a minimum of two senators plus an additional one for each 200,000 people, and a minimum of two representatives plus an additional one for each 100,000 people (Kline, 1983:73).

Because of factional competition, voters are normally presented with many different party lists. Between 1974 and 1982 there was an average of 5.2 lists for the Liberal party, 3.5 lists for the Conservatives, 1.5 lists for leftist opposition parties, and 1.4 other lists were offered per department in each election (Hoskin, 1985). Colombians may mix lists for different offices, but few do so. Elections for the relatively unimportant posts of departmental assemblymen and municipal councilors take place every two years using the same list system, but when these contests occur in the middle of a presidential term, they generate very little voter enthusiasm (less than 30 percent of the electorate voted in 1984).

From 1974 through 1986 the two traditional parties have captured over 93 percent of the vote in every congressional election (see Table 6.1). The fragmented opposition on the left has failed to mount any serious electoral challenge and has been unable to gain a popular following outside of the largest cities and a few isolated pockets in the countryside. The data also confirm that the Liberal party has maintained the majority status achieved in the 1930s. Since interparty competition was restored in 1974 the Liberals have won a consistent 56 percent of the vote, compared with the Conservatives' 37 percent average.

The large Liberal vote margins have naturally resulted in comfortable Liberal congressional majorities, as most recently reflected in the makeup of the 1982–1986 Congress (Senate: Liberals, 62; Conservatives, 51; Left, 1. House: Liberals, 114; Conservatives, 84; Left, 1) and the 1986–1990 Congress (Senate: Liberals, 68; Conservatives, 45; UP, 1. House: Liberals, 107; Conservatives, 82; UP, 10). Within the dominant Liberal party, the lists associated with the Turbay-López faction have collected far more votes than the lists aligned with Galán's dissident New Liberalism movement. New Liberalism lists collected only 10.2 percent of the total congressional vote in 1982, then fell to 6.6 percent of the vote in 1986, a sum sufficient to elect only eight senators and seven members of the House.

In spite of the fact that many more Colombians identify with the Liberals than the Conservatives, the minority party has managed to run very close races in two of the four presidential elections held since 1974 (Table 6.2). Conservatives have remained competitive by appealing to the growing segment of independents and weak partisans more effectively than the majority party has and by taking advantage of Liberal divisions. In 1974 and 1986, when the Liberals ran a single candidate against Alvaro Gómez (a Conservative whose family name still evokes memories of *la Violencia*), they won the presidency by landslide margins comparable to the size of its congressional victories. In contrast, in 1978 and 1982, when the Conservatives nominated populist Belisario Betancur, a more congenial personality from a humble social background, the party was able to attract large numbers of independents and disgruntled Liberals, earning nearly half of the national vote.

TABLE 6.2
Colombian Presidential Election Results, 1974–1986 (in percentages)

1974		
Alfonso López Michelsen	Liberal	56.3
Alvaro Gómez Hurtado	Conservative	31.4
María Eugenia Rojas	ANAPO	9.5
Hernando Echeverri Mejía	UNO	2.6

1978		
Julio César Turbay	Liberal	49.5
Belisario Betancur	Conservative	46.6
Other candidates		3.9

1982		
Belisario Betancur	Conservative	46.8
Alfonso López Michelsen	Liberal	41.0
Luis Carlos Galán	New Liberalism	10.9
Other candidates		1.3

1986		
Virgilio Barco Vargas	Liberal	58.2
Alvaro Gómez Hurtado	Conservative	35.8
Jaime Pardo Leal	UP	4.4
Other candidates		0.6

Sources: Keesing's Contemporary Archives (September 24, 1982), p. 31720, and (December 1986), pp. 34801–34802, and J. Mark Ruhl, "Party System in Crisis? An Analysis of Colombia's 1978 Elections," Inter-American Economic Affairs 32 (Winter 1978), p. 45.

Most recently, in 1982, Betancur ran at the head of the National movement, a coalition that added several small political groups (Christian Democrats, ANAPO remnants, and a few Liberals like leftist Gloria Gaitán) to the Conservatives, in order to reinforce its candidate's progressive and nationalist credentials. In a well-managed campaign combining traditional *gamonal* voter mobilization with a sophisticated mass-media appeal designed by U.S. and Colombian consultants, Betancur was able to defeat his two Liberal opponents (Hoskin, 1983:9). In Bogotá, Betancur captured 65 percent of the independents and 14 percent of the Liberals (as well as 93 percent of the Conservatives) and, unusual for a Conservative, ran better in popular-sector zones than in the more affluent districts (Hoskin, 1983:32, 46). The official Liberal candidate, former president López Michelsen, suffered from the hard-line reputation he had earned during his 1974–1978 term and was ill-served by an old-fashioned, highly partisan Liberal campaign that made less effective use of new campaign technologies. In addition, López lost Liberal votes to dissident Galán, who could not be persuaded to withdraw his presidential candidacy after the New Liberalism faction's lists lost to pro-López lists in the 1982 congressional elections (which often serve as a substitute for a presidential primary system).

Galán's poorly organized New Liberalism movement lost momentum after 1982, and his congressional lists took such a small portion of the March 1986 congressional vote that he decided not to participate in the May presidential elections, rejoining the parent party in 1988. In addition, the Conservative party was weakened by the declining popularity of the economically troubled Betancur administration and by the party's failure to find a candidate with broader appeal than the aristocratic Gómez. As a result, the pragmatic, centrist Virgilio Barco Vargas, a Liberal, won the 1986 presidential election handily—carrying all but two departments.

Interestingly, the Liberals' partisan advantage narrowed considerably in the 1988 municipal elections, when mayors were popularly elected for the first time. Preliminary results indicated that approximately 48 percent of the electorate turned out in the nation's 1,008 municipalities, electing 430 Liberals, 412 Conservatives, 14 UP candidates, and 162 representatives of coalitions and small local parties.

Long-Term Trends

Colombia is one of Latin America's few durable liberal democracies, and the Liberals and Conservatives who dominate it are two of the world's oldest active political parties. The nation's political system has clearly demonstrated its viability in spite of its justifiably criticized elitism, clientelism, and injustice (Peeler, 1976:223). Broad, traditional party identification has been the mainstay of the two-party system, however, and recent studies have documented a decline in partisan attachments. The growing segment of uncommitted urban voters represents an important new electoral element that urbanization will increase and that new political forces one day could mobilize.

Thus far, alternative political parties (e.g., populists, Marxists, and others) have completely failed to capitalize on the erosion of traditional party identification. Although greater unpredictability has been introduced into the future of Colombian politics, the established parties continue to show remarkable institutional resiliency. Unfortunately, in spite of their impressive political adaptability, neither of the traditional parties has been able to reverse the worsening climate of drug-connected and guerrilla-related violence that threatens the country's stability in the late 1980s.

References

Dix, Robert A. 1987. *The Politics of Colombia*. New York: Praeger.
Hoskin, Gary. 1980. The Attempted Restoration of the País Político. In R. Albert Berry, Ronald G. Hellman, and Mauricio Solaún, eds., *Politics of Compromise: Coalition Government in Colombia*. New Brunswick, NJ: Transaction.
———. 1983. The Colombian Party System: The 1982 Reaffirmation and Reorientation. Presented at the Latin American Studies Association meeting, Mexico City.

———. 1985. The Democratic Opening of Colombia: How Do Party and Electoral Behavior Relate to It? Presented at the Congreso Internacional de Americanistas meeting, Bogotá.

Kline, Harvey F. 1983. *Colombia: Portrait of Unity and Diversity.* Boulder, CO: Westview.

Peeler, John. 1976. Colombian Parties and Political Development. *Journal of Interamerican Studies and World Affairs* 18:203–224.

Ruhl, J. Mark. 1981. Civil-Military Relations in Colombia: A Societal Explanation. *Journal of Interamerican Studies and World Affairs* 23:123–146.

———. 1978. Party System in Crisis? An Analysis of Colombia's 1978 Elections. *Inter-American Economic Affairs* 32:29–45.

Sharpless, Richard E. 1982. Colombia. In Robert J. Alexander, ed., *Political Parties of the Americas.* Westport, CT: Greenwood.

7

URUGUAY

Party politics in Uruguay has emerged through four distinct historical periods. The first period, from independence in 1830 to approximately the beginning of the twentieth century, was one of instability and civil wars. It was during this period that organizations were formed that would evolve into the two traditional Uruguayan parties, the Colorado party (PC) and the National party (PN), the members of the latter more commonly known in Uruguay as the "Blancos."[1] The second period lasted until about 1973 and was one of stable politics, free elections, and vigorous party competition; these realities began to deteriorate as military intervention slowly increased, beginning in the mid-1960s. By 1973 the military was firmly in control of the government and party politics was suspended. The third period, from approximately 1973 until 1984, was one of military dictatorship. Party organizations and leaders were repressed and elections were not held. The fourth period began in 1984 with the reestablishment of party politics, elections, and civilian government. Of the four periods, our emphasis will be on the second, the time in which party politics was established and the institutions solidified. Although there have been new political realities, personalities, and issues since 1984, the basic style of party politics is that of the earlier period, and it is premature to state which recent changes in party politics will become permanent features of the system.

There was little evidence during the first seventy-five years following independence that Uruguay would eventually achieve a sustained period of democratic, civilian politics and relatively visionary public policy. Civil wars between rival coalitions of caudillos and international intervention from Brazil, Argentina, and Britain kept the country in constant turmoil. Stabilization came through the efforts of a remarkable politician, José Batlle y Ordóñez, in the first decade of the twentieth century. Batlle had both a vision of a modern, representative, self-sufficient Uruguay and an ability to work out political compromises and institutionalize them. He created an environment in which stability and democracy were possible. Both sides in the civil wars transformed their organizations into mass-based political parties and provided the country with more than sixty-five years of democracy and political stability. But this experience was based on a critical assumption of continuing economic growth and increasing prosperity, an assumption that fell victim to international economic realities following World War II and eventually led to the decay of the political system and the gradual rise of military influence. By the mid-1960s, economic stagnation and political paralysis had encouraged both a revolutionary movement and a growing involvement of the military. By the early 1970s the military was firmly in control of the government. The country had lost its democratic processes and liberties and was controlled by an authoritarian, repressive military regime until democratic politics was restored in 1985.

Two patterns have characterized Uruguayan politics: coparticipation and parity. Coparticipation is a belief that losers should share in the exercise of formal political power; parity is an assumption that such participation should be somewhat proportional to the relative electoral strength of the principal contenders. These two assumptions have found expression in several ways. The two major political groups, the Colorados and the Blancos, first practiced coparticipation as early as 1872 when they agreed to divide the country regionally into two blocs of provinces (departments) over which they could each exercise preponderant if not exclusive political control. Coparticipation found its ultimate expression in 1954 with the establishment of the National Council to replace the presidency. The council included six members from the stronger party and three members from the weaker one (Weinstein, 1975:50–85). Parity was achieved by formalizing the influence of the two parties in accordance with the relative strength of each, in 1872 by their military strength and in 1954 by their electoral strength. The issue of regional parity was finally resolved by the Pact of 1897, but behind that pact was a premise of continuing economic growth, modernization, and prosperity.

Coparticipation and parity also extended to the structures and leadership of the parties themselves. Party factions built around individual leaders were reinforced and guaranteed by a unique, complex electoral system known as the "lema law," the provisions of which defined the factional balances within the parties and guaranteed parity based approximately on their electoral strength. Control over political parties became not a question of winners or losers but a balance that guaranteed influence to all who adhered to the system.

The Evolution and Context of
Uruguayan Party Politics

The evolution of the traditional Uruguayan political parties began in 1830 at independence. For the remainder of the nineteenth century two militia groups, organized by coalitions of traditional caudillos, fought periodic civil wars to expand their regional influence and control the national government.

These two groups were identified by the arm bands they wore, red and white, the Colorados and the Blancos. The Colorados were stronger in the capital city of Montevideo and its adjoining departments. The Colorados' supporters grew as European immigrants streamed into the capital in the late nineteenth century. The Blancos were stronger in rural areas. During the civil wars the Colorados received aid from Brazil and several European nations, whereas the Blancos received assistance from Argentina, which had significant economic investments in rural areas. The period was dominated by those who had guns and could use force, and the country was ruled by political bosses. Effective national control had yet to be achieved, but the competing militias slowly were transformed into organizations that ultimately became the two traditional political parties.

With the emergence of the great Colorado leader, José Batlle y Ordóñez, at the end of the nineteenth century, came the development of modern Uruguayan politics. Few men have had so profound an impact on their country's party politics as did Batlle. He belonged to a family that had been central in Uruguayan politics since independence. Strongly nationalistic, anticlerical, and committed to the concept of stable, representative government, he developed sophisticated ideas about economic development and about the causes of political instability and dictatorships, which he saw as major plagues in Latin American cultures. He advocated programs for national control of economic resources and development, programs of social welfare, institutional limits on executive power, and even international guarantees of the rights and integrity of small nations—ideas that were visionary at the time. But his ideas and programs were also rooted in a very pragmatic desire to ensure the viability of the Colorado party and to build a strong electoral base for it among Montevideo's residents and immigrants. Batlle served twice as president (1903–1907, 1911–1915) and continued to dominate his party and his nation's politics until his death in 1929. In some ways contemporary party politics in Uruguay is still defined by the Batlle heritage.

Following the national election of 1903, Batlle and the Colorados won a decisive victory in the raging civil war with the Blancos and finally put an end to the political violence. As a pragmatist, Batlle understood the need to come to terms with the Blancos. He encouraged a party system congenial to the Blancos so that they would remain within a democratic system and compete in nonviolent ways. The objective of nonviolent competition coincided with his assumption that mass unrest in modern nations was the result of social and economic inequalities and that addressing those inequalities would strengthen political and governmental institutions and lessen the likelihood of dictators' coming to power.

Among his schemes was a controversial plan to abolish the presidency and replace it with a collegial executive. A referendum in 1916 for that plan failed, but it was ultimately approved in 1954. Batlle also designed and implemented an unusual electoral system, the lema law (Taylor, 1955:19–21), which stabilized Uruguayan politics through coparticipation and parity for factional leaders in the national party organizations. His programs were the foundation of modern, mass political parties and politics, which he and his party came to dominate through their substantial and growing electoral strength in the capital city and its surrounding region.

The Colorado party was divided into pro-Batlle and anti-Batlle groups, the former spawning a Batlle family political dynasty. His two sons, César and Lorenzo, became leaders of a faction known as "list 14," identified with *El Día*, while his nephew Luis Batlle Berres led a somewhat more orthodox Batlle list 15 and served as the country's president from 1947 to 1951. The difference between these two Batlle lists was more personal than political. A third group made up of anti-Batllista Colorados was led for many years by Amílcar Vasconcellos and other politicians who were either uncomfortable or unwelcome in the two Batlle groups. In the early 1960s a fourth Colorado faction gained national significance, list 99, led by Zelmar Michelini. This group was the most reformist of the Colorado factions and ultimately broke with the Colorado party to support an alliance of leftist groups in the 1971 election.

The major divisions in the National party emerged from long-standing traditions of strong Blanco leaders affectionately known by their supporters as the "great caudillos." Perhaps the best known of these romanticized, rural leaders was Luis Herrera, but there were others, such as Benito Nardone, whose *ruralista* group had a populist, perhaps fascist orientation. In the 1960s these groups joined forces under the leadership of Sen. Martín Echegoyen, forming a faction known as Herrerismo-Ruralismo-Movimiento Popular Nacionalista, the largest component of the National party. A more moderate group known as Reform and Development, list 400, was the next largest of the party's factions. Prior to the suspension of party politics by the military, the National party was divided and without strong leadership, with its leaders building complex coalitions by cross-endorsing and cross-listing candidates under the lema law.

Minor political parties or lemas have always been a part of Uruguayan politics, although their electoral strength even when combined has rarely been significant. The oldest of these "third" parties is the Uruguayan Communist party (PCU), whose principal support has been in the Uruguayan labor movement. For most of its history, the PCU has participated openly in elections. There is also a Socialist party (PS) and the Civic Union party (UC), a conservative Catholic group originally organized to respond to the anticlericalism of the Batlle factions. In the 1960s left-oriented leaders of the UC broke with the party and formed a Christian Democratic party (PDC).

The shift to electoral politics following Batlle's reforms gave priority to party organization. In Montevideo and most of the towns and villages, leaders formed clubs to support the candidacies that were identified with the party factions, or sub-lemas. These clubs, particularly in the capital, were neighborhood organizations that served social as well as political functions. It was through the clubs that voters kept in touch with the candidates they supported and adherents gained access to patronage and services. Clubs for both traditional parties, often several factions of both parties, could be found in many neighborhoods, and they provided the organizations necessary for political campaigns. By providing stable political organizations and access to patronage, these clubs constituted an exchange of goods and services between candidates and their constituents; they were in many ways the heart of Uruguayan party politics.

Uruguayan parties evolved with a close relationship to newspapers and journalists. Most major parties and factions have been affiliated with a newspaper. Moreover, many prominent Uruguayan politicians have had backgrounds and careers in journalism, and those who have not frequently have become associated with newspapers as columnists as their political careers have evolved (McDonald, 1971b:113–120). Batlle himself established the tradition when he founded *El Día*, serving as its publisher until his death. One of South America's most influential newspapers, *El Día* was a vehicle for Batlle's political ideas and was the principal organ of the Colorado party. It remained under the control of the Batlle family, some of whom have become prominent leaders and presidential candidates. Newspapers have played an extraordinary role in the evolution of Uruguayan party politics, forging strong ties between a free and competitive press and a free and competitive political system. Today television is beginning to share that function.

Uruguayan political parties maintained a balance in their evolution between modern bureaucratic structures and traditional personalistic leadership. The two traditional parties achieved a stable political balance through a distinctive system of coparticipation and parity designed to prevent violent conflict between them and protect the careers and constituencies of party leaders.

Throughout most of its history Uruguay appears to have had a vital, competitive two-party system with a few third parties participating. But this characterization is somewhat misleading. The Colorado party has prevailed in all but two elections, even though the National party has retained its influence and participation in national government. The stronger factions in each party have traditionally dominated elections, but minor factions have maintained their influence and participation in party leadership through a parity defined by their electoral strength. Uruguay's distinctive means of formalizing and dividing political power produced an unusual two-party system in which the losers maintain parity and participation in national government as well as in party structures and processes. By protecting minorities the system produced remarkable stability, political freedom, and competition, qualities normally associated with democratic politics. But this stability also produced what by the mid-1960s came close to political paralysis. This inertia had a stabilizing influence on Uruguayan politics only as long as the challenges were long-term and the needed adjustments were incremental. The party system, faced with the need to deal with the country's economic decline and the political threats from outside the traditional party system, could not adjust and respond.

Regional parity and party coparticipation were based on a crucial premise: spontaneous and continuing economic growth and modernization. Politics was seen as a process of distributing affluence among Uruguayans rather than a process of assuring or stimulating more affluence. When by the mid-twentieth century this assumption proved false, the traditional parties were unable to respond to the growing problems of economic decline and austerity, and the need to stimulate economic growth (Taylor, 1963:62-68).

Apart from the distinctive party system, the country's democracy followed traditional forms. Regular elections were held and the results were respected. At least in principle, elections were open to all parties that chose to take part, even if that participation was not on an equal basis with the two traditional parties. Electoral participation was high, and campaigns were vigorous, noisy, and competitive. Laws and programs were formulated and executed through institutions that included a functioning legislature, following procedures defined by the nation's constitution. National security, both internal and external, was controlled by civilians, and expenditures for this purpose were kept at a minimum. Uruguay's democratic heritage became a matter of national pride, particularly by contrast to the authoritarianism and instability of its neighbors, Paraguay, Brazil, and Argentina. Uruguayans welcomed political exiles from other Latin American nations, sustained a fiercely independent and competitive press, and maintained an impressive system of public education. The assumptions of "progress" and growth that underlay Uruguayan democracy spawned highly advanced, even visionary programs of social welfare that provided extensive benefits in education, health, social security, and retirement to its citizens, at levels beyond those common in Europe or the United States at the time. Party leaders competed to take credit for these benefits, trying to maximize their own personal influence and the electoral strength of their party factions. Until economic decline set in following World War II, many outside observers characterized Uruguay as the "Switzerland of South America"—inappropriately, as it turned out.

The decline of Uruguayan democracy, shown by the growing paralysis in the party system and a rise in civil violence, encouraged a gradual ascendancy of military influence in politics over almost a decade, from 1965 to 1973 (McDonald, 1975:25-27; Kaufman, 1978:8-12). This decline was rooted in the structural defects and intransigence of the country's economic system and in the assumption of continued, spontaneous economic growth. The fact that the rise of the military to power was gradual made the results no less decisive. Civilian institutions and leaders became increasingly isolated from national decisionmaking and ultimately were replaced by military ones.

The period of military dictatorship was one of confusion and uncertainty and contrasted sharply with the stability and near predictability of the preceding democratic period. Faced with growing national and international opposition and their inability to manage the economic problems, military leaders eventually, if reluctantly, agreed to reestablish civilian control. The transition from military to civilian control ("redemocratization") in Uruguay was a confrontational, chaotic process despite its being controlled not by the military but by the civilian politicians and parties.

Electoral Laws and Representation

There is no more profound influence on political parties, campaigning, and voting in Uruguay than the unusual electoral laws and practices that regulate them (Taylor, 1955:19–42). Uruguay employs a variation on proportional representation—known as "Double Simultaneous Voting" (DSV)—which is built around the d'Hondt distributive formula and a closed-list ballot. Representation in the lower house, the National Assembly, is keyed to population in the nineteen departments of the nation; there are ninety-nine members. The thirty-member Senate is elected at large from the nation. Under the constitution, the vice-president of the republic also presides over the National Assembly.

A unique feature of the system is its formalization of party factions, which are known as "sub-lemas," and their relationship to the parties, which are known as "lemas." Voting, which is compulsory, is done by party and sub-lema lists, which are printed and distributed by the sub-lemas following a form prescribed by the government. For the purposes of campaigning and voting, sub-lemas are distinguished as numbered lists whose titles are clearly identified with a leading personality or cause. Hundreds of different lists exist for national elections, and separate numbers are used for each sub-lema in each district. The sub-lemas that have received formal recognition from the lema print and distribute the ballots, sometimes requesting a campaign contribution from the voter in exchange for a ballot. Individuals vote for sub-lema candidates and, in so doing, also vote for the lema. After balloting, each sub-lema's votes are totaled separately, then all sub-lema votes in a lema are totaled to determine the overall number of seats awarded to the party. Sub-lemas receive their share of the total awarded to the lema according to the proportion they contributed to the total lema vote. Under this arrangement, a sub-lema benefits or suffers in relation to the general fortunes of the lema and shares proportionately to its specific vote in the election. Individual candidates are elected according to their position in the rank-order of candidates on the sub-lema list; if that position is high enough, they are included in the share allotted to the sub-lema by its vote and the total lema vote.

Following the basic d'Hondt formula for allocating representation, a sub-lema's total vote in a department (or in the case of the Senate, the entire nation) is divided by consecutive divisors (1, 2, 3, 4, etc.), and each sub-lema's quotients are arranged in descending order. Seats are awarded successively according to the highest remaining quotient until all seats won by the party (based on its percentage of the total vote) are distributed. Any vote for a sub-lema contributes to the total vote for the lema, and the sub-lema is rewarded by sharing its proportion of the total representation. Under the collegial system (1954–1966), the lema that won control of the legislature received two-thirds of the seats on the National Council, and the Opposition gets the remaining one-third; the majority sub-lema of the majority lema gained control of the two-thirds majority (McDonald, 1971a:694–708).

The unusual lema law was designed specifically for Uruguayan elections more than seventy-five years ago. The strongly personalistic party politics and the relatively autonomous position that many leaders have within the broader party structure required innovative laws. Through the lema law parties have been coalitions of organizations and leaders at the sub-lema level. And the strength and influence of these sub-lemas within the lema have been dependent on their electoral strength. What has tended to hold together these sub-lemas within the structure of the lema is that a vote for any sub-lema helps other sub-lemas by increasing the total for the lema and, consequently, expanding the number of seats to be awarded to the lema and subsequently, the sub-lemas. The sub-lema and its leaders are thus the real center of power in the party. It is they who have built the party organizations and who have controlled the vast systems of patronage in the country.

The lema law affects both legislative and presidential elections. Uruguayan elections customarily have a number of candidates running for the presidency in each of the major lemas; usually they are leaders of the large sub-lemas. Theoretically at least, any sub-lema leader is a potential presidential candidate. The presidency is won by the lema with the largest national vote and by the candidate of the lema whose sub-lema receives the largest share of the lema vote. Under this system it is possible for a candidate from a lema with multiple candidates to be elected, even though he might receive fewer votes than a candidate from the opposition lema, if the total vote for the latter is less than that for all the candidates of the opposition lema. This occurred in 1971, when a Colorado candidate won over a Blanco candidate who received more votes (Gillespie, 1986:231).

The lema law has many political implications. It creates a kind of primary election within the general election, giving the voter considerable latitude in selecting his representatives as well as the president. As long as a sub-lema and its candidate can receive sufficient votes to gain representation, it remains a viable force within the lema and exists independently from the other sub-lemas and leaders. The more representatives a sub-lema elects, the greater its influence within the lema. This makes campaigning vigorous to say the least: while all sub-lemas benefit from votes for other sub-lemas in the party, they are also competing with each other for a share of the lema vote. Therefore, service to the voter and patronage become important preoccupations between elections, although this practice seems to be declining (Rial, 1986:257).

The lema law was a principal obstacle to the reestablishment of civilian rule in Uruguay in 1986 (McDonald, 1987:173–188). The military rulers were strongly opposed to the return of powerful sub-lema leaders, who the military rulers felt were responsible for the economic and political malaise that "forced" them to take power in the first place. The new constitution drafted by the military and defeated in the referendum of 1980 would have drastically changed the former system of party organization and voting (Handelman, 1986:210–211). The military continued to oppose the system through protracted negotiations (1980 to 1985) with the civilian leaders. In one of the many ironies of Uruguayan politics, the military regime twice lost its effort to reform the system—first to the voters who rejected the new constitution in the referendum, and second to the political leaders who stubbornly refused to agree to a change in the electoral laws.

Although almost any group can register with the national electoral commission and print a list of candidates, use of the lema symbol and name is controlled by the lema itself and therefore by the leaders whose sub-lemas control the lema. New sub-lemas generally benefit the lema because they attract additional votes, and recognition has therefore been readily extended. Often, the new sub-lemas are no more than repackagings of existing ones, with a difference in the first name on the list, that of the sub-lema leader. This process accounts for the often dismaying number of electoral alliances and cross-alliances made during elections. Candidates may adopt a specific sub-lema for their district, placing their name at the top of the list, thereby creating a new list and a new number. In such a case, the sub-lema list in a given district may account for no more than the addition or substitution of a name or names in the printed hierarchy of another list. The smaller, district-level sub-lema benefits from the publicity and popularity of the major sub-lema leadership and campaign while pursuing its own personalistic ends in specific legislative races. Both the lema and the sub-lemas ultimately benefit from the system. Historically, the losers have been the "third-party" movements, which must register and compete as lemas but which actually resemble sub-lemas in size and vote. The system, in other words, subsidizes and supports the two major parties and has made electoral competition with them very difficult. By custom, party unity and cooperation prevail in the legislature following elections—but a great deal of backroom negotiation takes place to achieve it.

Contemporary Political Parties

Beginning in the 1960s and clearly by the election of 1971, fundamental changes, which established the foundations for contemporary parties, had begun to occur in Uruguayan party politics. Most of the changes in the traditional parties were evolutionary, but new party organizations also appeared. These changes lay dormant during the decade of military rule, and their significance will not be totally clear until after the 1989 election.

As military influence increased in the 1960s, two Colorado presidents, Jorge Pacheco Areco (1967–1971) and Juan María Bordaberry (1971–1973), came under military control. Pacheco Areco had been elected vice-president in 1966 as running mate of Oscar Gestido, a retired military officer who won the presidential election with a new sub-lema of the Colorado party created exclusively for that purpose. Gestido died shortly after taking office, Pacheco Areco assumed the presidency, and military influence began to increase rapidly. After his term ended, he received diplomatic posts from the military regime as ambassador first to Spain and subsequently to the

United States. Bordaberry was elected in 1971, but ultimately he was forced to resign by the military in 1973 and was replaced by a puppet president appointed by the military. This experience divided the Colorados into new groups, those acquiescing in the military rule, represented by Pacheco Areco and Bordaberry, and those opposing it.

Until the military dictatorship, the Blancos had been united by their opposition to Batlle and his Colorado followers but were profoundly divided by personalities and traditions. One of their leaders, Wilson Ferreira Aldunate, became a major critic of the military regime during the dictatorship, rallying opposition to it both nationally and internationally. His leadership consolidated the National party and overcame many of its traditional divisions.

The emergence of the Tupamaro revolutionary movement, more precisely known as the Movement for National Liberation (MLN), created a new political force in Uruguay in the mid-1960s. Apart from its revolutionary activities, the MLN was instrumental in forming a coalition for the 1966 election that included the Socialist and Communist parties. The coalition was the "Leftist Front of Liberation," more ominously known by its Spanish acronym "FIDEL." The coalition ran candidates in 1966 using the Communist party lema, list 1001. As conditions deteriorated during the next few years, the coalition broadened to include the Christian Democratic party and the Colorado party list 99, led by Zelmar Michelini, and was renamed the Broad Front (FA). The presidential candidate of the Broad Front in 1971 was Líber Seregni, a former military officer who like Blanco leader Ferreira had been persecuted and imprisoned by the military regime. Seregni reemerged during the 1984 election as a major political leader, but like Ferreira the military had barred him from running for the presidency in that election.

Some Uruguayan politicians cooperated with the military regime or at least refrained from public criticism of it (Handelman, 1981:215–220). Other leaders, like Ferreira and Michelini, went into exile. While he was in Argentina Michelini was assassinated, many believe in a plot organized by the Uruguayan military. In 1980 the military sponsored a constitutional referendum. The referendum failed, but it further regrouped traditional party factions according to those supporting and those opposing the military proposal.

Ferreira returned to Uruguay in 1984 just before the national election campaign and was immediately imprisoned by the military. Many Blanco leaders wanted him as their presidential candidate, but he declined to press the issue with the military, wishing to avoid a direct confrontation with the regime, a confrontation that might prevent the country's return to democracy. After the Colorado victory in that election, Ferreira and his supporters—Carlos Julio Pereyra, Jorge León Otero, Gonzalo Aguirre, among others—assumed control of a relatively united National party and had at least the potential of becoming a formidable challenge to the Colorados in the 1989 election. But in March 1988 Wilson Ferreira Aldunate died, and leadership of the Blancos fell to Pereyra, Alberto Zumarán, and Luis Alberto Lacalle.

The emergence of FIDEL and subsequently the Broad Front challenged the political hegemony of the two traditional parties. The ability of the

Colorado and Blanco politicians to run the country was in doubt for many voters, a doubt shared by the military leaders. The traditional party system, so carefully conceived by Batlle and so assiduously nurtured for generations by politicians, lost control of the nation's politics and ultimately lost control of its government. The formula that had produced political stability for so many years was by now producing political paralysis. Coparticipation, exemplified by the sub-lema system and the brief but disastrous experiment with the collegial executive, obstructed strong political leadership at a time when the country desperately needed it. Batlle's romantic assumption about steady and inevitable economic development, nationalism, and a modern Uruguay of expanding affluence could no longer support the visionary programs of a modern welfare state or sustain the political parties and leaders who advocated and promoted them. The possibility of economic decline had not been considered.

Elections, Campaigns, and Voting

According to the 1967 constitution, elections for municipal, legislative, and presidential offices are held simultaneously every five years; before 1967 they were held every four years. The final election before the miltary takeover took place in 1971. In 1980 a referendum was held on a military-sponsored constitution; an election to select party leaders followed in 1982. The election that reestablished civilian government took place in 1984. Until the advent of the military regime, Uruguayan parties were among the best organized, most sophisticated and institutionalized in Latin America and were thoroughly integrated within the broader political and governmental processes of the country.

The lema system and double simultaneous voting are regarded as extraordinarily complex by many outside observers. As complex as they appear, the practices are not complicated for voters familiar with them. Decisions are made from the top of the lists down, and the alternatives diminish in that process. A voter first chooses a party (lema), a choice that normally does not change from one election to another. Then one of the presidential candidates is selected (if there is more than one for the lema), followed by the first choice for the Senate. After that, voters can select a list for a specific candidate for the National Assembly. Decisions concerning local candidates rarely become a factor in the selection. The voter's decisionmaking is also facilitated by the fact that the elections are organized around sub-lemas and, more important, around personalities who are sub-lema leaders. As we have already noted, Uruguayan elections are highly personalistic, and it is the sub-lema leaders who are most visible during the campaigns. Considering the fact that the voter actually marks no ballot, the system provides remarkable flexibility, providing in some respects a primary election within the general election. National parties, i.e., the lemas, become composites of the sub-lemas' fortunes, with individual leaders exercising influence in the national parties more or less according to their ability to attract votes for their sub-lemas and to make alliances with other sub-lema leaders in their own party.

Sub-lemas not only organize the voting in Uruguay, but they also provide the basic organization of the parties themselves. Sub-lema organizations, particularly in cities and especially in Montevideo, are extensive and highly institutionalized. As we have seen, the center of party organization, at least until the military assumed power, was a vast network of political clubs. The importance of these clubs has been strangely overlooked by most observers of Uruguayan politics (an exception is Campiglia, 1969), yet their presence was obvious to anyone visiting the country. The political clubs in Montevideo, which are the most numerous and most active ones, resembled the system once common in large U.S. cities such as New York—except in Montevideo the major parties maintained neighborhood clubs in the same areas and competed for adherents. These neighborhood clubs were identified with sub-lemas through their traditional list number and their long, colorful names. During election campaigns, their brightly painted headquarters organized campaign workers and solicited campaign funds, providing workers to distribute campaign literature and solicit votes by direct, personal exchanges and appeals.

The clubs were held together between elections by patronage and client services, which were provided by the clubs' agents or, if necessary, by the politicians whose sub-lemas the clubs advocated. An estimated one out of four Uruguayans received some kind of direct service or payment from the government. At its peak the system touched almost every family in the country in some way or another. Bureaucratic mistakes and confusion and the need for special advocacy put the sub-lema leaders in positions as congressmen and politicians to serve the club members. This service, or the possibility of it, is what created the personal bond between the club-related voters and their politicians. Politicians, in return, were indebted to clubs for campaign work, loyalty, and contributions. Not all the club activity was political. Clubs were neighborhood social units. But they mostly provided a grass-roots political organization that benefited parties, their leaders, and the voters. Personal bonds are both possible and critical in so small an electorate as Uruguay.

In the past three legislative elections (1966, 1971, and 1984) there has been little stability in the sub-lemas of the Colorado and National parties (Table 7.1). The changes in sub-lema names, however, is less significant than might be assumed, because the leadership has remained relatively constant. The different sub-lemas tend, rather, to be regroupings of previous ones—coalitions being redefined with each new election.

In addition to the three congressional elections, there have also been two special elections since 1966. One, in 1980, was a military-sponsored constitutional referendum; the other, in 1982, was a special primary election to select party leaders prior to the organization of the 1984 national election.

The constitutional referendum of November 30, 1980, was part of the military regime's plan to restructure Uruguayan politics (particularly the

TABLE 7.1
Principal Sub-lemas in Uruguayan Elections, 1966–1984

Party	1966	1971	1984
Colorado	Desarrollo y Justicia	Batllismo Unido (list 15)	Batllismo Unido (list 15)
	Batllismo Unido	Re-elecionismo	Unión Colorado
	Evolución y Gobierno del Pueblo (list 99)	Tercer Frente	Batllista Independiente
	Batllismo	Por la Unión del Partido	Libertad y Cambio
	Unión Colorado y Batllista		
	Unidad y Reforma		
	Antorch de Batlle		
National	Herrerismo-Ruralismo	Por el Triunfo del Partido	Por la Patria
	Reforma y Desarrollo	Por la Soberania Blanca	Movimiento Herrerista Nacional
	Herrera-Haedo	Nacionalista y Justicia Social	Unión Nacional Herrerista
	Movimiento Popular Nacionalista	Soberania y Desarrollo Por la Patria	Movimiento de Rocha

parties and their practices) before returning the government to civilians through elections. The government did not release the text of the constitution until November 1, and the referendum was strictly controlled. A massive propaganda campaign was also launched in favor of the proposed constitution. The opposition was relatively disorganized and without funds. They also lacked sufficient press freedom to criticize the government's proposal. Despite these adverse conditions, the proposal was voted down. 43 percent of the voters cast ballots in favor of it, 57 percent voted against it; 85 percent of the electorate participated. Rarely if ever has a military dictatorship had to admit defeat in a constitutional referendum it so tightly controlled. The defeat opened up new negotiations between the military regime and the civilian party leaders over terms for returning power to the civilians. The civilians prevailed on most of the crucial issues, including the continuation of the lema system of elections.

Two years later, in November 1982, a special primary election, mentioned above, was held to select leaders for the two major parties. The task, unprecedented in Uruguayan political history, was undertaken by the military so as to empower civilians that least opposed the military as party leaders. Again, the military failed to achieve its objective. Of those voting within the Colorado party, 69 percent voted for strong opponents of the military regime; in the National party, 85 percent of the vote went to the regime's opponents. Participation in this election was 61 percent, low by Uruguayan

TABLE 7.2
Participation and Party Vote in Uruguay, 1966–1984 (in percentages)

	1966	1971	1980[a]	1982[b]	1984
Participation	75	93	87	61	88
Party Vote					
Colorado	49	41			41
National	40	40			36
Broad Front		18			21
Other[c]	11	1			2

[a]Referendum.
[b]Election of party leaders.
[c]Other signifies a blank, protest vote.

Source: Official Uruguayan electoral results compiled by the Corte
Electoral (Montevideo), 1966–1984.

standards (Table 7.2). Unlike other elections, voting was not compulsory. Also, voters failed to see the election as critical in the process of restoring democracy (Gillespie, 1986:219).

Several conclusions can be drawn regarding voting behavior in Uruguay, as revealed by the results of the five most recent elections.

1. Uruguay can boast of uncommonly high levels of voter participation in national elections, usually in excess of 80 percent of those eligible. This is all the more remarkable when one considers that many Uruguayans are now permanent residents of other countries (estimates of at least 20 percent are common) who must either return to Uruguay to vote or make arrangements for voting through an Uruguayan consulate. Voting has been compulsory in all but the 1982 election.

2. Throughout the twentieth century there has been a relatively even balance between the vote for the two major parties, suggesting considerable stability. A comparison of the outcomes of the 1971 and 1984 elections is particularly striking (see Table 7.2). The Colorado party received exactly the same percent of the national vote (41 percent) in 1984 that it had received in 1971; the National party received 40 percent in 1984 and 36 percent in 1971, a modest increase. Thirteen years of military rule and a vigorous campaign by the military to reorient and restructure party politics apparently had no effect on the electorate. Normalization of Uruguayan politics in 1984 meant precisely that, a return to virtually the identical voting patterns that existed in 1971.

3. The Colorados have remained throughout this century the stronger of the two major parties. The National party won only the elections of 1958 and 1962. The Colorados have advocated and implemented significant changes in Uruguay, but they have also become the political establishment. The

TABLE 7.3
Party Representation in the Uruguayan Legislature, 1962–1985

	Deputies				Senate			
Party	1962	1966	1971	1985	1962	1966	1971	1985
Colorado	45	50	41	41	14	16	13	13
National	46	41	40	35	15	13	12	11
Christian Democrat	3	3	0	0	0	0	0	0
FIDEL	3	5	0	0	1	1	0	0
Broad Front	0	0	18	21	0	0	5	6
Other	2	0	0	2	0	0	0	0
Total	99	99	99	99	30	30	30	30

Source: Official Uruguayan electoral results compiled by the Corte Electoral (Montevideo), 1962–1985.

National party victories in 1958 and 1962 may have resulted primarily from dissatisfaction with the country's deteriorating economic and social conditions. Ferreira's strong leadership and opposition to the military regime and his return to head the National party after the 1984 election may have set the stage for the Blancos to become the stronger party in 1989. Much depends on how voters judge the performance of the Colorado regime since 1985 (Rial, 1986:261).

4. The major variable in voting since 1966 has been the third parties, or more precisely the coalitions. In 1966 this was FIDEL, dominated by the Communist party; in 1971 and 1984 it was the Broad Front. Nontraditional parties received 11 percent of the vote in 1966, 18 percent in 1971, and 21 percent in 1984. These percentages reflect considerable discontent with the traditional system as well as demands for reform in policies and improvement in living standards. By late 1988 it was unclear just how cohesive the Broad Front would be for the coming election. Could the Colorado party recapture this disenchanted vote? Or would it be channeled toward the National party or the Broad Front? These are key questions in contemporary Uruguayan party politics.

5. Although Uruguay has a very competitive, largely two-party system, neither of the major parties has won a majority of the vote in recent elections. This has translated into a national legislature that no party can control, making alliances and shifting coalitions critical to the outcome of legislative endeavors (Table 7.3). This is one of the principal factors in the government's political paralysis in the 1960s. Given the outcome of the 1984 election, this could happen again. For the Colorado party to govern Uruguay, it must maintain the solidarity of its own lema in the legislature and obtain support from the National party or the Broad Front.

6. There is a strong regional bias dividing Uruguay. The Colorado party traditionally has enjoyed overwhelming support in Montevideo and those departments contiguous to it, in the densely populated regions, and in a band of rural northwestern departments. The National party has been strongest in some rural departments in central Uruguay. A band of departments lying between these strongholds can be won by either party. In 1971 the Colorados carried only five departments with 39 percent of the vote; they carried eleven with the same 39 percent in 1984. In 1971 the National party carried fourteen departments with 40 percent of the vote. But in 1984 they carried only six departments with 36 percent of the vote. Of the fourteen the Blancos won in 1971, five were won by fewer than three thousand votes. Given the nature of representation in Uruguay, the number of departments won or lost has little political significance.

Several Latin American nations have a long tradition of national opinion polls. Uruguay, having an affiliate of the Gallup organization, is foremost among them. Little analysis of this data has been done, but the polls contain few surprises. Insofar as class is a basis for party preference, one poll taken prior to the 1971 election showed upper-class voters about as likely to support the Broad Front as the Colorado party; they were least likely to support the National party. The middle class and lower class were more disposed toward the Colorado party, less so toward the National party and the Broad Front. Male voters were somewhat more disposed then females toward the Broad Front. Voters over the age of thirty-five were about equally divided between the two major parties and were less likely to support the Broad Front. Younger voters (ages eighteen to twenty-four) were clearly more disposed toward the Broad Front, with little difference evident between males and females (La Mañana [Montevideo], July 7, 1971:1).

By 1984 party disposition had changed slightly, and some provocative trends emerged. Colorados received greater support from lower-income voters than did the other groups, and received least support among the upper-middle-class voters. The Blancos received least support from the wealthiest voters, while the Broad Front generally did least well among the poorer voters. Polls taken prior to the 1982 primary election showed support for the Broad Front increased in relation to higher levels of income and education; it also attracted the younger voters (Gillespie, 1986:233–237). These surveys also showed that the young were less committed to the two traditional parties, that most voters made up their minds about their choice fairly early in the campaign, and that a substantial proportion of voters expressed a preference for a national-unity government over a government controlled by the winning party (Rial, 1986:262–265). The Colorado party won the presidential elections of 1966, 1971, and 1984, but the victories were somewhat Pyrrhic. Oscar Gestido, elected in 1966, died a few months after taking office, elevating Jorge Pacheco Areco to the presidency. Pacheco, a rightist with little popular support, had the misfortune to preside over the country during the height of political tensions in the late 1960s. He contributed to the decline of representative government by acceding to most of the demands of his military advisors.

Juan María Bordaberry was elected in 1971, only to be deposed by the military after he tried to assume dictatorial powers himself. Julio Sanguinetti, a traditional, centrist candidate, won in 1984. But his two most prominent opponents—Wilson Ferreira of the National party and Líber Seregni of the Broad Front—had been imprisoned by the military and denied their political rights. The vice-president elected with Sanguinetti was Enrico Tarigo, a journalist who had been a strong opponent of the military regime. As vice-president, Tarigo became a leading contender for the 1989 presidential election and was endorsed by Jorge Batlle, the principal Colorado party leader in the Senate. Sanguinetti's tasks of rebuilding the economy and building confidence in the Colorado party were challenging if not impossible. Sixty percent of the voters cast their ballots for Sanguinetti's stand-in opponents, Alberto Zumarán for Ferreira and Juan Crottogini for Seregni. Yet, the Broad Front's mayoral candidate for Montevideo, the coalition's strongest area of support, lost to the Colorado candidate. Voting in the 1984 elections seemed to suggest a tendency toward moderation and the political center, a tendency visible even in the leadership of the Broad Front (Rial, 1986:260).

The issue of human-rights abuses perpetrated by military officers during the dictatorship plagued the Sanguinetti administration. The government extended amnesty to former Tupamaros shortly after taking office and proposed legislation that would also extend amnesty to the military and police accused of human-rights violations. The amnesty law proposed by the government was eventually passed, amid great controversy, by the legislature in 1986. But, subsequently, opponents of amnesty initiated a petition drive to force a plebiscite on the issue. By June 1988 the supporters of the plebiscite claimed sufficient signatures, about 25 percent of the electorate, for the referendum. If these are certified, a referendum must be held.

Long-Term Trends

Of the nearly 2,000,000 voters who cast ballots in 1984, about 630,000 were new voters who were too young to have voted in 1971. Political polls suggest this group is less disposed to support the traditional parties, more disposed to support the Broad Front. It remains to be seen whether this represents a leftist trend, a disenchantment with the traditional parties and leaders, a dissatisfaction with economic conditions and a search for new and more radical solutions, or is merely as yet weak party identifications. The ability of the two major parties to retain their control over Uruguayan politics is at stake, and these voters can make a significant difference in the future.

It also remains to be seen how effectively the Colorado government can rule and how effectively it can meet the formidable economic problems it faces. The government's control over the legislature is weak, and it is vulnerable to attack. The traditional sources of patronage and clientelism that sustained the Colorado dominance have been weakened by economic austerity. The military remains an imponderable factor. Most of the officers who participated in the miltiary regime have retired, many involuntarily, but the military itself may not yet have retired completely from politics. Political immobility, economic decline, or civil insurrection could create a scenario for another intervention.

Continued civilian rule may depend on the government's ability to solve some of the nation's economic problems. These problems include a revitalization of the economy and economic growth, resolving the burden of a large international debt and debt payments, inflation, the limitations of a small economy with traditional exports, and a pent-up demand for a return of government programs and services that were decimated by the military regime. Uruguay also remains sensitive to events in other countries, including the economic viability and political stability of its neighbors, Brazil and Argentina.

On the basis of recent polls there seems to be no logical class division in party support in Uruguay. Indeed, the Broad Front, the most radical group, seems to draw more support from the more affluent and better-educated Uruguayans, while it does less well among the poor, whose interests it advocates. Support for the concept of a national-unity government would suggest that partisanship is less a priority than problem-solving for many voters.

The political climate of the 1984 election was an artificial one. Two of the principal national leaders, Ferreira and Seregni, were prohibited from participating, and the return to civilian rule overwhelmed other issues. The 1989 election will be critical, with full participation and a wide range of issues. At stake is a possible realignment of the traditional party system and the ability of the Broad Front to penetrate it effectively.

Batlle's vision of a progressive and activist government laid the foundations for a democratic Uruguay and a dominant Colorado party, but his assumption of continuing and expanding economic growth and prosperity for his country created a contradiction in modern Uruguay. Eventually, the contradiction contributed to the political paralysis and unrest that encouraged the military to intervene. Batlle's vision may persist, but there are formidable problems in implementing it given Uruguay's new political and economic realities.

Notes

1. The National party is commonly known in Uruguay as the Blanco party. For our purposes here, the formal title "National party" is used to refer to the organization, and "Blancos" to its adherents.

References

Campiglia, Nestor. 1969. *Los Grupos de Presión y el Proceso Político*. Montevideo: Arca.

Gillespie, Charles G. 1986. Activists and Floating Voters: The Unheeded Lessons of Uruguay's 1982 Primaries. In Paul W. Drake and Eduardo Silva, eds., *Elections and Democratization in Latin America, 1980–1985.* San Diego: Univ. of California, San Diego.

Handelman, Howard. 1981. Uruguay. In H. Handelman and T. G. Sanders, eds., *Military Government and the Movement Toward Democracy in South America.* Bloomington: Indiana Univ. Press.

———. 1986. Prelude to Elections: The Military's Legitimacy Crisis and the 1980 Constitutional Plebiscite in Uruguay. In Drake and Silva, eds., *Elections and Democratization.*

Kaufman, Eli. 1978. *Uruguay in Transition.* New Brunswick, NJ: Transaction.

McDonald, Ronald H. 1971a. *Party Systems and Elections in Latin America.* Chicago: Markham.

———. 1971b. Legislative Politics in Uruguay: A Preliminary Analysis. In Weston H. Agor, ed., *Latin American Legislatures: Their Role and Influence.* New York: Praeger.

———. 1975. The Rise of Military Politics in Uruguay. *Inter-American Economic Affairs* 28:25–43.

———. 1987. Redemocratization in Uruguay. In George A. Lopez and Michael Stohl, eds., *Liberalization and Redemocratization in Latin America.* Westport, CT: Greenwood.

Rial, Juan. 1986. The Uruguayan Elections of 1984: A Triumph of the Center. In Drake and Silva, eds., *Elections and Democratization.*

Taylor, Philip B. 1955. The Electoral System in Uruguay. *Journal of Politics* 17:19–42.

———. 1963. Interests and Institutional Dysfunction in Uruguay. *American Political Science Review* 58:62–74.

Weinstein, Martin. 1975. *Uruguay: The Politics of Failure.* Westport, CT: Greenwood.

———. 1988. *Uruguay: Democracy at the Crossroads.* Boulder, CO: Westview.

8

HONDURAS

Only two political parties have figured significantly in Honduran politics, the Liberal party (PLH), founded in the 1890s, and the National party (PNH), created a quarter-century later. Both of these rival parties are patron-client networks more interested in amassing patronage than in developing effective programs, yet most of the poor and predominantly peasant electorate still identifies with them. As in Colombia, widespread traditional party identification has posed a major obstacle to would-be third parties.

Beginning with the administration of Tiburcio Carías (1933–1949), the National party dominated the party system for almost half a century. Conflict between the two parties persisted, however, ultimately leading, in 1956, to the country's first modern military coup. In the thirty years that followed, the army gradually replaced the traditional parties as the nation's most important political actor. After an extended period of military rule, often in collaboration with the PNH, the armed forces agreed to reestablish free elections in the early 1980s. Despite impressive Liberal victories in 1980 and 1981, however, the U.S.-enlarged military under right-wing Gen. Gustavo Alvarez Martínez grew more influential than ever.

When General Alvarez was deposed in an internal military coup in 1984, many observers hoped progress toward democracy finally would begin. But instead of working to consolidate new democratic institutions, President Roberto Suazo Córdova, a Liberal, abused his power in an unsuccessful effort to extend his mandate beyond the legal limit. He became the first constitutionally chosen president since 1933 to transfer authority, albeit reluctantly, to a freely elected successor. In 1986 Liberal José Azcona del Hoyo took office weakened by divisions within his party and faced with economic decay and civil wars on two borders. In this context, the army and the U.S. Embassy remained more powerful than either of the traditional parties.

The Evolution and Context of Honduran Party Politics

The self-styled "generals" and rural political bosses who struggled for power following Honduras's independence sometimes adopted Liberal or Conservative labels, but there were no organized parties in Honduras until very late in the nineteenth century. Liberal views predominated by the 1870s, but factional conflict and chronic instability delayed the formal creation of any party until 1890. Established by Policarpo Bonilla, the PLH was plagued by personalist infighting. With no cohesive Liberal aristocracy, the U.S. banana companies that dominated the country after 1900 exploited Liberal divisions for their own purposes. Between 1916 and 1919 a dissident group of nominal Liberals associated with Manuel Bonilla organized the National party, which was neither socially nor ideologically distinguishable from the other factions of the period (Stokes, 1950). Both the PLH and PNH were loose coalitions of rural landowners and their unsophisticated peasant followers.

Between 1923 and 1932 the Nationals, supported by the United Fruit Company, and the Liberals, backed by the Cuyamel Fruit Company, competed in a series of fairly honest elections. National party candidate Tiburcio Carías Andino won a plurality in 1923 in a contest with two Liberal opponents, but the Liberal Congress refused to confirm his victory. Carías mounted an armed rebellion that brought U.S. intervention and eventually resulted in his PNH running mate taking office in his place. Five years later, in 1928, the factionalized Liberals agreed on a single candidate and defeated Carías, who raised his political stature after the election by refusing to promote another armed revolt. By the early 1930s Carías, with the endorsement of United Fruit (which had absorbed Cuyamel), had become the nation's most powerful and popular caudillo.

After winning the presidency legitimately in 1932, Carías soon outlawed the Liberal party and established a dictatorship that lasted until 1949. The Liberals staged several unsuccessful uprisings but eventually began to disintegrate. With most of its leaders in exile and its supporters cut off from patronage, the party atrophied (Morris, 1984:9). In contrast, the National party prospered in its role as the official party. When Carías decided to step down, the PNH remained firmly in control under President Juan Manual Gálvez, Carías's minister of war, who was elected unopposed in 1948.

The Gálvez administration, however, ushered in a welcome period of political liberalization and also encouraged economic development. The Liberal party was permitted to reorganize under reformist physician Ramón Villeda Morales, who expanded the party's appeal by attracting new urban middle-class and working-class elements. In addition, after a massive banana workers' strike in 1954, the PNH government recognized labor's right to organize. Predictably, Gálvez's conciliatory style angered Carías and split the hegemonic National party. When free elections were held in 1954 for the first time in two decades, dynamic Villeda Morales won a 48 percent plurality in a three-way race with the aged former dictator, running as the official PNH candidate (31 percent), and a dissident National Reformist movement (MNR) nominee (21 percent).

After the election, the two PNH factions cooperated to prevent the Congress from choosing a president. In the meantime, Gálvez was stricken by a heart attack and his vice-president, Julio Lozano, took advantage of the confused circumstances to seize power. Lozano repressed the Liberals but gained little support from the PNH for his troubles. He therefore formed his own short-lived National Unity party (PUN), and his ouster in 1956 by the small Honduran military was well received. After fourteen months in power, the army supervised a new round of elections for a constituent assembly that resulted in a landslide Liberal victory.

Liberal president Ramón Villeda Morales (1957–1963) modeled himself after Latin American Social Democrats such as Venezuela's Rómulo Betancourt. While in office, he instituted a modern labor code, an urban social security system, and a fledgling land reform. Villeda's reformism was opposed by the PNH and by many conservative rural bosses within his own party, most of whom rallied around rival Liberal strongman Modesto Rodas Alvarado. To make matters worse, the president's creation of an autonomous civil guard incensed the military. By 1963 Villeda had lost control of his party, and the PLH nominated the fiery Rodas as its presidential candidate. In addition, the National party had rallied around a compromise candidate and developed a close relationship with the armed forces.

Although he represented the right wing of the Liberal party, Rodas campaigned in 1963 on a reformist and antimilitary platform and was expected to win. Shortly before the election, the military (with PNH encouragement) intervened to prevent his triumph. Armed forces commander Col. Oswaldo López Arellano took power and ruled the country from 1963 to 1971 with the assistance of astute National party politician Ricardo Zuñiga. The conservative, authoritarian civil-military government suppressed popular organizations and rigged the electoral machinery to assure National party victories in the 1965 and 1968 elections.

Honduras's defeat in the 1969 war with El Salvador intensified popular frustration with the corrupt and repressive López-Zuñiga regime. Under pressure particularly from moderate business groups and organized labor, López agreed to relinquish power to a bipartisan civilian government in 1971. Drawing on the successful example of the Colombian National Front arrangement, the two Honduran traditional parties pledged in a pact of national unity to share patronage equally and to cooperate on a common reform program. But, instead of embracing Colombian principles of legislative parity and presidential alternation, the Honduran parties determined that the winning party in the next election would receive both the presidency and a one-vote majority in the unicameral Congress. The 1971 electoral contest produced an unexpected PNH victory for conservative Ramón Cruz, who showed little inclination to implement reforms or to operate a truly bipartisan government. Liberals soon protested, and popular unrest spread.

With land reform stalled, peasant groups threatened by expanding commercial agriculture disrupted the political system by invading disputed lands and staging mass demonstrations.

In a remarkable turnabout, former right-wing chief executive General López Arellano took advantage of the situation by deposing the Cruz government in late 1972 and forming an alliance with labor unions, peasant groups, and reformist business sectors. Inspired to some extent by the post-1968 Peruvian military regime, the populist and nationalist military government headed by López expanded the role of the state and instituted a significant agrarian-reform program. Yet, after being accused of accepting a bribe from the United Brands Company (formerly United Fruit) for reducing the banana-export tax, López was ousted in an internal military coup in 1975. Military conservatives began to reassert control, and by the late 1970s the armed forces again were repressing popular organizations and reestablishing ties with the National party.

Not long after the fall of the Somoza regime in Nicaragua, U.S. officials persuaded the military of the wisdom of instituting a democratic transition. Full-scale party activity resumed and, in 1980, elections for a new constituent assembly drew a large (81 percent) and enthusiastic turnout. In the first electoral contest in nine years, antimilitary sentiment gave the Liberals an unanticipated victory with 49 percent of the vote and thirty-five of the seventy-one Assembly seats. The Nationals gained 42 percent of the vote and thirty-three seats, while a small new centrist party, the National Innovation party (PINU), drew 3.5 percent and three seats. But in spite of the Liberals' success, the military under Col. Policarpo Paz García retained control of the executive branch, and National party figures served in many important administrative capacities. Moreover, in return for promising to allow general elections to take place in 1981, the army compelled civilian party leaders to agree to ignore past military corruption and to give the armed forces a voice in future government appointments.

The 1981 election produced another Liberal victory with an increased margin (54 percent) and brought Modesto Rodas's close associate, rural physician Roberto Suazo Córdova, to the presidency over Ricardo Zuñiga (42 percent). The small remainder of the vote was divided between PINU and a tiny, left-of-center Christian Democratic party (PDCH). The Liberal success raised expectations for democracy but, before long, it became obvious that the armed forces still were very much in control. From his appointment as armed forces chief in 1982 to his exile after an internal coup in 1984, right-wing Gen. Gustavo Alvarez Martínez (who had formed a close political alliance with Suazo) was considered the country's most powerful figure (Rosenberg, 1983). Despite the reestablishment of formal democracy, human rights abuses mounted and pluralism declined while the Alvarez-Suazo coalition ruled the country. After Alvarez's fall, Suazo showed no greater respect for democratic institutions and resorted to every means possible to keep himself in power beyond his constitutional term (Rosenberg, 1986). The president used bribery and his control of the National Electoral Tribunal (TNE) and Supreme Court to elicit compliance from the PLH and the PNH in order to manipulate the presidential nomination process. Suazo's actions severely factionalized both parties and, in 1985, precipitated a constitutional crisis requiring military mediation after his opponents in Congress had attempted to legally replace some of the president's Supreme Court justices. The crisis was resolved by an agreement to permit all party factions to run separate candidates in the 1985 elections under an Uruguayan-like electoral system (see Chapter 7, Electoral Laws and Representation).

The Nationals increased their share of the vote in 1985, but the divided Liberals still managed to win while minor parties continued to have little success. The new president and leader of the largest Liberal faction (46 of the 134 PLH congressmen) was José Azcona, a Suazo opponent. Shortly after the contest, Azcona strengthened his government by forming a coalition with the National party's Rafael Callejas, for whom more Hondurans had voted than for any other candidate. The Azcona-Callejas arrangement entailed no agreement on legislative program, but the cabinet portfolios, Supreme Court control, and other patronage received by the Nationals reduced a potential source of opposition and gave the government a bipartisan appearance. Although the breakup of the coalition was announced in 1987, PNH officeholders retained their positions.

With the restoration of democratic elections in the 1980s, Honduran political parties regained formal control of the governmental apparatus, yet, neither the ruling Liberals nor their PNH opponents have devoted serious attention to the nation's pressing problems. Instead, the overriding purpose of traditional party politics has remained the provision of *chamba*, or patronage, to party bosses and their followers (Rosenberg, 1986:2–3). In recent years the Honduran military and the U.S. government have shown more interest in and influence over policymaking than have either of the anachronistic parties.

Most Honduran generals are motivated by simple greed and a lust for power. But in the early 1970s General López Arellano presided over the most important reformist era in the country's history. A few years later Argentine military academy graduate Gustavo Alvarez committed the armed forces to conservative, anti-Communist national security doctrines. The army became the nation's dominant political actor during the López era and, under Alvarez and his successors, has continued to exercise control over foreign policy and security affairs and to wield veto power over most other government activities (Shepherd, 1986:135–136).

Alvarez was unseated by officers who resented his attempt to monopolize power (and his willingness to allow the United States to train Salvadoran soldiers in Honduras). Since his departure, control of the military has been shared among the fifty-odd members of the Superior Council of the Armed Forces (Meza, 1988). Although the armed forces have continued to expand in accordance with U.S. designs for the region, factionalization along generational and ideological lines has increased. Participation in the narcotics trade by an indeterminate number of senior officers has further divided the army. Nevertheless, the military continues to press its common institutional priorities and to enjoy unprecedented opportunities for corruption provided by the massive U.S. aid and the Nicaraguan *contra* supply system. In addition, after a brief decline following the fall of Alvarez, human rights abuses attributed to the armed forces have once again increased.

The U.S. Embassy, like the Honduran military, recognizes the advantages of maintaining democratic appearances, and the two institutions worked together to resolve the 1985 constitutional crisis. As in the case of El Salvador, high levels of U.S. economic and military assistance have bought the U.S. government great influence. Without U.S. inducements, in fact, democratic elections and party competition would not have been restored in 1980, nor would Honduras have assumed such a central role in U.S. Central American strategy.

Other influential political actors include the private sector and organized labor, both of which operate very independently of the traditional parties. The U.S. banana companies, especially United Brands, still produce the country's principal export, and their cooperation remains essential to any government. Domestic business, represented by organizations such as the Honduran Council of Private Enterprise (COHEP) and the right-wing National Federation of Honduran Agriculturists and Stockraisers (FENAGH), has also become an important force since economic diversification began in the 1950s. In both military and civilian governments, COHEP and FENAGH provide many of the cabinet officers charged with economic affairs.

Business influence is moderated to some extent in Honduras, however, by the existence of Central America's best-organized independent labor movement. In recent years, the moderate AFL-CIO-linked Confederation of Honduran Workers (CTH)—based in the banana workers and the more militant, Social Christian General Central of Workers (CGT)—have cooperated with each other to advance basic worker and peasant economic demands and to support democracy. Neither traditional party has been able to enlist organized labor in its ranks on a permanent basis, although the Liberals consistently draw more votes in unionized areas (Morris, 1984:79). In addition, in spite of the unusual importance of organized peasant groups such as the CTH-connected National Association of Honduran Peasants (ANACH) and the CGT-associated National Peasants' Union (UNC), the Liberals and Nationals have both failed to address the country's worsening land-tenure situation (Ruhl, 1984).

◾ Contemporary Political Parties

The two principal Honduran political parties are very much alike. Controlled by traditional agrarian and commercial interests, both are conservative supporters of the socioeconomic status quo and of the nation's intimate alliance with the United States (although, since 1987, the PNH officially has become less supportive of the Nicaraguan *contras'* basing in Honduras). Yet, the two parties, ideologically weak, are far more concerned with patronage than policy. After the Villeda Morales administration, the Liberals possessed a more reformist and antimilitary image than the Nationals, but the right-wing Suazo government erased that impression. Unlike the Nationals, the Liberals do encompass a reformist minority wing.

The PLH and PNH both are patron-client political machines that integrate a large number of locally based personalist networks. In each party, central control is exercised by a party president and a central executive committee, which traditionally have had considerable influence on nominations and patronage distribution. Both parties also maintain extensive grass-roots organizations and provide various local services for the party faithful. Factionalization has usually created more difficulties for the Liberals than for the Nationals, but both parties have been troubled by personalist divisions. Internal primaries to determine the relative popularity of competing factions have often been marred by fraud.

In the early 1980s the Liberals were divided into two formally organized factions, the conservative Rodista Liberal movement (MLR), a dominant force representing the traditionalist followers of the late Modesto Rodas, and the much smaller Popular Liberal Alliance (ALIPO), a progressive, urban-based group. Yet by 1985 Suazo's drive to stay in power had splintered the party into five factions, of which all but ALIPO (which backed Azcona) ran separate candidate lists in the general elections. Azcona and Efraín Bu Girón, formerly Suazo's allies in the MLR, created their own factions, and the most reformist element of ALIPO, under Social Democrats Carlos and José Antonio Reina, left the group to form the Liberal Democratic Revolutionary movement (M-LIDER). Three rival National party factions, including one backed by Suazo, contested the 1985 elections. But the Nationalist Rafael Callejas movement (MONARCA), named after a young conservative, collected almost all of the PNH votes. The National party was not as unified as MONARCA's success seemed to indicate: Several different party groups had endorsed Callejas.

Both the Nationals and Liberals are multiclass parties that benefit from widespread hereditary party attachment. An estimated 60 percent of registered voters are identified with the traditional parties, with the Liberals reported to have about a 5 percent edge over the Nationals. Voter support for the Liberals traditionally is strongest in urban areas, e.g., industrial San Pedro Sula, and in the economically more developed North Coast departments (Cortés, Atlántida, Colón); but the party also has rural strongholds such as El Paraíso and Suazo's native La Paz. The National party shows its greatest electoral strength in the more backward and isolated rural regions (Lempira, Intibuca) and in the southern agricultural departments of Choluteca and Valle, but it has developed a sizable urban following, too. In 1985 the PLH and PNH ran almost even in Francisco Morazán department in which the nation's capital and largest city, Tegucigalpa, is located.

Two minor reformist parties have become active during the 1980s, but neither has been able to collect more than about 2 percent of the vote. The Honduran Christian Democratic party (PDCH) grew out of the Catholic church's social activism of the 1950s and 1960s and developed into a more left-of-center party than either the Guatemalan or Salvadoran Christian Democrats. The PDCH is highly critical of the traditional parties' disinterest in social reforms and human rights issues and of their subservience to U.S. interests. Christian Democratic leaders come mostly from the urban middle class, but interestingly, in 1985, the party's strongest electoral support materialized in three backward rural departments that border on El Salvador (Ocotepeque, Lempira, Intibuca). The other minor party that has won congressional seats is the National Innovation party (PINU), an urban-based, centrist group headed by progressive businesspeople and middle-class professionals.

Parties of the radical left, seldom tolerated by Honduran officials, have failed to amass an appreciable following. The pro-Moscow Communist party (PCH), dating from 1927, is the most important revolutionary group, but it has been plagued by personalist and ideological divisions. The PCH has its greatest influence on the working class through close association with the United Federation of Honduran Workers (FUTH), a Marxist group. Independent leftist candidates who ran in the 1980 and 1981 elections were harassed by the authorities, winning very few votes, and in 1985 radical groups either boycotted the election or directed their adherents to cast ballots for the PDCH or PINU. The four small and ineffective Marxist guerrilla groups operating in the country condemned the electoral process.

Elections and Voting

The restoration of democratic elections in the 1980s brought Hondurans to the polls in great numbers. Voting was nominally compulsory for everyone over eighteen years of age who was not in the armed forces, but no penalties were applied for abstention. Overall, more than 80 percent of the electorate participated in each of the three electoral contests held after 1980 (Table 8.1), a sizable increase over participation rates in the three previous elections (1957, 1965, 1971). Moreover, despite some signs of increasing public cynicism, the recent elections have been held in a carnival-like atmosphere more akin to Costa Rican elections than to the tense electoral climates of neighboring El Salvador or Guatemala. Because of the strength of the traditional parties' rural campaign organizations, electoral participation was as high in the countryside as it was in the cities.

Under the arrangements established in the 1982 constitution, the Honduran president is elected by plurality and may serve only a single four-year term. But, in order to resolve a 1985 constitutional crisis, all party factions had agreed to a modified electoral system similar to Uruguay's, whereby the presidency is awarded to the leading candidate of the party whose combined factions garnered the most votes. The unicameral Congress is elected concurrently with the president using a proportional representation system and closed party lists. Congressional seats are allotted to each of the country's 18 departments according to population (1 deputy for every 35,000 inhabitants) and were increased from 82 to 134 for the 1985 election. Because

TABLE 8.1
Electoral Participation and Party Voting in Honduras, 1954-1985 (in percentages)

	Voting	Liberal	National	Other[a]	Invalid
1954	--	47.9	31.2	20.9	
1957	65.1	61.5	29.8	8.7	
1965	75.4	44.3	54.6		1.1
1971	67.5	44.4	49.3		6.3
1980	81.3	49.4	42.2	3.5	4.9
1981	80.7	52.4	40.4	4.3	2.9
1985	84.0	49.2	43.9	3.4	3.5

[a]MNR in 1954 and 1957; PDCH, PINU, and Independents, 1980-1985.

Sources: Adapted from James A. Morris, Honduras: Caudillo Politics and Military Rulers (Boulder, CO: Westview, 1984), p. 37, and Honduras: Boletin Informativo (January 1986), 11.

of the special circumstances surrounding the race, party nominating conventions, which normally select and rank order congressional candidates, were bypassed in 1985. Instead, Liberal and National party factions ran separate lists just as if they were independent parties like the PDCH or PINU. (After the 1985 election the electoral law was changed to require internal party elections to determine nominations in 1989.) No split-ticket voting is possible in Honduras because the single ballot used for presidential, congressional, and municipal elections forces voters to select a party's entire slate.

Honduran elections are supervised by the National Electoral Tribunal (TNE), which is composed of a Supreme Court judge and one representative from each of the four legally inscribed political parties (PLH, PNH, PDCH, PINU). Assisted by the National Register of Persons, the TNE is responsible for conducting the electoral census, registering parties and their official leadership bodies, establishing voting regulations, overseeing balloting, and tabulating returns. As in neighboring El Salvador, most of the funds required for these tasks have been provided by the United States. Although electoral fraud has been a common feature of Honduran politics, all three elections supervised by the TNE since 1980 were free of serious irregularities. Nonetheless, the institution has come under criticism. Suazo gained control over the TNE and used it to give official sanction to unrepresentative leadership cadres in both major parties. In addition, when PNH candidate Callejas disputed the 1985 electoral pact as unconstitutional, arguing that the candidate receiving the most votes individually should win the presidency, the TNE behaved irresponsibly—refusing to come to a decision until the day before the election.

The results of the three elections held since 1980 (Tables 8.1 and 8.2) demonstrate the continued dominance of the two historic parties. In every election, the Liberals and Nationals together amassed more than 95 percent

TABLE 8.2
Honduran Election Results by Party, 1981 and 1985

		Valid Votes	Total	Congress Seats
1981				
Roberto Suazo Córdova	LIB	636,392	53.9	44
Ricardo Zuñiga	NAT	491,089	41.6	34
Miguel Andonie Fernández	PINU	29,419	2.5	3
Hernán Corrales Padilla	PDCH	19,163	1.6	1
Independents	Left	3,997	0.3	0
Total		1,180,060	99.9	82
1985				
José Azcona	LIB	424,358	27.5	46
Oscar Mejía Arellano	LIB	250,519	16.3	18
Efraín Bu Girón	LIB	64,230	4.2	3
Carlos Reina	LIB	43,373	2.8	0
Votes for party only		4,114	0.3	0
Liberal party total		786,594	51.0	67
Rafael Callejas	NAT	656,882	42.6	63
Fernando Lardizábal	NAT	22,163	1.4	0
Juan Urrutia	NAT	20,121	1.3	0
Votes for party only		2,240	0.0	0
National party total		701,406	45.5	63
Hernán Corrales Padilla	PDCH	30,173	1.9	2
Enrique Aguilar Cerrato	PINU	23,705	1.5	2
Minor party totals		53,878	3.5	4
Total		1,541,878	100.0	134

[a]Percentage totals sometimes do not add up because of rounding.

Sources: Adapted from James A. Morris, Honduras: Caudillo Politics and Military Rulers (Boulder, CO: Westview, 1984), p. 57, and Honduras: Boletín Informativo (January 1986), p. 11.

of the valid votes cast and neither of the minor reformist parties drew more than token support. The 1980, 1981, and 1985 returns also all have confirmed the Liberal party's majority status. The PLH has won each of the three elections with more than half of the valid vote and has beaten its perennial rival with an average margin of 8 percent. Nevertheless, the Liberal party's victory margin declined noticeably in 1985, suggesting that its control over the party system would not go unchallenged.

The Liberals' most convincing triumph came in the 1981 elections, when antimilitary sentiment helped the party to capture 54 percent of the vote and to carry all but four departments. Campaigning under false reformist colors, Roberto Suazo Córdova bested National party conservative Ricardo Zuñiga and assumed office with a decided Liberal congressional majority (forty-four seats to the PNH's thirty-four).

Because of the novel electoral format, the 1985 election was a much more complex contest, and it also produced a closer outcome. Nine presidential candidates and accompanying congressional lists competed. They represented four Liberal factions, three National factions, and the two minor parties. The three most important contestants for the presidency were José Azcona Hoyo, a center-right Liberal and former Suazo ally now opposed to the president; Liberal Oscar Mejía Arellano, a longtime Rodista (MLR) politician controlled by Suazo; and the National party's young Rafael Callejas (born 1943), an ex-minister of agriculture and former associate of General Alvarez. The 1985 campaign was marked by an increasingly effective use of mass media advertising, particularly by the conservative, U.S.-educated Callejas, and cost more than any previous race (only partly subsidized by the government). Yet, in spite of the expensive and hard-fought campaign, all three major candidates avoided saying anything of substance about important national issues such as the future of the agrarian economy or the Nicaraguan *contras'* presence in Honduras, devoting most of their time to slandering one another (Shepherd, 1986:151).

The returns revealed that the four Liberal party candidates had amassed 51 percent of the vote. Hence, under the terms of the electoral pact, the Liberal front-runner José Azcona, with only 27.5 percent of the ballots (compared to 16 percent for Suazo's crony Mejía) was elected chief executive. Although growing anti-Suazo sentiment helped Azcona defeat Mejía, it cost the PLH votes as a whole. The National party's attractive candidate Rafael Callejas (MONARCA) also drew votes away from the Liberals and received greater support than any other candidate (43 percent). But because the other two National party candidates were able to add only 2 percent to the PNH total, Callejas's presidential ambitions were frustrated for the time being.

The Nationals were pleased by their party's improved performance and by the majorities they were able to build in seven departments, but the military made it clear that no constitutional challenges to Azcona's victory would be accepted. National party tempers cooled somewhat when the winning Liberal candidate quickly set about forming an alliance with Callejas that assured the PNH of a significant share of power and patronage. With only 46 of the 134 members of the Congress committed to him, Azcona desperately needed the support of some of MONARCA's 63 deputies.

The 1985 elections confirmed once again the limited appeal of leftist candidates to a predominantly peasant electorate still identified with the conservative traditional parties. The only genuinely progressive major party faction in the election, M-LIDER, won less than 3 percent of the vote, while the reformist PDCH and PINU collected 3.4 percent between them.

Long-Term Trends

Two parties have monopolized Honduran party politics since the 1920s. Although the Liberals and the Nationals both are conservative, patronage-based organizations that have shown little interest in addressing national problems, they retain the support of the majority of the predominantly peasant mass population. The three elections held during the 1980s have demonstrated the dominance of the traditional parties and have also shown that the Liberal party has replaced the National party as the strongest member of the two-party system. However, the relatively close 1985 result and the Liberals' more serious factionalization problems indicate that the current PLH advantage is not necessarily a permanent one.

It is also important to reemphasize that although the traditional parties continue to control the party system, the armed forces dominate Honduran politics. The military has been the nation's most influential political actor for the past two decades, and U.S. efforts to expand the armed forces as part of the U.S. Central American strategy have only enhanced its power. Whether democratic elections and civilian government persist or not, the army is unlikely ever again to recede into the background.

References

Meza, Victor. 1988. The Military: Willing to Deal. *NACLA Report* 22:14–21.

Morris, James A. 1984. *Honduras: Caudillo Politics and Military Rulers*. Boulder, CO: Westview.

Rosenberg, Mark B. 1983. Honduran Scorecard: Military and Democrats in Central America. *Caribbean Review* 12:12–15, 40–42.

———. 1986. Can Democracy Survive the Democrats? From Transition to Consolidation in Honduras. Presented at the Latin American Studies Association meeting, Boston.

Rosenberg, Mark B., and Philip L. Shepherd., eds. 1986. *Honduras Confronts Its Future*. Boulder, CO: Lynne Rienner.

Rudolph, James D., ed. 1984. *Honduras: A Country Study*. Washington, DC: U.S. Government Printing Office.

Ruhl, J. Mark. 1984. Agrarian Structure and Political Stability in Honduras. *Journal of Interamerican Studies and World Affairs* 26:33–68.

Shepherd, Philip L. 1986. Honduras. In Morris J. Blachman, William M. LeoGrande, and Kenneth Sharpe, eds., *Confronting Revolution: Security Through Diplomacy in Central America*. New York: Pantheon.

Stokes, William S. 1950. *Honduras: An Area Study in Government*. Madison: Univ. of Wisconsin Press.

Volk, Steven. 1981. Honduras: On the Border of War. *NACLA Report* 15:2–37.

PART THREE

Emerging
Two-Party Systems

VENEZUELA

9

Venezuela has received considerable attention from political scientists over the past quarter-century, and the reason is not difficult to find. Like Cuba at the end of the 1950s, Venezuelan politics underwent an unprecedented transformation. Unlike Cuba, Venezuela instituted a system of democratic politics encompassing strong party organizations, regular and impartial elections, vital competition between candidates and political parties, and guaranteed political freedoms. All of these conditions stand in sharp contrast to Venezuela's unstable and authoritarian past. In any event, political power since 1958 has been peacefully transferred from one elected regime and party to another, not a common process elsewhere in Latin America.

Venezuela's conversion to democratic politics occurred in 1958 with the ouster of dictator Marcos Pérez Jiménez. But one could trace the origins of democracy back even further, to a group of political leaders known as the "Generation of '28" (Martz, 1964). Pressures for democratization were stimulated by the development of the country's petroleum industry, which revolutionized the export economy and provided the means for rapid modernization. The full impact of petroleum on the economy was slow in coming, and it produced problems as well as opportunities. (Even today it has only marginally improved the fundamental welfare of Venezuelans and is not a sufficient explanation for the dramatic changes in Venezuelan politics.)

These changes can be easily summarized. All of Venezuela's political parties are "modern" ones, created either to promote the democratic experience or having resulted from it. None of the contemporary political parties has roots in the nineteenth century, or for that matter even existed prior to 1928. Venezuela did produce political parties during its first century of independence; Manuel Vicente Magallanes in his encyclopedic survey of Venezuelan parties (1973) identified no fewer than 294 of them, of which at least 108 preceded all of the contemporary ones. But most were of passing interest and had little if any impact on the nation's political history. Modern

Venezuelan parties were conceived as mass-based parties, instruments to mobilize large numbers of people. Toward this end, most are ideologically center or left of center, advocating nationalistic interests and those of the less-advantaged in Venezuela. Party identifications are relatively new and unstable: little more than a generation has passed since parties became politically salient. As a result they have been in a state of flux and evolution. In addition, substantial changes have occurred in party competition since 1958, resulting in a dismaying number of choices for voters as parties have multiplied, divided, changed, or disappeared from the scene. Personal political ambitions, particularly at the presidential level, have often overwhelmed party organizations, defined party competition, and created divisions in existing parties and the bases for new ones. Campaigning, political appeals, and communication generally have been profoundly affected by modern technologies of mass communication, sophisticated public relations, advertising techniques, and public-opinion polling, to mention only the more obvious ones.

During the three decades of modern party politics, there has been an important pattern in its evolution that helps to explain its success. In 1958 the major political parties united in their determination to make democracy work. The largest of these groups, Democratic Action (AD), and its principal leader, Rómulo Betancourt, had been prime movers in establishing the democratic system that replaced the Pérez Jiménez dictatorship in 1958. It dominated other parties and embraced many leaders with presidential ambitions. As politics evolved during the Betancourt administration (1958–1963), new political parties emerged and AD began to divide into rival political factions, some of which became full-fledged parties. Venezuelan politics began to dissipate, control became more fragmented and competition more diverse. This proliferation of parties (from approximately 1963 to 1978) had only a marginal impact on the electoral outcomes because most new parties failed to attract large numbers of voters. Interestingly, since 1978 an opposite tendency has become evident. Parties began to consolidate, leaving Venezuela now dominated by two strong, competitive parties, AD and a Christian Democratic party known by its acronym, COPEI (Committee of Independent Electoral Political Organization).

Of course, party competition may experience additional mutations or may fluctuate from one mode to another. As time passes, however, AD and COPEI are becoming increasingly more institutionalized and imbedded in Venezuelan political culture, making it more difficult for new organizations to challenge them. For a country that had enjoyed only three years of elected civilian government prior to 1958, the changes in Venezuela are remarkable. Within the context of Latin American politics they are unprecedented.

The Context of Venezuelan Party Politics

Three distinct historical periods have shaped Venezuelan party politics: a period from independence in 1810 until 1936, characterized by dictatorships, a major civil war, and general political instability; a period from 1936 until 1958, in which modern political forces, including new political parties, emerged and tried to gain control over the nation's politics, albeit with limited success and against considerable opposition; and the period from 1958 to the present, when modern political parties emerged to control the nation's politics and achieved many of their original goals. During the first two eras, several significant and distinctive political traits characterized Venezuelan politics: the lack of a strong nineteenth-century party tradition; the virtual destruction of the rural oligarchy that controlled the country following independence; the emergence of a highly pragmatic national politics, oriented almost exclusively to the interests of strong leaders rather than to the conflicts of classes, ideologies, or even regions; sudden and rapid modernization, facilitated by the development of the petroleum-export economy and the creation of a professional military; the growing dominance—economic, demographic, and political—of the capital city of Caracas; and the development of generational cleavages, especially among leaders, that created a context for rapid evolution and renovation of the political system. In the discussion below, I shall describe each of these three eras.

Following independence, the entrenched landed aristocracy took over Venezuela and formed the Conservative party (PC), advocating their rural economic interests, the church, and strong central government. These objectives were little more than a rationalization for their own privileges and power, and eventually a rival faction emerged and came to be known as the Liberal party (PL). These "parties" were never organized nor did they solicit mass support. In the absence of elections, they played only a minor role in Venezuelan politics.

The conflict between these two rival groups eventually deteriorated into a protracted civil war, which lasted from 1859 to 1864. It is estimated that about a quarter of the national population perished. The conservative aristocracy was decimated, leaving Venezuela without one of the bases for the class conflict that has habitually plagued party politics in other Latin American countries. The victors, those who identified themselves as liberals, ruled the country through a series of dictatorships from 1848 through 1935. The last of the traditional, patrimonial dictators, Juan Vicente Gómez, held power for twenty-eight years (1908–1935).

Like other strong, centralized dictatorships in Latin America at the time, the Gómez regime was reasonably successful in initiating economic development, specifically the exploration and exploitation of the country's petroleum resources. Petroleum became a useful, although not critical, export in the early years of the twentieth century; there were ample supplies of it worldwide and demand was limited. The income from natural-resource development permitted the regime to establish a modern army, and with it an increasingly professionalized military elite. This elite, particularly by the second generation, became identified with the goal of national development, and some younger officers saw the need for major political changes, including an end to the traditional dictatorships. This new generation of officers coincided with a new generation of civilian leaders who would later transform Venezuelan politics, the so-called Generation of '28 (Martz, 1964). This generation of young Venezuelans enjoyed the advantages that typically accompany economic modernization, including a university education. The Central University in Caracas was especially influential in this regard, producing young political leaders united in their opposition to the dictatorship and committed to making fundamental changes in Venezuelan politics. Most of the national political leaders who were to emerge in subsequent years, and the nuclei for groups that later emerged as the country's major political parties, trace their origins back to the Central University.

Venezuela's population relative to its national territory is very small. By 1900 there were no more than 2.5 million people in an area about the size of Texas. Settlement patterns created one large city, Caracas, which had been the colonial center of a broad region. With economic development in the twentieth century, Caracas's population gradually grew, assuming an increasing share of the national population. Economic development benefited the city disproportionately, and stimulated urban migration. By the 1950s urbanization had become the most rapid in Latin America. Caracas's growth and increasing prosperity created more modern political views and made the city the center of Venezuelan political change. Apart from the effect of economic modernization on the country's political evolution, two historical factors also contributed to change. One was a lack of strong party traditions rooted in the nineteenth century. Also, early in Venezuela's history the power of traditional socioeconomic elites had been contained. Finally, a new generation of leaders, both military and civilian, emerged. They were committed to the transformation of national politics and to ending the long series of dictatorships.

The absence of strong party traditions combined with the lack of significant regional and class confrontations concentrated Venezuelan politics by the mid-twentieth century on a single issue—that of establishing a democratic system supported by parties and elections, with established rules to regulate and limit the behavior of elected officials. A consensus about these rules included military as well as civilian leaders, and a vigorous, competitive system of party politics evolved.

The Evolution of Contemporary Parties

Contemporary Venezuelan political parties originated during the dictatorship of Juan Vicente Gómez, who ruled from 1908 to 1935. Most of the parties were organized at the Central University in Caracas as student movements involved with national politics. The Gómez dictatorship was one of absolute control, without political opposition, parties, or elections, and the dictator mistrusted the political activism at the Central University. The Venezuelan Federation of Students (FEV) was dissolved on several occasions by Gómez, but in 1927 it was again reorganized by the students and it served as a vehicle for those opposed to the dictatorship. Many of the student leaders active in the FEV and other campus political organizations at that time went on to become prominent national political leaders, including Rómulo Betancourt, Raúl Leoni, Jóvito Villalba, Gonzalo Barrios, and Rafael Caldera, among others. After an attempt to overthrow Gómez in 1929, many of the student activists went into exile, but the dictator weathered these challenges and remained in power until his death in late 1935.

Younger military officers were also opposed to the Gómez regime. Gómez used officers and cadets at the military college for, among other things, nonmilitary activities such as working on his personal lands. They initiated an abortive coup in 1928 and were sympathetic to the changes advocated by their civilian counterparts. That shared opposition of the two young elites to the regime was critical later in shaping civil-military relations in Venezuela (Burggraaft, 1972).

The exiled student leaders of 1928 formed a clandestine organization known as the Revolutionary Group of the Left (ARDI), which maintained communication with and solidified their political objectives. With the death of Gómez, most of the original opposition leaders returned to the country, and new political organizations began to emerge, including the Republican National Union (UNR), the Democratic National Bloc (BDN), the Movement of Venezuelan Organization (ORVE), and the Progressive Republican party (PRP). The UNR was an organization of younger Venezuelan businessmen who saw opportunities for continued economic growth and modernization, which they associated with a more open, democratic political system. Both regional and reformist in orientation, the BDN began as a regional organization in Maracaibo, the center of petroleum production in the country. The ORVE contained most of the leaders of the Generation of '28 and was formally constituted on March 1, 1936. Specifically aimed at Venezuela's younger generation, ORVE was explicitly conceived as a multiclass organization capable of transcending class differences and achieving national unity through democratic processes (Martz, 1964:26–27). The PRP was a Marxist group and the most radical.

A new constitution was promulgated after the death of Gómez, and a congressional election was held in January 1937. Participation in the election was highly restricted by an indirect electoral system and limited suffrage. Three political groups (ORVE, PRP, BDN) joined with the FEV and two labor organizations to form the National Democratic party (PDN). When it became clear that the government intended to control the results of the election, the PDN leaders protested, their supporters demonstrated, and a few weeks later most of the leaders went into exile again. The effort, although frustrated, was nevertheless a valuable experience in how to construct modern political parties in Venezuela. Forced to operate either in exile or clandestinely, the PDN leaders soon recognized the importance of organization. One legacy of this experience is that contemporary Venezuelan political parties are among the most effectively and explicitly organized in Latin America.

The PDN decided to present at least a token opposition in the scheduled elections of 1941, which were held primarily to formalize a change in the presidency (a successor was personally selected by the incumbent). The PDN nominated Rómulo Gallegos, an internationally known and respected author. The government candidate, former minister of war Isaías Medina Angarita, easily defeated Gallegos. Undeterred, PDN leaders formally petitioned the new government for legalization of a new party, Democratic Action. The more than thirteen years experience in trying to establish a modern, democratic political party had taught its leaders important political lessons. Through their efforts, AD would ultimately succeed.

Under increasing pressure to establish more democratic processes and after considerable instability, the government scheduled elections for 1946. By this time additional political parties had been formed, including several Marxist ones. Two of the more important new groups were the Democratic Republican Union (URD), founded in December 1945, and what had by then become known as COPEI, or the Christian Democratic party. The URD was identified with Jóvito Villalba, one of the original leaders of the Generation of '28, and was a vehicle for his presidential ambitions. COPEI had its origins in the FEV, students who differed with their peers over religious questions. In 1936 COPEI and its principal leader, Rafael Caldera, formed the National Student Union (UNE). Caldera was part of the Generation of '28, but broke with other leaders on the issue of the church. The UNE became a political party and in 1938 was called Electoral Action (AE), in 1942 as National Action (AN), and finally in 1946 as COPEI.

The 1946 election for a constituent assembly was held in a much more open political environment. AD won a resounding victory, receiving 79 percent of the vote and 137 of the 160 seats in the assembly, demonstrating both its organizational skills and popular support. After a new constitution was adopted in 1947 another set of elections was scheduled for later that year to select a new president, congress, and municipal legislators. The AD nominated Rómulo Gallegos again for the presidency, COPEI nominated Rafael Caldera, and the URD nominated Jóvito Villalba. The Venezuelan Communist party (PCV) also competed in the elections, nominating its leader Gustavo Machado for president. Again AD won a commanding victory, with Gallegos receiving 74 percent of the vote and the party electing 38 of the 46 senators and 83 of the 110 deputies. The period of electoral activity and elected government from 1945 to 1948 is known as the *Trienio*, an important period in the evolution of Venezuelan party politics and democracy (Table 9.1).

The new Gallegos-AD government took power in early 1948, but in November of that year the military intervened, ending the *Trienio* and producing a dictatorship that ultimately came to be dominated by Maj. Marcos Pérez Jiménez. Crude, repressive, and irresponsible, the dictatorship lasted until January 1958, when mass uprisings and increasing pressure from the military itself forced Pérez Jiménez to resign. During this period, most of the country's party leaders were in exile again, and when they returned to the country in 1958 they faced many of the same problems in reestablishing democracy that they had faced a decade earlier. By this time the Generation

TABLE 9.1
Party Vote for Trienio Elections, 1946-1947 (in percentages)

	AD	COPEI	URD	PCV	Other
1946					
Constituent Assembly	79	13	4	4	1
1947					
Congress	71	21	4	4	1
Presidential	74	22		3	

Source: Official Venezuelan electoral results compiled by the
Consejo Supremo Electoral (Caracas), 1946-1947.

of '28 was middle-aged, but their experience over the previous thirty years had hardened their resolve to succeed in establishing democratic politics in Venezuela. They succeeded.

The Electoral System

Just as there was no strong tradition of party politics in Venezuela in the century following independence, so too there was no tradition of elections. Even when elections were held, their consequences were limited by the severe restrictions on enfranchisement and voting procedures. The constitution of 1936 did little to improve the situation. Enfranchisement was still limited to literate males, and all national officials were elected indirectly. The constitution of 1947 finally established universal adult suffrage. Prior to that time no more than 20 percent of the adult population over the age of eighteen was eligible to vote. In the 1947 presidential election, only 21 percent of the total population participated, a relatively low level even by Latin American standards. When elections resumed in 1958, however, Venezuela had a large potential electorate, and, without much preparation, the country marched suddenly into an environment of mass politics.

Venezuela is a federal system, at least theoretically and constitutionally. The capital city, Caracas, is the federal district, and there are twenty states and two territories. "Federalism" had been the battle cry of many political confrontations in the past, and the federal arrangement was thus part of the 1947 constitution, although, as a compromise measure, federalism is retained in principle, but in reality it has little or no political significance (Martz, 1966:71).

Elections are held every five years, and all offices are elected at that time, including the president, the entire Senate, the Chamber of Deputies, as well as the state legislative assemblies and municipal councils. Former presidents become lifetime members of the Senate. Voting is by simple party ballots, prepared and distributed by the Supreme Electoral Council (CSE). There are two ballots for each election, the "large ballot" used for the presidential election, and the "small ballot" used for all other contests. Each party ballot contains the name of the party, a registered symbol for the party, and is printed in a color assigned to the party. Those who are illiterate can make their selection by either the color or the symbol on the ballot. Voters are assigned polling stations following registration, with each polling station servicing three hundred voters.

Representation in Venezuela is allocated proportionally, adhering to the d'Hondt formula. One of the most generous of the proportional representation systems, the d'Hondt formula makes it easier for smaller parties to obtain representative status than other formulas. This procedure, particularly when combined with the relatively lenient legal requirements for establishing a political party, has opened the electoral system to new groups, allowing them a greater opportunity for representation and participation than is usually found in Latin America.

Representation of small parties is further encouraged by a unique procedure known as the "national quotient." Allocation of seats under the national quotient is different for each election, and it is calculated only after the standard d'Hondt formula has been applied to the voting returns. The total valid legislative vote for all parties is divided by the total number of fixed legislative seats to arrive at a national quotient. Each party's total national vote is then divided by the national quotient. If the party's representation gained through the fixed seat quota is less than that produced by the national quotient, the party is awarded additional legislative seats to bring it up to that total. No party can receive more than four Senate seats under the national quotient formula. This device means that the total size of the legislative chambers varies with each election, depending on the results of the national quota. In 1963, for example, eleven additional seats in the Chamber of Deputies were allocated to six different parties, and four parties received additional Senate seats; two minor parties that were unable to win any seats under the d'Hondt formula were awarded one seat in the Chamber of Deputies under the national quotient.

Although the system may seem complex, it is not by comparison with others used in Latin America. Moreover, it has two very important implications within the evolutionary context of Venezuelan party politics. The system encourages a maximum voter participation through compulsory voting, universal enfranchisement, a simple party ballot that need not be marked, and the use of colors and symbols to assist illiterate voters. The system also encourages the participation of new and smaller political parties by making their legal registration simple and by providing the national quotient system to ensure that parties with a smaller vote have a chance of gaining representation in the national legislature. The possibility of access to political power rather than exclusion from it may be a critical consideration for smaller political organizations, as they weigh the advantages and disadvantages of working within the established political system. This support for small and new political groups was particularly well suited to the political realities of 1958, specifically, a highly mobilized population and the absence of strong party traditions and voter identifications. Overall, the electoral laws have probably contributed to the success of the party system and to the general political stability of the nation.

Contemporary Political Parties

When the dictatorship of Marcos Pérez Jiménez ended on January 22, 1958, the exiled party leaders of AD, COPEI, and URD reached a "tri-party" agreement to cooperate in restoring democracy. The agreement called for party cooperation after a national election to be held in December, a pledge to honor the outcomes of that election, and a government of national unity with the victorious candidate designating cabinet members from all three of the parties. In the 1958 election three principal candidates ran for the presidency: Rómulo Betancourt for AD, Rafael Caldera for the COPEI, and Wolfgang Larrázabal for the URD; Larrázabal also had the endorsement of the Venezuelan Communist party and the small Independent National Electoral movement (MENI). Larrázabal, a retired vice admiral, had served as provisional president of the country in 1958 following the overthrow of Pérez Jiménez. Betancourt received just under 50 percent of the national vote, Caldera 16 percent, and Larrázabal 35 percent. Venezuela began its new experience with democratic government with what seemed to be relative unity. The major parties formed a government coalition, AD the strongest of the groups, but by no means wholly dominant.

For the next ten years Venezuela's party system went through a period of rapid fragmentation, followed by a period of gradual contraction and concentration. By 1983 the system was dominated by AD and COPEI. Partly a product of the lenient electoral laws that encouraged new political parties to form, fragmentation also resulted from the lack of strong party identities and voting patterns within the electorate. But fragmentation also occurred within the political parties themselves, particularly in the AD in the years immediately following the 1958 election. The AD was in fact the principal variable in post-1958 Venezuelan politics—its divisions, controversies, and successes defined the opportunities for the opposition for at least a decade.

After 1958 AD was plagued by three general problems: generational divisions, ideological divisions, and conflicts in personal ambitions (Martz, 1966). Two years after the 1958 election, the unity of the government generally and AD specifically had begun to erode. URD withdrew from the coalition, and, while Betancourt continued to work with COPEI leaders in Congress, Caldera himself withdrew from any formal association with the coalition to pursue his own presidential ambitions for 1963.

The first major division within AD was the result of the disaffection of its youngest leaders, who by virtue of their generation and ideological orientation were impatient with the programs and methods of the older leaders who controlled the party organization. These younger leaders, including Domingo Alberto Rangel, eventually withdrew from the party and formed the Movement of the Revolutionary Left (MIR). In 1962 many members of the MIR joined with some Communist supporters to launch a vigorous guerrilla campaign against the government that lasted about seven years. The MIR itself underwent divisions, and many of its leaders—including Rangel—were captured and jailed. Rangel's supporters joined with several other small groups—including the Popular Nationalist Vanguard (VPN), a URD splinter group, and the National Revolutionary party (PRN), an AD splinter group—to form the Revolutionary Party of Nationalist Integration (PRIN). PRIN endorsed the candidacy of Luis Beltrán Prieto, himself a disaffected former leader of AD who at the time had formed the Electoral Movement of the People (MEP). Electoral failures and further divisions within the leadership of the PRIN had all but destroyed the organization by the 1973 election.

While the MIR division threatened to rob the AD of its younger generation, another division within the party was even more serious. Yet another generational group had emerged in the party by the time of the 1958 election. Younger than the AD's "old guard" but older than those who had formed the MIR, this group became known by the nickname ARS. By 1962 much of it had split from the formal AD organization. The ARS formed a new political party, originally known as AD-OP but later as the National Revolutionary party (PRN). By the early 1970s most of the dissident ARS leaders rejoined AD and supported the 1973 candidacy of Carlos Andrés Pérez, who was of their generation. The defection of ARS had caused many problems for AD—first in congress, as AD-ARS representatives withdrew support from the government and voted with the opposition, and subsequently in the 1968 national elections, when AD lost to COPEI with the lowest level of the national vote the party has ever received, 28 percent. The victorious COPEI presidential candidate in 1968 was Rafael Caldera, the party's longtime leader.

The AD easily won the elections of 1973. Its presidential candidate, Pérez, received a plurality of 44 percent of the national vote in a context of many presidential candidates and much party competition. But AD lost the 1978 election amid charges of corruption leveled against the Pérez regime, charges made by even the AD candidate that year, Luis Piñerúa Ordaz. COPEI presidential candidate Luis Herrera Campíns won with 47 percent of the vote. In 1983 AD scored its greatest political victory since 1947. Its presidential candidate, Jaime Lusinchi, received 57 percent of the popular vote, and AD won commanding victories in the legislature—about 66 percent of the Senate and 60 percent of the Chamber of Deputies. The AD also won control of all the state legislatures but one, and carried every precinct in Caracas.

The fragmentation and gradual reconsolidation of the AD from 1958 to 1983 is a complex story. The party's early internal divisions certainly played a role: the generational and ideological divisions that produced MIR and the loss of its younger generation, in addition to the generational and personal conflicts that gave rise to the ARS and its subsequent defection.

But the difficulties of the party were also in part caused by its very successes, which were redefining the basic political issues in the country faster than AD could accommodate them. Many of these successes came in the early years under Betancourt's leadership: the restoration of representative democracy; the transfer of power for the first time from one constitutionally elected president to another (1963); programs of land reform and industrialization, including the development of the nation's potential for steel production; and the gradual movement toward control of the nation's major source of wealth, its petroleum industry. Venezuela was instrumental in the creation of the Organization of Petroleum Exporting Countries (OPEC), and by 1976 had acquired total national control over its petroleum resources and production under programs initiated by Betancourt. In 1968, when Democratic Action lost the national election, power was transferred from one constitutionally elected party to another for the first time in Venezuelan history. Betancourt's achievements, his charisma, and his enormous influence threatened the ambitions of other leaders in the party, creating opposition and hostility. COPEI, meanwhile, was gradually maturing as the principal opposition party, and its electoral strength grew steadily. That AD suffered to some extent from its own successes is perhaps less surprising than the fact that it was able by 1983 to emerge as a stronger electoral power than before.

COPEI, since 1958 the principal opposition to AD, has twice won the presidency. Unlike its Chilean counterpart, COPEI has been relatively untroubled by ideological conflicts. In its earlier days COPEI embraced a wide range of Christian ideology, and its left- and right-wing supporters had major differences. The right wing became discredited and some members were expelled for cooperating with the military government of 1948. One of the major differences between COPEI and Chile's Christian Democratic party (PDC) has been the relatively narrow range of ideological divisions compared with those of Chile. In both cases, the ideological complexion of the societies has been reflected in the Christian Democratic parties.

The Democratic Republican Union, once a major contender in Venezuelan party politics, has steadily declined in importance since 1958. Its fate has been closely tied to that of its principal leader, Jóvito Villalba, one of the original members of the Generation of '28. The URD presidential candidate of 1958, Wolfgang Larrázabal, received 31 percent of the national vote. Villalba ran for the presidency in 1963 and 1973, but he received only 18 percent of the vote in the former and 3 percent in the latter. In 1973 URD's legislative representation fell drastically. In 1978 the URD endorsed the candidacy of the COPEI candidate, Herrera Campíns, but received no representatives in either chamber of the legislature.

Since 1958 the Communist party has had a difficult and largely unsuccessful experience in Venezuelan party politics. Many of its leaders supported the revolutionary activities of the MIR and its attempt to overthrow the government of Betancourt—an effort that Fidel Castro supported, thus fomenting a bitter personal feud between the Cuban leader and Betancourt. After two serious uprisings and other incidents, Betancourt in 1962 suspended the legal status of both the MIR and the PCV. In 1970 the PCV was reinstated, and in 1973 it joined a coalition known as the Broad Front (FA), which included the URD, the MEP, and other groups. The front was conspicuously modeled after a Chilean coalition of the same name, which had come to power only two years previously. In the 1973 election the front's candidate received just 1 percent of the vote, and the PCV elected only one member to the Chamber of Deputies. In 1978 the PCV nominated its own presidential candidate, who received less than 1 percent of the vote; in 1983 it received less than 2 percent of the national vote.

Socialist parties have never fared well in Venezuela. Two small parties—the Agrarian Socialist party (PSA) and the Socialist Workers party (PST), a splinter of the PSA—survived the collapse of the *Trienio*. The PSA changed its name to the Venezuelan Socialist party (PSV) in 1958 and again in 1967 to the Democratic Socialist party (PSD). It has participated in several electoral alliances but has been unable to elect candidates to the national legislature. The PST likewise has failed to attract voters. In 1961 it merged with other small groups to form the Progressive Republican movement (MRP), which did not survive the 1963 elections. In 1973 the PST again merged with another small group but disappeared after that year's election. Neither the PST nor the PSD was affiliated with the Socialist International, but the AD and the MEP were.

Many other minor parties have participated in Venezuelan politics since 1958. Besides the PRIN, the MEP, and the MIR, there have been the Movement to Socialism (MAS), made up of former PCV leaders who broke with PCV for personal and ideological reasons; the Independent National Electoral movement (MENI), which formed in 1958 to support Larrázabal's candidacy and supported other candidates in 1963 and 1968 and then disappeared; the Nationalist Civic Crusade (CCN), formed in 1965 to support a return of Pérez Jiménez, survived only marginally until 1978; the Popular Democratic Force (FDP), resulting from a split in the MIR in 1962, later supported COPEI candidates and elected several candidates to the Chamber of Deputies running on COPEI lists. All of these parties resulted from personal rivalries or ideological divisions within larger party organizations, and none of them had a significant impact on Venezuelan party politics.

Up to 1988 the AD had elected four presidents (Betancourt, 1958; Leoni, 1963; Pérez, 1973; and Lusinchi, 1983); COPEI had elected two (Caldera, 1968; Herrera Campíns, 1978). The AD presidential candidate supported by Lusinchi for the 1988 election lost the party nomination to former president Carlos Andrés Pérez. COPEI in 1988 nominated Eduardo Fernández, once a protégé of former president Caldera; the URD nominated Isménia Villalba, the first female presidential candidate in Venezuelan history; nine other candidates also ran. Pérez won the 1988 election, receiving approximately 56 percent of the vote.

The fragmentation of Venezuela's dominant party, AD, during the 1960s, accompanied by the proliferation of small parties, was gradually replaced

TABLE 9.2
Venezuelan Electoral Participation, 1946-1983 (in percentages)

	Adult Population Registered	Registered Voting	Population Voting
1946	--	92	36
1947	--	92	30
1958	87	92	37
1963	83	92	37
1968	98	94	40
1973	91	94	43
1978	91	92	43
1983	92	87	48

Source: Official Venezuelan electoral results compiled by the Consejo Supremo Electoral (Caracas), 1946-1983.

by an increasing concentration of political power around two party organizations, AD and COPEI. Thus, what had initially appeared to be an increasingly chaotic situation gradually stabilized into a vital two-party system. And this all occurred within a relatively narrow range of ideological diversity, and prevented effective challenges from either ideological extreme.

Elections, Voting, and Public Opinion

A substantial amount of research has been published over the past quarter-century on elections, voting, and public opinion in Venezuela. In part this is a result of the interest of political scientists in Venezuela's unusual experiment with democratic party politics. But interest has also been aroused by the availability of good survey research and public-opinion data, census data, and electoral data. The moderate size and relative homogeneity of the country have also focused the analytic questions more precisely than is possible in many other Latin American nations.

On balance, the research has produced few surprises for anyone familiar with Venezuela's recent history and institutions. In contrast to most other Latin American nations, Venezuela has demonstrated little change or growth in levels of electoral participation since 1946, when its first modern election took place. Registration and voting levels have remained high throughout the period (Table 9.2). Voting is compulsory in Venezuela, and one might be inclined to attribute the high levels to that requirement. But voting is compulsory in other Latin American nations, and their voter turnouts have not been as high, although patterns of steady growth can be seen over an extended period. The percentage of voters for the total Venezuelan population has increased—caused, perhaps, by a slight rise in the population's median age. The electoral data suggest that Venezuela entered its modern period in 1946 with high levels of social mobilization and that it was able to cope with such levels even without well-established party and electoral institutions.

TABLE 9.3
Venezuelan Presidential Vote by Party, 1958-1988 (in percentages)

	AD	COPEI	URD	PCV	Other
1958	49	16	35	0	0
1963	33	21	18	0	28
1968	28	29	0	0	43
1973	49	35	3	1	12
1978	43	47	0	1	9
1983	57	29	0	0	14
1988	56	42	0	0	2

Note: The URD and the PCV endorsed other candidates in those elections where no vote is shown.

Source: Official Venezuelan electoral results compiled by the Consejo Supremo Electoral (Caracas), 1958-1988.

Presidential elections have basically become contests between two parties, AD and COPEI. Between them they have received an increasing share of the national presidential vote—from a low combined total of 54 percent in 1963 to a high of 90 percent in 1978 (Table 9.3). In 1958 Larrázabal, the URD candidate, received more votes than the COPEI candidate, but that was the only time the URD received more votes than the COPEI. Moreover, candidates of minor parties and coalitions have received a combined total of only 10 percent to 14 percent of the total national presidential vote, regardless of how many competed with the major party candidates. This suggests a more or less permanent number of independent, alienated, and special-interest voters in the country rather than a real challenge to the major political parties.

Presidential campaigns, held simultaneously with all other elections in the country, have been aggressive, noisy affairs even by Latin American standards. Estimates of presidential campaign expenditures suggest that more money is spent per voter in Venezuela during national campaigns than in the United States; particularly in the past several elections, modern techniques of campaigning have been widely employed. Television and the mass media have become especially important, as has the use of public relations firms to organize and manage the presidential campaigns. Many of the campaign techniques commonly employed in the United States have been used in Venezuela, although their effectiveness is not yet clear.

If one looks at the impact of elections on party representation in the Chamber of Deputies and the Senate (Table 9.4), several trends are immediately apparent—the most significant appearing from 1958 to 1968. The AD's representation from 1946 to 1968 in the lower house steadily and precipitously declined from 137 to 63 members. It increased to 102 in 1978 and to 118 in 1983, even though it lost the 1978 presidential election. COPEI

TABLE 9.4
Legislative Representation by Party in Venezuela, 1946–1983

	AD	COPEI	URD	PCV	Other	Total
Chamber of Deputies						
1946	137	19	2	2	0	160
1947	83	19	8	6	1	117
1958	73	19	34	7	0	133
1963	65	40	29	0	45	179
1968	63	59	20	5	66	213
1973	102	64	5	2	27	200
1978	86	86	3	1	23	199
1983	112	61	3	3	16	195
Senate						
1947	38	6	2	2	0	48
1958	32	6	11	2	0	51
1963	26	6	11	2	6	51
1968	19	16	3	1	13	52
1973	28	13	1	0	7	49
1978	21	21	0	0	5	47
1983	28	14	0	0	2	44

Source: Official Venezuelan electoral results compiled by the Consejo Supremo Electoral (Caracas), 1946–1983.

received the same number of deputies in the three elections from 1946 to 1958 but has since increased its total delegation to about 60 members. Since 1958 URD representation has declined to the point where, in 1983, it received none. Other parties received about 25 percent of the legislative seats in 1963, 30 percent in 1968, but only 13 percent in 1978.

With the 1968 election the number of senators elected by AD fell to nineteen from a high of thirty-eight in 1947, and since then its total has fluctuated mildly. In 1968 COPEI significantly increased its number of senators from six to sixteen, and, like AD, its total has fluctuated mildly since then. The PCV has managed to elect one or two senators, and other parties have been able to send only five to seven senators to Caracas, with the exception of 1968 when their combined total reached thirteen senators.

To some extent this pattern since 1958 of the growth and demise of alternate parties merely reflects the political vicissitudes of the AD. But the growth of COPEI, the decline of URD, and the stabilization of minor political party strength at a low level also contribute to the trend. The deteriorating economic conditions in the country since 1978 have not as yet been translated into voter disenchantment with the major party organizations, although that conceivably could happen if conditions were to continue or worsen.

Some of the more visible effects of modernization on Venezuela over the past century have been the growth and increasing affluence on its capital city, Caracas. The growing demographic importance of the city and its environs (roughly the Federal District) has been pointed out frequently in the literature

TABLE 9.5
Comparison of Venezuelan National Party Vote and Federal District (Caracas)
Vote, 1958-1978 (in percentages)

	AD		COPEI		URD		PCV		Other	
	FD	Nat.	FD	Nat.	FD	Nat.	FD	Nat.	FD	Nat.
1958	23	49	19	16	58	35	0	0	0	0
1963	13	33	13	21	10	18	0	0	64	28
1968	17	28	16	29	7	12	0	0	60	31
1973	43	49	40	35	2	3	1	1	14	12
1978	41	43	43	47	0	0	1	1	15	9

Note: The URD and PCV supported other candidates in some elections where no
vote is shown.

Sources: Adapted from David J. Myers, "Urban Voting, Structural Cleavages,
and Party System Evolution: The Case of Venezuela," Comparative Politics 8
(October 1975), pp. 125, 132, and official Venezuelan electoral results
compiled by the Consejo Supremo Electoral (Caracas), 1978.

(Martz and Meyers, 1977:284). In 1847 Caracas contained only 2.6 percent
of the national population, and in 1926 it had 7.6 percent. But in 1971 21.5
percent of the country's population lived in Caracas, and the trend has
continued. The growing dominance of Caracas raises the question of what
political effects, if any, the city and its high rate of population growth have
had on national politics.

If one compares the party voting patterns in Caracas with the national
patterns for the period 1958–1978 (Table 9.5), several trends are apparent.
For example, from 1958 through 1968, AD received less than half of the
vote in Caracas. After 1968, however, the AD vote in Caracas came much
closer to that of its national average. COPEI also received a smaller share
of the Caracas vote than it did the national vote, except for 1973 when its
vote in the capital slightly exceeded its national vote. The major beneficiaries
of this low vote for the two major parties in Caracas were the URD and
smaller parties. In 1958 the URD presidential candidate received 68 percent
of the vote in Caracas, compared to only 35 percent nationally. In 1968
smaller political parties won 60 percent of the Caracas vote while receiving
only 10 percent of the national vote.

Two conflicting conclusions can reasonably be drawn from these voting
patterns. First, Caracas is more responsive to the appeals of minor parties
and new organizations, to the subtle changes and currents in Venezuelan
politics. In part this is because the capital region has a greater diversity of
interests and political orientations than other parts of the country have. It
is also because smaller parties campaign harder and are more visible in
Caracas. Thus voters there know more about the parties and their candidates.
Second, major parties have become more effective in soliciting votes in
Caracas, and perhaps voters increasingly see the major parties as the only

realistic choices. If this trend persists, the difference between voting patterns in Caracas and those elsewhere in the country may be of decreasing significance.

Caracas has other distinctive voting patterns. Martz and Harkins (1973) found lower voter turnouts in Caracas, which they attributed to a cultural characteristic of *caraquenos* (residents of Caracas), rather than to nonvoting of lower classes. They also saw a predictable correlation of class membership and ideological preferences, with lower-class citizens more likely to vote for leftist parties. Most of Venezuela's minor parties are leftist, which explains the relatively higher levels of minor-party voting in Caracas. Martz and Harkins also observed a trend from their data through the 1973 election for voting in Caracas to become increasingly centrist while voting outside Caracas was becoming somewhat more leftist. They argue that in each case the shift can be explained by the growing political sophistication of Venezuelan voters generally.

Meyers (1975) found that party voting clearly responded to socioeconomic pressures, that there was an increasing tendency until 1968 for "antisystem" voting in Caracas, and that from the perspective of the 1973 election the prospects for a two-party system and for continued democracy in Venezuela were not "confirmed." He speculated that in future elections AD and COPEI would compete with parties more oriented toward the traditional than the modern political culture, and that the changes in the region would not favor the modern parties. Subsequent elections have not supported Meyers's interpretation.

The impact of the mass media on Venezuelan politics is an important question given their relative sophistication and their freedom to function. Considerable research exists on the subject, and numerous studies have been published. In his study of the media and the 1978 campaign, O'Connor (1980) draws some conclusions regarding the media in that campaign: (1) the media provided conduits for the parties' and the candidates' communications; (2) they enjoyed freedom of expression and were generally nonpartisan; (3) their influence was greatest in the capital; and (4) television specifically had begun to play a major role in influencing national campaigning and the media were increasingly important generally in Venezuelan politics.

Extensive studies have also been done on political socialization in Venezuela. Blank (1973), who reviews research conducted jointly in 1968 by the Massachusetts Institute of Technology and the Central University of Venezuela Center for the Study of Development, draws some predictable conclusions. He found that the higher-status social and economic groups tended to give greater priority to economic-development issues, while lower-status groups identified programs of agrarian reform and housing along with other efforts to equalize the distribution of wealth as their highest priority. In response to questions concerning individual loyalty, the vast majority of respondents identified "the family" as the primary loyalty. The same study suggests that Venezuelans do not commonly join organizations for political purposes, and that among the urban groups only the barrio dwellers appear "locked into an isolated, near-paranoid distrust of people outside of the family group" (213).

Martz and Baloyra (1976:256) discovered that at the time of the 1973 campaign most Venezuelans (94 percent of those polled) felt the outcome of the election was important and 68 percent cared about which party won the election; but only 43 percent of those polled believed that the campaign had helped them choose. In a subsequent book (Baloyra and Martz, 1979:62) the same authors reported, on the basis of their 1973 data, a more distinctive relationship between ideological preference and socioeconomic status. They found that the lower the status of the class, stratum, or reference group, the greater the frequency of a rightist orientation. But they also found that the reverse did not hold; that is, while preference for the right declined with increased status, a preference for the left did not emerge. Their interpretation is that the lower strata's preference for the right is less an endorsement of corporatism than a reaction to efforts by the left to destroy a popularly, democratically elected government. They also failed to find a strong middle-class support for the right. They concluded that (1) ideological orientations according to socioeconomic groups is based on the preference of part of the lower classes and strata for the right, particularly the poor and peasants; (2) women as a group are very rightist throughout all the strata; and (3) a relatively strong preference for the left can be found on the basis of group identifications, not on that of class images or social stratification—specifically among those who identify themselves as students or workers. Additional research on student political attitudes tends to confirm this finding (Arnove, 1971).

The survey research provides rich data for understanding contemporary Venezuelan politics. Most conclusions based on this research confirm the generalizations from survey research conducted in other Latin American countries. A few factors influencing political socialization, identifications, and attitudes, however, are distinctive to Venezuela.

Long-Term Trends

During a cycle when most Latin American nations were resorting to authoritarian rule—including the long-standing democracies of Chile and Uruguay—Venezuela was implementing a democratic political system, apparently with effective and enduring results.

There are two key ingredients in the success of Venezuelan party politics over the past thirty years, and both are critical to its continued survival. First, the system has been able to generate extraordinarily high quality of political leadership generally and party leadership more specifically. Second, a remarkable consensus has evolved among political leaders and the general public regarding the proper rules of the game for Venezuelan politics. This consensus has included the critically important military elites, the majority of whom seem to have shared the values and aspirations of Venezuela's civilians. The extended period of dictatorships, and particularly the self-serving and grossly incompetent rule of Marcos Pérez Jiménez, probably helped to promote this consensus.

There are both distinctive and universal characteristics in the Venezuelan experience. The distinctive ones are perhaps the more obvious: the civil strife of the nineteenth century reduced the political power of the traditional, rural upper class, leaving a vacuum that military elites filled for many generations. But the civil wars also had the effect of eradicating a potentially troublesome oligarchy as the country moved toward a context of mass politics. The political containment of this traditional oligarchy also tended to diminish the seriousness of class conflicts and class politics as the masses became more politically aware and politically active. As a result, political competition in Venezuela has not been as polarized by class conflict as it has in other Latin American nations. Regionalism, an important factor in nineteenth-century Venezuela, no longer has much political salience in the country, thereby removing another source for political conflict that characterizes many other Latin American nations—although a residue of regionalism still lingers in the Venezuelan concept of federalism, at least constitutionally. The country's political context is also distinctive, if not unique, in that it has had no long-established tradition of political parties, all of which are of recent origin. Identifications with them are therefore relatively weak and are based on modern values and expectations rather than on traditional ones. But parties that are not well established and institutionalized are also vulnerable to fragmentation and instability. The advantage, however, is the elimination of another source of conflict and potential paralysis in the party system: archaic political parties that have little relevance to contemporary problems and issues but remain influential by virtue of their longevity.

Venezuela also possesses what appear to be distinctive and widespread political values. The country's consensus about the rules of the game, whereby party politics is for gaining momentary advantage over the opposition rather than for exterminating it, has created in Venezuela a value system as pluralistic as it is corporatist; this is truly an unusual context in Latin American politics. These values can be seen clearly and dramatically in the willingness of one party to yield power to another after an election, in the apparent willingness of the supporters of one party to accept temporary defeat without abandoning the premises of the system, and for a tradition of a "loyal opposition" to emerge among Venezuelan political parties.

Finally, there has been an unusual and almost unique willingness on the part of Venezuela's political elites to tolerate, even subsidize, minority political interests in the country, including small and new political parties and divergent electoral patterns. This willingness has kept the system open—perhaps more so than in any Latin American nation except democratic Costa Rica—and has unquestionably encouraged the smaller groups to remain within the system rather than resorting to undemocratic methods. Interestingly, those who have not remained within the system have been consistently unsuccessful, and many have returned to the mainstream to argue and pursue their objectives.

Other characteristics of Venezuelan party politics over the past three decades have been more universal, more common to other Latin American systems. The nation's politics has been influenced by the increased social mobilization in the country, although that influence is not revealed by electoral data. With the establishment of democratic politics in 1946, Venezuela began with a relatively high level of social mobilization owing to fundamental changes in the society that had begun a half-century before. Electoral participation has not increased in Venezuela since 1946, but it has been sustained at a high level.

Caracas resembles other primary cities of Latin America in that it has become an increasingly dominant force in its country—demographically, economically, and politically. Like primary cities elsewhere, it has been more responsive to dissident political movements (which explains the success of small and new political parties in the capital region) and is less likely to support the dominant parties. During the past decade, however, the country's two dominant political parties, AD and COPEI, have made remarkable progress in expanding their political base in Caracas—a trend that is potentially very important to Venezuelan politics if it continues and is consistent with mature political systems.

Survey research in Venezuela seems to suggest attitudinal patterns commonly found elsewhere in Latin America. The high level of priority given to family loyalty and identification persists in the country, even in the face of growing modernity and modern values, as it does in other Latin American nations. Female attitudes toward politics seem, if not more conservative, at least more orthodox than male attitudes, a contrast also commonly found throughout the region. Portions of the lower classes are as likely if not more so to identify with rightist groups as they are with leftist groups. This tendency deserves considerable qualification and specification for Venezuela, for it is not true of all the lower-class groups in the nation and it exists within a relatively narrow ideological range. However, comparable tendencies have been found in Chile, Argentina, and Uruguay, to mention only three other examples.

The continuation of the present political system and its increasing institutionalization depend essentially on two factors. First, the country generally and the parties specifically must continue to generate effective leadership and to recruit effective leaders into politics. Second, the government has to address Venezuela's economic problems and its process of development, particularly the critical balance between sustained aggregate economic growth and increased equalization of economic welfare. This balance was relatively easy to achieve from 1958 through the 1970s because of the profitable petroleum exports. But with the economic challenges brought on in the 1980s by the stagnation of petroleum prices and demand and the country's growing international debt, the economic problems have become much harder to manage. The potential for political hostility toward traditional parties and leaders could thus increase. The country's success in these two areas will determine whether the current consensus about the system can be sustained. On balance, will the benefits perceived by the public from the system outweigh the hardships and deprivations created by it?

References

Alexander, Robert J. 1969. *The Communist Party of Venezuela.* Stanford, CA: Hoover Institution Press.

Arnove, Robert F. 1971. *Student Alienation: A Venezuelan Study.* New York: Praeger.

Baloyra, Enrique A., and John D. Martz. 1979. *Political Attitudes in Venezuela: Societal Cleavages and Political Opinion.* Austin: Univ. of Texas Press.

Blank, David Eugene. 1973. *Politics in Venezuela.* Boston: Little, Brown.

Burggraaft, Winfield J. 1972. *The Venezuelan Armed Forces in Politics, 1935–1959.* Columbia: Univ. of Missouri Press.

Magallanes, Manuel Vicente. 1977. *Los Partidos Políticos en la Evolución Histórica Venezolana.* Caracas: Monte Avila Editores.

Martz, John D. 1964. Venezuela's Generation of '28: The Genesis of Political Democracy. *Journal of Interamerican Studies anu World Affairs* 6:17–32.

———. 1966. *Acción Democrática: Evolution of a Modern Political Party in Venezuela.* Princeton, NJ: Princeton Univ. Press.

Martz, John D., and Peter B. Harkins. 1973. Urban Electoral Behavior in Latin America: The Case of Metropolitan Caracas. *Comparative Politics* 53:523–49.

Martz, John D., and David J. Meyers, eds. 1977. *Venezuela: The Democratic Experiment.* New York: Praeger.

Martz, John D., and Enrique A. Baloyra. 1976. *Electoral Mobilization and Public Opinion: The Venezuelan Campaign of 1973.* Chapel Hill: Univ. of North Carolina Press.

Meyers, David J. 1975. Urban Voting, Structural Cleavages, and Party System Evolution: The Case of Venezuela. *Comparative Politics* 8:119–51.

O'Connor, Robert E. 1980. The Media and the Campaign. In Howard R. Penniman, ed., *Venezuela at the Polls: The National Elections of 1978.* Washington, DC: American Enterprise Institute.

Ray, Talton F. 1969. *The Politics of the Barrios in Venezuela.* Berkeley and Los Angeles: Univ. of California Press.

10

ARGENTINA

Political parties have played an unusual but important role in Argentine politics over the past century. Their existence has been complicated in part by internal problems of leadership and organization and in part by the presence of strong organizations and interests that are unsympathetic to electoral activity. What has therefore emerged historically in Argentina is a shifting and evolving electoral competition, generally organized by two parties, or clusters of parties. Additional parties have competed within this context, and new or smaller parties have generally been permitted to form and to participate in elections. Argentine parties have been factionalized and unstable, and some important political interests have failed to take shape as coherent and enduring organizations.

There have been two important reform movements in twentieth-century Argentina, generally characterized as "radicalism" and "Peronism." Both spawned political parties that proliferated and evolved in response to different political realities. Today, parties derived from these reform movements constitute the dominant ones in Argentina. Radicalism and Peronism have both failed to achieve their objectives or to satisfy the expectations and demands of their supporters. With the resumption of elections and party politics in 1983, the party organizations that inherited these traditions are anachronisms. Their survival, perhaps the survival of electoral politics, depends on their ability to modernize, strengthen their organizations and political appeals, and respond to contemporary problems and demands rather than dwell on the confrontations of the past.

Party politics in Argentina has several distinctive characteristics. Over the past half-century power has alternated between civilian and military leaders. The country thus has no experience with or tradition of orderly, democratic transfers of power as a result of an election. Under such circumstances it has often been difficult for Argentines to regard electoral processes and outcomes as politically decisive or even important. This is not to say that elections are taken lightly. Most Argentine elections have seen intense competition, strenuous campaigning, and high levels of voter participation. In fact, voter participation is regularly among the highest in Latin America. But these experiences have often had an air of artificiality—more rituals than processes with which voters can associate their individual or collective welfare.

Argentine party politics, like the society itself, is permeated by rigid class divisions. As in other Latin American nations, there is a striking difference between Argentina's wealthy and the poor. Argentina differs, however, in that it has a large middle sector, which by Latin American standards is relatively affluent, educated, urban, and politically sophisticated. The majority of Argentine voters are by expectation and self-definition, if not reality, middle class. But it is a middle class pressured and dominated by an upper class and fearful of encroachment by lower classes. It is also a class at war with itself, with almost limitless gradations in status and expectations and chronic rivalries. Argentina is a fractious society that has produced equally contentious parties and leaders who are not normally disposed to accept either compromise or defeat.

Outside Latin America it is commonly assumed that political instability is a product of poverty and deprivation, and that as countries became more modern, affluent, better educated, and more middle class, they become more politically stable and more democratic. Argentina challenges these assumptions, for it is the most middle-class in Latin America and is one of the most modern, affluent, and best-educated nations in the hemisphere. Yet, it has also been one of the most politically unstable and periodically produces oppressively dictatorial regimes. This apparent contradiction can be partly explained by the nation's party politics.

The Context of Argentine Party Politics

Viable party organizations have been thwarted by the country's lack of cohesiveness, expressed partly by its regionalism and interprovincial hostilities. At the time of independence, effective control of the country rested in the hands of provincial rulers who acted more or less autonomously. Their power reinforced by independence, provincial rulers were free to develop their own political machines. But nationhood threatened provincial autonomy and raised the possibility that smaller provinces would be controlled by larger and stronger ones like Buenos Aires. The fear of domination found expression, as it did elsewhere in Latin America following independence, as a contest between centralization and decentralization of "federalism." The issue of federalism spawned a period of considerable violence among the provinces and encouraged alliances of some provinces against others.

The regional dimension of Argentine party politics evolved in the nineteenth century into a new configuration with the rapid growth of the capital city, Buenos Aires. Throughout the late nineteenth and early twentieth centuries, European immigrants caused the population of Buenos Aires to expand until the city contained about one-third of Argentina's population and dominated the remainder of the country demographically as well as economically. The rivalry between Buenos Aires's urban interests—commercial, financial, and, eventually, industrial—and the rural interests of the provinces found expression in the growth of political parties and the demand for national elections. Argentina has long had comparatively high levels of social mobilization and political participation. European immigrants, literacy, and political awareness, encouraged by a tradition of public education and considerable urbanization, have all contributed to this. The growth of Argentina's middle sectors occurred very rapidly—over no more than a few generations. The political orientations and economic expectations of the European immigrants generated the principal political issues. In addition, these immigrants proved difficult for the political system to absorb, especially because of their concentration in Buenos Aires. In fact, Argentina's two reform movements, radicalism and Peronism, were largely fueled by demands from the middle sectors for changes in traditional Argentine politics; they established confrontations that persist today. Although Argentina has undergone further social mobilization during the twentieth century, it has gone from high to higher levels, not from low to higher levels as is characteristic of other Latin American nations.

The Argentine export economy is based on cattle and grain and was developed and largely owned by Argentines. Latin American exports were often developed by international organizations. Ensuing patterns of industrialization and urban growth created domestic elites without ties to the traditional rural sectors. In Argentina, however, rural elites controlled much of the export economy and subsequently controlled the diversification of the national economy. Few differences or conflicts therefore emerged between traditional rural elites and the modernizing urban ones. The traditional Argentine agricultural economy became transformed into an "export industry," largely run and managed by domestic elites. Sectors of the export economy were foreign-owned, including the important meat-packing industries, and foreigners participated extensively in Argentine economic development. But the rural landowners became both wealthy and powerful as a result of their participation in the burgeoning export economy. It created a level of wealth and a degree of elite consensus uncommon elsewhere, and with it a formidable basis was formed for political influence and control.

Organized elites in Argentina are not limited to economic ones. The country's rapid industrialization in addition to the government's high degree of participation in public services over the past fifty years have created a vast sector of public employees. They are well organized and constitute a formidable political force in Argentine politics.

Another powerful, well-organized interest group is the military. For many years, the officers corps of the Argentine military was disproportionately recruited from the upper classes, a practice not dissimilar to the British military during the same period of time, particularly the British navy. Argentine military officers were therefore more comfortable with the viewpoints and interests of the Argentine upper classes than with the emerging interests of other sectors of society. The recruitment of officers has broadened in recent decades, becoming more middle class, but the outlook of the officers has changed little. The military's mistrust of politicians, parties, mass politics, and reformist movements such as Peronism and Marxism is deeply rooted in its traditions. Since the mid-1960s, the Argentine army has ruled the country longer than have the party politicians.

Argentines succeeded as well or better in their economic development as Europeans until the postwar reconstruction of Europe. Since then they have not kept pace. This slackening economic development, coupled with the political turmoil of the same period, has given rise to a national malaise that has overwhelmed an already vulnerable system of party politics. No solution to this dilemma has yet been found, and it is difficult in the short run to imagine what a solution might be.

The Evolution of
Traditional Argentine Parties

The evolution of Argentine political parties can be divided into three principal periods: (1) from independence about 1819 to 1912, when the Sáenz Peña electoral reform laws were approved; (2) from 1912 to the end of the first Perón regime, in 1955; and (3) from 1955 to the present.

Political parties did not play important roles in Argentina during the nineteenth century. Indeed, none of the prominent political parties of the twentieth century has had strong roots in the country's history. Argentina's first national party, the Liberal party (PL), emerged in 1852 following the overthrow of dictator Juan Manuel de Rosas. It advocated a national, constitutional government and the imposition of limitations on the provincial governments that had cooperated with the Rosas regime. The Liberal party remained a force in Argentina until the mid-1870s, and several of its leaders were subsequently elected president—Domingo Sarmiento, Bartólome Mitre, and Nicolás Avellaneda. Two other minor parties emerged during this period, the Republican party (PR) and the National Autonomist party (PAN). The former was a national party, but its strength was concentrated in the suburban areas of Buenos Aires province, among the middle class and the farmers. Formed in 1878 by former Liberals, the PR advocated the institution of democratic processes in the country. At that time the PAN was taken over by Julio Roca, who had been elected president and proceeded to use the party as a way of consolidating provincial support, transforming it into his own political machine. From the late 1870s until the Radical Civil Union (UCR) came to power in 1916, Argentina was ruled by its presidents and controlled by the oligarchy, which also controlled the rural economy, exports, and virtually everything else in the country.

What was to become Argentina's first genuinely mass-based political party emerged in 1889 in opposition to the country's authoritarian regimes: In that year the Civic Union of Youth (UCJ) proclaimed itself a party, and to broaden its support was renamed the Civic Union (UC) the next year. The

UC responded to the Argentines' disenchantment with authoritarian regimes and the interests of Buenos Aires' emerging middle class—particularly those of the increasingly numerous immigrants from Europe.

The Radical Civic Union (UCR), which evolved from and then encompassed the UC, became an instrument of reform in Argentine politics. The landed aristocracy, which dominated the country, was the UCR's political target. The party's specific objective was to achieve electoral reforms that would give it a chance to gain national power. Under the electoral system then in effect, the UCR had virtually no chance of victory. Reform finally came in 1912, broadening enfranchisement, establishing procedures for honest elections, and creating a representational system that was more responsive to opposition parties. The UCR leader and presidential candidate Hipólito Yrigoyen won the presidential election of 1916, the first under the new regulations. The middle sectors had for the first time gained entrance into Argentine politics, and, given the context, the event was indeed "radical."

Yrigoyen served a full term, from 1916 to 1922, and was reelected in 1928; but in 1930 he was removed from office by the military. His role as a reformer in Argentine politics is a controversial one and in some respects resembles that of Chile's Arturo Alessandri of the same period. As a party, the UCR had no clear program and met overwhelming resistance from the legislature. By 1928 Yrigoyen had lost his vigor and effectiveness; on balance, UCR's tenure in office was characterized by frustration and failure. The UCR did, however, retain the loyalty of many voters, between one-third and one-half, and functioned as the only organized opposition from 1930 to 1955. But its internal divisions were profound and its policies so diffuse and contradictory that it became little more than a residual opposition force in Argentine politics.

Marxist parties have a long tradition in Argentina, dating at least from 1896, with the formation of the Socialist Labor party (PSO). But the socialist movement was riven with chronic divisions and factionalization and over the years produced a variety of competing "socialist" parties. One such division resulted in the formation in 1918 of the International Socialist party (PSI), which eventually became the Communist Party of Argentina (PCA). The socialist movement produced several prominent political leaders and played a visible, if limited, role in Argentine politics during the 1920s and the 1930s. Marxist parties later had great difficulty in deciding how to deal with Peronism, a situation aggravated by their competition with Peronists over control of the emerging labor movement. When Juan Domingo Perón came to power in 1946, the labor movement came almost wholly under the control of his party. The Marxist parties were repressed and their leaders persecuted by the regime.

Like the radical movement before it, the Peronist movement represented a major change in Argentine politics. A detailed analysis of Perón and his regime is beyond our scope here. What is important is that Peron's political party, under various names, was used by him to consolidate his political power and control over the nation. The Peronist party (PP) as such was formed in mid-1946 out of three parties that had supported Perón's presidential candidacy in 1946—the Labor party (PL), which was established late in 1945 by pro-Perón union leaders; the Renovating Radical Civic Union (UCRR), Peronist supporters from the UCR; and the Independent party (PI), which was formed in 1945 to draw support from nonunion voters to Perón. Through the efforts of Perón and his wife, Evita, women were enfranchised for the first time in the new constitution of 1949. Evita also sought to politicize women through the Feminist Peronist party (PPF) and to rally support for her husband's regime. Formally two separate organizations, the PP and the PPF were part of the same movement and controlled by the same leaders.

The Peronist parties ran candidates for the legislature, campaigned, and organized voters. Yet, fundamentally, the organizations were devices of Perón and originally had no existence independent of him. The PP was very hierarchical, with Juan and Evita Perón making decisions that the organization carried out. At their zenith of power and popularity in the early 1950s, the Peronist parties contained most of the organized labor movement, a strong youth contingent, much of the middle class, and the newly enfranchised women, who identified with the regime. The parties also had considerable support from the church and some military leaders. Unions and their leaders used the PP to gain access to the regime. Students viewed it as a reform and nationalist movement (much as their grandfathers had viewed the UCR two generations earlier), and many women viewed the PP and Evita specifically as their advocates. The strength of the party depended on these supporters and their organizations. Perón rationalized his movement with a diffuse, somewhat incoherent ideology of justice known as "*justicialismo.*" As the regime consolidated its power, provincial Peronist parties emerged to support the movement, and vestiges of these remained after the regime's demise.

Peronism is impossible to categorize ideologically. Perón cloaked his movement in appeals to nationalism, international autonomy, and reform that were particularly directed toward workers and their unions. Perhaps a more fruitful way to view Perón and his party is as a reform movement responding to the demands of large numbers of Argentines for inclusion in the political system and for social change, as well as to diffuse aspirations for national identity and integrity. With the fall of Perón in 1955, the PP ceased to exist, and the military waged a brutal campaign in what proved to be a futile effort to exterminate all vestiges of Peronism. It continued to exist underground, not as an organization, but through its component organizations—principally labor unions and provincial organizations.

Conservative parties had been an important force in Argentina until the rise of Perón. Conservatives dominated the country until 1916, although not through a party so much as through their influence with the government. But the Conservatives, like the Radicals and Marxists, could not maintain a cohesive, independent political organization. There was no single Conservative party, not even an opposition, during the brief period in the nineteenth century when the Liberal party prevailed. Conservative parties formed and disappeared, often functioning in electoral contexts as coalitions and alliances. Like other Argentine parties, most were provincial rather than genuinely national political organizations.

After 1916 and the UCR's accession to power, many provincial conservative parties emerged, including one called the Conservative party (PC) in the populous province of Buenos Aires. It became allied with other provincial conservative organizations, but these coalitions were never able to create or sustain a unified national organization capable of challenging the mass support of the UCR or, later, the PP. In fact, from 1916 to 1946 there were only two national political groups that had substantial mass support and competed nationally throughout the country. And even they depended on provincial organizations and, in the case of the Peronists, affiliated organizations. Although many minor parties competed in elections, most of them did so in a few provinces. Fourteen parties competed in the 1916 congressional election; in 1924, twenty-seven competed; and in 1934, thirty-four competed. Even in the 1946 elections, which swept the Peronists into power, twenty-eight parties competed for legislative seats.

Historically, it is obvious that there is no systematic pattern in the evolution of Argentine political parties and no institutionalized organizations capable of transcending a single generation. The only exception was the UCR, which did survive. But from its inception until 1958, the party had elected only two presidents, Yrigoyen in 1916 and 1928, and Alvear in 1922. The Peronist party, which was not formed until after Perón was elected president in 1946, was suppressed after Perón's fall in 1955 until 1973, when once again it elected Perón as president. Both groups spent more of their years opposing governments rather than organizing them. All Argentine parties, with the arguable exception, at times, of the Peronists, have been highly factionalized and chronically divided, often into opposing political parties. Regionalism played an important role in causing these divisions, which have plagued Argentine politics since independence. Personal rivalries and ambitions also divided the groups, as did ideology.

The failure of parties to institutionalize on a national basis—to transcend the issues and leadership of more than one generation—is an important characteristic of the evolution of Argentine party politics. But perhaps this failure was inevitable, given the fractious and confrontational political environment and the power of individuals and organizations outside the party arena. Nevertheless, the absence of institutionalized party organizations and traditions is somewhat surprising because of Argentina's economic development, social mobilization, and apparent homogeneity. Argentine parties were conspicuous and active during electoral periods, and they often mobilized important sectors of the society. But their influence on national government was overwhelmed by other organizations, interests, and leaders, and their ultimate influence on national policy was minimal.

Electoral Systems and Representation

National elections in Argentina have been held under a variety of electoral systems. Representational formulas have generally evolved in favor of opposition political parties, and, historically, political demands have played a role in this evolution.

The 1853 constitution, the nominal document regulating Argentine government (except for the 1949–1955 period under Perón), specifies that the president and vice-president be elected through an electoral college, that the lower legislative chamber be directly elected by the people, and that the Senate be elected by a plurality of votes in the provincial legislatures. The number of presidential electors is equal to twice the congressional delegation of each province. Each province is assigned two senators, as is the federal capital; the number of deputies for the lower house is based on the population of a province, each province being guaranteed a minimum of two.

The electoral system underwent a major change in 1912, producing what has come to be known as the "Sáenz Peña law," after then president Roque Sáenz Peña. The law, which took effect for the 1916 elections, allowed the UCR to take power in Argentina and contained many provisions designed to eliminate electoral fraud. It created a permanent register of voters, established a secret ballot, made voting compulsory, prohibited many fraudulent practices, and made the federal judiciary responsible for supervising elections (Remmer, 1984:91). It also established a new formula for representation, known as an "incomplete list system." The formula provided that the selection of presidential electors, all national deputies, and senators from the capital be selected by a two-thirds incomplete list. Each voter could choose two-thirds (but no more) of the number of positions to be filled; candidates who obtained the most votes would be proclaimed winners, regardless of their party lists (Snow, 1965a:332). Generally, this meant that whatever party received the largest share of the vote in a province received two-thirds of the legislative seats; the party with the second most got one-third. However, as elections were conducted on a provincial basis, the national totals for the parties did not necessarily reflect a two-thirds / one-third balance; the plurality party could actually receive more than or less than two-thirds depending on the specific vote of each province when combined—specifically, what parties were participating and their relative strengths. The Sáenz Peña system tends to overreward strong parties, particularly those competing in enough provinces so that they can place first or second in each. The only other nations that have used a similar system have been Nicaragua (under Somoza) and Paraguay (under Stroessner), where the superior resources of the government parties and the context of controlled elections always assured the ruling party of a two-thirds share of the national legislature while maintaining the illusion of an opposition holding one-third of the seats, enough to be visible but not enough to be threatening to the regimes.

The 1912 reforms met the political objective of the conservatives, who by that time had decided that the UCR posed less of a threat to their economic interests than did a civil war. The reforms also more or less protected the interests of strong provincial parties and interprovincial alliances. But the new electoral laws hurt the small, weak national parties whose vote was spread thin throughout many provinces and whose legislative representation would always be less than their total national vote.

The reforms remained in operation until a new constitution was adopted in 1949 during the Perón regime. That constitution called for the direct election of the president and senators and, through a special election law of 1951, the election of all deputies at large; it reserved at least ten seats in the lower chamber for the opposition, even if an opposition party could not win ten seats.

Suffrage was extended in 1912 to all male Argentine citizens over the age of eighteen. In 1947, as a part of his overall political strategy to mobilize women, Perón extended the right to vote to women, although few managed to register until the 1951 election. Literacy is not, nor has it ever been, a requirement for voting in Argentina.

Following the overthrow of Perón in 1955 and the constitutional convention of 1957, the principal provisions of the Sáenz Peña law were restored. The military government, fearful of an eventual return to power by the Peronists, let it be known that it favored some form of proportional representation, a suggestion that was also endorsed by the many small parties. However, the constitutional convention decided not to implement such innovations.

The military's fear of the Peronists was reinforced by the large, Peronist-inspired blank vote in 1958 and 1960, and by the large Peronist vote in 1962, which went to a group standing in for the suppressed party. The military intervened in 1962, nullifying the election. It subsequently issued a decree that the d'Hondt formula would be used for the national elections scheduled for 1963. Particularly after the 1962 election, the military believed that the Peronists were strong enough nationally to take control of the congress and ultimately the presidency, and that the Sáenz Peña system was working in their favor.

The d'Hondt system of proportional representation uses closed-list ballots, with the hierarchy of candidates established by the party. Voters may split their voting, as between legislative and presidential ballots, or rearrange and add names to the lists, but few do. Until 1962 provinces had considerable latitude in choosing the rules for their own elections. Most adopted the national Sãenz Peña procedures, but there was no uniformity. So, when in 1962 the government decreed that provinces use proportional representation, this created both opposition and experimentation (Snow, 1965a:335).

Since 1962 the issues of d'Hondt versus Sãenz Peña has been raised periodically. While a change of procedures would affect the balance of parties in the legislature, the results of a change are by no means predictable. Given the national legislature's limited role since 1962 and the absence of any political crisis resulting from proportional representation, inertia has worked against changing the system any further.

The lower chamber has grown over the years, given that representation is fixed according to population. In 1912 there were 60 deputies; 120 in 1916; 158 from 1920 to 1949; 192 from 1960 to 1963; 243 in 1973; and 254 in 1983. The Senate has remained the same (46) with two for each province and two for the federal capital, except in 1973 when there were 3 for each province and the capital, making the total 69. In that election, senators were chosen by popular vote, with the majority party receiving two senators, and the minority party getting one.

The presidential term, historically six years without reelection, was changed to four years with reelection possible for the 1973 election. In 1983 the traditional term was restored. Since 1916, twenty-seven persons have held the presidency in Argentina, of whom only ten gained office by election. Of those ten, only four completed their terms in office. None have done so since Perón in 1953.

Contemporary Political Parties

The expulsion of Perón in 1955 initiated a reorientation of the Argentine party system that has continued to redefine party competition. As we have seen from our earlier discussion, two groups have dominated Argentine politics: the Radicals and the Peronists. Both have been divided and factionalized, with the former producing two separate Radical parties from 1957 to 1973. When the Peronist parties were illegal, the principal competition was between them. The Peronist vote during those periods was divided, some going to provincial Peronist parties, some to one of the Radical parties, and the rest being cast as blank ballots. Following the overthrow of Perón in 1955, the new military leaders tried to destroy all remnants of Peronism and to exorcise its influence from Argentine culture, but their efforts were in vain. Peronism continued to be on the cutting edge in Argentine party politics through the 1987 national elections.

Radical parties. Peronism provoked a split in the Radical party when electoral politics was reestablished in 1957. Leaders of the UCR disagreed over the issue of whether to reintegrate Peronists into Argentine politics—essentially the same issue that had divided the Radicals when Perón came to power in 1946. In any event, the disagreement produced the Intransigent Radical Civic Union (UCRI) and the People's Radical Civic Union (UCRP). The UCRI was led by Arturo Frondizi, who had taken a moderate position regarding cooperation with Perón and who saw Peronists as a potential source of electoral support. The UCRP, one of whose leaders was Ricardo Balbín, was uniformly opposed to the Peronists and constituted in a sense the "old guard" of the Radical party. Frondizi's effort to take leadership of the UCR is what precipitated the split, and the two groups competed with each other for influence and votes from 1957 until 1973.

In the 1963 national elections, the UCRI nominated Oscar Alende, who had opposed Frondizi's effort to build an alliance with the Peronists. But Alende was defeated, and Frondizi left the UCRI and formed the Development and Integration movement (MID). By 1965 the UCRI's vote had fallen significantly, and in 1972, when the right to use the name Radical Civic Union was awarded to the UCRP, the UCRI renamed itself the Intransigent party (PI).

The UCRP won the presidency in 1963 after nominating an obscure but honest governor from Córdoba, Arturo Illia; it captured 37 percent of the deputies and senators. Illia was overthrown by the military in 1966, and Balbín reemerged as the leading figure in the party. He was nominated for the presidency in 1973 but lost to Perón's stand-in, Héctor Cámpora. After a long and particularly repressive right-wing military dictatorship (1976–1983), the UCR coalesced for the 1983 national election behind Raúl Alfonsín, who won a commanding victory in the presidential race, but the party won only a slim majority in the lower house. The UCR increased its congressional margin slightly in the by-elections of 1985, only to lose ground, and its majority, in the 1987 elections.

Peronist parties. The Peronists were repressed by the government and beset with internal divisions following Perón's ouster in 1955. Barred from the elections of 1957 and 1958, the Peronists nevertheless garnered massive blank votes in the elections of 1957 and 1960 (in both cases, about 25 percent of the total vote); in the 1958 election, UCRI candidate Frondizi received many Peronist votes at the urging of the group's exiled leader.

In 1962 the Peronists functioned more openly in the by-elections for Congress, urging support for pro-Peronist and neo-Peronist parties at the provincial level. The Peronists were able in the 1962 legislative elections to win about one-third of the popular vote through provincial parties, an achievement that prompted the military's intervention, mentioned earlier, and the decision to implement proportional representation for the 1963 elections. Because the Peronists were proscribed from nominating candidates for the presidency and vice-presidency, the blank vote, which had been only 1 percent for the 1962 congressional elections, rose again to about 22 percent. It was not until 1973 that the party was again permitted to function at a national level, which it did as the Justicialist party (PJ). It participated again in 1983 and afterward under the same name.

Many other vehicles were used by Peronists after 1955. One prominent one was the Popular Union party (UP), controlled by Peronist labor leaders, which participated in the legislative elections of 1962 and 1963. A more militant group of Peronists within the labor movement formed the Peronist Revolutionary movement (MRP), but it did not participate in any elections. The Peronists' greatest successes between 1957 and 1973 were scored by provincial parties, particularly in the 1962 legislative elections, when they captured 44 of the 192 seats. They fared less well the next year under proportional representation, capturing only six seats through provincial parties. Although, as we saw earlier, Perón himself was barred from running for the presidency in 1973, his surrogate, Héctor Cámpora, ran openly on the promise that, if elected, he would schedule new elections that would allow Perón to participate. Cámpora won just under 50 percent of the vote.

A few months later, new presidential elections were held in which Perón received 62 percent of the vote. The PJ also captured about two-thirds of the legislative seats in 1973. In 1983 the PJ's presidential candidate, Italo Luder, received about 40 percent of the vote, unexpectedly losing to the UCR's Raúl Alfonsín, who received 52 percent. But the Peronists did well in the 1987 by-elections, increasing their congressional representation and receiving a large vote in the provinces and 16 of 22 governor's races, including the important contest in Buenos Aires province, where the UCR candidate lost. Presently, at least one-third of the electorate seems willing to support Peronist candidates, and even more who will vote Peronist as a protest.

Marxist parties. Just as Peronism divided the UCR party, so, too, did it cause a rift in the Argentine Socialist party (PSA), whose mainstream leadership had been strongly anti-Peronist since the mid-1940s, when the Peronists replaced the Socialist leadership in the labor movement. The issue of cooperating with the Peronists divided the party in two, with the hard-liners breaking off to establish the Democratic Socialist party (PSD) and the more conciliatory, if not necessarily pro-Peronist, group continuing to call itself the Argentine Socialist party (PSA). Both parties continued functioning separately thereafter, dividing the Socialist vote between them.

The Communist party also fractionated over ideological questions, dating back to disagreements between Stalin and Trotsky supporters in addition to more current disputes having to do with the Peronists. In 1946 the party opposed Perón, although some of its leaders subsequently formed an electoral alliance with the Peronists. In the 1960s several extremist groups broke with the party, following Maoist and Castroist ideological lines and supporting revolutionary tactics against the regime. One of these groups formed the Workers Revolutionary party (PRT), and another, committed to revolutionary tactics, became known as the Revolutionary Army of the People (ERP). By 1983 the Communists had broken with the Peronists. Electoral support for the Communist party has been low, their positions and potential strength co-opted by the Peronist parties and the labor unions.

Conservative parties. Conservative parties were as fragmented and dissipated following 1955 as they had been before Perón's fall. National organizations were alliances of provincial parties—such as the National Federation of Conservative parties (FNPC), which was organized in 1958. Later, other organizations formed, including the Federal Popular Alliance (APF) in 1973, and the Federal Republican Alliance (ARF). The FNPC was able to elect only twelve deputies in 1963, and its strength has never been substantial. Scores of conservative parties, mostly provincial ones, formed and participated in elections between 1957 and 1987, but their cumulative influence was and continues to be minimal.

The Center Democratic Union (UCD), led by a retired military officer, Alvaro Alsogaray, won 4 percent of the legislative votes in 1985, but in 1987 it won 6 percent of the vote nationally, gaining 18 percent from the province of Buenos Aires, which suggests considerable dissatisfaction in the capital region with the two traditional party alternatives.

During the nearly thirty years following the overthrow of Perón, literally hundreds of political parties participated in one way or another in Argentine elections. Some were personalistic vehicles for their founders, perhaps the most important of which was the Union of the Argentine People (UDELPA), organized to support the candidacy in 1963 of Gen. Pedro Eugenio Aramburu, who had served as provisional president of the country from 1955 to 1958. Others, such as the Christian Democratic party (PDC) organized in 1954, tried without success to create an alternative to the Radicals and the Peronists.

More than forty years have passed since Perón first came to power, and the movement he created is still a potent force in Argentine politics. Its presence caused major divisions in the Radical, Socialist, and Communist parties, and its share of the vote, whether cast as blank ballots, for provincial parties, or for the PJ, continued to command a sizable portion of the Argentine electorate. It persists in spite of Perón's death in 1974 (his second wife, Isabel, succeeded him), serious factionalization within the movement, and long periods of government repression. Although it lost the 1983 presidential election, it received 40 percent of the presidential vote, captured more than one-third of the seats in the lower chamber of the legislature, and more Senate seats than any other party. In 1987 its electoral success was even greater. No other organization, neither on the left nor the right, is as serious a threat to the UCR. The country's two frustrated reform movements, radicalism and Peronism, continue to dominate the nation's party politics with as yet no viable alternatives.

Elections, Voting, and Public Opinion

Voter participation and registration is high in Argentina; indeed, the levels approximate those normally found in other modern countries. The only significant increase occurred in 1951, when women, who had been enfranchised a few years before, registered and voted. Female voting levels began at a high level and have remained there. Participation from 1912 to 1983 (Table 10.1) does not reveal any pattern of progressive change, neither does the mobilization of new voters explain the country's political trends.

Longitudinal patterns in party voting also reveal little that is not otherwise apparent. Moreover, there were important mitigating conditions in most of the elections after the 1916–1928 period. In the 1930s elections were frequently fraudulent and controlled; in the 1940s the phenomenon of Peronism overwhelmed the electoral process. Elections in the next three decades were further distorted by controls imposed by the military, particularly against the Peronist parties, and until 1973 by the bifurcation of the UCR. Aggregate voting in presidential elections for the period 1916–1983 is shown in Table 10.2.

There seems to be remarkable stability in party voting in Argentina, if one allows for voting restrictions and internal party divisions. The popular presidential vote for the UCR in 1983 was virtually identical to what it had been in 1916—about half the vote. In 1973 Perón (in the second presidential

TABLE 10.1
Participation in Argentine Elections, 1912-1983 (in percentages)

	Population Registered	Registered Voting	Population Voting
1912	13	69	9
1914	13	5	7
1916	15	56	9
1918	16	57	9
1920	16	53	9
1922	17	55	10
1924	16	41	7
1926	17	49	9
1928	17	81	18
1930	17	75	13
1931	17	73	13
1934	19	65	13
1937	18	76	14
1938	19	68	13
1940	18	70	12
1942	19	65	13
1946	22	85	19
1948	24	72	18
1951	51	87	45
1954	52	81	42
1957	51	87	45
1958	52	90	47
1960	50	87	45
1962	55	83	43
1963	55	86	46
1965	55	81	42
1973	56	89	49
1983	62	84	51

Sources: Adapted from Dario Cantón, Elecciones y Partidos Políticos en la Argentina: Historia, Interpretación, y Balance, 1911-1966 (Buenos Aires: Siglo XXI, 1973), pp. 267-277, and La Nación (Buenos Aires), 1973, 1983.

election) received almost exactly the same percentage of the national vote that he received in 1951, when his regime was well established and in control. Notwithstanding the dozens of minor national and provincial parties that participated in the elections, none of them seriously challenged the position of the radicals and Peronists. Apart from these two groups, the next highest level of voting in many elections was blank voting.

Voting trends are also difficult to interpret for Argentina because of the demographic dominance of the capital region. Approximately 40 percent of the total national vote comes from Buenos Aires province and the federal district. That vote dominates and skews any interpretation of a "national" vote in Argentina.

TABLE 10.2
Argentine Presidential Vote, 1916–1983 (in percentages)

	1916	1922	1928	1931	1937	1946	1951	1958	1963	1973	1983
Radical	50	48	64	a	41	44	32				52
UCRP								29	25	24	
UCRI								45	16		
Peronist						52	63	b	b	62	40
Conserv.	22	18	14	60	54		2				
Socialist	9	9	5	a	3		1	3	.01	2	
Blank/Null	4	6	7	10	2	4	2	8	21		4
Other	15	19	10	30				15	37	12	4

[a]Abstained from election.
[b]Prohibited from participating.

Sources: Adapted from César Reinaldo García, Historia de los Grupos y Partidos Políticos de la Republica Argentina (Buenos Aires: Sainte-Claire Editora, 1985), and La Nación (Buenos Aires).

Regionalism, however, has not differentiated major competing groups. Its principal influence has been the proliferation of minor parties. In the 1962 legislative elections, for example, the two Radical parties and the estimated Peronist vote (combining the vote for the provincial pro-Peronist parties and the sizable blank vote nationally) garnered 78 percent of the national vote. The remaining 22 percent was divided among the minor parties, about sixty-four of them, most with regional bases of support (Table 10.3). Because many of these minor parties have loose associations with each other and with national parties, they do contribute to the overall strength of national organizations. These minor parties have left control over what otherwise would be national movements indisputably in the hands of provincial politicians.

The Socialist and Communist parties have found support only in the federal capital and surrounding province. The Peronist vote has been strongest in the same area, but with important regional centers of strength as well. The UCR tends to enjoy support throughout the country, although when it functioned as two separate parties (1957–1973), its component groups had their own regional specializations. Given the historic importance of the rivalry between the capital region and the outlying provinces, there have been fewer differences between them in party voting than one might expect.

If one compares the voting for males and females (each vote separately) there is very little difference between them, far less than can be found in neighboring Chile. There were only slight differences between male and female voting in the federal capital for the years 1951–1973 (Snow, 1979:41), when women evinced a slight preference for the Radical party—more so, in any event, than men during the period. More women also voted for the Christian Democratic party during this period than did men, although the difference declined over time.

TABLE 10.3
Principal Minor Parties in the 1962 Election

Party	Provincial/Regional Focus
Autonomist Party (PA)	Corrientes
White Party (PB)[a]	Tucumán, Río Negro
Conservative Party (PC)	Córdoba, Río Negro, Neuquén
Popular Conservative Democratic Party (PDCP)	Jujuy
Liberal Democratic Party (PDL)	La Rioja
White Flag Provincial Defense (DPBB)	Tucumán
Liberal Democratic Party (PDL)	Entre Ríos
Justicialist Front (FJ)[a]	Chabut
Justicialist Party (PJ)[a]	Entre Ríos
Labor Party (PL)[a]	Córdoba, Santa Fe, Tucumán, La Pampa
National Labor Party (PLN)[a]	Salta
Liberal Party (PL)	Corrientes
Democratic Federal Movement (MFD)	Salta
Neuquén Popular Movement (MPN)[a]	Neuquén
Popular Radical Movement (MRP)	Santiago del Estero
Radical Recuperation Movement (MRR)	Santa Cruz
Populist Party (PP)[a]	Santa Cruz, Catamarca, Corrientes
Three Flags (TB)[a]	Santiago del Estero, Santa Fe, Mendoza, Entre Ríos, Federal Capital
Progress and Work Party (PTP)	Santa Fe
Conservative Union (UC)	Buenos Aires
Radical Civic Union (UCR)	Santiago del Estero
Blocking Radical Civic Union (UCRB)	San Juan
Renovating Cross of the Radical Civic Union (UCR-CR)	San Juan
Popular Union (UP)[a]	Misiones, Federal Capital, Buenos Aires
Provincial Union (UP)	Salta

[a]Peronist-affiliated party.

An analysis of female voting by Lewis (1971:438–440) reaches much the same conclusion. He found a higher turnout by women than men for the period 1958–1963, but the difference was slight. He also concluded that women appeared to vote somewhat more conservatively than did men, but again the difference was slight and mostly confined to the Christian Democratic party, as mentioned above. When broken down by class, Lewis found no significant differences for women and men, and women no more or less likely to switch parties from election to election than men were.

Differences in party voting by class are fairly predictable and consistent in Argentina. Germani's pioneering work (1955) for the critical period of the 1940s shows a high correlation between occupation and party vote in the 1946 national election for the federal capital and a significant realignment from the 1940 election for the same region. The principal change, of course, was in the vote for Perón. Predominantly working-class districts were strongly Peronist, while districts that were predominantly white collar, professional, and affluent were more likely to vote for Radical candidates. The much higher correlations between occupation and party preference in 1946 than in 1940 illustrates the growing importance of class in Argentine politics generated by the Peronist movement.

A study of the post-Perón period by de Imáz (1962) also shows a class orientation to party voting, most strikingly for the Peronist vote, which was significantly stronger among the lower classes. Snow's analysis of the 1957 party voting in the federal capital also shows a clear basis for Peronist voting increasing as class levels decline (Snow, 1979:166). He correctly cautions, however, that while the conservative parties tended to receive most of their electoral support from upper and upper-middle classes, Peronist support was not limited to the lower class, nor was radical support limited uniformly to the middle classes. Both groups cut across class lines in their support, the Radicals with a less consistent pattern than the Peronists. The same data suggest that the Socialist parties did best among lower-middle classes and rather poorly among the lower class, which remained a domain of the Peronists. The two Radical parties found their support spread more evenly among all the classes.

The competition for lower-class support seems to be between the strong Peronist movement and the Marxists, with the latter making little if any headway against the former. The competition, of course, extends far beyond the party structures themselves, involving principally the labor movement and control over it. What is significant in this struggle is that the Peronists draw support from many sources, including the middle classes. Moreover, their principal opposition, the Radicals, also draw support across class lines, although their heaviest and most consistent support has been from the middle classes. Little found evidence (1973:282) that the Peronists also received support from a variety of different elite groups, notwithstanding their heavy reliance on urban and rural working classes for electoral support. Smith attributes Peronist strength (1969:48) to the "pre-existing political frustration of the lower class," which was in turn conditioned by the attitudes and actions of the ruling political elites that had controlled the country since the 1930 military takeover.

In his summary of survey research on Argentine politics, Turner (1975) postulates the effect of continuing economic frustration on political attitudes and partisanship, specifically the gap between high economic expectations and poor performance, inadequacies of leadership, and strong nationalistic appeals (75). Kirkpatrick (1971) found a strong correlation between Peronist sympathies in 1965 and the more authoritarian members of the lower class (221–222).

TABLE 10.4
Results of the Argentine Elections of 1983, 1985, and 1987

Party	1983 Presidential Election				Deputies			Senate
	Candidate	Vote	%	Elec. Coll.	1983	1985	1987	1987
Radical	Alfonsín	7,659,530	52	317	129	132	129	18
Peronist	Luder	5,936,556	41	269	111	106	98	20
Intransigent	Alende	344,434	2	14	2	3	6	1
Other		842,640	5	10	12	13	21	7
Total		14,783,160	100	610	254	254	254	46

Source: La Nación (Buenos Aires), 1983-1987.

The frustration of Argentines with the performance of their economy and their political leaders is further suggested by survey research. Studies from a project known as "Opiniometro," reported by Turner (1975:92), show in 1971 and 1972, for example, that less than 10 percent of those interviewed in the federal capital were satisfied with their economic situation, but that an equally small percentage believed that the military regime could remedy the situation. Another study conducted by the Analistas de Empresa & Consultores de Dirección showed that while 66 percent were content with the military coup of 1966, within two years 70 percent had come to believe that the military government was as bad or worse than the one it replaced, and 86 percent of the working class blamed their plight on the government (Turner, 1975:92-93).

The 1983 national elections restored power to a unified UCR (Table 10.4). Their presidential candidate, Raúl Alfonsín, won an impressive victory with 52 percent of the vote. The UCR also won a majority of seats in the lower house of the legislature, 129 out of 254, with the Peronists receiving 111. Neither party gained control of the Senate, but the Peronists captured several more seats than did the UCR. In the by-elections of 1985 the UCR picked up several more seats at the expense of the Peronists. The future of Peronism without Perón was still unclear, as was the ability of Alfonsín to rally his own party and enough support from the electorate to meet the extraordinarily difficult economic and financial problems facing the regime. In the 1987 by-elections, the UCR lost seats to the Peronists, with neither receiving a majority in the chamber; the Peronists showed strong regional support. The Radicals lost all but two of the seven governorships they had held, including the important province of Buenos Aires. The primary beneficiaries of the decreased UCR vote were parties on the right and, to a lesser extent, the Peronists. The by-elections in 1987 were important for the regime, as parties and politicians looked toward the presidential election scheduled for 1989.

Long-Term Trends

In light of the levels of conflict, governmental instability, and military intervention in Argentina for more than half a century, one of the remarkable qualities of Argentine party politics during the period has been the general level of stability and persistence of the nation's political parties. The Radical Civic Union party in its many forms and mutations has remained a central force in Argentine politics, challenged since 1946 by the Peronist parties. No other political party has been able to penetrate this competition in any meaningful way. Both groups have been able to rely on about a third of the popular vote in any relatively free election, and each has been able to obtain a clear majority in national elections. Both represent the traditions and remnants of significant reform movements that essentially failed to change or restructure their society and consolidate their achievements. The power of the upper class and the military, whose interests frequently converge, has been a significant factor in the parties' relative weakness. It is significant that the upper class has been able to maintain its control from outside the party system; it has never had a viable national party that could win elections or maintain relative organizational unity.

Class divisions, class interests, and class politics have dominated Argentine politics, yet political parties have not been defined solely on class bases. Regionalism has been an important component in Argentine politics, but it has persisted as much within political parties (especially the UCR and the Peronist parties) as among them. The basic divisions in Argentina have not changed for generations. What has changed is the ability of parties and politicians to respond to them.

High levels of social mobilization—reflecting relatively advanced economic development, high levels of urbanization and education, and a large middle sector—have yielded consistently sizable voter turnouts. With the exception of female enfranchisement, there has been little change in participation levels over the years. In addition to the limits placed on party politics by strong, autonomous groups, limits have also been created by self-serving leaders, Perón and Frondizi to mention only two, and by unsuccessful or impotent ones, such as Yrigoyen and Illia. Party factionalization has been a symptom of ineffective political leadership, not the cause of it.

Discussions of party politics in Argentina often dwell on the failures of party politics and the defects of the party system (Snow, 1979:40–48), yet radicalism and Peronism have managed to dominate party politics in the country even in the face of a proliferation of competing parties. The "failures" of the party system reflect the failures of Argentine society to generate an effective consensus and a commitment to means as well as ends in politics. The lack of effective political leadership is a problem that has plagued military as well as civilian regimes.

The problems facing any regime—civilian or military, Radical or Peronist— in the late 1980s are formidable ones, and the ability of an Argentine government to respond to the chronic economic frustrations of the population is necessarily limited by the country's many financial and economic dilemmas.

Until a new political force emerges that can persuade Argentines of an alternative solution and mobilize their support, the traditional civilian conflicts reflected in the party system will likely continue. There is no evidence to suggest that a new force in Argentine politics is either imminent or likely.

References

Bugatti, Enrique. 1975. *Breve Historia del Parlamento Argentino, 1813–1974.* Buenos Aires: Alzamor.

Cantón, Dario. 1968. *Materiales para el Estudio de la Sociología Política en la Argentina.* Buenos Aires: Editorial del Instituto Tercuato di Tella.

_____. 1973. *Elecciones y Partidos Políticos en la Argentina: Historia, Interpretación, y Balance, 1911–1966.* Buenos Aires: Siglo XXI.

Ciria, Alberto. 1974. *Parties and Power in Modern Argentina, 1930–1946.* Albany: State Univ. of New York Press.

de Imaz, José Luis. 1962. *Motivación Electoral.* Buenos Aires: Instituto de Desarrollo Economico y Social.

_____. 1964. *Los Que Mandan.* Albany: State Univ. of New York Press.

Gerassi, Marysa Navarro. 1965. Argentine Nationalism of the Right. *Studies in Comparative International Development* 1 (1):181–194.

Germani, Gino. 1955. *La Estructura Social de la Argentina.* Buenos Aires: Editorial Raigal.

_____. 1969. Mass Immigration and Modernization in Argentina. In Louis Horowitz, ed., *Latin American Radicalism.* New York: Vintage.

Huntington, Samuel P. 1968. *Political Order in Changing Societies.* New Haven, CT: Yale Univ. Press.

Johnson, Kenneth F. 1969. *Argentina's Mosaic of Discord, 1966–1968.* Washington, DC: Institute for the Comparative Study of Political Systems.

Kirkpatrick, Jeane. 1971. *Leader and Vanguard in Mass Society: A Study of Peronist Argentina.* Cambridge: MIT Press.

Lewis, Paul H. 1971. The Female Vote in Argentina: 1955–1965. *Comparative Political Studies* 3:425–441.

_____. 1975. *The Governments of Argentina, Brazil, and Mexico.* New York: Crowell.

Little, Walter, 1973. Electoral Aspects of Peronism, 1946–1954. *Journal of Interamerican Studies and World Affairs* 1:515–524.

O'Donnell, Guillermo A. 1973. *Modernization and Bureaucratic-Authoritarianism.* Berkeley and Los Angeles: Univ. of California Press.

Potash, Robert A. 1959. Argentine Political Parties, 1957–1958. *Journal of Interamerican Studies* 1:515–524.

Puizzros, Rodolfo. 1956. *Historia Crítica de los Partidos Políticos Argentinos.* Buenos Aires: Editorial Argumentos.

Ranis, Peter. 1966. Peronismo without Perón: Ten Years After the Fall, 1955–1965. *Journal of Interamerican Studies and World Affairs* 8:112–128.

Remmer, Karen. 1984. *Party Competition in Argentina and Chile: Political Recruitment and Public Policy, 1890–1930.* Lincoln: University of Nebraska Press.

Rock, David. 1975. *Politics in Argentina, 1890–1930: The Rise and Fall of Radicalism.* London: Cambridge Univ. Press.

Rowe, James W. 1964. *The Argentine Elections of 1963: An Analysis.* Washington, DC: Institute for the Comparative Study of Political Systems.

Smith, Peter H. 1969. Social Mobilization, Political Participation, and the Rise of Juan Perón. *Political Science Quarterly* 84:30–49.

———. 1974. *Argentina and the Failure of Democracy: Conflict Among Political Elites.* Madison: Univ. of Wisconsin Press.

Snow, Peter G. 1965a. The Evolution of the Argentine Electoral System. *Parliamentary Affairs* 18:330–336.

———. 1965b. *Argentine Radicalism.* Iowa City: Univ. of Iowa Press.

———. 1968. *Argentine Political Parties and the 1966 Election.* Iowa City: Department of Political Science, Univ. of Iowa.

———. 1979. *Political Forces in Argentina.* New York: Praeger.

———. 1985. Argentina: Politics in a Conflict Society. In Howard J. Wiarda and Harvey F. Kline, eds., *Latin American Politics and Development.* Boulder, CO: Westview.

Turner, Frederick C. 1975. The Study of Argentine Politics Through Survey Research. *Latin American Research Review,* 10:73–116.

Wynia, Gary W. 1986. *Argentina: Illusions and Realities.* New York: Holmes and Meier.

11

COSTA RICA

The Costa Rican political system diverges significantly from the Latin American norm. Liberal democratic traditions, which have yet to develop in most of the region, are deeply embedded in Costa Rica. In addition, the nation's small armed forces never interfere in politics. Since 1920 dictatorship and political repression have been almost unknown. Not surprisingly, this enviable democratic record has earned the country's political institutions an exceptionally high level of popular legitimacy in spite of persisting socio-economic inequalities and recent economic problems.

Political parties have thrived in this liberal democratic environment, but most Costa Rican parties have been little more than personalist electoral vehicles. An exception has been the National Liberation party (PLN), which has developed into an institutionalized party with both a coherent Social Democratic program and a substantial grass-roots organization. A product of the 1948 revolt against the populist regime of Rafael Angel Calderón Guardia, the PLN has been the most important player in Costa Rican politics since its initial electoral victory in 1953.

Yet, its position has not been unchallenged, because less than half of the population identifies itself with the National Liberation party. On three occasions, multiparty opposition coalitions have been able to defeat the PLN in presidential contests. Currently, the Costa Rican party system appears to be evolving toward a competitive two-party model because the parties that composed the Unity coalition (the latest anti-PLN political force) merged formally into the Social Christian Unity party (PUSC) in 1984.

The Evolution and Context of
Costa Rican Party Politics

Throughout most of the nineteenth century, Costa Rican politics was dominated by a coffee-planter elite, although the country continued to be known for its egalitarian social values formed before the coffee era (Ameringer, 1982:16; Booth, 1984:159). During the rule of the coffee oligarchy, the liberal, secular consensus among the elite and the small size of the eligible literate electorate (10 percent of adults) made political parties unnecessary. Politicians simply formed temporary, informal networks of followers (Peeler, 1985:61, 64). Unfortunately, intense competition among powerful families sometimes degenerated into violence and electoral fraud. Ultimately, it produced a military dictatorship under Col. Tomás Guardia (1870–1882), a progressive who succeeded in curtailing the power of the coffee planters (Ameringer, 1982:17).

In 1889 Costa Rica held its first completely free and competitive (although still indirect) election. This marked the beginning of the Liberal Republic, which lasted until the late 1940s (Ameringer, 1982:19). During this era, democratic elections, honest civilian public administration, and peaceful transfers of power gradually became standard practices (although interrupted by the unpopular 1917–1919 dictatorship of Col. Federico Tinoco). The dominant political organization of the time was the Republican party, founded in the 1890s as a loosely organized electoral platform for liberal elite politicians. Challengers to the Republicans included the Catholic Union party of the 1890s, which opposed anticlerical legislation, and the influential, socially progressive Reformist party of the 1920s, as well as a number of personalist vehicles whose labels seldom endured beyond a single election. Of these competitors, only the Reformist party (founded by devout Catholic Jorge Volvio), armed with a Social Christian and antioligarchical program, managed to enlist a genuine mass following. Although the Reformist party disappeared after the deadlocked 1924 elections in which Volvio agreed to support the Republican candidate in return for the vice-presidency (Ameringer, 1982:24), it had already created a new social agenda for the country. It had also paved the way for future cooperation between the Catholic church and lower-class unions (Booth, 1984:163).

Liberal patriarchs such as Ricardo Jiménez Oreamuro and Cleto González Víquez led the Republican party, which was held together more by patronage than by program. Republican presidents were nevertheless responsible for the introduction of direct elections (1914), the rapid expansion of public education, and other valuable reforms. With the consequent rise of literacy, the electorate swelled to include fully half of the adult male population by 1928, when the secret ballot was first introduced (Ameringer, 1982:20). Moreover, by the 1930s the Republicans had to contend with the rise of a new labor movement and Communist party, which became strongly entrenched among the largely Jamaican workforce of the coastal, banana-producing areas (Peeler, 1985:65). The Republican party was therefore forced to increase its ability to mobilize voters.

In the 1936 elections, coffee barons (opposed to popular demands for social reform and increased taxation of the wealthy) backed conservative, antilabor candidate, León Cortés Castro. He took control of the Republican party and ousted its aged leadership. In 1940, after four years in office,

Cortés connived to continue in power by selecting a pliable successor. He chose pediatrician Rafael Angel Calderón Guardia, who ran as the candidate of the newly renamed National Republican party (PRN) and was elected against token opposition. Calderón, however, soon proved to be very independent-minded. In fact, during the 1940s, he introduced a broad program of populist social reform and was supported by an unlikely alliance of the Catholic church and the Communist party, which Volvio's Reformist party had foreshadowed. Armed with ample patronage and other material inducements, Calderón was also able to wrest control of the PRN from Cortés. To oppose Calderón, Cortés and other PRN defectors founded the Democratic party (PD).

Cortés and his party represented conservative interests endangered by Calderón's reformism and his mobilization of the working class. But the anti-Calderón forces also included middle-class liberals and Social Democrats who accepted the need for reform but criticized the regime's growing authoritarianism, corruption, and clerical/Communist ties. In 1944 opposition forces put aside their differences and backed Cortés against Calderón's ally, Teodoro Picado, who headed a Victory Bloc composed of the PRN and the Popular Vanguard party (PVP), a Communist group. Picado won the 1944 elections, but the opposition screamed fraud. Electoral irregularities also marred midterm elections two years later, and Picado was forced to agree to an impartial electoral tribunal.

The onset of the cold war made Calderón's alliance with the Communists more of a liability when he ran for a second term in 1948. Conservative and reformist opposition elements favored by the United States rallied again behind a single candidate, newspaper publisher Otilio Ulate, chief of the recently formed National Union party (PUN) and a moderate conservative. A key component of this electoral coalition was the new Social Democratic party. Created in 1945, the party comprised reform-minded PD activists led by longtime Calderón opponent José Figueres and middle-class professionals who were associated with the Center for the Study of National Problems. Although the new electoral tribunal declared Ulate the victor in 1948, it was Calderón's turn to cry fraud, and he used his congressional majority to annul the results. Opposition forces under José Figueres responded by ousting the government in a bloody six-week civil war pitting them against both armed Communist workers and the small Costa Rican army.

Figueres headed an eighteen-month provisional junta that dissolved the army and the Communist party and instituted several important reforms, including a tax on wealth, a nationalized banking system, and full political rights for women. However, after Ulate's PUN won the most seats in subsequent constituent assembly elections, Figueres's badly defeated Social Democrats were unable to control the drafting of the new constitution, which emerged as only a modest revision of the liberal 1871 constitution.

After turning power over to Ulate as promised, Figueres and the Social Democrats embarked on an extensive recruitment campaign that resulted in the foundation of the National Liberation party (PLN) in 1951. Despite the firm imprint of "Don Pepe" Figueres's personality, *Liberación* stood for more than the advancement of its leader's personal interests. The party advocated a comprehensive and detailed Social Democratic program emphasizing state-promoted social welfare reform and a mixed economy. The PLN won power for the first time in 1953, with Figueres capturing 65 percent of the vote. He ran against a Democratic party candidate who had also been endorsed by Ulate's National Union party.

The National Liberation party has remained Costa Rica's most important party since its triumph in 1953. The PLN has won six of the nine presidential elections held since then and has gained a plurality in the Legislative Assembly in all but one contest. No other single party has become strong enough to challenge the PLN. The opposition has therefore regularly resorted to anti-PLN electoral coalitions.

Calderón's supporters, drawn particularly from the urban lower classes, reorganized under the old Republican party label and quietly backed the PUN candidate, Mario Echandi, in 1958. This informal coalition narrowly defeated the National Liberation party, which had become bitterly divided during the Figueres administration. A reunified PLN under Francisco Orlich easily beat a fragmented opposition in 1962, winning 50 percent of the vote to the PR's 35 percent (for Calderón) and the PUN's 14 percent (for Ulate). But four years later, *Liberación* again confronted a united opposition.

In 1966 the two principal anti-PLN parties—Calderón's Republicans (PR) and Ulate's more conservative National Union party (PUN)—allied with former president Echandi's newly formed personalist party, the Authentic Republic Union (PURA), to form the National Unification (UN) coalition. In an extremely close race, UN candidate José Joaquín Trejos beat his PLN rival by a single percentage point. However, the parties composing the UN coalition agreed on very little beyond their distaste for the PLN. Consequently, the National Unification government (1966–1970) was characterized by dissension and a lack of direction, a record that proved a handicap in the next election. When Ulate's PUN pulled out of the UN coalition, the PLN's José Figueres was assured of an easy victory over Mario Echandi.

Continued division among the PLN's opponents enabled *Liberación* to maintain control of the government in 1974, despite waning electoral support that had produced only 43 percent of the vote for its candidate Daniel Oduber. The PR survived the death of its founder in 1970 by rallying around his son, Rafael Angel "Junior" Calderón Fournier, and by renaming itself the Calderonist Republican party (PRC). But the PUN collapsed with the death of Ulate in 1973. With support mostly limited to the PRC, the National Unification coalition did poorly in 1974, dividing the large anti-PLN vote with two independent opposition candidates: Jorge González Martén of the National Independent party (PNI) and prominent PLN defector Rodrigo Carazo of the Democratic Renewal party (PRD).

The National Liberation party (PLN) suffered its greatest defeat in 1978. It lost control of the presidency and the Legislative Assembly to the new four-party Unity (*Unidad*) coalition. Unity's 1978 presidential candidate was

Rodrigo Carazo, whose Democratic Renewal party (PRD) was composed of PLN members—particularly from the youth sectors—disaffected with *Liberación's* old guard leadership. Carazo, who had lost to Figueres in a battle for the 1970 PLN presidential nomination, promised a continuation of the basic elements of the welfare state but pledged to administer it more efficiently and more honestly. Carazo's PRD was joined in Unity by the Calderonista Republicans and two smaller parties—the centrist Christian Democratic party (PDC), which had run independent candidates in 1970 and 1974, and the Popular Union party (PUP), a front for conservative coffee interests. Unity obviously contained contradictory political elements, but with the PLN tarnished by charges of corruption, the opposition won by a large margin.

Once elected, the Unity government, like that of the earlier UN coalition administration, was plagued by internal divisions and incoherent policy. Unity also had the misfortune to be in office when oil prices were soaring and coffee earnings were falling. Carazo's economic mismanagement made matters worse; his government also came under attack for its close association with the Sandinistas (and related arms-sales profiteering).

Rafael Angel Calderón Fournier, who had recently served as foreign minister, was therefore severely disadvantaged by the Carazo government's unpopularity when he became Unity's presidential candidate in 1982. He was soundly defeated by the PLN's Luis Monge, whom Carazo had so easily bested four years earlier. Shortly after the election, Calderón began the arduous task of transforming Unity into an ideologically coherent and better-organized single party. His efforts seemed to bear fruit in 1984, when the four component parties of Unity merged into the Social Christian Unity party (PUSC). Although Calderón lost in 1986 to the PLN's Oscar Arias Sánchez, his party-building efforts helped to reduce the margin of defeat.

Party politics and elections are especially important in Costa Rica because no professional military since 1948 existed to interfere in the political process. The small civil guard and rural guard are both patronage-based police forces that wield no independent political influence. Thus, the power to govern the country actually does reside with the democratically elected president and Legislative Assembly; civilian party politicians dominate Costa Rican political life. Nevertheless, the lack of party discipline and the limitations placed on presidential power by the constitution make Costa Rica difficult to govern.

The single-term Costa Rican president is weak by Latin American standards. Civil service reforms have restricted his powers of appointment, and legislative and budgetary authority must be shared with a coequal legislative branch. The Legislative Assembly, rather than the president, chooses the magistrates of the Supreme Court, an institution that has frequently used its powers of judicial review to overrule executive actions. In addition, the Costa Rican government is composed of more than 130 autonomous agencies over which the chief executive has little control. In fact, members of the huge (25 percent of the country's wage earners) and well-paid state bureaucracy and public sector—represented by organizations such as the

National Association of Public Employees (ANEP)—constitute one of the nation's most important interest groups.

If Costa Rican parties were highly disciplined, it still might be possible to implement a coherent governmental program despite this fragmented and decentralized institutional structure. But Costa Rican parties have seldom displayed enough unity to make the government function effectively. Victorious anti-PLN electoral coalitions of parties with competing policy goals, personalities, and interests have had little hope of sustaining unity once in power and have also found the largely PLN-affiliated bureaucracy resistant to their central direction. When in power, the PLN has demonstrated greater cohesion, and the bureaucracy has also proved more cooperative. But the National Liberation party also has been troubled by uncertain party discipline in the legislature.

Because of the weakness of party discipline and the decentralized nature of the Costa Rican governmental system, pressure groups are able to exert influence over policymaking (Arias Sánchez, 1978). Costa Rica has few large corporations, but business organizations such as the conservative National Association for Economic Development (ANFE) and the Costa Rican Chamber of Commerce have become very active in politics. Although these private-sector organizations have failed to stop PLN governments from intervening in the economy and from expanding the welfare state, they have been influential enough through lobbying and informal contacts to prevent more serious redistributive actions.

With the exception of the powerful and predominantly middle-class public-employee groups, organized labor is a weak political force in Costa Rica. The blue-collar labor movement is small and divided among at least half a dozen competing union federations. Working-class consciousness has never been highly developed in Costa Rica outside of the banana-producing zones, and the country's labor code contains strike restrictions and social guarantees that hinder union organization. The Communist-led United Confederation of Workers (CUT), which has a strong following among manual laborers, is a constant critic of the government but has little influence. Conversely, the moderate PLN-linked Costa Rican Confederation of Democratic Workers (CCTD) and National Confederation of Workers (CNT) enjoy more direct access to government decisionmakers.

In spite of their problems with internal discipline, Costa Rican political parties, and particularly the PLN, are the nation's most important political actors. Indeed, in light of the extreme weakness of the armed forces and the modest political roles played by the private sector and the unions, the relative importance of political parties may be greater in Costa Rica than anywhere else in Latin America.

Contemporary Political Parties

Since the 1950s the ideology of the National Liberation party has been expressed in a basic charter that commits the PLN to liberal democracy, a mixed economy, and an ambitious Social Democratic program of state-directed socioeconomic reform. However, the party always has been more pragmatic than ideological. In recent years, for example, deteriorating economic conditions have made it difficult to promote further expansion of social welfare, and the PLN has begun to place greater emphasis on the need to stimulate economic growth. In foreign policy, the traditionally anti-Communist National Liberation party is usually an ally of the United States, although it parted company with the Reagan administration when President Arias orchestrated the Central American peace accord (Esquipulas II) in 1987.

The PLN is the country's best-organized major party. Party affairs are directed by its National Executive Directory composed of the National Executive Committee (party president, secretary-general, and treasurer), the head of the PLN Legislative Assembly delegation, and ten national secretaries in charge of various party activities and auxiliary bodies (Tartter, 1983:213). The directory administers a nationwide grass-roots organization that is extensive but tends to be relatively inactive between elections. Party cantonal assemblies are responsible for nominating PLN municipal candidates and for choosing delegates to the seven *Liberación* provincial assemblies. These provincial assemblies select delegates to the PLN National Assembly and recommend candidates for the Legislative Assembly. The PLN National Assembly makes the final decisions on Legislative Assembly slates and also selects the party's National Executive Committee. In addition, the PLN National Assembly formally ratifies the party's presidential nominee, who is chosen by a direct vote of all active party members.

Factionalization has troubled the National Liberation party since its inception, and the party is presently divided along both personalist and policy lines. Personal enmities exist among many of the PLN's traditional leaders; and each of the former presidents Figueres, Oduber, and Monge has a private following. Other less-prominent party figures who aspire to high office also have their own loyal networks. The PLN has also been split into competing wings over the party's recent endorsement of austerity policies and its deemphasis of its social welfare commitments.

Former secretary-general Oscar Arias represented the rise to power of a new generation within the PLN. A party centrist, Arias won the nomination with the support of about 60 percent of active PLN members, defeating a candidate backed by both Figueres and Oduber. As president, however, Arias has failed to gain full control over the PLN after his election, as evidenced by the election of Walter Coto, a candidate he strongly opposed, as PLN secretary-general in 1988.

Mass support for the National Liberation party is concentrated in Costa Rica's sizable middle class, especially among those employed in the large public sector. Although the middle class has become the core of the PLN, *Liberación* also draws votes from the rural peasantry and from blue-collar workers associated with the PLN-linked unions. In elections the PLN now does about equally well in urban and rural Costa Rica and in all of the country's provinces—except for banana-producing Limón, where it is traditionally weak, and Cartago, where it usually gains its strongest support (Seligson, 1987:169; Ameringer, 1982:214; Denton, 1972:72–73).

The principal opposition party to the PLN is the Social Christian Unity party (PUSC), which was formed in 1984 by the formal, if still tenuous, merger of the Calderonist Republican party (PRC); the Democratic Renewal party (PRD), started by Rodrigo Carazo; the small Christian Democratic party (PDC); and the coffee elite's tiny Popular Union party (PUP). In 1986 Jorge González Martén, whose personalist National Independent party (PNI) competed in the 1974 election also brought his followers into the PUSC. In spite of the diversity of the PUSC's component parts, the party has been able to agree on a conservative platform that clearly differentiates it from the PLN. Under the young, dynamic party leader Rafael Calderón, the PUSC advocates orthodox neoliberal economic policies and major reductions in the size of the state bureaucracy. Fierce advocates of free enterprise, the PUSC is also strongly anti-Communist and was a highly vocal supporter of U.S. policy in Central America under Reagan. At this point, the party's promises to preserve the nation's social safety net are the only remaining historical tie to the social paternalism of Calderón's father.

The PUSC has clarified itself ideologically but has not yet been able to develop an organizational apparatus comparable to that of the PLN. Its component parties still maintain separate identities, and no elaborate PLN-like party structure has been constructed to organize the party's mass following. Rafael Calderón is the party's undisputed leader and the most important member of its only significant organized body, the National Political Directory. However, many other aspiring party leaders and their loyalists jockey for subordinate positions and power within the PUSC. In addition, when the Social Christians moved decisively to the right, some party members resisted the change of ideological tone.

The PUSC naturally gains strong support from conservative business leaders and landowners and from among more privileged social strata not dependent on public-sector employment. Yet, the party also has an important following among the working class and marginal groups that have backed *Calderonista* parties since the 1940s. Growing contradictions between the PUSC's conservative program and the welfare needs of much of its electorate may pose a serious dilemma for the party. In the last two elections the PUSC and its Unity predecessor ran more or less equally well in both urban and rural Costa Rica. The party did best in Guanacaste province on the Nicaraguan border; its poorest provincial results were obtained in PLN stronghold Cartago and in Limón where the radical left traditionally does well.

Radical critics of the PLN and PUSC claim that, despite their differences, the two major parties are quite similar in their defense of the nation's dependent capitalist order and in their neglect of popular-sector interests. Led by urban intellectuals, Marxist parties offer Costa Ricans an anti-U.S. and revolutionary alternative but have failed to attract more than a small following in San José and in the banana zones. The most important leftist party is the orthodox pro-Soviet Popular Vanguard party (PVP), which has been active since 1931 despite its having been officially outlawed from 1948 to 1975. The PVP is directed by a central committee and political bureau and organized along traditional Communist party lines with affiliated unions and ancillary groups. In 1978 and 1982, the communists allied with three smaller Marxist groups in the United People (PU) electoral alliance, managing to win an average of 7 percent of the electorate. However, when a more militant faction replaced longtime Communist leader Manuel Mora in 1983, the coalition became factionalized. Pro-Mora dissidents formed the splinter Costa Rican People's party (PPC) and remained in the United People (UP) coalition. Excluded from this coalition, the Popular Vanguard party organized the competing Popular Alliance (AP) by allying with another radical group. In the 1986 elections, the two Marxist coalitions divided the much reduced radical vote relatively equally.

Public Opinion, Political Participation, and Elections

Public opinion studies conducted over the past twenty years have shown that Costa Ricans strongly endorse their country's political institutions (Gómez and Seligson, 1986; Goldrich, 1966). Even the country's recent economic decline has not lessened Costa Ricans' popular faith in democracy (Gómez and Seligson, 1986:23). The nation's major parties are also viewed favorably: more than three-quarters of the voting population (over the age of eighteen) identify with the PLN or its opponents.

Considering the modest number of thorough public opinion analyses available, it is more difficult to reliably characterize the political orientations of the mass public. Widespread support for most existing social programs seems to persist, but some recent studies have suggested a conservative shift in attitudes. In 1984, 80 percent of Costa Ricans said they would vote for Ronald Reagan if given the chance and an even larger majority expressed hostility toward Nicaragua's revolutionary regime (Furlong, 1986:7; Gómez and Seligson, 1986:27).

Costa Ricans characterize themselves as uncooperative, individualistic, and hard to mobilize, but, in fact, they participate vigorously in the electoral process and in other forms of political activity (Booth, 1984:165). Since the *Calderonistas* were fully reintegrated into electoral politics in 1962 (Gómez and Seligson, 1986:11), an average of 80 percent of the voting-age population has turned out to vote (Table 11.1). In fact, elections have become a national passion in Costa Rica, a high-spirited *fiesta cívica*, in which large segments of the population dress in party colors, display party banners, and involve themselves in mass rallies, parades, and other campaign events. Technically speaking, voting is obligatory, but there are no penalties for abstention.

Elections to choose the Costa Rican president and the unicameral Legislative Assembly (fifty-seven members) are held concurrently using separate

TABLE 11.1
Costa Rican Legislative Assembly: Election Returns by Party and Rates of
Participation, 1953-1986 (in percentages)

	PLN	PD	PUN	PR	UN	Unidad	Left	Other	Voting
1953	65	21	7					7	67
1958	42		21	22				15	65
1962	49		13	33			2	3	81
1966	49				43			8	82
1970	51				36		5	8	83
1974	41				25		4	30	80
1978	39					43	8	10	81
1982	55					29	6	10	79
1986	--					--	--	--	82

Sources: Adapted from John A. Peeler, Latin American Democracies:
Colombia, Costa Rica, Venezuela (Chapel Hill, NC: University of North
Carolina Press, 1985), p. 100, and Miguel Gòmez and Mitchell A. Seligson,
"Ordinary Elections in Extraordinary Times: The Political Economy of Voting
in Costa Rica," paper presented at the 1986 Latin American Studies
Association meeting, Boston, p. 11.

ballots once every four years. The candidate who wins more than a 40 percent plurality of the vote is declared president, otherwise a runoff election between the two top contenders has to be scheduled (this has yet to happen). Presidential candidates may not hold any high government posts in the year prior to the election, and since 1969 presidents have been limited to a single term. Legislative Assembly deputies are selected in each of the country's seven provinces by proportional representation (the d'Hondt system) using closed party lists. The number of seats allotted per province is determined by population. Deputies are not immediately eligible for reelection.

Costa Rican elections are supervised by the independent and impartial Supreme Electoral Tribunal (TSE). Chosen by a two-thirds vote of the Supreme Court, this body is composed of three magistrates and six alternates, none of whom may be affiliated with a political party (Furlong, 1986:2–3). The TSE inscribes parties and oversees the Civil Registry, which issues voters' identity cards and produces the data from which the TSE creates a current list of eligible voters. The tribunal also monitors campaign practices for violations of election law and certifies the final election results.

After the election returns are tallied, the TSE is charged with the distribution of public campaign funds to all parties winning more than a minimum of 5 percent of the vote. A substantial portion of these funds are paid out in advance during the campaign on the basis of shares of the party vote won in the last election. There are no limits on private campaign donations and no ceilings on a party's total campaign spending, but public campaign funding is limited by law to no more than 2 percent of the government budget, a sum equal to U.S.$10 million in 1986 (Furlong, 1986:7).

TABLE 11.2
Costa Rican Legislative Assembly: Distribution of Seats by Party, 1953-1986

	PLN	PD	PUN	PR	UN	Unidad	Left	Other
1953	30	11	1					3
1958	20		10	11				4
1962	29		8	19		1		0
1966	29				27			1
1970	32				22			3
1974	27				16			14
1978	25					27	4	1
1982	33					18	4	2
1986	29					25	2	1

Sources: Compiled from Ronald H. McDonald, Party Systems and Elections in Latin America (Chicago: Markham, 1971), p. 162, William L. Furlong, "Elections and the Election Process in Costa Rica in 1986," USFI Reports 12 (September 1986), p. 7, and Keesing's Contemporary Archives (March 4, 1974), p. 26391, (June 2, 1974), p. 26535, and (May 21, 1982), p. 31499.

The National Liberation party (PLN) has had a dominant, but not unassailable, position within the Costa Rican party system (Tables 11.1 and 11.2). In Legislative Assembly elections held between 1953 and 1986, the PLN gained the support of an average of just over one-half of the electorate and won a plurality of deputy seats in all but one election (1978). In contrast, since 1966 the National Unification and Unity electoral coalitions—and the Social Christian Unity party (PUSC) that has emerged out of them—have attracted an average 35 percent of the voting population. The Marxist left, in its various combinations, has garnered a mean 6 percent of the vote in Legislative Assembly contests and a mere handful of deputies since returning to electoral competition. PLN victories seldom have been overwhelming, however, except in 1953 and 1982, and the party has often governed with a slim, one-vote legislative majority. On three occasions (1958, 1974, 1978) opposition parties have combined to win enough legislative seats to deny the PLN a majority.

Disadvantaged by the greater organizational strength of the PLN and its broader popular following, the anti-PLN opposition has had to rely on short-term forces to succeed in presidential elections. It has won three presidential contests since 1953 by rallying around attractive candidates and by taking advantage of PLN divisions and public dissatisfaction with PLN administrations. The Calderonistas have formed an indispensible part of each of these winning opposition combinations (1958, 1966, 1978). Most recently, in 1978, the Unity electoral alliance captured the presidency by uniting behind PLN dissident Rodrigo Carazo, who was able to enlist many independent voters and wavering PLN partisans by attacking corruption in the Oduber and Figueres administrations.

The anti-PLN opposition has essentially remained unified since 1978 and has found another appealing candidate in Rafael Angel Calderón Fournier.

TABLE 11.3
Costa Rican Presidential Election Results, 1974-1986 (in percentages)

1974		
Daniel Oduber	PLN	42.6
Fernando Trejos	UN	30.2
Jorge González Martén	PNI	11.0
Rodrigo Carazo	PRD	9.7
Other candidates		6.5
1978		
Rodrigo Carazo	Unity	48.8
Luis Alberto Monge	PLN	42.3
Rodrigo Gutiérrez	PU	7.3
Other candidates		1.5
1982		
Luis Alberto Monge	PLN	58.7
Rafael Angel Calderón	Unity	33.6
Mario Echandi Jiménez	Mov. Nac.	3.8
Rodrigo Alberto Gutiérrez	PU	3.3
Other candidates		0.6
1986		
Oscar Arias Sánchez	PLN	52.3
Rafael Angel Calderón	PUSC	45.7
Other candidates		2.0

Sources: Keesings Contemporary Archives (March 4, 1974), p. 26391, and (May 12, 1978), p. 28975, Charles D. Ameringer, Democracy in Costa Rica (New York: Praeger, 1982), p. 120, and William L. Furlong, "Elections and the Election Process in Costa Rica in 1986," USFI Reports 12 (September 1986), p. 7.

But the poor performance of the Unity administration (1978–1982) was a major factor behind PLN victories in the last two presidential elections (Table 11.3). As Carazo's foreign minister, Calderón was closely identified with the discredited president and saddled with his dreadful administrative record. Thus, in 1982, PLN presidential candidate Luis Monge won in a landslide, carrying all of Costa Rica's seven provinces and collecting nearly 59 percent of the vote. The PLN's share of the Legislative Assembly vote was almost as large (55 percent) giving the party assured control of the body with thirty-three deputies. Only about one-third of the electorate endorsed Calderón, and the Unity coalition garnered just eighteen seats in the Legislative Assembly. None of the four other presidential candidates drew as much as 4 percent of the vote.

Four years later, memories of the disastrous 1978–1982 Unity administration had not entirely faded, and former president Carazo was still rated in polls as the nation's most unpopular politician. In contrast, in spite of its austerity measures, the incumbent PLN administration was viewed very positively by most Costa Ricans because of falling inflation and renewed economic growth, aided by large infusions of U.S. economic assistance. A 1986 Gallup poll ranked affable President Monge the most popular politician in Costa Rica. The contrasting public evaluations of the Carazo and Monge administrations were an important asset to PLN candidate Oscar Arias Sánchez (scion of a wealthy coffee-planter family) and a major obstacle for the PUSC in the 1986 race. Unwisely, *Liberación* nearly squandered this advantage when the party's internal struggle over the presidential nomination produced a major schism.

In spite of early campaign problems, however, Arias and the PLN went on to win a convincing victory in 1986. Faced with a possible PLN defeat, former presidents Figueres and Oduber swallowed their disappointment at failing to stop the Arias candidacy and campaigned tirelessly for the PLN ticket. In addition, under the guidance of U.S. media consultants, the PLN launched an effective mass media campaign that linked Arias to the popular Monge and gave a bit more warmth to the British-educated candidate's cold, intellectual image.

Backed by a core of highly committed PUSC militants, Rafael Calderón waged a tenacious and unusually ideological campaign (aided by funding from conservatives abroad) and enjoyed the endorsement of most of the nation's press. Yet, his hard-line positions on economic and foreign policy issues probably cost him more votes than they gained. Although not inclined to like the Sandinistas, most Costa Ricans preferred Arias's plan for peace and normalization of relations with Nicaragua to Calderón's talk of the possible need to help defend Honduras. In addition, Arias's vaguely defined promises to cut government spending without sacrificing critical social services were more palatable than the drastic budget cuts proposed by his opponent.

The PLN's victory in 1986 with 52 percent of the vote marks only the second time that *Liberación* had been able to elect two presidents back to back. The PUSC greatly improved on its 1982 showing, however, winning almost 46 percent of the vote for Calderón and twenty-five seats in the Legislative Assembly. The four other presidential candidates representing the two feuding Marxist coalitions and two tiny right-wing groups collected only 2 percent of the vote.

Long-Term Trends

Costa Rica is regarded as Latin America's most genuine liberal democracy. Since 1948, when a brief civil war succeeded in restoring democracy, the nation's political leadership has been chosen peacefully every four years in free and competitive elections. Costa Rica continues to be spared the political violence, military intervention, and repression that have plagued most of Latin America. In recognition of these achievements, Costa Ricans display great pride in their governmental system and participate actively in its electoral process. Despite persisting social inequalities and economic conditions that threaten the nation's social welfare protections, the spirit of compromise and the unusually high legitimacy of Costa Rican institutions remain secure.

Political parties play a central role in this classic liberal democratic context, but until recently most have been rather weakly organized personalist vehicles. The social democratic National Liberation party (PLN) became the first large party to develop both a coherent program and a durable grass-roots organization. With a firm base of support in the middle class and the peasantry, the PLN has gained a dominant, but not impregnable, position within the party system. Although the PLN has won six of the last nine presidential contests, opposition party coalitions have won the other presidential races and have often prevented the National Liberation party from gaining a dependable legislative majority. The most recent of these multiparty coalitions, Unity, has attempted to transform itself into a single party with a common program and an improved organizational structure. Led by Rafael Calderón, the new Social Christian Unity party (PUSC) came close to defeating the PLN in 1986 and could well mount another serious challenge in 1990.

References

Ameringer, Charles D. 1982. *Democracy in Costa Rica*. New York: Praeger.

Arias Sánchez, Oscar. 1978. *Quién Gobierna en Costa Rica?* San José, Costa Rica: Editorial Universitaria Centroamericana.

Booth, John A. 1984. Representative Constitutional Democracy in Costa Rica. In Steve C. Ropp and James A. Morris, eds., *Central America: Crisis and Adaptation*. Albuquerque: Univ. of New Mexico Press.

Denton, Charles F. 1971. *Patterns of Costa Rican Politics*. Boston: Allyn and Bacon.

Furlong, William L. 1986. Elections and the Election Process in Costa Rica in 1986. *USFI Reports* 12:1–8.

Gómez, Miguel, and Mitchell A. Seligson. 1986. Ordinary Elections in Extraordinary Times: The Political Economy of Voting in Costa Rica. Paper presented at the meeting of the Latin American Studies Association, Boston.

Goldrich, Daniel. 1966. *Sons of the Establishment: Elite Youth in Panama and Costa Rica*. Chicago: Rand McNally.

McDonald, Ronald H. 1971. *Party Systems and Elections in Latin America*. Chicago: Markham.

Peeler, John A. 1985. *Latin American Democracies: Colombia, Costa Rica, Venezuela*. Chapel Hill: Univ. of North Carolina Press.

Seligson, Mitchell A. 1987. Costa Rica and Jamaica. In Myron Weiner and Ergun Ozbudun, eds., *Competitive Elections in Developing Countries*. Durham, NC: Duke Univ. Press.

Tartter, Jean R. 1983. Government and Politics. In Harold D. Nelson, ed., *Costa Rica: A Country Study*. Washington, D.C.: U.S. Government Printing Office.

Woodward, Ralph L., Jr. 1976. *Central America: A Nation Divided*. New York: Oxford.

PART FOUR

Multiparty Systems

12

CHILE

Chile's experience with party politics has been unusual and dramatic. It is unusual in that party politics have mattered historically both in government and in the daily lives of Chileans. The tradition of competitive party politics was established shortly after the 1818 independence, and persisted with few interruptions until the military coup of 1973. Elections offered real choices between candidates, policies, and, often, ideologies, and they had an enviable record for honesty and impartiality. Chilean elections attracted international attention from some who tried to influence them and from others curious about the implications of the Chilean experience for other developing nations. A country of modest size, limited affluence, and persistent economic problems, Chile tried for generations to govern and reform itself by democratic means, an effort that brought chronic frustration and ultimately ended with a protracted and brutal military dictatorship.

Chilean party politics has stimulated many contrasting interpretations. One study, by Federico Gil (1966), interprets Chilean politics as a search for reform, a solution to underdevelopment and inequality. Gil sees this search as transcending ideology, although ideological rhetoric clearly emerged from politicians and parties responding to the Chilean quest. Frustrations and disillusionment in seeking easy or painless solutions created new and often more radical proposals, ultimately resulting in an increasingly polarized society. A second interpretation of Chilean politics stresses the impact of modernization on the country. Increasing levels of education have resulted in greater expectations and demands. In addition, political awareness and participation has encouraged an expanding enfranchisement over the past half-century (Huntington, 1969). A third interpretation reflects a Marxist view, stressing Chile's capitalistic development over the past century; its economic dependence on, and hence vulnerability to, international pressures; and the growing diversification and confrontation of class interests.

On the surface, the Marxist interpretation is persuasive. Chile's economic development was capitalistic. It did produce a society in which the means

185

of production were highly concentrated and monopolistic. A confrontation did result between those who controlled Chile's wealth and production and those who provided its labor. It is also true that Marxists' and anti-Marxists' final confrontation occurred just prior to the military takeover. Chile was dependent internationally, its exports subject to price fluctuations beyond its control, its imports tied to critical commodities such as food, energy, resources, and manufactured goods. Yet, Marxist groups and leaders have had a long and generally unhindered involvement in Chilean politics. Studies of voting and public opinion raise some doubts and add qualifications to the Marxist interpretation. Our purpose here is to describe Chile's extended experience with party politics and to explore these and other interpretations that help to explain it.

The Context of Chilean Party Politics

Organized political parties emerged in the generation following Chilean independence in 1818. With the exception of two brief civil wars (in 1829 and 1891) and a short military regime (1927–1931), Chile was peacefully ruled by civilians. Many parties endured for generations, including several that were important up until 1973. Literally hundreds of parties have functioned in Chile since independence, multiplying with remarkable facility.

This proliferation of parties followed a general pattern that penetrated Chile's socioeconomic class structure until virtually all classes were politicized and had vehicles advocating their interests and soliciting their support. The abundance and diversity of parties encouraged coalitions between parties for elections. Many of the parties themselves were actually political coalitions whose organizations were diverse and often confusing. Coalitional politics tended to diffuse political and ideological options, confuse the responsibility for ineffective policies, and heighten political frustration.

Class interests and politics had an unusual relationship, particularly in the earlier years of Chilean democracy. The upper-class economic rivalry between the landed aristocracy and the urban, commercial, financial elite had little importance in Chile. The common nineteenth-century issues of centralization vs. decentralization and the role of the church in society were resolved early in Chile's history. The wealth of the country generated by its export economy was largely in the hands of foreigners by the turn of the twentieth century, and the traditional rural and urban elites each tried to derive what they could from the newfound wealth. To a large extent, the rural and urban elites merged their interests and assimilated into a relatively homogeneous class.

The urban middle class gained entrance early on into Chilean politics and did so with considerable success. Their interests were tolerated by the late nineteenth century within a context of rapid economic growth, and they benefited significantly from expanding government services, particularly education. Sharp party differences were blurred by this early absorbtion of the middle class into politics, although subsequent expansion of the party system to include lower classes brought eventual confrontations.

Chilean politics has been distinctively national rather than regional. Notwithstanding its obvious geographic regionalism, Chile achieved a relatively homogeneous national culture and was spared the violent confrontations that regionalism often imposed on the party politics elsewhere.

Chile has maintained a tradition of political experimentation since its independence. Toward the end of the nineteenth century, Chile had a strong, centralized, conservative regime, which was replaced in 1891 by a parliamentary system with a weak president, and in 1925 by a more balanced division of powers between a congress and a president. Since the 1930s Chile has been ruled, however briefly, by a Socialist republic, a popular front coalition, a reinstated dictator (Carlos Ibáñez) who ruled constitutionally, in the 1960s by increasingly ideological parties, and by a Marxist regime in the early 1970s.

These "experiments" were based on an ironic but common assumption: that the political system in Chile was not working, and without changes Chile could not be governed. In a sense, the same assumption underlies the reasoning of the present military regime, permitting officers to believe that Chile's historic political processes were not working and could not work. The paradox was caused by frustration, by Chile's failure to achieve fundamental reforms in the social and economic systems and greater affluence through development.

The pressures for reform came as the political system expanded to include the middle and lower classes, and the frustrations were essentially economic. It was impossible to bring living standards into line with expectations generated by mass education. Chileans seemed permanently dissatisfied with governments and leaders, making opposition coalitions more visible and viable than governing ones. Chilean parties historically tried to mobilize and attract this frustration and translate it into votes. Ironically, those parties and coalitions that succeeded and came to power subsequently found they were vulnerable to the same forces.

The ideological distinctions in Chilean politics coexist with strongly personalistic elements. This is suggested both by voting patterns and by public opinion surveys. Charismatic leaders have emerged to build support irrespective of their ideological orientations. Arturo Alessandri, Carlos Ibáñez, Jorge Alessandri, Eduardo Frei, and perhaps Salvador Allende were such personalities. The phenomenon has been no less important historically in Chilean presidential politics than in U.S. presidential politics. But in Chile this tendency has been tempered and sometimes overwhelmed by ideological considerations.

Chilean politics might seem to have been one of the most "pluralistic" in Latin America, measured by the diversity and multiplicity of political interests encompassed in the party competition. But Chilean politics, even prior to 1973, was no less corporatist than is commonly found elsewhere in Latin America. Virtually all Chilean political groups functioned with corporatist assumptions: namely, that there was a natural order for their society, that nothing would function effectively or justly until that order was achieved, and that the objective of political action was to pursue that proper order. Those parties and alliances that came to dominate Chilean politics generally shared this corporatist orientation, different as they may have been in interpreting what the "natural and just order of society" should be. It was true for the right, the left, and even for one major centrist party, the Christian Democrats, who had their own vision of the proper structuring of society and stubbornly resisted views held by the right and the left.

The Chilean experience with party politics raises important issues. Can democratic party politics persist in meaningful, nonviolent ways in a political culture dominated by corporatist values, or is confrontation and instability inevitable? How far and how rapidly can societies be reformed by governments without precipitating instability and armed confrontation? Is the present military regime an inevitable consequence of the premises and context of Chilean party politics, or is it an anomalous interlude to be followed by the resumption of party politics? The military leaders, at least those now in control, seem to envision a transition to a new system more harmonious with their orientation to corporatist values.

The Evolution of Contemporary Party Politics

Chile's first significant political parties emerged in the mid-nineteenth century, specifically the Liberal party (PL), the National party (PN), the Conservative party (PC), and the Radical party (PR), in that order. All but the National party survived in one form or another up until the 1973 military intervention. Two sequential patterns can be seen in the evolution of the Chilean party system: first, one of proliferation, and second, one of contraction. Proliferation, which began almost from the outset, expanded the number of parties competing in elections and diversified the political orientations embraced by them. For example, the Liberal and Conservative parties dominated Chilean politics in the nineteenth century, but they did not have exclusive control over the party system. "Third" parties represented an important component in the dynamics of the system and, through alliances, could often tip the scales toward one of the two dominant parties. This proliferation of parties accelerated until about 1958. But Chilean party politics began to undergo a major change at about that time, contracting from about 1958 to 1967. From 1967 to 1973 the system became polarized. The intense, uncompromising confrontation could not be resolved by traditional political processes and it eventually overwhelmed the system.

The Liberal and the Conservative parties, the first ones in Chile, emerged over the issues of centralization and the role of the church in society. Although there was considerable competition between the groups in the nineteenth century, the Conservatives generally dominated the country until 1871; the Liberals were preeminent afterward. The Liberals organized first as an opposition force in the 1840s, and the Conservatives about a decade later. A third group, known as the National party, organized at the same time as the Conservatives but differed from them primarily on the bases of personal loyalties and leadership rather than on policy or philosophy. The National party remained a political factor for about seventy-five years, declining rapidly in the 1920s and officially disbanding in 1933.

During the administration of President Manuel Montt (1851–1861), the Conservatives formed an alliance with the dominant faction of the Liberal party, a coalition that caused a rift in the Liberal organization and gave rise to yet another party, the Radical party, that was to play a critical role in Chilean politics. The Radicals became the principal advocate of the emerging Chilean middle class in the late nineteenth century, a role it would continue to play, albeit with variable success and considerable fragmentation, until 1973.

The Radicals were "radical" only within the context of the time. They advocated in their first national convention (1888) complete separation of church and state, elected provisional assemblies that would devolve some authority from the central government, free public education, proportional representation, and guarantees for individual rights and liberties. By the turn of the century their constituency had become primarily white-collar workers, bureaucrats, teachers, merchants, and small farmers—i.e., the enfranchised portion of the Chilean masses, those who were literate and had the right to vote. In the fifty years prior to the 1973 military coup, the Radical party, having achieved its original goals, came to encompass a wide range of political viewpoints and orientations. Held together by political expediency, Radicals made alliances with a variety of other political parties, several of which were electorally successful, usually with increasingly influential political coalitions. The Radicals' success with their initial programs, however, served to destroy their ideological focus. They were eventually superseded by new "radical" parties that appealed directly to the lower classes as they were enfranchised and became politically active.

By the late nineteenth century the religious issue had been resolved in favor of secularization. Centralization, however, remained an issue. In 1891 a civil war broke out in Congress, where there was growing hostility to presidential power generally, and to José Manuel Balmaceda's increasingly dictatorial rule specifically. After a brief confrontation between Balmaceda's troops and Congress, the regime collapsed and Balmaceda committed suicide. From then until the 1920s, Chile was governed by its legislature, a parliamentary system in which the presidency was little more than a formality.

The Democratic party (PD) emerged in Chile just prior to the 1891 civil war. The party was known as the "Partido Demócrata" and the "Partido Democrático"—sometimes the different names referred to different factions. It eventually evolved through complex mutations into the National Democratic party (PADENA), which remained a minor group up to the 1973 coup. The Democratic party comprised dissident Radical party members in addition to leaders of a fledgling labor movement. In the first party convention (1889), its leaders called for universal suffrage, which would clearly benefit their party; social security; and industrial protectionism, which would benefit the labor movement by protecting jobs in the burgeoning but inefficient industrial sector. The organization is often considered the first Socialist party in Chile, although its origins were not Marxist. It later affiliated with the Socialist International, and in time its more radical leaders parted with PADENA to form Socialist parties with Marxist programs and ideology. Just as the Radical party had represented an expansion of the party system to include the newly emerging middle sectors of the society, the Democratic party tried to incorporate society's lower-class sectors. Like most Chilean parties, it was beset with factions, some of which evolved into still more political parties.

The parliamentary experiment was the first challenge to the traditional oligarchy. The oligarchs did not disappear or lose their political influence but continued to participate through their political parties with considerable success. They were, however, by then only one of an expanding number of organized political interests. The expansion of the party system was encouraged by the elevation of the legislature and parties to a primary position of power and the increase in the importance of elections. The 1891 civil war changed the rules and the participants in Chilean party politics, but it was not a broadly based social revolution that changed other conditions in Chile. More Chileans were drawn into politics as they sensed that party activities could affect their well-being, and more diverse political organizations formed to solicit their support. But the price of expansion was legislative instability and paralysis. In the sixty years prior to the 1891 civil war there had been 31 cabinets in Chile, whereas in the thirty-three years of the succeeding parliamentary period there were 121 cabinets and 530 ministers (Gil, 1966:50). Legislative chaos made consensus about genuine reform almost impossible.

The frustrations with reform ultimately produced a new reform leader, Arturo Alessandri, a presidential candidate supported by Democrats, Radicals, some Liberals, and minor parties. Alessandri was elected, but his term as president was turbulent. His reform efforts were frustrated by legislative opposition. The military intervened in 1924, dissolved the Congress, and forced Alessandri into exile. He returned the next year, only to be forced to resign again a few months before the end of his term. He was replaced by a military officer with presidential ambitions, Col. Carlos Ibáñez. In 1925 a new constitution was promulgated. Restoring a balance between the presidency and the legislature, the new constitution was in many ways visionary. It strengthened parties and elections by establishing a system of proportional representation and staggering national legislative and presidential elections. Ibáñez ultimately assumed dictatorial powers and ruled Chile from 1927 to 1931, when he was deposed by some military officers who imposed a short-lived "Socialist republic" on the country.

As the party system expanded during the parliamentary period, a group of Marxist parties was formed. Chilean parties generally have factionalized, but the Marxist parties have no peer in this regard. No less than twenty-two Socialist parties were formed between 1892 and 1973, most with a common lineage. Seven Communist parties emerged during the same period, although the most dramatic expansion in the number of Marxist parties came during the 1930s and 1940s. For the most part, expansion was tolerated and the organizations were allowed to compete freely with other parties for legislative representation. The Communist Party of Chile (PCCh) was formed in 1920 and was affiliated with the Third International. It was declared illegal briefly during the Ibáñez dictatorship (1927–1930) and again in 1937 and 1939. It was banned for only one extensive period, from 1948–1958.

Christian Democracy evolved in Chile during the 1930s largely among university students at the Catholic University. These students shared with their parent's generation a commitment to Catholicism, but found the Conservative party too conservative. In 1938 this generation founded the National Falange, a youth movement that was originally part of the Conservative party. The Falange was soon joined by the Popular Corporative party (PPC), a small group founded during the Socialist republic that shared many of the Falangists political ideas. In the 1940s, the Falange elected several deputies and a senator. In 1957 it joined with still other small parties, including the Social Christian Conservative party (PCCS) and the National Christian party (PCN) to establish an alliance that finally became the Christian Democratic party (PDC).

The expansion of the Chilean party system reached a climax in the 1950s. In 1949 ten parties were represented in Congress and ten more had registered for the 1949 congressional elections. By 1953, twenty parties were represented in Congress out of thirty-six that had competed in the election. The strongest parties were the traditional ones—Radical, Conservative, and Liberal, in that order. Together they constituted about two-thirds of each chamber of the legislature. They were forced to make coalitions and electoral alliances, however, with smaller parties, which acquired considerable leverage as a result.

The evolution of political parties in Chile saw a continual expansion of the number of parties and the range of their political orientations from the original nineteenth-century organizations through the 1950s. From then on the number and diversity of Chilean parties decreased, and, ultimately, the system polarized. These evolutionary patterns reflected fundamental, long-term changes in Chilean society, particularly in its electorate and its economy. Its course was facilitated and encouraged by (1) the electoral system, (2) the parliamentary experience after the 1891 revolution, and (3) the provisions of the 1925 constitution. The result was a political environment that permitted the political expression of fundamental conflicts and aspirations in the society through the party system and elections, and encouraged democratic politics in a context of underdevelopment and deprivation to a degree rarely known elsewhere.

Electoral Systems and Representation

The Chilean electoral system has undergone many changes, historically, particularly ones affecting enfranchisement and party representation. The

TABLE 12.1
Registration and Participation Levels in Chile, 1915–1973 (in percentages)

Year	Election	Population Registered	Registered Voting	Population Voting
1915	Congress	5	81	4
1918	Congress	10	54	5
1921	Congress	12	51	5
1925	President	8	85	7
1932	President	11	70	7
1937	Congress	10	87	9
1938	President	10	88	9
1941	Municipal	14	70	10
1941	Congress	11	78	9
1942	President	11	80	9
1944	Municipal	15	65	9
1945	Congress	12	70	8
1946	President	12	76	9
1947	Municipal	12	84	10
1949	Congress	10	80	8
1950	Municipal	14	74	11
1952	President	18	87	16
1953	Municipal	18	69	13
1953	Congress	18	72	13
1956	Municipal	18	62	11
1957	Congress	19	68	13
1958	President	22	84	18
1960	Municipal	24	70	17
1961	Congress	25	75	19
1963	Municipal	33	81	27
1964	President	36	87	32
1965	Congress	37	85	27
1967	Municipal	38	80	26
1969	Congress	39	70	26
1970	President	36	84	28
1971	Municipal	36	75	27
1973	Congress	42	81	34

Source: Official Chilean electoral results compiled by the Dirección del Registro Electoral, Oficina de Informaciones (Santiago), 1915–1973.

net result was a party system that embraced an increasing number and variety of voters and parties.

From independence to the 1891 revolution, participation in Chile was highly restricted. In the 1864 election there were only 22,000 "qualified" voters out of a total population of about 2 million, or about .01 percent of the population. Registered voters had risen to 10 percent by 1938 and by 1970 to 36 percent of the population (Table 12.1). About 9 percent of the total population voted in 1938, and about 28 percent participated in 1970. The largest increases came in the 1960s.

These changes were largely the result of expanding suffrage. Until 1891, eligibility to vote was restricted to those who were literate males over twenty-five years of age who met minimum income requirements and owned property. To qualify to vote one had to be certified by local officials, who in turn were under the control of the national government, making fraud and control of voting a common and easy matter for regimes. Restrictions on suffrage were eased after 1891, and the registration and voting procedures were made more impartial. With the 1925 constitution suffrage was extended to all literate males over the age of twenty-one. In 1952 women were enfranchised, and in 1972 the voting age was lowered to eighteen and the literacy requirement was eliminated. The literacy qualification was particularly important in the earlier years before Chile had reached relatively high levels of education, for it selectively worked against those of lower socioeconomic status.

Voting in Chile was by means of an "open list" ballot rather than the "closed list" more commonly employed by countries that used a proportional-representation system. Chile was the first and almost the only Latin American country to use the open list. In the more common closed list ballot, parties submit lists of candidates for multimember districts with the names of the candidates hierarchically arranged by the party. The voter votes by party, not candidate, and candidates are elected according to their hierarchical position on the list and by how many candidates a party elects. With the open list ballot, candidates are listed by party in an order determined by lot, and the voter marks his or her ballot for a specific candidate. Those candidates with the most votes are chosen according to the number of seats the party won as a whole. This system allows greater leeway for personal maneuvering by candidates, for they are campaigning not only against other parties but also against candidates of their own party. The system weakens party discipline, however, because elites are not free to move uncooperative candidates to lower positions on the ballot, thus destroying their chances for election. A popular candidate who personally attracts a large vote is an asset to other candidates, given that the larger the party's total vote the larger its share of seats, which in turn increases the candidate's value and influence in the party. The system, while complicated, combines to some extent a primary and a general election, and encourages personalism in electoral politics.

The most important reformation of the electoral system was the adoption, decreed by the 1925 constitution, of proportional representation to allocate seats in multimember districts following the d'Hondt formula—the most commonly employed system in Latin America and in Europe. Of the many variations of proportional representation, the d'Hondt is one of the most generous in allocating seats to weaker parties. The system therefore reinforced the tendency for Chilean parties to multiply after 1925.

One of the consequences of proportional representation in Chile was the inability of any one party, with few exceptions, to win control of the legislature, which further encouraged alliances and electoral coalitions. These coalitions were often successful in winning elections but not in running the government once they got into office. The tendency to form coalitions was not entirely a result of proportional representation, however, but had characterized Chilean multiparty politics from the outset. Alliances ranged from informal and often unstable cooperation between like-minded politicians on specific issues to formal electoral coalitions designed explicitly to maximize the number of seats the alliance could win.

As parties proliferated in the 1930s and 1940s, party coalitions were increasingly blamed for the failure of the legislature to take decisive action and to implement coherent programs. Although the blame was partially misdirected, it produced by 1958 a movement to prohibit electoral coalitions altogether. It was not coincidental that the process of electoral coalition—which had for many generations favored right-wing parties—was by 1958 beginning to benefit parties on the left. The prohibition of coalitions produced one important change in Chilean politics: it decreased the residual influence of small parties, which was based on their willingness to enter into alliances with stronger parties—a phenomenon that helped lead to the general contraction and polarization of the party system.

In spite of the prohibition against electoral coalitions, Chilean politicians found a way around the obstacle, and two important leftist coalitions played a critical role in the 1960s and 1970s—the Popular Action Front (FRAP) and Popular Unity (UP). The prohibition ruled out several parties endorsing a single candidate, but the FRAP and UP made informal agreements not to run separate candidates in specific electoral contests against each other. Candidacies were assigned to a candidate that had the best chance of winning in a specific district. The procedure met the letter of the law if not the intent of the prohibition. The Radical party, whose political influence had been the result of alliances and coalitions, finally tipped the scales in favor of the left. In 1962 it had joined with the Conservative and Liberal parties in the short-lived "Democratic Front." And in 1964, by withdrawing from the presidential campaign, it encouraged the election of a Christian Democratic president. By the late 1960s the majority of its leadership joined the Popular Unity alliance, which elected Salvador Allende. The Christian Democrats, largely for ideological reasons, refused at first to participate in coalitions—a fatal error. By 1973 the PDC, standing more or less alone in the center, finally initiated a coalition (the "Confederation for Democracy") with the National party and two factions of the Radical party. But it was too late to affect the course of events. The idea of a coalition resurfaced after the military intervention, when the Christian Democrats promoted a similar coalition during the Pinochet dictatorship.

The electoral system—its procedures, regulations, representative formulas, and administrative structures—defined the political options available and supported the evolution of party politics in Chile. Its incorporation of more and more Chileans into the electoral experience reflects the fundamental social changes in the country.

TABLE 12.2
Presidential Voting in Chile, 1938-1970

Year	Elected	Party	Percent of Votes	Number of Votes	Total Vote
1938	Aguirre Cerda	PR	34	143,140	421,000
1942	Ríos	PR	36	167,280	464,669
1946	González	PR	40	192,207	474,600
1952	Ibáñez	Ind	47	446,439	954,131
1958	Alessandri	Ind	34	389,909	1,235,552
1964	Frei	PDC	56	1,406,002	2,506,563
1970	Allende	PS	36	1,075,616	2,962,743

Source: Official Chilean electoral results compiled by the Dirección del Registro Electoral, Oficina de Informaciones (Santiago), 1938-1970.

Contemporary Political Parties

By contemporary parties in Chile, we mean those that functioned from the mid-1950s to the military coup of 1973 and its aftermath. The major parties involved in this period were the Liberal, Conservative (and, after 1966, the National party formed by a merger of the two), the Radical, Christian Democratic, Socialist, and Communist parties of Chile. Some minor parties also deserve attention. The results of the presidential elections from 1938 to 1970 are shown in Table 12.2.

Chilean parties are often conceptualized on an ideological spectrum: the right, composed of the Conservative, Liberal, and eventually the National party; the left, principally made up of the Socialist and Communist parties; and the center, the Radical and Christian Democratic parties (Gil, 1966:309; Valenzuela and Valenzuela, 1986:203). This is a reasonable approach, but it requires a few qualifications. There was often considerable ideological disagreement within many of the parties. Some leaders of the Conservative and Liberal parties were more willing to countenance change than others—particularly if they could supervise it—and to cooperate with more moderate groups. The Christian Democrats were divided between moderate and more radical groups representing different generations of leadership and differing over the pace of change and its scope. The Socialist party had similar divisions, with many Communist leaders even more cautious about implementing change than Socialist ones. The Radicals, while avoiding ideological positions, vacillated between the right and the left when forced to take sides. It would also be incorrect to assume that all Chilean voters were ideologically committed or motivated. The left and the right were more or less balanced electorally by the late 1960s, and tried to solicit support from the center. The apparent ideological shift to the left in 1970 may have been yet another effort by Chilean voters to find a vehicle for reform that would work. Both the right and the center had failed, and the left was the only remaining option.

An equally valid way of looking at Chilean politics is one of coalition building, which by 1973 produced two evenly matched ideological groups on the left and the right, and a weakened center. By lending support to Popular Unity, the Radicals tipped the scales in favor of the left and continued to function as an arbiter in coalition building. The irony of the experience was that the process of coalition building worked well in a narrow political sense—more or less evenly balancing the major contenders for power—but it created a vacuum in the center and a condition of paralysis in which no group could effectively rule.

The 1952 elections had left the Conservative party divided and weakened. In 1958 they joined with Liberals to support the successful presidential candidacy of Jorge Alessandri. They endorsed no one in 1964, leaving their supporters with a choice between Frei and the Christian Democrats or Allende and the FRAP. In the parliamentary election the following year, the Conservatives suffered such enormous losses that they joined in 1966 with the Liberals to form the National party (PN).

The union of the two former rivals brought success in the 1969 parliamentary elections, substantially increasing their representation in both houses of congress. In 1970 the National party endorsed the candidacy of Jorge Alessandri. His candidacy seemed a plausible one: the Christian Democrats were divided ideologically, they had a less than attractive candidate in 1970, and they carried the burden of incumbency. Alessandri enjoyed a great deal of personal popularity and benefited from the nostalgia of being an ex-president; moreover, the alternative, Allende, created fears that unified the center and the right. The National party lost the 1970 presidential election, but not by much. It fared better, in any event, than the incumbent Christian Democrats did. In the 1973 congressional elections the National party formed a loose alliance with the Christian Democrats and the conservative splinter of the Radical party ("Radical Democracy") to oppose Popular Unity candidates. In this election, the National party won an additional Senate seat and three additional deputies.

The principal role of the Radical party from 1952 to 1973 was one of arbitrating party politics, its strategy one of building coalitions. However, it was frequently disunified, with separate factions pursuing separate strategies. In 1952 one faction ("Doctrinal Radical party") supported Carlos Ibáñez and, in 1957, the FRAP. Later the same group divided between Allende and Alessandri in the 1958 election and disappeared in the mid-1960s. In 1958 the Radicals ran their own presidential candidate, who finished fourth. They originally opposed the Alessandri administration, but in the last year joined his cabinet. Prior to the 1964 election the Radicals affiliated with the Liberal and Conservative parties and nominated their own party candidate, but the Conservatives and Liberals, sensing defeat and the possible election of Allende, withdrew from the alliance. Most of their supporters voted for Frei, as did most of the Radical party voters; the Radical presidential candidate received only 4 percent of the vote in the three-way race. After the 1964 presidential election the majority of the Radical party, sensing a shift in power to the left, supported the FRAP. Those who opposed this affiliation were expelled from the party in 1969 and formed Radical Democracy (DR), which supported Alessandri in the 1970 election.

Although the Christian Democratic party can trace its origins to 1930, it did not appear under that name until 1957. It nominated Eduardo Frei for president in 1958, who came in third after Alessandri and Allende. In the 1961 congressional elections the PDC emerged as the strongest single party in Chile, a position it was to retain until the 1973 coup. But unlike the other Chilean parties, the PDC's position was one of self-imposed isolation from other parties until the futile effort it made with other groups to oppose Popular Unity in the early 1970s. In 1964 it won a majority of the presidential vote (an almost unprecedented achievement in Chilean politics made possible by what was essentially a two-way race with Allende), and the next year the party won an equally unprecedented majority of the seats in the Chamber of Deputies. The PDC did not win control, however, of the Senate, and its programs of reform were often, but not always, defeated in the Senate. Many of its programs, particularly those of tax reform, were unpopular and alienated the middle class, a serious strategic blunder.

Increasingly factionalized (particularly by the extreme left, which criticized Frei's administration as too gradual and too moderate), some Christian Democrats urged an alliance between the PDC and the parties of the left. The Christian Democrats lost seats in the 1969 legislative elections and suffered yet another reversal in 1969 when a splinter group formed the United Movement of Popular Action (MAPU) and joined forces with Popular Unity to support the candidacy of Allende. The PDC candidate finished a distant third in the 1970 presidential race. When the PDC leadership in the early 1970s finally agreed to a loose affiliation with forces opposed to Popular Unity, it was too late to reverse the trend, and Popular Unity did well in the 1972 congressional elections.

In their own way the Christian Democrats were a very "ideological" party, whose program was defined by the modern and mostly liberal doctrines of the church rather than Marxism. As ideologues they found compromises and expedient alliances difficult and distasteful, and their rapid rise to power failed to provide them the critical experience necessary in building coalitions to rule Chile. They fell from power as rapidly as they had risen.

Chile's Socialist party was predictably divided for the election of 1952. One group, which ultimately controlled the official party designation, had supported the 1948 legislation to outlaw the Communist party; the other, led by Salvador Allende, had opposed the legislation and ultimately formed the Popular Socialist Party of Chile (PSP). Allende ran for the presidency in 1952, but lost. Committing itself to more rigid Marxist-Leninist principles, the PSP was supported by the Socialist branches of the copper miners' unions. Allende ran for the presidency against Alessandri in 1958, and his vote increased over what it had been in 1952. In 1964, in what became a two-way race with Frei and the Christian Democrats, Allende obtained 39 percent of the vote, the largest he was ever to receive in a presidential race. After his defeat in 1964, Allende urged formation of a new party to take on the Christian Democrats, one that would include the Radical party. Ultimately, the Communist party concurred with this, and Popular Unity was formed prior to the 1970 presidential election. The Socialists dramatically increased their vote in the 1971 municipal elections, much more so than the Communist party did; the Popular Unity coalition obtained nearly half the national vote. Leadership of the Socialist party during the Allende presidency gravitated to the extreme left of the party, which often opposed Allende—particularly his later efforts to solicit support from Christian Democratic leaders, a reversal of his earlier strategy.

Although Allende himself was a Socialist, he received more reliable support following his election in 1970 from the Communist party than he did from his own party. The Communists supported his efforts to reach an accommodation with the Christian Democrats and opposed some of the more extreme actions being advocated by the left wing of the Socialist party. They proclaimed their willingness to allow an opposition party to assume the presidency in the scheduled 1976 election should it win, a guarantee that was conspicuously not forthcoming from some Socialist leaders.

Throughout its history, the Communists were far more unified, more consistent, and in some respects less radical than other Marxist groups in the country, including most of the Socialist party. Their base of support in the labor movement was solid and was slowly if not dramatically increasing. They were not involved in nor had they supported an armed struggle to overthrow the political system. Indeed, they seemed particularly eager to prove that they could function within the traditional system itself and would respect the democratic outcomes it produced. By comparison with other Chilean parties of the late 1960s, the Communist party was unified in its organization, cautious in its strategies, and realistic about what it could accomplish.

One could argue that the radicalization of Chilean politics from 1952 to the military coup of 1973 was less a result of fundamental changes in Chilean society or voters than of the decisions made at critical junctures by Chilean politicians as they tried to define and redefine coalitions, alliances, and new parties that could maximize their voting strength. As the issues increasingly became ideological for the Marxist parties, the right, and the center, the options for coalitions became more complex and contributed to severe internal divisions within the Christian Democratic, the Socialist, and ultimately the Radical parties. The extent to which such ideological divisions affected the majority of Chileans can be seen through voting patterns and public opinion.

Chilean party politics ended with the military intervention of September 11, 1973, and the imposition of a brutal and vengeful military dictatorship. One of the first actions of the military rulers was to suspend all political parties; it subsequently banned them altogether. Many party leaders were arrested, particularly those of Marxist groups, and others went into exile. The depth, extent, and duration of the repression was unprecedented for Chile (Valenzuela and Valenzuela, 1986:153). Three of the principal leaders during the time preceding the military intervention are now dead. President Allende died in 1973 during the coup, Frei in 1982, and Alessandri in 1986.

Seven years after the intervention—exactly seven years—on September 11, 1980, the military government held a plebiscite on a new constitution. It was reported that 93 percent of the electorate voted, 67 percent in favor and 30 percent against. The plebiscite sanctioned Gen. Augusto Pinochet remaining in power at least until 1989, and provided for a controlled democracy afterward with the armed forces playing an active role. The constitution allowed the armed forces to nominate a candidate for president who would run unopposed in a plebiscite scheduled sometime between late 1988 and early 1989, a candidate that could be General Pinochet or another selected by the armed forces. If the vote on the plebiscite were affirmative, the military candidate would take office in 1989 and rule for eight years until 1997, twenty-four years after the intervention. If the vote were negative, a new election with party candidates for the presidency and the congress would occur within a year. The plebiscite was held on October 5, 1988, with more than 90 percent of the electorate participating. Sixteen parties united in a successful effort to defeat the proposal. Almost 55 percent of those voting voted against it. As a result of the plebiscite Pinochet's term as president will end in March 1990, and open presidential and congressional elections are scheduled to be held in 1989.

Following the 1980 plebiscite a bipartisan group of party leaders, supported by church leaders, promoted a new national accord designed to move Chile toward democracy—a proposal rejected by the government. Subsequently, many of the former parties under Christian Democratic leadership formed the Democratic Alliance in 1983 to pressure the government into reforms and a return to democratic politics. Christian Democratic leaders called for a new coalition of parties to prepare for the 1989 election and to present a single candidate to oppose the government. The Chilean Communist party called for an alliance with the PDC in 1985, which the latter rejected, and also affirmed its pledge to support the next democratic government, whoever might win.

Violence and protests continued throughout the military dictatorship, culminating in an attempt to assassinate Pinochet in 1986 just five days before the thirteenth anniversary of the military intervention. Early the following year a process for legalizing non-Marxist parties was proclaimed, and soon afterward new coalitions began to form. Three principal groups emerged: the Party for Democracy (PPD), consisting of eight parties formerly in the Democratic Alliance but excluding the PDC; the United Left (IU), composed of leftist organizations and former leftist parties; and the National Renewal party (PRN), composed of supporters of General Pinochet. There were profound divisions as parties tried to coalesce within an unstable and unprecedented political context. After the defeat of the plebiscite in 1988, it was still unclear just which new groups would become established parties, which coalitions of former parties would become new, unified parties, or for that matter, precisely what the status of the still illegal leftist parties would be. If the scheduled presidential and congressional elections are held in 1989, it is clear that one result will be a restructured party system in Chile.

Elections, Voting, and Public Opinion

The two most dramatic events in Chilean party politics have been the election in 1970 of a Marxist president, Salvador Allende, whose regime was committed to changing Chile in fundamental ways, and the 1973 military coup that established the regime of General Pinochet and ended party politics in Chile. The first question these events raise is whether some fundamental change in Chilean party politics or some shift in public opinion was responsible for the events, and second, whether they represent a "failure" of some kind in the country's party politics.

There have been extensive studies of Chilean elections, voting behavior, and public opinion. Electoral and census data are available for Chile, and the data are generally reliable. During the critical years from 1958 to 1973 extensive polling was done. Both kinds of analysis point to the same tentative but consistent conclusion: that fundamental changes in Chilean voting behavior and public opinion did not occur during the period, and that the election of Salvador Allende and the movement toward the left were more a result of the structural realities of the system and the continuation of long-established patterns of party preference and voting.

One useful measure of Chilean party politics is the voting by party for members of the legislature, particularly the Chamber of Deputies, where the full range of party alternatives were available and other factors, especially personalistic ones, were less characteristic than in presidential and Senate contests. Representation in the lower house (Table 12.3) for the period of 1949–1973 closely parallels party vote owing to proportional representation. Representation during the period shows a dramatic contraction of the party system, particularly the declining ability of small parties to gain representation in the chamber. The major parties were all well represented, of course. Nontraditional parties peaked in representation in 1953, a year after the election of Carlos Ibáñez as a "nonparty" president. Many of his supporters were drawn from the ranks of the Conservative and Radical parties, which suffered heavy losses in 1953. By 1953 nontraditional parties controlled more than half the seats in the lower chamber. In the subsequent congressional election (1957) their representation collapsed, however, returning to the more traditional level of about a quarter (thirty-five) of the total seats. In 1961 nontraditional parties elected only twelve deputies, dropping in 1965 to three and in 1969 to none.

Parties of the left gained slight increases up until 1973. Socialist party representation from 1957 to 1973 remained essentially the same; Communist

TABLE 12.3
Party Representation in the Chilean Legislature, 1949–1973

Party	Chamber of Deputies							Senate			
	1949	1953	1957	1961	1965	1969	1973	1961	1965	1969	1973
Conservative	31	16	22	17	3			4	2		
Liberal	33	22	29	28	6			9	5		
National						34	36			5	8
Radical	34	20	36	39	20	24	5	13	10	9	3
Ch.Dem.	3	4	14	23	82	55	50	4	12	23	19
Socialist	11	7	11	12	15	15	28	7	7	5	7
Communist					16	18	22	25	4	6	6	9
Other	35	78	35	12	3	0	6	4	3	2	4
Total	147	147	147	147	147	150	150	45	45	50	50

Source: Official Chilean electoral results compiled by the Dirección del Registro Electoral, Oficina de Informaciones (Santiago), 1949–1973.

party representation (after it resumed activity as a legal party in 1961) showed modest gains in each election, but not dramatic or significant ones. In the 1965 election following the strong 1964 electoral victory of Eduardo Frei, Conservatives and Liberals had little change in their representation. The Radical party until 1965 followed no distinct trend, experiencing a significant loss of seats only in 1953 owing to the candidacy of Carlos Ibáñez. In 1965 Christian Democratic representation increased fourfold, giving the party a clear majority of seats in the lower chamber—an unprecedented achievement in Chilean party history. Most of that increase was drawn from the Conservative, Liberal, and Radical parties.

In 1969 the Christian Democrats lost seats and their majority control over the chamber, but that loss was not to parties on the left but to the newly formed coalition of the former Conservatives and Liberals—the National party—which won back some of the seats lost in 1964. The Radical party representation in 1969 was essentially the same as it had been in 1965. Even in 1973 during the Allende administration there were only incremental changes in party representation. The Socialist party had the largest relative gain, but it amounted to only thirteen additional deputies. The Communist party continued its steady but gradual growth, gaining three more deputies in 1973 than it had in 1969. The only party whose representation was significantly altered by the 1973 election was the Radical party, whose delegation fell from twenty-four to five deputies. Party representation during the period shows two general trends: a contraction in the number of parties represented, and a polarization of the parties remaining, skewed slightly but increasingly toward the left.

This polarization led some to interpret Chilean party politics as "moving toward the left." If one aggregates the parties on a conventional ideological spectrum from left to right, three groups emerge: on the left, the Communist and Socialist parties with a total of 53 seats in 1973; the National party

TABLE 12.4
Chilean Party Vote by Right, Center, and Left for Chamber of
Deputies, 1941-1973 (in percentages)

	Right	Center	Left	Other
1942	31	32	34	3
1945	44	28	23	5
1949	42	47	9	2
1953	25	43	14	17
1957	33	44	11	12
1961	30	44	22	4
1965	13	56	23	9
1969	20	43	28	9
1973	21	33	35	11

Source: Adapted from official Chilean electoral results compiled
by the Dirección del Registro Electoral, Oficina de Informaciones
(Santiago), 1941-1973.

on the right with 39 seats; and in the center, Christian Democrats and
Radicals with a combined total of 55 seats. If one traces the representation
of the two center parties in the congressional elections of 1965, 1969, and
1973 (Table 12.4), their combined total fell from 102 to 70 then to 55.
During the same period the right increased its representation by 25 seats,
the left by 20 seats. Changing party representation did constitute a realignment, but not a strong shift to the left. It produced a greater differentiation
between the left and the right—both sides increasing in almost equal
proportions—and a weakening of the center; in other words, a polarization
of the party system.

If one looks at party voting directly, the pattern is even clearer. Center
and left voting in Chile in 1941 were virtually identical to what they were
in 1973, less than a percentage-point different in each case. The principal
variables were the decline in nontraditional party voting and a shift from
the right, first to the nontraditional groups and then to the Christian
Democrats. Until 1973 left voting in Chile remained more or less stable,
declining from 1949 to 1961 as a result of the Communist party being
outlawed, then returning to approximately the same level it had been in
the early 1940s. The pattern was not an evolutionary one in which the left
steadily increased its vote at the expense of the other groups. Of the three
ideological groups, the left was the most stable of all.

Historically, there was a steady increase in voting levels owing to the
expansion of the franchise, which eventually embraced all Chileans over
the age of eighteen without regard for sex, literacy, or other restrictions.
The changes in the party system, however, seem not to have been the result
of this process, nor of increased levels of participation or the incorporation

TABLE 12.5
A Comparison of the Chilean Presidential Vote: National and
Santiago Province (in percentages)

	Allende		Alessandri		Frei		Tomic		Other	
	NAT	SAN	NAT	SAN	NAT	SAN	NAT	SAN	NAT	SAN
1958	29	28	31	35	21	21			19	16
1964	39	36			56	61			5	3
1970	36	35	35	38			28	23	1	4

Source: Adapted from official Chilean electoral results compiled
by the Dirección del Registro Electoral, Oficina de Informaciones
(Santiago), 1958–1970.

of large numbers of previously unmobilized voters into the Chilean political system (Valenzuela and Valenzuela, 1986:193–197). The assumption by Huntington and others that increased social mobilization within the context of stagnant or declining standards of living will by itself radicalize or destabilize a political system is not a persuasive explanation of the Chilean experience (Huntington, 1968:53–58).

It is also unconvincing to assume that the fortunes of the left were tied to its appeals to the mobilized but impoverished sectors of the society (Valenzuela and Valenzuela, 1986:197–198). Chileans simply have not identified with parties strictly on this basis. Alejandro Portes has persuasively demonstrated (1971, 1972, 1976) that the gap between expectations and realities, what Gurr termed "relative deprivation" (1970:24) does not explain the patterns of left voting or party preference in Chile. Indeed, Portes found that the lower the socioeconomic status of Chileans, the less likely they were to support the left, and that status inconsistency and social frustration were not associated with leftist voting. He found no greater tendency toward leftist voting for them than for other Chileans. Their voting patterns were "quite similar to those exhibited by the highest and frustrated category— intermediate services and white collar" workers (Portes, 1976:217). This conclusion is similar to what has also been observed in Uruguay, where leftist voting has not been identified with the less-advantaged or most frustrated in society but, if anything, has been more characteristic of higher socioeconomic groups.

There also seems to be little inclination for those living in the most modernized portion of Chile, Santiago province, to vote for the left more than Chileans living elsewhere in the country. If one compares presidential voting in 1958, 1964, and 1970 for Santiago province (Table 12.5), this characteristic is clear. In each election Allende received a slightly smaller proportion of the vote for Santiago province than he did from the nation

TABLE 12.6
Chilean Presidential Vote by Gender, 1958–1970 (in percentages)

	1958			1964			1970		
	Total	Male	Fem.	Total	Male	Fem.	Total	Male	Fem.
Allende	29	32	22	39	45	32	36	42	31
Alessandri	32	30	34				35	32	29
Frei	20	19	24	56	50	63			
Tomic							28	26	30

Source: Adapted from Official Chilean electoral results compiled by the Dirección del Registro Electoral, Oficina de Informaciones (Santiago), 1958–1970.

as a whole, as did Frei in 1964. If one combines Alessandri's vote from 1958 with Frei's from 1958, the total is about equal to what Frei alone received in 1964 when the rightist National party abstained from nominating a candidate. Allende's vote in Santiago was almost exactly the same in 1964, 35 percent, as it was in 1970, 36 percent, despite the fact that the 1964 presidential race was essentially a two-way contest and the 1970 election was a three-way race. What may have existed in Santiago was rather stable patterns of party preference with a greater inclination for protest voting.

One distinction that is apparent is that between male and female voting. Because votes are tallied separately in Chile, it is possible to learn exactly how each group voted. In three presidential elections (Table 12.6), the male vote for Allende was substantially higher than was the female vote. The female vote for Allesandri was significantly higher in 1958 and 1970 than the male vote. The greatest proportional difference between male and female vote, however, was for Frei in both 1958 and 1964, when he received a substantially greater share of his total vote from females. These differences are not unexpected or unusual. Latin American women tend to be, if not more conservative, more "orthodox," apparently less willing to risk changing the status quo. The lower likelihood of women voting for Allende was offset by the greater level of men participating in the elections.

Voting studies and public opinion surveys tend to confirm that, notwithstanding the apparent "shift to the left" in Chilean party politics to 1973, there was little change in either public opinion or in voting trends. Prothro and Chaparro (1974:23–41) describe the shift to the left in Chile between 1952 and 1972 as occurring without a corresponding shift in ideology and found a "remarkable stability" in leftist support rather than a mass movement to the left. They observe an "immobilization" in the Chilean party system during the twenty-year period and suggest that the changes were brought about by alterations in the structure of party competition. Chileans, they argue, were most motivated by pressing personal needs and were therefore looking for a formula that would make the necessary adjustments and changes in their lives. Socialism was a way to meet long-standing needs, not an end in itself. Chilean socialism can trace its origins in the country to before the turn of the century and had been accepted as a legitimate alternative within the party system. Prothro and Chaparro confirm what Gil (1966) had argued previously, that the Chileans had been frustrated historically by their efforts to win major reforms through elections, a crusade that began in the 1920s with their vote for Arturo Alessandri and continued through the 1950s with their support of the "nonparty" presidential candidates Carlos Ibáñez and Jorge Alessandri. Frei offered a similar reformist vision of a "new" Chile in the 1960s, a vision that was frustrated and thus only partially implemented. Allende was the last in a series of reformers, all of them sharing the experiences of frustration and, ultimately, failure.

If Allende's election was not caused by a shift in public opinion or voting disposition to the left, then what was its cause? More than anything it was the coalitional nature of Chilean politics, a characteristic that had dominated the country's party politics since the founding of the first political parties. Governing multiparty Chile has always depended on coalitions, and electoral outcomes have been a product of them. The success of the left in Chile was caused by two factors: (1) the particular options created by party leaders through their decisions regarding alliances and coalitions and (2) the gradual exhaustion of alternatives other than socialism for solving Chile's innumerable socioeconomic problems.

The role of the Radical party for the twenty years leading up to the military intervention was critical for the party balances in Chile, just as it had been since the nineteenth century. The right and the left had clearly defined and constraining ideological positions that limited their options in building coalitions. The Christian Democrats, whose ideological position in the center was just as inflexible as those of the right and the left, had similarly limited options. Buoyed by their rapid and unprecedented electoral successes of the 1960s and deeply committed to the purity of their religious doctrines, the Christian Democrats were unable and unwilling to form centrist coalitions. The only party that could (and had been doing so effectively for generations) was the Radical party. Chronically divided over ideology, Radical leaders were by class and social background sympathetic to the right. They were nevertheless aware of the political expediency of appealing to the left. The growing polarization of the party system found the Radicals torn apart by their own ideological contradictions and vacillations, an ambivalence that had characterized the party throughout its history. In the 1950s Radicals had been allied with the right. In the 1960s they tried to function without alliances and failed. The ultimate decision of the majority of the party to support Popular Unity—only when it became unavoidably evident that such a coalition could win—fractured the party and virtually destroyed its legislative representation. The tension between the left and the right in the party had never been resolved but, instead, had only been finessed in the practical interest of achieving power. By the late 1960s the rift could no longer be finessed. Given the disinclination of the Christian Democrats to deal with it, a coalition with the left or with the right was the only option. The choice was not difficult.

Chilean politics did shift to the left, but the realignment resulted from political expediency (party leaders trying to win elections) rather than from a substantive shift of political sympathies among Chilean voters. Prothro and Chaparro (1974) suggest that Chilean party politics underwent "a change in the structures of competition." Popular Unity gained a greater share of the popular vote in the two elections that followed the 1970 election of Salvador Allende (the 1971 municipal and 1973 congressional elections), but the changes were modest, less than the Christian Democrats gained after their own presidential victory in 1964. Like coalitions before it, Popular Unity found cohesion a far more vexing problem in governing than it had been in reaching power.

Long-Term Trends

The Chilean experience with party politics has been remarkable in many respects: party politics evolved early in the country's history and resolved some divisive issues—centralization and the church—fairly easily. Evolving in response to the changing realities and demands in Chile, the parties sustained individual liberties and democratic processes. With few and minor exceptions, the Chilean military stayed out of politics and accepted civilian control over public policy. In these respects, Chilean politics was unusual not only for Latin America but also worldwide.

But the country's political leaders and parties confronted formidable problems: economic development, economic redistribution, and international dependency. They also had to solve these problems in the context of an increasingly educated, urban, and politically active electorate. The search for reform and solutions to the economic problems has therefore been a preoccupation of Chilean party politics throughout the twentieth century. This search has encouraged experimentation and has embraced new proposals but with chronically frustrating and disappointing results. What made the system viable for many years was the ability of diverse groups to form alliances and coalitions, but these coalitions had to function within a context which was increasingly polarized, confrontational, and internationalized. Coalitions worked well for the purposes of opposition, but for the political tasks of governing coalitions were self-defeating. The polarization and the failure of coalitional politics contributed to the paralysis that emerged in the 1970s, and provided the rationalization for military intervention and the brutal regime of General Pinochet.

The years since 1973 have been traumatic and painful ones in Chile, as the remnants of the political parties have tried to regroup and to adjust to the new realities while under surveillance and persecution by the regime.

Yet, it is unlikely that the military, for all its oppression, has been able to extinguish the fundamental democratic values that had evolved in Chile. An eventual return to a civilian government that rules with the support of the Chilean people is inevitable; the questions are how and when that return will occur, through violent or nonviolent means, with or without the cooperation of the military, and with what configuration of political parties.

When democratic processes are restored, the repressed demands for reform will reappear with a vengeance, and political parties will have to contend with demands for change more powerful than those predating the intervention. The major difference will be the recognition of the possibility of failure by the party system and the consequences failure can bring. The legacy of the military dictatorship has become a part of Chilean politics, the price of political paralysis. The task of renewing and stabilizing democratic party politics will undoubtedly preoccupy Chileans for another generation.

References

Alexander, Robert J. 1982. Chile. In Robert J. Alexander, ed., *Political Parties of the Americas*. Westport, CT: Greenwood.

Daugherty, Charles H., ed. 1963. *Chile: Election Factbook*. Washington, DC: Institute for the Comparative Study of Political Systems.

Gil, Federico G. 1966. *The Political System of Chile*. Boston: Houghton Mifflin.

Gurr, Ted Robert. 1970. *Why Men Rebel*. Princeton, NJ: Princeton Univ. Press.

Huntington, Samuel P. 1968. *Political Order in Changing Societies*. New Haven, CT: Yale Univ. Press.

Parrish, Charles J., Arpad J. von Lazar, and Jorge Tapia Videla. 1967. *The Chilean Congressional Election of March 7, 1965: An Analysis*. Washington, DC: Institute for the Comparative Study of Political Systems.

Portes, Alejandro. 1971. Political Primitivism, Differential Socialization, and Lower-Class Leftist Radicalism. *American Sociological Review* 6:820–835.

———. 1972. Status Inconsistency and Lower-Class Radicalism. *Sociological Quarterly* 13:361–382.

———. 1976. Occupation and Lower-Class Political Orientations in Chile. In Arturo Valenzuela and J. Samuel Valenzuela, eds., *Chile: Politics and Society*. New Brunswick, NJ: Transaction.

Prothro, James W., and Patricio E. Chaparro. 1974. Public Opinion and the Movement of the Chilean Government to the Left, 1952–1972. *Journal of Politics* 36:2–43.

Stevenson, John R. 1942. *The Chilean Popular Front*. Philadelphia: Univ. of Pennsylvania Press.

Valenzuela, Arturo. 1977. *Political Brokers in Chile: Local Government in a Centralized Polity*. Durham, NC: Duke Univ. Press.

Valenzuela, Arturo, and J. Samuel Valenzuela, eds. 1976. *Chile: Politics and Society*. New Brunswick, NJ: Transaction.

———, eds. 1986. *Military Rule in Chile: Dictatorship and Oppositions*. Baltimore: Johns Hopkins Univ. Press.

Wiarda, Howard J., and Harvey F. Kline, eds. 1979. *Latin American Politics and Development*. Boulder, CO: Westview.

13

PERU

For approximately the last sixty years, the American Popular Revolutionary Alliance (APRA, or Apristas), one of Latin America's few disciplined mass parties, has been the most important participant in Peru's multiparty system. Yet, until its electoral victory in 1985, it seemed destined never to attain power. Traditionally hostile to the Apristas, the Peruvian military frequently banned the populist party or suspended the electoral process altogether. In fact, generals have dominated Peru for most of its history. Only once since 1920 has an elected civilian president managed to transfer his office to a freely elected successor. APRA was also prevented from winning control of the government before 1985 because (with one exception in 1945) whenever the Apristas were permitted to offer candidates, the party could attract no more than about a third of the electorate. In addition the party's militancy and its reputation for opportunism have generated strong anti-APRA feelings on both right and left. Such sentiments have aided the many personalist parties with which APRA has competed through the years.

In the early 1980s, APRA was divided and in disarray following the death of its charismatic founder, Victor Raúl Haya De la Torre, and a humiliating electoral defeat. Yet, under the dynamic leadership of Alan García, the party was able to heal its wounds and broaden its mass support. Profiting from the declining reputation of Fernando Belaúnde's center-right Popular Action (AP) administration and the dissension in the radical United Left (IU) coalition, APRA finally captured the presidency and both houses of Congress in 1985. Unfortunately for President García, his inability to solve Peru's severe economic problems or to combat a growing guerrilla insurgency led by the Shining Path (*Sendero Luminoso*) caused his popularity to erode rapidly in the late 1980s and threatened APRA's hold on power.

The Evolution and Context of
Peruvian Party Politics

After independence in 1824, Peruvian politics revolved around competing regions and strongmen and was monopolized by military officers (Palmer, 1980:36). The country's first political party, the Civil party (PC), was organized in the late 1860s to campaign for an end to army domination. From the election of Manuel Pardo in 1872 to the beginning of the 1919–1930 dictatorship of Augusto Leguía, the aristocratic *Civilistas* were Peru's most influential political group. Although armed intervention occurred at times during this era, civilian rule became the norm.

Competitive elections disappeared with the authoritarian Leguía regime, causing the *Civilistas* and the other weakly organized nineteenth century parties to atrophy. During the 1920s, more radical parties, claiming to represent the emerging middle class and popular sector, arose to take their place. The best organized of these parties was the American Popular Revolutionary Alliance (APRA), founded in Mexico in 1924 by Victor Raúl Haya De la Torre, a university student exiled for fomenting unrest.

Initially envisioned as a pan-American movement for the liberation of the entire region from oligarchical rule and U.S. imperialism, APRA gained a popular following only in Peru, where it was also known as the Peruvian Aprista party (PAP). In its early years, APRA was a revolutionary nationalist group advocating expropriation of foreign investment, redistribution of wealth, state economic control, and equal rights for the oppressed Indian majority. A fiery orator and skillful organizer, populist Haya De la Torre used these themes to attract the urban and coastal lower and middle classes to his party. Although preaching fundamental change, he rejected Marxism and became a bitter rival of José Carlos Mariátegui's small Socialist party, which later formed the core of the Peruvian Communist party (PCP).

Haya De la Torre ran for president in 1931 against Col. Luis Sánchez Cerro, who had earned wide popularity for deposing the Leguía dictatorship. Despite an incoherent platform, the better-known Sánchez, heading a hastily created Revolutionary Union (UR), was able to defeat Haya in a reasonably fair election (Stein, 1980:190). APRA nevertheless charged fraud and condemned the new government as illegitimate. Shortly thereafter, the new president declared the Apristas illegal, and, in 1932, an armed APRA uprising began in Haya's native city of Trujillo in northern Peru. After bloody excesses on both sides, the military crushed the rebellion, giving rise to a deep army-APRA enmity that was to endure for many decades.

The Apristas were hounded by the authorities from 1932 until 1939, but when the civilian government of Manuel Prado (1939–1945) allowed APRA to emerge from underground, the party quickly resumed its drive to expand membership. During the 1940s Haya De la Torre toned down the party's earlier anti-U.S. rhetoric. By 1945, when free elections were held for the first time in fourteen years, APRA formed the most important part of presidential candidate José Bustamante's winning Democratic Popular Front

(FDP). APRA nominees running under a People's party (PP) label also won a majority in the Senate and a plurality in the Chamber of Deputies.

The APRA-Bustamante alliance, however, soon collapsed as Haya and Bustamante competed over control of government policy. During the next three years, on orders from Haya, APRA legislators refused to cooperate with the progressive president. Party members also became implicated in antigovernment violence, and, after a naval mutiny supported by some Apristas miscarried, APRA was again outlawed. Subsequently, a military coup led by Gen. Manuel Odría put an end to the civilian regime.

To the delight of Peru's conservative landed oligarchy, APRA was repressed during the Odría dictatorship (1948–1956), and Haya De la Torre spent much of the time as a refugee in the Colombian embassy. Once more facing an indefinite period of exclusion from office with no hope of taking over by force, APRA began to further moderate its party doctrine and to move closer to the political center. The formerly intransigent Haya also resolved to consider any political alliance that could enhance his chances of gaining power, even if it involved collaboration with the right wing.

In return for a promise of legalization, APRA in 1956 endorsed the Peruvian Democratic movement (MDP), a personalist vehicle for conservative former president Manuel Prado, against reformer Fernando Belaúnde's middle-class Popular Action party (AP). After the victorious Prado lifted the official ban on the Apristas, APRA cooperated with the Prado administration and was allowed to renew its organizational activity. But the party's desertion of its traditional ideals profoundly damaged its credibility and compelled many left-leaning younger party activists to resign.

APRA's declining popularity was evident in the 1962 elections. Although finishing first, Haya De la Torre failed to collect the necessary one-third of the vote to be declared president in a race with Belaúnde's AP and the right-wing populist National Odriist Union (UNO) of former dictator Odría. With the presidential selection constitutionally transferred to Congress, Haya negotiated a power-sharing deal with Odría, but the army intervened before it could be consummated. In a military-supervised election in 1963, Belaúnde, strengthened by support from the small Christian Democratic party (PDC) and the Communists (PCP), won the presidency with 39 percent of the vote over Haya (34 percent) and Odría (24 percent). The congressional plurality APRA managed to garner was small consolation to party militants, many of whom were disillusioned by the cynical APRA-UNO alliance.

The moderate Popular Action government could make little headway against a Congress controlled by the obstructionist APRA-UNO legislative coalition. Fearing that a successful AP government would attract support away from APRA, the Aprista hierarchy instructed its congressmen to vote against Belaúnde even when he proposed reforms that APRA always had advocated. With the president weakened, Haya hoped that APRA could win the 1969 elections, but a military coup in 1968 prevented that contest from ever taking place.

Frustrated with Belaúnde's floundering administration and APRA's irre-sponsibility, the armed forces under Gen. Juan Velasco Alvarado seized power and began a twelve-year period of direct military rule. Between 1968 and 1975 the Peruvian armed forces pursued the most ambitious program of military reformism ever attempted in Latin America. The populist Velasco government vastly increased the economic role of the Peruvian state and introduced major redistributive policies, such as a land reform and worker participation in industry. A number of foreign companies were expropriated by the nationalist government and more stringent rules were imposed for future foreign investment. Moreover, the authoritarian military regime by-passed the civilian parties, all of which it viewed as corrupt and divisive, and encouraged the creation of new popular organizations such as the National System to Support Social Mobilization (SINAMOS).

SINAMOS attracted members away from all of the country's change-oriented political movements, including APRA, and functioned in many ways like an official party (Stepan, 1978:150). However, the army high command never allowed the organization to gain institutional autonomy or to acquire any real influence in decisionmaking. In time, popular sector groups began to view SINAMOS simply as a means of social control. Yet, as strikes and mass demonstrations mounted, military officers worried that SINAMOS and other new popular organizations were causing mass mobilization to get out of hand. After an internal coup in 1975, a more conservative military junta headed by Gen. Francisco Morales Bermúdez dismantled SINAMOS and many of the Velasco government's leftist programs.

At this point, the army reached a truce with APRA. In fact, other political groups complained that the Morales Bermúdez government (1975–1980) unfairly favored APRA's organizational efforts during the transition period that preceded the 1978 constituent assembly elections. But even with Belaúnde's Popular Action (AP) boycotting the contest, these elections produced only a 35 percent Aprista plurality. Nonetheless, by cooperating with the Popular Christian party (PPC)—a conservative 1966 defector from the PDC—APRA was able to dominate the drafting of the new constitution.

The biggest surprise of the 1978 elections, however, was the capture of one-third of the electorate by the new six-member Marxist Popular Front of Workers, Peasants, and Students (FOCEP) and four other left-wing groups despite limited campaign funds and harassment by the authorities (Woy-Hazelton, 1982:37). Evidently, the lower-class politicization achieved under the military, plus APRA's drift away from its original ideology, was paying dividends to the once insignificant left.

The two major elections since 1978 have shown that the multiparty system that has developed in the wake of military rule is divided into three segments: the Popular Christians (PPC) and Popular Action (AP) on the right, the tenuous United Left (IU) electoral coalition on the left, and APRA in the middle. After losing badly to AP in 1980, APRA made a remarkable comeback in 1985 and collected more than half of the valid vote. The radical left, after experiencing extreme fragmentation in 1980, coalesced into the United Left (IU) coalition in 1985 and finished second, backed by a full quarter of the electorate. Greatly disadvantaged by President Belaúnde's ineffectual performance, AP's fortunes declined drastically in the early 1980s; the combined conservative forces, including the Popular Christians (PPC) and a dissident APRA faction, amassed less than a fifth of the 1985 vote.

Traditionally, the armed forces, the oligarchy, and foreign corporations—not the political parties—have been Peru's most powerful political actors. The populist military regime implemented reforms, however, which undermined both the traditional oligarchy and foreign capital. Moreover, after twelve years in power, the army itself returned to the barracks discredited and divided. This temporary situation created an unusual opportunity for political parties to increase their role. Indeed, the Popular Action (AP) government headed by Fernando Belaúnde (1980–1985) and the APRA government led by Alan García (1985–) had more real freedom to govern Peru than any democratically chosen civilian regime had in recent memory. The relative autonomy to design government policy, of course, did not guarantee its success. His economic incompetence and the poor export prices, not military intervention or capitalist collusion, caused Belaúnde's failures. By 1988, Peru's dependent and poverty-stricken economy had defeated García's energetic (although misguided) efforts as well.

Despite their demoralized condition, the armed forces remain a major, but cautious, political actor. With little enthusiasm for reassuming governmental authority, the military has ceased to interfere in decisionmaking on topics not directly related to national security or to its own jealously guarded budget. In fact, strengthened by his initial popularity, President García was able to demonstrate greater civilian influence even in these areas of high military priority. Some of his measures, such as reducing foreign-arms purchases, displeased the officer corps, but the high command recognized that, for all its populist rhetoric, the APRA government was a moderate one that posed no real threat to the armed forces. In addition, as the *Sendero* insurgency continued to expand during his term and APRA officials became prime targets for assassination, García relied increasingly on the military to maintain order.

The political power of Peru's landed oligarchy and associated traditional elites was decimated by the Velasco government's agrarian reform. Nonetheless, aggressive new groups involved in industry, finance, mining, and real estate have begun to assert themselves (Lowenthal, 1983:426). Dominant in important interest associations, such as the National Industrial Society (SNI), and influential in the expanded state bureaucracy and mass media, modern business elites are becoming a significant political factor. In 1987 the failure of Peruvian business leaders to support Garcia's expansive economic policies led the president to attempt to nationalize much of the private banking system. But because this policy caused the angry private sector to reduce investment, the move only added to the government's economic woes.

Organized labor emerged far stronger from the era of military reformism because of the popular sector's increased mobilization. Still, the Peruvian trade union movement remains highly factionalized and closely linked to competing political parties. President García usually could rely on the support of the moderate Confederation of Peruvian Workers (CTP), which has been associated with APRA since the 1940s. In contrast, the radical General Confederation of Peruvian Workers (CGTP), which has expanded rapidly since 1968, is controlled by the Communist party (PCP) and is unalterably opposed to APRA. After García's economic policies had helped to bring about Peru's worst economic crisis in decades in 1988, he was forced to institute harsh austerity measures, which generated opposition among all sectors of organized labor.

With the military hesitant to exercise its power, the new private-sector groups still building their strength, and a segment of the union movement under its influence, the APRA government began its term with considerable room for maneuver. However, the abject failure of García's heterodox economic program, as well as the continued spread of the guerrilla insurgency, has led to increasingly strong opposition on both the left and right. By 1988 the once popular and powerful APRA government was described by many observers as weakened and "beleaguered" (Werlich, 1988:37).

Contemporary Political Parties

The American Popular Revolutionary Alliance (APRA) today is best understood as a pragmatic, Social Democratic party of the center-left. APRA continues to emphasize its traditional nationalism (as demonstrated by its fervent support for nonalignment and by its commitment to limit Peruvian debt repayments), but the party opposes communism and is not strongly hostile to the United States. In addition, although the Apristas continue to call for social reform to aid the poor, they also claim to recognize the need to create a favorable climate for business.

APRA is one of Latin America's most highly centralized, hierarchical, and disciplined mass parties. As we have seen from the discussion above, the party has been ruled throughout most of its history by its authoritarian founder, Victor Raúl Haya De la Torre, the author of all of the party's primary ideological texts (Alexander, 1973:20–21). After his death in 1979, competing left- and right-wing factions, led respectively by Armando Villanueva and Andrés Townsend, engaged in a bitter struggle for supremacy. Ultimately, Villanueva won the contest and expelled his adversary from the party. After his poor performance as APRA's 1980 presidential candidate, however, the old guard (born 1915) party chief lost his position in 1982 to young (born 1949), European-educated Alan García, a former Villanueva supporter and Haya protégé, who promised to reconcile rival factions.

In 1988, García continued to head APRA as party president, assisted by two general-secretaries and a national executive committee. Growing internal dissension, however, was in evidence since 1987 when Luis Alva Castro, a party leader who opposed the controversial bank nationalization, was elected head of the party's congressional delegation over the president's opposition. Subordinate committees direct party activities at the departmental, provincial, district, and municipal levels, and specialized groups are designated to handle such tasks as union relations, students, finance, and cadre training. Between elections, the APRA party organization remains active in the fashion of a European mass party, and local grass-roots party chapters maintain *Casas del Pueblo*, which offer a range of activities and services to the party faithful.

Although APRA always has been a multiclass party, its most dependable sources of electoral support have been concentrated in the urban and coastal popular sectors (e.g., sugar workers) and in northern departments such as La Libertad and Lambayeque (Palmer, 1980:88; Chang-Rodríguez, 1982:601). The party has traditionally been weak in the center and south (including the Indian highlands), in the Lima/Callao area, and among higher socio-economic groups. (Interestingly, in 1985, APRA ran unusually well in both Lima/Callao and in the central region [Taylor, 1986: 124].)

The second most important electoral force in Peru is the Unified Left (IU), a loose and often fractious Marxist coalition. At the time of the 1985 elections, the IU included the orthodox, pro-Moscow Communist party (PCP) founded in 1930, a Maoist PCP splinter called the Union of the Revolutionary Left (UNIR), the Velasquista Revolutionary Socialist party (PSR), the Unified Mariateguista party (PUM), the Castroite Revolutionary Communist party (PCR), Hugo Blanco's Trotskyist Workers' Revolutionary party (PRT), and the remnants of the Popular Front of Workers, Peasants, and Students (FOCEP).

The United Left has created an elaborate party structure complete with a national executive committee, membership standards, and a unified national convention system, but its component groups still refuse to relinquish their separate institutional and ideological identities. Competition over candidate selection and policy definition within the United Left has been intense, and the IU's composition could well change. Some elements threaten to leave the coalition and campaign independently, as the Puno-based Nationalist Left party (PIN) has done since 1978.

In spite of their conflicting revolutionary visions, the urban intellectuals who dominate the IU's leadership have succeeded in agreeing on a common program. If elected, the IU promises to expropriate major mining corporations and to institute a broad policy of redistribution to benefit the urban working class and peasantry. Funds for expanded lower-class assistance are to be derived, in part, from a moratorium on debt repayments. Although highly critical of capitalism and U.S. imperialism, the United Left tries to project an image of political realism and does not advocate complete state control of the economy or a prohibition on foreign investment. With respect to the guerrilla war, the radical coalition expresses sympathy for the peasants who have become involved in Abimael Guzmàn's Maoist, Ayacucho-based *Sendero Luminoso* and in other smaller armed groups such as the Tupac Amaru Revolutionary Movement (MRTA), but it criticizes their resort to violence.

United Left voters now constitute about a quarter of the electorate and are concentrated in the nation's popular sector, particularly among trade unionists associated with the large PCP-controlled CGTP confederation and other leftist unions. Geographically, the IU, like the radical unions, is strongest in southern Peru, especially in the departments of Puno, Tacna, Cusco, and Arequipa (Taylor, 1986:124).

With the near demise of Belaúnde's Popular Action (AP) in 1985, the most important party to the right of APRA and the United Left became the small, personalist Popular Christian party (PPC) led by Luis Bedoya Reyes, a former mayor of Lima. Modeling itself after European Christian Democratic parties, the PPC is a forceful advocate of the free-enterprise system and of the need to reduce restrictions on domestic and foreign business. The party is also strongly anti-Communist and favors a military solution to the guerrilla problem. Left-leaning Christian Democrats who find the PPC's stances too conservative have remained in the tiny, APRA-aligned Christian Democratic party (PDC), from which Bedoya defected.

The PPC essentially is an extension of Bedoya's personality and, as such, possesses only a rudimentary party organization. It often resorts to alliances with other parties. The Popular Christians cooperated with APRA in the constituent assembly and then participated in Belaúnde's cabinet in the early 1980s. After the AP rejected Belaúnde's advice to adopt Bedoya as a joint AP-PPC presidential candidate in 1985, the PPC formed the Democratic Convergence electoral coalition (CODE) with the moderate Hayista Bases movement (MBH) headed by ousted APRA politician Andrés Townsend. With Bedoya as its standard-bearer, CODE collected 11 percent of the vote with electoral support centered in the Lima/Callao metropolitan area, the PPC's traditional base. The party has always been popular with the capital's upper and middle classes.

Belaúnde's once powerful center-right Popular Action (AP) party managed to salvage only a meager 7 percent of the vote in 1985 and did not campaign at all in the 1986 municipal contests. The AP has long depended on its aging founder's popularity. Now that he has lost public confidence, the group's future is unclear. Popular Action lacks a genuine program beyond a vague commitment to cautious reform and moderate nationalism and has never developed a serious grass-roots organization. In addition, with Belaúnde's control weakened, the AP has been prone to competing personalist and generational factions. Amid claims of fraud in the AP's internal elections, a younger group of party members (critical of the monetarist economic policies pursued by Belaúnde) gained the upper hand in 1984 and named their leader, Javier Alva Orlandini, as the party's presidential candidate (Taylor, 1986:105). Popular Action once enjoyed broadly based electoral support with particular strength in the educated, urban middle class and in Belaúnde's native southern Peru, e.g., Arequipa. Yet, in 1985, AP votes declined precipitously among all social groups in all geographical regions.

To protest the García government's bank nationalization policy, Peruvian novelist Mario Vargas Llosa organized a conservative, urban, middle-class-based Freedom movement in 1987 and later joined forces with the PPC and AP in the Democratic Front (FREDEMO), an electoral alliance that planned to nominate a joint presidential candidate in 1990.

Political Participation and Elections

Encouraged by the military regime's initial populist phase, mass involvement in public demonstrations, strikes, and other political activities accelerated greatly during the 1970s, remaining high in the 1980s. Nonetheless, a highland Indian population still exists as a large, culturally distinct element. Constituting about 40 percent of the population, these Peruvians have not been integrated into national political life. Although voting became compulsory in 1980 for illiterates as well as literates (between the ages of eighteen and seventy), great numbers of *sierra* Indians either did not register or chose not to vote. After exceeding an 80 percent rate in 1978 before illiterate citizens were added to the electorate, Peruvian voter turnout fell to 62 percent in 1980, rising to roughly 70 percent in 1985 (Dietz, 1984:812). In addition, as in Guatemala (another country with a large Indian population), an unusually high number of voters cast blank or invalid ballots (22 percent in 1980 and 14 percent in 1985).

Public opinion in the aftermath of military rule is difficult to determine with any precision because of the underdeveloped state of survey research in Peru (Taylor, 1986:115). Nearly all poll samples are limited to the Lima/Callao area and, beyond documenting the low level of political information possessed by Peruvians, the weakness of party identification, and the importance of economic issues and candidates' personalities, public opinion studies have not yet revealed a great deal (Dietz, 1986–87:143, 152–155). The strong electoral support received by the radical left and the conspicuous unpopularity of the extreme right, however, suggest that attitudes are skewed more toward the center-left of the political spectrum in Peru than in most other countries in the region.

The 1979 constitution mandates that presidential and congressional elections be held concurrently at five-year intervals. If no presidential candidate collects more than 50 percent of all votes cast, including blank and invalid ballots, a second round contest is supposed to take place between the two top vote-getters (beginning in 1985). The president is elected on the same ticket with two vice-presidents and may not run for reelection until he has been out of office for at least one term. The 60-member Senate is elected on a separate ballot, entirely at large, by a proportional representation system using national party lists that permit voters to indicate individual preferences. The 180 members of the Chamber of Deputies are elected on a third ballot using party lists drawn up separately for each of the nation's twenty-seven departments and a similar PR system. Each department has at least one deputy; otherwise, seats are allocated by population.

All elections are supervised by the autonomous National Electoral Commission (JNE). With the cooperation of the Electoral Registry, the JNE is responsible for establishing voting regulations, registering parties, overseeing balloting, and tabulating election returns (Rudolph, 1981:175). Competing parties receive free airtime on state-owned radio and television during campaigns; the JNE's regulation of this media access has become an important function. With nearly 40 percent of the voters concentrated in the greater

TABLE 13.1
Peru: Constituent Assembly and Congressional Election Results by Party, 1978-1985

| | Constituent Assembly, 1978 | | Congress, 1980 | | | Congress, 1985 | |
	Total(%)	Seats	Total(%)[a]	Senate	Chamber	Senate	Chamber
APRA	35.3	37	27.6	18	58	32	107
AP			40.9	26	98	5	10
Left/IU	36.3	34	20.8	10	14	15	48
PPC/CODE	23.8	25	9.4	6	10	7	12
Others[b]	4.6	4	1.4	0	0	1	3
Total	100.0	100	100.1[c]	60	180	60	180

[a]Valid votes in Senate election.
[b]In 1985 this category included one National Left senator, one National Left deputy, and two Independent deputies.
[c]Percentages do not add to 100 because of rounding.

Sources: Adapted from Sandra L. Woy-Hazelton, "The Return of Partisan Politics in Peru," in Stephen M. Gorman, ed., Post-Revolutionary Peru: The Politics of Transformation (Boulder, CO: Westview, 1982), pp. 36, 55, and Keesing's Contemporary Archives (September 1985), p. 33836.

Lima area, mass media have become a significant part of Peruvian political campaigning.

The two major elections that have been held since the military left power in 1980 have produced strikingly different results (Tables 13.1 and 13.2). The 1980 election, the first presidential contest to take place since 1963, resulted in an impressive victory for Popular Action (AP). Winning 45 percent of the valid vote in a field of fifteen candidates, Fernando Belaúnde regained the presidency from which he had been ousted by the army in 1968. Belaúnde ran ahead of his rivals in all but five departments; the AP congressional tickets won a majority in the Chamber of Deputies and a plurality in the Senate.

APRA finished a disappointing second in 1980 with only a little more than a quarter of the vote—well below the 35 percent it had won two years earlier. The badly factionalized left, with nine different presidential candidates, also lost votes in comparison with the 1978 constituent assembly contest. All of the leftist candidates together polled less than 17 percent and their congressional slates performed only slightly better (21 percent). Furthermore, because the radical vote was scattered among so many competing parties, the left acquired just 10 percent of the seats in Congress. Finally, the conservative Popular Christians (PPC), whose vote share was inflated in 1978 owing to AP's nonparticipation, shrank to about 9 percent of the vote.

Popular Action's 1980 triumph was based on many factors—including Belaúnde's personal popularity and statesmanlike campaign. In addition, some Peruvians simply voted for the AP candidate as a slap against the military or because they feared the consequences of an APRA regime. A sizable number of radicals, for example, split their tickets to vote for Belaúnde

TABLE 13.2
Peruvian Presidential Election Results, 1980 and 1985

	Valid Votes[a]	%
1980		
Fernando Belaúnde Terry (AP)	1,870,864	45.4
Armando Villaneuva (APRA)	1,129,991	27.4
Luis Bedoya Reyes (PPC)	394,592	9.6
Left Candidates (9)	690,934	16.8
Other Candidates (3)	37,395	0.9
Total	4,123,776	100.1[b]
1985		
Alan García Pérez (APRA)	3,457,030	53.4
Alfonso Barrantes Lingán (IU)	1,606,914	24.8
Luis Bedoya Reyes (CODE)	733,705	11.3
Javier Alva Orlandini (AP)	472,627	7.3
Other Candidates (5)	198,930	3.1
Total	6,469,206	99.9

[a]Total votes cast equaled 5,307,465 in 1980, of which 1,183,689 (22.3%) were invalid or blank. Total votes equaled 7,557,182 in 1985, of which 1,087,976 (14.4%) were invalid or blank.
[b]Percentages do not add to 100 because of rounding.
Sources: Adapted from Sandra L. Woy-Hazelton, "The Return of Partisan Politics in Peru," in Stephen Gorman, ed., Post-Revolutionary Peru: The Politics of Transformation (Boulder, CO: Westview, 1982), pp. 45, 55, and Keesing's Contemporary Archives (September 1985), p. 33836.

because they felt that an APRA government would be a greater threat to their position in the unions and other popular organizations (Cotler, 1986: 170). Unfortunately for APRA, Armando Villanueva's reputation for intolerance and the use of strong-arm tactics was reinforced by his drive to take over his divided party.

Popular Action followed up its presidential and congressional victories with a good showing in the municipal elections held later that year by winning 36 percent of the vote, while APRA sank to an all-time low (23 percent). Yet, by the time the next set of municipal contests took place in 1983, AP, plagued with Belaúnde's abysmal economic record, was already in steep decline and APRA was resurgent. APRA led all parties with a third of the 1983 municipal vote, while the leftist IU coalition came in second with 29 percent in addition to winning the Lima mayoral race.

The Apristas continued their climb back from near-collapse by winning a stunning victory in 1985. In a complete reversal of the 1980 results, APRA almost doubled its vote (to 53 percent) and won in twenty-five of Peru's twenty-seven departments. Alan García was elected easily to the presidency and APRA captured majorities in both houses of Congress. The United Left (IU), unified behind Lima's urbane Marxist mayor Alfonso Barrantes, finished a distant second, although it increased its vote share to 25 percent and became the largest opposition force in Congress. Although García won slightly less than half of the total number of valid and invalid/blank ballots cast, Barrantes chose not to contest a second presidential round.

The parties to the right of APRA and the IU suffered a devastating defeat. Bedoya's Popular Christians (PPC), as part of the Democratic Convergence (CODE) coalition, held their own with 11 percent of the vote, but Belaúnde's Popular Action (AP), with Javier Alva Orlandini at the head of its ticket, was decimated. In sharp contrast to its success five years earlier, AP came in fourth with a demoralizing 7 percent of the vote.

García himself was an indispensible element in APRA's amazing comeback because of his reunification of the party and his personal appeal to Peruvian voters. Having learned from Villanueva's errors in 1980, García's well-financed campaign and slick television advertising communicated an image of a youthful, caring leader heading a party committed to responsible reform (Taylor, 1986:116). Under the advice of European political consultants, García courted independents and new voters by presenting APRA as a safe, middle-ground alternative between the revolutionary left and the insensitive conservatives.

Obviously, the Apristas also benefited from the rising inflation, unemployment, and debt associated with the AP. Some of the same antigovernment sentiment aided the United Left as well, but the radicals were handicapped by limited financial resources and an unfriendly news media. Deteriorating urban services under Lima's Marxist administration, although not actually the fault of Mayor Barrantes, also cost the IU coalition votes as did a widespread belief that an IU victory would bring military intervention. APRA followed up its 1985 victory by beating the IU handily in the 1986 municipal elections.

Long-Term Trends

After a history of military intervention and dictatorship broken only intermittently by periods of civilian rule, Peru embarked on a new liberal democratic experiment in the 1980s when the military relinquished control to President Fernando Belaúnde of Popular Action (AP). But Belaúnde's subsequent economic difficulties quickly eroded his support and created an opportunity for APRA, the most important party in Peru since the 1920s, at last to win power. Reunified by Alan García after the death of its legendary founder, APRA scored a resounding electoral victory in 1985.

Because of the reluctance of the army to interfere and the political inexperience of new private-sector interests, the center-left APRA government initially enjoyed ample room to maneuver and hoped to realize Haya De la Torre's dream of making APRA Peru's permanent governing party. Yet, the economic problems and guerrilla war that destroyed Belaúnde's popularity undermined García's as well. Given the high volatility of Peruvian voter preferences, the country's future became increasingly difficult to predict. Either the radical United Left (IU) coalition or the new conservative Democratic Front (FREDEMO) could gain from APRA's decline. However, although the military might welcome a resurgent right, Peru's new democratic institutions seem too frail to support an elected Marxist government. The armed forces are not eager to reassume power, but neither are they prepared to serve under a Marxist chief executive.

References

Alexander, Robert J. 1973. *Aprismo: The Ideas and Doctrines of Victor Raúl Haya de la Torre*. Kent, OH: Kent State Univ. Press.

Chang-Rodríguez, Eugenio. 1982. Peru. In Robert J. Alexander, ed., *Political Parties of the Americas*. Westport, CT: Greenwood.

Cotler, Julio. 1986. Military Interventions and Transfer of Power to Civilians in Peru. In Guillermo O'Donnell, Philippe C. Schmitter, and Laurence Whitehead, eds., *Transitions From Authoritarian Rule: Latin America*. Baltimore: Johns Hopkins Univ. Press.

Dietz, Henry. 1984. Republic of Peru. In George E. Delury, ed., *World Encyclopedia of Political Systems and Parties*. New York: Facts on File.

———. 1986–87. Electoral Politics in Peru, 1978–1986. *Journal of Interamerican Studies and World Affairs* 28:139–163.

Lowenthal, Abraham F. 1983. The Peruvian Experiment Reconsidered. In Cynthia McClintock and Abraham F. Lowenthal, eds., *The Peruvian Experiment Reconsidered*. Princeton, NJ: Princeton Univ. Press.

Palmer, David S. 1980. *Peru: The Authoritarian Tradition*. New York: Praeger.

Rudolph, James D. 1981. Government and Politics. In Richard F. Nyrop, ed., *Peru: A Country Study*. Washington, DC: U.S. Government Printing Office.

Stein, Steve. 1980. *Populism in Peru*. Madison: Univ. of Wisconsin Press.

Stepan, Alfred. 1978. *The State and Society: Peru in Comparative Perspective*. Princeton, NJ: Princeton Univ. Press.

Taylor, Lewis. 1986. Peru's Alan García: Supplanting the Old Order. *Third World Quarterly* 8:100–136.

Werlich, David P. 1988. Peru: García Loses his Charm. *Current History* 87:13–16, 36–37.

Woy-Hazelton, Sandra L. 1982. The Return of Partisan Politics in Peru. In Stephen M. Gorman, ed., *Post-Revolutionary Peru: The Politics of Transformation*. Boulder, CO: Westview.

14

BOLIVIA

Bolivian party politics is both distinctive and paradoxical. Given the socioeconomic realities of the country and its history of instability and military intervention, the mere existence of political parties is somewhat surprising. They do exist, and a good many have been functioning for decades. But parties have generally had little success in governing Bolivia or even in exerting political influence. There have been only three instances in the twentieth century when one elected president has transferred power to another at the end of his term—arguably not as a result of very democratic processes. Bolivia has had about as many unplanned changes in governments as it has had years of independence and possesses many times more political parties than it has had regimes. Few political parties in the Bolivian multiparty system, once formed, ever entirely disappear; they remain even in spite of their irrelevance. But Bolivia has also had a "revolution," believed by many to have been both genuine and similar in importance to the Mexican experience. The Bolivian revolution occurred in 1952, rather quickly and without protracted violence.

Bolivian party history falls into several distinct periods, and some important evolutionary patterns are in evidence in spite of its apparent instability. Our purpose here is not to reconstruct that history—for it has been done elsewhere (Alexander, 1958; Klein, 1969; Malloy, 1970)—but to focus specifically on the evolution of parties, their interaction with and their relationship to elections, and their distinctive if limited role in Bolivian national politics. Bolivia is a country isolated by culture and geography, and its party politics has been largely unrelated to what exists elsewhere in the region. But within its own context there have been important evolutionary patterns.

The Context of Bolivian Party Politics

Several preoccupations permeate Bolivian political history, none of which has been satisfactorily resolved and all of which continue to define party

223

competition and much of the political conflict in the country. Foremost, perhaps, has been the search for national identity. The population of the country is predominantly Indian, descendants of the ancient Inca civilization, which in pre-Columbian times ruled much of what today is Bolivia, Peru, and Ecuador. These peoples were systematically subjugated and exterminated by the Spanish during colonial times, and their lot did not improve much after independence. By its history, culture, and demography, Bolivia is an Indian country. But until 1952 this overwhelming reality was not reflected in either its social or political priorities. The Mexican revolution in 1910, which was part of that country's search for its Indian identity, struck a sensitive nerve in Bolivia. From that time on, the country edged toward a confrontation on the issue that finally erupted in the 1952 revolution. Whatever the successes or failures of that event, it at least addressed a fundamental contradiction in the country.

Bolivia also has been preoccupied with securing its national autonomy. Its ill-defined boundaries at independence in 1825 eventually led to international conflicts and, unfortunately for Bolivia, the loss of national territory, to Chile in the War of the Pacific (1879–1884) and to Paraguay in the Chaco War (1932–1935). But Bolivia has also endured foreign incursions of another kind, the economic influence of more powerful nations. Tin and petroleum, its two principal resources, have been exploited by U.S. corporations throughout the twentieth century, and Argentina has generally viewed Bolivia as a virtual economic colony. Political intervention has also been common, particularly over the past fifty years. Political intervention came first from Nazi Germany in the late 1930s, and then from the United States in response to the German influence. Following World War II, and particularly since the late 1960s, U.S. covert activities in the country have been continual. In the mid-1960s Che Guevara, with the assistance of Cuba, entered Bolivia clandestinely and tried unsuccessfully to foment another revolution. More recently, since the 1970s, the country has come close to being completely controlled by another international interest, the organizations that market and distribute cocaine. Their influence has had a nearly paralytic effect on the nation's politics and economy.

Finally, Bolivia historically has been preoccupied with development, particularly economic development. The poorest of the Hispanic nations in the Western Hemisphere by almost any measure, Bolivia remains without many essential services, without much industry, and almost stagnant economically.

These three preoccupations—the search for identity, for autonomy, and for development—all fueled the 1952 revolution. But that event did not resolve the problems, and the rising importance of illegal cocaine exports has further exacerbated them. Cocaine trafficking has corrupted the nation's military beyond reasonable levels, created excessive inflation and economic imbalances, and contributed to political corruption and the penetration of organized crime in the country. This in turn has promoted further intervention by the United States, the primary market for Bolivian cocaine, in an effort to control the cocaine traffic by controlling Bolivia.

The political context in Bolivia has not been conducive to either democratic politics or stable party competition. The country since independence has been controlled more frequently by military leaders than by civilian ones, and military intervention for assorted political reasons has been the rule. The military has functioned as an interest group, a mixture of collegial decisionmaking, personal ambitions, and greed, and it remains one of the least professional armed forces in the hemisphere. Foreign elites through their political and economic influence have often exercised an effective veto over Bolivian politics, corrupting and controlling its military and civilian leaders. Cocaine has accentuated this pernicious influence; the value of illegal cocaine exports is commonly estimated to be greater than the total value of all legal Bolivian exports and may in fact exceed the official value of the entire Bolivian economy.

Yet, despite these grim conditions, Bolivia has had an unusually large number of national political parties that have functioned, however limited their influence. These parties have drawn upon and contributed to the social mobilization of several important sectors of the society. Efforts to mobilize the Indians began well before the 1952 revolution, and with some success. The access to the Indian culture was to a large extent by way of the organized tin miners, Indians who were subsequently recruited for political objectives and who helped politicize those in their own communities and villages. The building of the railways also created unions composed of Indians and reinforced the labor movement in the country. The capital city saw a small middle sector arise with the export of tin and the secondary economic activity it stimulated—an embryonic middle class that has had a disproportionate influence in Bolivian politics generally and political parties specifically. Its influence has resulted, not from its size, but from the absence of effective alternatives. Bolivian party politics has also been influenced by the personal ambitions of its leaders, both civilian and military, who have used political movements and have preyed on popular aspirations for their own benefit. Neither unusual nor unexpected, this personalism is of a very traditional kind where strength and success often take priority over other political values and issues.

Two political traumas have also influenced the evolution of Bolivian party politics—the War of the Pacific and the Chaco War. Of these two the latter is the more directly relevant. The influence of the Chaco War on Bolivian politics is controversial. Alexander (1958:22) describes it as having "disorganized the economy, discredited the Army, spread new ideas among the urban workers and miners, and sowed discontent among the intelligentsia." By contrast, Klein (1969:xii) suggests that although "most commentators have assumed that the Chaco War created social discontent and economic dislocation, a careful examination of the post-war period reveals neither of these effects. . . . The impact of the war must rather be seen in terms of political dislocations and basic changes in the political structure of national leadership and ideology." There seems to be agreement only that the war discredited the traditional civilian elites who were responsible for initiating it and the traditional military elites who lost it. The war also mobilized large numbers of Bolivian Indians, who became aware of the extent to which they had been used and exploited. Following the Chaco War, new groups formed to draw on the growing disenchantment of Indians and the more general disillusionment created by the outcome of the war. The most important of these produced in 1941 a new political party, the Nationalist Revolutionary movement (MNR), led by Víctor Paz Estenssoro. That organization ultimately catalyzed the 1952 revolution, and subsequently became a principal force in civilian politics.

The Evolution of Contemporary Parties

From independence in 1825 until the end of the War of the Pacific in 1883, Bolivia had no political parties. Factions evolved around individual leaders, but they had no organization, separate identity, or longevity. When parties began to emerge in 1883 they took a familiar form, Liberals and Conservatives. The Liberal party (PL) was formed in 1883, committed to the economic interests of northern Bolivia and the capital city, La Paz. The Conservative party (PC) was formed a year later in 1884, primarily to advocate the mining interests of central and southern Bolivia. The two parties precipitated a civil war in 1889, leaving the Liberals in control until 1920 when the Republican party (PR), which had emerged in La Paz in 1914, through a coup replaced the Liberals in power. It subsequently divided over personal issues, producing the Socialist Republican party (PRS) and the Genuine Republican party (PRG)—the remnants of which reformed again in 1946 as the Republican Socialist Union party (PURS). Several regime parties were formed, the Nationalist party (PN) in the 1920s and the State Socialist party (PSE) in the 1930s. Both enjoyed no more than a brief period in power.

In 1937 another party was formed that did survive the vicissitudes and chaos of Bolivian party politics. Indeed, it still competes in Bolivian elections. Known as the Bolivian Socialist Falange (FSB), the organization was a right-wing nationalist organization that advocated Fascist ideas and appealed to the country's small urban middle class. After the 1952 revolution the FSB became the most outspoken opponent of the Nationalist Revolutionary movement (MNR), to be discussed below, and organized several plots to overthrow the MNR regime. At its peak in 1956 it managed to poll about 15 percent of the national vote, and in 1971 it participated in a government controlled by its archenemy, the MNR. It continues to exist today as a minor party.

Another political party that came to be identified as a principal opponent of the MNR was formed in 1940, originally as the United Socialist party (PSU). Its founders were united primarily on personal grounds to advocate the presidential ambitions of Gen. Enrique Peñaranda, who served briefly as president from 1940 to 1943. After the overthrow of Peñaranda, the party divided. Some of its leaders formed the Independent Socialist party (PSI), which later joined with the Genuine Republican party (PRG) and the Socialist Republican party (PRS) to form the Party of the Republican Socialist Union (PURS). That organization continued its opposition to the MNR and Paz Estenssoro right up to the 1952 revolution, after which it became inactive, although it legally existed through the 1970s. "Socialism" was more a catchword for the organization and did not seem to reflect any commitment to Marxism as such.

By far the most important organization was the Nationalist Revolutionary movement, the MNR, led by Víctor Paz Estenssoro. Apart from Paz, whose political career spanned more than four decades, the organization originally had other leaders, many of whom withdrew from the MNR over personal disagreements with Paz but continued to play an important role in national political life in subsequent decades. Principal among these leaders was Juan Lechín Oquendo, organizer and leader of the powerful mine-workers union; Walter Guevara Arce; and Hernán Siles Suazo. The MNR was the first Bolivian party to develop a genuinely mass base for its power and, along with its principal leader, Paz Estenssoro, has been the principal catalyst in Bolivian politics since its formation.

The MNR is perhaps best characterized as a nationalist and reformist political party. Ideologically it has embraced a wide range of thought and has evolved through several historically distinct periods. Originally the party drew most of its supporters from the same middle-class base as the other groups of the time. But this orientation, once expressed through Fascist symbols and doctrines, expanded into what came to be defined as a "revolutionary alliance" of workers, peasants (meaning, of course, Indians), and the middle class. It was strongly nationalistic, opposed to international influences in the country—particularly (through Lechín's influence) those international corporations that were involved with tin mining. Through the efforts of Lechín's miners and idealistic student supporters, the MNR was reasonably successful in communicating its principles to large numbers of Bolivian workers and peasants. Its primary objectives were land reform, nationalization of the mines, and integration of the Indians into national life with full equality and dignity—truly "revolutionary" ideas for Bolivia. Responding both to the grievances of the past—the oligarchical, militaristic, and racist regimes that had controlled the country—the MNR had a vision for a modern Bolivia. The MNR won an electoral plurality in the 1951 elections, but the military refused to permit Paz to become president. The MNR responded by organizing an uprising of the workers, peasants, and the middle class, with the help of the national police, who sided with the MNR; it came to power in April 1952. This was not the first uprising the MNR had attempted, but it was the first one to succeed. Bolivian politics would never again be quite the same.

After taking power, the inherent contradictions in the MNR alliance became manifest as rival political ambitions surfaced and competing economic interests began to erode the unity of the organization. Paz, for whatever reasons, was unable to maintain unity and cohesion within the party. These different economic, class, and ideological orientations combined with the personal ambitions of those leaders advocating them to produce several serious divisions within the MNR. Ultimately, several new political parties were formed. Guevara, frustrated in his pursuit of the presidency, broke with Paz and formed the Authentic Revolutionary party (PRA) in 1959. Lechín, who earlier had prevailed over Guevara, broke with Paz and the MNR to form the Revolutionary Party of the Nationalist Left (PRIN) in 1963. The other principal leader in the original MNR, Hernán Siles Suazo, did manage to become president following the revolution. But eventually he, too, broke with Paz in the late 1970s, forming a rival MNR group, known as the National Revolutionary Movement of the Left (MNRI). Paz retained nominal control over what was left of the MNR for more than thirty years following the revolution, but he increasingly became identified with the more conservative elements of the MNR. With the defections of Lechín and, ultimately, Siles, Paz by inclination and default was ideologically isolated to their right.

In the period just prior to the MNR revolution, one other political party emerged, which had some political visibility on the right—the Social Democratic party (PSD). It was organized in 1944 by younger, conservative Bolivians committed to modernization and the technological and technocratic strategies they believed necessary to achieve it. The PSD entered into alliances with the FSB and opposed the MNR. By the mid-1960s some of its leaders cooperated with the military regime that had since come to power. Their influence no doubt was stimulated by the growing prominence of "technocrats" in the military dictatorships of Brazil and Argentina. One of the PSD leaders, Adolfo Siles Salinas, was the half-brother of Hernán Siles Suazo. Siles served as vice president during the military regime of Gen. René Barrientos. Upon the latter's death in 1969, Siles briefly served as president; he was deposed by the military after five months in office. The PSD became inactive after that, although Siles Salinas continued to pursue his presidential ambitions.

Marxist political parties in Bolivia have a long, fragmented, and generally unsuccessful, if not ineffectual, history in the country. They have been divided ideologically, by personal rivalries, and by different international allegiances and influences. The situation is made somewhat more complex by the fact that several prominent Bolivian parties have used the term "Socialist" (the Bolivian Socialist Falange, the State Socialist party, the United Socialist party, among others) without actually having any serious Marxist connection. Conversely, some Marxist parties have identified themselves as "revolutionary" while other "revolutionary" parties have clearly not been Marxist.

The earliest party to identify itself as Marxist was the Socialist party (PS), formed in 1920. Organized by young intellectuals in La Paz, it advocated principally the interests of workers and survived only a few years. The first "Communist" party established in Bolivia was the Revolutionary Workers party (POR), formed in 1934. The organization advocated a Trotskyite position when Trotsky was still alive, albeit in exile. That position called for worldwide and "permanent" revolution to be led by the industrial proletariat, which in Bolivia meant the tin miners. The organization developed considerable influence in the labor movement through the miners but suffered from the vagaries imposed by the chaotic nature of Bolivian politics, as well as from serious internal divisions and rivalries.

One of the early divisions in the POR resulted in the expulsion of one of its leaders, Gustavo Navarro, and the formation in 1938 of the Bolivian Socialist Labor party (PSOB). Navarro also sought to build a political base among the tin miners, an effort that failed as Lechín and the MNR became the principal influence in the miners union. The PSOB cooperated with the right-wing regime of Enrique Hertzog (1946–1952), which preceded the MNR revolution. But that alliance effectively destroyed the credibility of the organization and its leader.

The Party of the Revolutionary Left (PIR), established in 1940, was the first Communist party in Bolivia oriented toward the prevailing Stalinist ideological position. The organization was torn by internal divisions, by the international shifts in Soviet foreign policy, and by its failure to build its own constituency in Bolivia. In its eagerness to oppose the MNR in the late 1940s, it also became identified with the right-wing regime that tried to prevent the MNR from reaching power. The party was dissolved in 1952 but was subsequently reestablished in 1956 as a small "Socialist" party.

The first Communist party to use the name was the Bolivian Communist party (PCB), established in 1950, not an auspicious time in the evolution of Latin American Communist parties. Its organizers were originally younger supporters of the PIR who left that organization in disgust over its cooperation with the right-wing regime of the late 1940s. But its subsequent history is generally seen as the least aggressive and militant of any Communist party in Latin America. It cooperated with several regimes in an effort to gain influence, endorsing Paz Estenssoro in 1951 and, later, Hernán Siles Suazo. It failed, however, to support Che Guevara in his abortive revolutionary crusade in Bolivia in the mid-1960s, and there is speculation that some of its leaders may have actually betrayed him.

Following the 1952 revolution, more Marxist parties appeared, some as clandestine groups. Among the more conspicuous and legal ones were the Marxist-Leninist Communist party (PCML), formed in 1964, which took a pro-Beijing orientation, thereby giving Bolivians a choice of pro-Beijing, pro-Trotskyite, and pro-Soviet Communist parties. The party did little beyond attacking other Marxist parties for their "incorrect" ideological positions. It eventually made common cause with Juan Lechín's POR in his conflict with Siles Suazo, who in turn had been endorsed by the PCB. In the late 1960s a group of young militants from the Christian Democratic party (PDC) formed yet another "Marxist" party, known as the Movement of the Revolutionary Left (MIR).

In 1970 a second Socialist party was formed, which ultimately came to be known as the Socialist party-1 (PS-1) after a split in its ranks prompted the government's electoral authorities to assign the party name to another faction (PS-2). Its principal leader, Marcelo Quiroga Santa Cruz, was killed in an uprising in July 1980, and the party has languished since.

The problems for the Marxist parties in Bolivia have been threefold: they have found it difficult to co-opt the MNR's "revolutionary" appeals, ideology, and tradition; they have failed to build their own distinct constituencies; and they have all but destroyed each other through their ideological and internecine conflicts and divisions. They have also made tactical alliances that have damaged their credibility. None of the Marxist parties has had any electoral significance, and most have had little if any political influence.

The revolution of 1952 represents the major turning point in twentieth-century Bolivian history. Many of the parties that predate the revolution continue to exist, and some have had genuine political influence. The existence of so many small party organizations suggests the fragility and weakness of Bolivian multiparty politics, although to a limited extent these characteristics have been encouraged by the country's electoral laws.

The Electoral System

One of the major changes brought about by the 1952 revolution was the expansion of suffrage in Bolivia. Elections may never have been a central or decisive experience, but the right to vote has reflected the prevailing attitudes toward the status of individuals in the society.

Prior to 1952 only male voters who could pass literacy and property tests were permitted to vote. The exclusion of women automatically cut the voting population in half, and the other two restrictions, given the poverty and illiteracy of the nation, excluded most of the remainder. The right to vote was expanded in 1952 to include all Bolivians over the age of twenty-one, and those over eighteen years of age who were married. In the 1951 election, the last to be held under the old restrictions, only 120,000 Bolivians voted. In 1952, the first election after the change in enfranchisement, 958,000 Bolivians voted. All citizens between the ages of twenty-one and seventy are required to vote, and penalties for not registering or voting are rarely imposed. Since 1952 approximately 75 percent of the potential electorate has been composed of campesinos, a fact not lost on Bolivian politicians.

Bolivia is theoretically governed by a constitution adopted in 1967. Under that constitution, Bolivia is a unitary state with two legislative chambers, a Chamber of Deputies and a Senate. The lower chamber has 130 members, the Senate 27. Each department of the country has 5 deputies from its capital city, and 1 deputy for every 50,000 inhabitants, or fraction over 30,000, in the districts outside the capital. Each department also has 3 senators.

Representation is based in the Senate on a majority-type system using an incomplete ballot. Each party is permitted to nominate two candidates for each Senate district. The party with the most votes receives two senators, and the party with the second-largest vote gets one. Representation in the chamber is allocated by proportional representation, specifically the Hare system and a closed list ballot.

Voting is by secret ballot, which is identified by color and symbol to make voting easier for those who are illiterate. The Hare system is relatively complicated to administer, and given the problems with communication between centers of population as well as the problems in organizing and administering an election in Bolivia, the results take a long time to be announced. Charges of fraud and electoral manipulation are therefore commonplace. Such accusations would probably surface even under the best of conditions, and they discredit the integrity of the electoral process.

The president of Bolivia is elected by direct vote, but if no candidate receives a majority of the vote, a president is selected by Congress from the three candidates receiving the most votes. This process has caused serious political problems on several recent occasions. In 1985 the Congress selected Víctor Paz Estenssoro as president, even though he received fewer votes in the election than the former military dictator Hugo Banzer Suárez.

Contemporary Parties and Elections

The 1952 revolution was swift but comprehensive. It began to be organized following the national election held in May 1951, which the MNR and its presidential candidate, Víctor Paz Estenssoro, won. Paz, who received 54,000 votes compared to 39,000 for his closest rival, ran with support from the POR and the new Communist party, the PIR. The regime canceled the results of the election, charging among other things Communist infiltration of the MNR. After the election Paz fled to Peru, leaving command of the MNR in the hands of his vice-presidential running mate, Hernán Siles Suazo. Siles, with the cooperation of Juan Lechín, mobilized MNR supporters against the regime. During the next eleven months, Siles negotiated with one faction of the military to support a rebellion and to recruit the national police to join it. Lechín prepared the miners and organized labor for the confrontation. Fighting broke out on April 9, 1952, and was over in two days. The leaders of the previous regime fled the country and Siles announced formation of an MNR government. On April 15 Paz returned to Bolivia and was sworn in for a four-year term as president.

The revolution succeeded, owing in part to the organization of the MNR, particularly in La Paz and the provincial mining areas, and the relative solidarity among its leaders on the objective of overthrowing the regime. The MNR, and particularly Siles, had put together an effective coalition to support the party's effort to seize power, which included a broad spectrum among its own leaders, a faction of the military and the national police, most of the labor movement, and many middle- and working-class supporters from La Paz. The Indian campesinos had not been included in the coalition and, indeed, had not been effectively mobilized by the MNR to an extent that would permit their inclusion. The success of the revolution also resulted from the disorientation and dissolution of the traditional forces in Bolivia.

They simply could not mobilize a sufficient concentration of force or support to mount an effective resistance to the MNR.

The events of 1952 permanently changed the nature of Bolivian party politics, whatever its effects on Bolivia more generally. The MNR was no longer an opposition force trying to alter the entrenched social, political, economic, and military elites. After the revolution it was the government; the old elites were effectively displaced. The MNR regime instituted some fundamental changes, including land reform, nationalization of the mines, and an extension of political rights to the Indians. Historically, land tenure had been a particularly important issue in Bolivia (Fifer, 1972), and land reform was therefore a popular issue. But with power came internal dissent and factionalization, and although the MNR enjoyed more than a decade in power, it failed to consolidate its control over the political forces of the country. Military intervention returned to Bolivia, and during the period from 1964 to 1988 the country underwent many unscheduled changes in government. During the twenty years from 1964 to 1985 Bolivia had twenty-two presidents, most of them coming to power via military intervention (Table 14.1).

The serious divisions in the MNR after the revolution were caused by the inherently contradictory interests of some of the elements contained in the party, particularly the conflicting interests of the middle class and organized labor and by the conflicting political ambitions of many of its principal leaders. Paz could not control these divisions. His political skills and motivation were insufficient to maintain or enforce party unity.

The process of factionalization in the MNR after 1952 has been reviewed elsewhere (Mitchell, 1978), as have the problems facing the regime that helped to precipitate the factionalization (Malloy and Thorn, 1971). Essentially, each of the MNR's major leaders came to control a competing political party. Walter Guevara Arce pulled out of the MNR in 1960 to form the PRA, Juan Lechín withdrew in 1963 to form the PRIN, and Hernán Siles Suazo left in 1979 to form the Leftist Nationalist Revolutionary movement (MNRI), a name that arose out of a dispute between Siles and Paz over the use of the MNR label. Siles therefore called his party the "Leftist Nationalist Revolutionary movement," and Paz called his the "Historical Nationalist Revolutionary movement" (MNRH). These defections were as much as anything a personal rivalry among the leaders and Paz, whose desire to be president seemed insatiable. He was elected to office in 1952 and again in 1960, and was reelected in 1964 only to be overthrown by the military. From exile Paz planned for the next fifteen years to return to power, finally being elected again in 1985.

Elections were held during the post-1952 period, but most of them were, in one way or another, controlled or fraudulent affairs. Siles was elected president in 1956 in a process monopolized by the MNR, and Paz was reelected under similar conditions in 1960 and 1964. The military regime of generals René Barrientos Ortuño and Alfredo Ovando Candia held a carefully arranged election in 1966 that excluded Paz and the MNR. Two

TABLE 14.1
Bolivian Regimes Since 1952

Year Initiated	President	How Initiated[a]
1952	Paz Estenssoro	Revolution
1956	Siles Suazo	Election
1960	Paz Estenssoro	Election
1964	Paz Estenssoro	Election
	Ovando	Military coup
	Barrientos	Military change
1965	Ovando/Barrientos	Military change
1966	Ovando	Military change
	Barrientos	Election
1969	Siles Salinas	Death of president
	Ovando	Military coup
1970	Miranda	Military coup
	Torres	Military coup
1971	Banzer	Military coup
1978	Pereda	Military coup
	Padilla	Military change
1979	Guevara Arce	Congress Elected
	Natusch Busch	Military coup
	Gueiler	Congress elected
1980	García Meza	Military coup
1981	Cayoja Riart	Military change
	Torrelio Villa	Military change
	Bernal	Military change
	Torrelio Villa	Military change
1982	Vildoso Calderón	Military coup
	Siles Suazo	Congress elected
1985	Paz Estenssoro	Election

[a]"Military coup" indicates use of force, "military change" indicates decision made within military elite.

civilian politicians held the presidency briefly, both in 1979, after having been selected by Congress, Walter Guevara Arce and Lidia Gueiler Tejada, the country's first female president. The only reasonably credible elections held during the period were those of 1980 and 1985. The 1980 election was annulled, however, by a military coup; Paz won the 1985 election. Elections for constituent assemblies and congresses were held periodically during the post-1952 period.

Several new parties emerged after the revolution, but none of them were particularly significant. One of the first appeared in 1954 and was originally known as the Social Christian party (PSC) but after 1964 was called the Christian Democratic party (PDC). It participated in several elections, including those of 1958 and 1962. It refused to participate in the military-controlled election of 1966, but then in 1967 it accepted an appointment (the Labor Ministry) to the Barrientos government. That decision caused a split in the PDC, with its younger members leaving to help form the Movement of the Revolutionary Left (MIR), events that took place on the heels of the capture and execution of Che Guevara in 1967. Following that, the PDC associated itself with the ambitions of Siles; its leader, Benjamín Miguel, was Siles's vice-presidential running mate in 1980.

After the military takeover in 1964, General Barrientos formed the Popular Christian movement (MPC) to consolidate his political support and to draw on the heritage of the 1952 revolution (Mitchell, 1977:106–120). The organization did not survive his sudden death. Subsequently, a right-wing political party that identified itself with the Barrientos legacy was formed— the National Barrientista movement (MNB)—but it failed to achieve any prominence.

One of the more resilient regimes of the post-1952 period was the military dictatorship of Gen. Hugo Banzer Suárez, who held office from 1971 to 1978. Banzer's success largely resulted from his support by his two powerful international allies, the United States through the CIA and the crime syndicates that were profiting from the export of cocaine from Bolivia. After Banzer was overthrown, his lingering political ambitions were kept alive by a political party formed in his behalf, the Nationalist Democratic Action (ADN). The ADN participated in both the 1979 and 1980 elections, running third in each election with about 15 percent of the vote. Much of the ADN support came from former supporters of the Bolivian Socialist Falange (FSB), a right-wing party advocating a conservative nationalist position and is also known as an advocate of the regional interests of the department of Santa Cruz, a rapidly developing region with agricultural, manufacturing, and petroleum interests. Banzer ran again in 1985, and received a plurality of the votes; however, Paz's supporters won a plurality of the congressional seats in the same election, and because no candidate had received a majority of the presidential vote, the president was chosen by Congress. Banzer lost to Paz in that selection.

In the 1980 presidential election slightly more than 1 million votes were cast, representing a participation of about 17 percent of the total population, not high by Latin American standards but respectable given the difficulties of holding elections in Bolivia. In that election Siles received approximately 45 percent of the vote, Paz 23 percent, and Banzer 20 percent. In 1985 Banzer received 29 percent, Paz 27 percent, and Jaime Paz Zamora (MIR) 9 percent. Following the 1985 election the MNR and the ADN signed a "pact for democracy," in which both Banzer and Paz agreed to work within the framework of "democratic" politics toward common goals and both eschewed the use of violence to achieve political objectives. The MNR won control of the Senate in the 1985 election, obtaining 16 of the 27 seats, the ADN received 10 (Table 14.2). In the Chamber of Deputies, the MNR won a slim plurality of 43 seats out of 130, with the ADN receiving 41. The only other party to receive a significant number of seats was the MIR with 15. In principal, cooperation between Paz and the MNR and Banzer and the ADN could guarantee control over the legislature, but such cooperation seemed unlikely. Under strong U.S. pressure to remain outside politics for the time being, the Bolivian military (itself divided and discredited by scandals involving complicity of some of its officers in the cocaine trade)

TABLE 14.2
Bolivian Congressional Representation by Party Following the National
Election of July 14, 1985

	Senate	Chamber of Deputies
MNR	16	43
ADN	10	41
MIR	1	15
MNR-1[a]		8
MNR-V		6
PS-1		5
FPU		4
PDC		3
FSB		3
MRTK-L[b]		2
Total	27	130

[a]The MNRI divided in 1985 into two separate groups, the MNR-1 and the
MNR-V.
[b]The MRTK-L divided from the MRTK for the 1985 election, both groups
being small campesino parties.

Source: Adapted from Arthur S. Banks, ed., Political Handbook of the
World (Binghamton, NY: CSA Publications, 1988), pp. 65-67.

seemed content to let Paz wrestle with the nearly insolvable economic
problems facing the country in the late 1980s, at least "for awhile." Paz,
perhaps with no alternative, imposed a severe economic austerity on the
country that caused serious deprivations among its middle and lower classes.
Some regard him as having sold out to more conservative interests and the
United States, but others have always viewed Paz more generally as
representing the conservative wing of the MNR and becoming increasingly
conservative as he aged (he was seventy-eight years old at the time of the
1985 election).

Bolivia has historically been characterized by a substantial amount of
regionalism—defined geographically by distinct climatic zones, culturally by
different ethnic mixtures and isolation from other regions, as well as by
different economic interests. These regional patterns—particularly the rivalry
between the highland capital of La Paz and the regions of Santa Cruz and
Cochabamba—have been important politically, and military rebellions have
normally succeeded or failed depending on the ability of their leaders to
unite several regions in a common cause. Regionalism has been less important
in Bolivian party politics than might be expected, however. Some parties,
such as the ADN, have been somewhat specialized regionally, but the urban
populations of each are not sufficient to ensure a viable national power
base. The limited importance of elections has probably contributed more
than anything to the relative absence of regional differences in party voting
and politics. Data and experience are both insufficient for the purposes of

discerning any consistent patterns of party support or voting based on sex or class.

Long-Term Trends

Bolivia has had an unusual experience with party politics historically. Parties and elections seem more symbolic (or perhaps symptomatic) of the country's politics than central to its evolution. In terms of sheer numbers, they have been formidable, and many of them have survived long after they ceased to be politically relevant. The MNR had a major impact on the country's politics, having facilitated a revolution that redefined Bolivia's political and social identity. Yet, parties and their leaders have been unable to gain effective control over the country—their efforts limited both by chronic military intervention and by their own inability to organize and integrate diverse political interests into party structures. Even the MNR has failed to do this.

The explanation for this apparent paradox of a lively party history combined with ineffective elections and unstable party organizations can be found in the pervasive and persistent influence of traditional political values in Bolivia, a country that by most standards has scarcely been touched by modernization. Loyalty to individual leaders is still paramount. Strength in politics is often the highest value, and personal ambitions normally transcend ideological or political commitments.

However, Bolivia's political tasks and historical traumas would challenge any country's party politics and leadership. The country's search for a more comprehensive identity, for autonomy from foreign domination, and for development and improved standards of living has preoccupied its politics throughout the twentieth century. To some extent, Bolivia's national identity and its relative autonomy were facilitated by the MNR in the early years following the 1952 revolution. The two wars had a profound impact on the nation's politics. The loss of territory to Chile in the War of the Pacific made Bolivia the only completely landlocked country in Latin America. The Chaco War discredited the traditional political and military elites and set in motion new political forces for reform. The severe economic problems of the past twenty years, caused in part by the extraordinary economic and political consequences of the cocaine trade, appear nearly insurmountable.

Bolivian party politics has evolved, but the parties have not effectively consolidated their organizations to take advantage of these trends, perhaps because of the very difficult and unstable context. For most of the past fifty years the country has had a multiparty system subject to constant and unpredictable changes; in spite of its chaotic history, the MNR has provided the greatest continuity for Bolivian politics since 1952. Following the 1985 election two political parties prevailed, the MNR and the ADN, although their success is more that of their respective leaders, Paz and Banzer, and the absence of effective alternatives. There is no evidence or reason to believe that further realignments will not recur. Paz, by virtue of his age if not otherwise, is reaching the end of his political career, and Banzer can hardly be expected to endure.

The future of Bolivian party politics rests on many forces and how they come together, including the economy, the cocaine traffic and the organizations involved with it, the emergence of new leaders and parties, and international intervention. But, ultimately, the future of Bolivian party politics rests on the mobilization and political organization of the Bolivian campesinos, who represent at least 75 percent of the nation's population. The campesinos are primarily Indian, in whose name much of the MNR crusade has been based. The status of the Indian in Bolivia has changed since the 1952 revolution, and reforms—including land reform and the nationalization of the tin mines— have responded to some of the historic concerns of the peasants and the miners. But the reforms have had little effect on improving the standards of living for the campesinos and miners. Both have already been partially mobilized, but they have yet to be fully exploited by political parties even though their potential influence is enormous. Any political party or leader who can mobilize the Indians to their cause can influence and perhaps ultimately control Bolivian politics. Until that occurs, Bolivian politics will probably vacillate between civil and military control, with no fundamental changes in the general pattern since the 1952 revolution.

References

Alexander, Robert J. 1958. *The Bolivian National Revolution.* New Brunswick, NJ: Rutgers Univ. Press.

———. 1982. *Political Parties of the Americas.* Westport, CT: Greenwood.

Fifer, Valerie. 1972. *Bolivia: Land, Location, and Politics Since 1825.* Cambridge, Eng.: Cambridge Univ. Press.

Klein, Herbert. 1969. *Parties and Political Change in Bolivia, 1880–1952.* Cambridge, Eng.: Cambridge Univ. Press.

Malloy, James M. 1970. *Bolivia: The Uncompleted Revolution.* Pittsburgh: Univ. of Pittsburgh Press.

Malloy, James M., and R. Thorn, eds. 1971. *Beyond the Revolution: Bolivia Since 1952.* Pittsburgh: Univ. of Pittsburgh Press.

Mitchell, Christopher. 1977. *The Legacy of Populism in Bolivia: From the MNR to Military Rule.* New York: Praeger.

———. 1978. Factionalism and Political Change in Bolivia. In Frank P. Belloni and Dennis C. Beller, eds., *Faction Politics: Political Parties and Factionalism in Comparative Perspective.* Santa Barbara, CA: ABC-Clio.

15

PANAMA

Panama long has possessed one of Latin America's most fragmented and least institutionalized multiparty systems. Traditionally, Panamanian political parties have been nonprogrammatic, personalist groups highly prone to faction. Since the 1930s several parties have attempted to gain mastery over this complex and sometimes volatile party system, but none has succeeded. The most recent party to strive for control has been the Democratic Revolutionary party (PRD), established by populist Gen. Omar Torrijos. Yet, since the death of the general in 1981, the PRD, too, has demonstrated disunity, lack of program, and an inability to dominate Panamanian party politics. Only a clumsy electoral fraud perpetrated by the military enabled the official party coalition to defeat the opposition in 1984.

Currently, political parties play only a marginal role in Panamanian politics. The PRD-led civilian government is nothing more than a thin facade for military rule by Gen. Manuel Antonio Noriega and the Panamanian Defense Forces. However, growing dissatisfaction with the corrupt and increasingly repressive Noriega regime has led to widespread protests organized by an urban-based National Civic Crusade and to U.S. economic pressure for democratization. Nevertheless, by retaining the loyalty of the armed forces, General Noriega still was successfully resisting demands for his resignation and exile in early 1989.

The Evolution and Context of
Panamanian Party Politics

Panama was a virtual protectorate of the United States for more than three decades following its secession from Colombia in 1903. Throughout this era, U.S. forces stationed in the Canal Zone guaranteed public order and often supervised Panamanian elections. Immediately after independence, the U.S.-favored Conservative party, many of whose members had played prominent roles in the 1903 revolt, were the country's most important party, but Panama possessed neither the landed aristocracy nor the strong church normally associated with Conservative strength (Ropp, 1982:17). The nation's natural geographical appeal as an international trade and transit point had instead produced an urban commercial elite and an open, secularized society more attuned to Liberal values. Led by Belisario Porras, the National Liberal party (PLN) soon gained supremacy by building a broad-based multiracial following. By the mid-1920s, the Conservatives had disappeared almost entirely from Panamanian politics.

The PLN, which emerged as Panama's preeminent political party, was a highly factionalized grouping. Although policy differences among party members were minimal, the party was fragmented into numerous personalist cliques. Each faction built an independent campaign organization linking its socially prominent leaders to the mass population through job-seeking intermediaries (Ropp, 1982:18–19). Several of these factions began to function essentially as autonomous parties, each claiming to represent genuine liberalism. The party system of this period also encompassed many other small and often short-lived parties led by members of the oligarchy as well as a fledgling Communist party (1925) and a Socialist party (1933).

The intense competition of Panamanian elections did not disguise the fact that virtually all important offices were won by members of the white urban commercial elite of Panama City and Colón. Nearly everyone recognized that the country's real center of power was Panama City's elitist Club Unión where coalitional deals were negotiated among the various party factions. Over time, however, Panamanians came to resent this urban oligarchy because of its power monopoly, its corruption, and its subservience to the United States. Beginning in the early 1930s, opposition forces gravitated to a new nationalistic movement headed by Harmodio and Arnulfo Arias.

The Arias brothers were middle-class mestizos from rural Panama who had managed to obtain professional degrees abroad. They blamed pervasive U.S. influence for most of Panama's ills and thus demanded an end to U.S. interference. Arnulfo Arias also launched vicious racist attacks on the large, English-speaking Antillian black population employed by the United States in the Canal Zone, claiming that they threatened traditional Hispanic culture. These nationalistic themes were especially popular among lower-class, urban mestizos (Morales, 1984:796).

Although Arnulfo Arias overthrew a Liberal government by force in 1931, he and his brother quickly adapted themselves to the existing political system. Both the U.S. government and the urban elite were assured that their interests would be respected (LaFeber, 1978:92–93). In 1932 Harmodio Arias won the presidency running as a doctrinaire Liberal and served quietly until 1936 while his brother spent much of the period as a diplomatic representative in Europe. While abroad, however, Arnulfo met both Benito Mussolini and Adolf Hitler and found many elements of Fascist ideology attractive. When he returned to Panama, he capitalized on his personal magnetism to build up a new National Revolutionary party (PNR) that embraced a radically anti-U.S. and racist platform (Leis, 1984:65).

Arnulfo Arias formed an electoral coalition made up of his new party and several Liberal factions, including that of the powerful Chiari family (Ropp, 1982:24), and in 1940 captured the presidency. Before he was deposed in 1941 by the National Police acting with the approval of the United States, Arias pursued a series of controversial policies. He disenfranchised English-speaking blacks and other racial minorities and confiscated some of their property. In addition, Arias introduced populist social legislation, imposed authoritarian political controls, and implemented a pro-Axis foreign policy.

When, in the 1930s, the United States ceased to intervene militarily in Panamanian politics, the racially mixed and hitherto insignificant national police forces had assumed new importance. In fact, by the 1940s, the National Police, the country's only armed force, had become the principal arbiter for the many contending parties and factions in the Panamanian multiparty system. As its political role increased, the force expanded and professionalized, especially after Col. José Antonio Remón assumed command. Moreover, Remón participated more actively in politics than previous commanders had and used his control over the strengthened National Police to make and unmake presidents at will during the 1940s and 1950s. For instance, Remón collaborated with a Liberal coalition to defraud Arnulfo Arias's renamed Panamanian party (PP) of its 1948 electoral victory. Yet, a year later the National Police strongman shocked everyone by putting Arias back in office. Despite promises of moderation, however, Arias's tenure was marked by corruption, intimidation of the opposition, and attempts to create an armed counterweight to the National Police. Predictably, Remón deposed the *Panameñista* leader again in 1951 and stripped him of his political rights.

Remón ultimately created his own party, the National Patriotic coalition (CPN), and placed himself in the presidential palace in 1952 after the CPN defeated a Liberal coalition. Although heterogeneous and ideologically vague, the CPN assumed the role of official government party and seemed to represent a potentially dominant force in the highly fragmented party system. Remón's administration gained substantial popular support because of its reforms in education, public health, and economic-development policy in spite of damaging (and well-founded) rumors about the president's involve-ment with narcotics traffic and prostitution. Remón supporters included everyone from businessmen favored by his economic programs to lower-class blacks who appreciated his less discriminatory racial attitudes. Given time, the National Patriotic coalition might have solidified these bases of support, but Remón's assassination in 1955 wrecked the party before it could begin to institutionalize. Although the CPN managed to maintain sufficient unity to win the 1956 presidential election, the party gradually collapsed without Remón. With Arias still banned from politics and the National Police (renamed the National Guard) under less politically ambitious leadership, the factionalized Liberals were temporarily able to reestablish political control.

The 1960 elections were not marred by the usual incumbent-party electoral abuses common to Panamanian politics. Sixteen parties participated. The

CPN's decline was fully evident when an opposition coalition, the National Union of Opposition led by Roberto Chiari's National Liberal party (PLN), emerged victorious. Part of Chiari's success, however, rested on the votes he received from Arnulfo Arias's followers in return for a promise to restore their leader's political rights. Once allowed to compete again, Arias soon demonstrated that his *Panameñista* party was the largest in the system. Although the populist leader lost a highly charged '1964 presidential race to the PLN's Marco Robles and an eight-party coalition, the *Panameñistas* won the greatest number of seats in the National Assembly.

With seven presidential candidates, three major electoral coalitions, and nineteen parties participating, the 1964 contest demonstrated the extreme fragmentation of the Panamanian party system. For the most part, the political parties of the 1960s still were weak and poorly institutionalized instruments for the ambitions of individual politicians. Parties were created to compete for patronage at election time, not to represent any particular policy commitments or formally organized interest groups. Only the small Christian Democratic party (PDC), formed in 1960, and the tiny Marxist parties were organized around coherent ideologies. By now, even Arnulfo Arias had moderated his party's nationalist and populist programs so much that the *Panameñistas* no longer constituted a clear contrast to other parties. The many political parties controlled by the urban oligarchy, in fact, tried to gain votes from the popular sector and deflect criticism from themselves by using strident, Arias-like anti-U.S. campaign rhetoric (Rudolph, 1981:146).

In order to attract U.S. Alliance for Progress funds, the Robles government (1964–1968) championed tax reform and advocated entry into the Central American Common Market. These measures caused a schism in the PLN by the time preparations began for the 1968 elections. When the Liberal party convention chose Robles's ally David Salmudio as its standard-bearer, more traditional Liberals such as the Chiaris threw their support to their old adversary Arnulfo Arias. At the head of a coalition of seven political parties, Arias thus easily defeated Salmudio's four-party alliance.

Arias's tenure in office was brief. Because of the Guard leadership's close ties to the Chiari Liberals and Arias's pledges of noninterference in military affairs, the National Guard did not engage in its usual efforts to harass the *Panameñista* campaign in 1968. But when the newly elected president broke his promises by trying to remove a number of Guard officers, he was swiftly deposed. Col. Omar Torrijos gradually emerged from the power struggle that ensued as the nation's new strongman. One of his first actions was to ban all parties.

Since the 1968 coup, Panama has been ruled by the Panamanian Defense Forces (called the National Guard until 1983). From 1968 to 1978, General Torrijos and a small circle of officers on the general staff exercised direct control of the government and restricted opposition political activity. Since 1978 Torrijos and his successors have chosen to govern indirectly through pliable civilian presidents and to allow greater political opposition. After being completely excluded from politics for a decade, political parties were permitted to renew their activities in 1978 and to compete in elections in 1980 and 1984 against the Democratic Revolutionary party (PRD), an official party established by Torrijos. Unfortunately, in spite of the return of competitive elections involving fourteen parties, the party system remains a peripheral factor. Military officers and, secondarily, Panamanian urban economic elites are still the principal domestic political actors.

General Torrijos's military regime was never as revolutionary as it claimed to be in its early stages and was as permeated with corruption as any other in Panama's sorry history. Nonetheless, the charismatic general's populist and nationalist policies won him a large mass following. His modest agrarian reform gave him a firm base among the long-ignored small farmers, while his provision of basic services to Panama City's squatter settlements enlisted the support of the urban marginal population. In addition, his nationalistic posture toward the United States during the Panama Canal treaty negotiations was popular with Panamanians of all social classes.

Despite organizational assistance from the Panamanian Communists, Torrijos had less success within the chronically fragmented union movement, largely because of his government's fairly conservative labor policies. On the other hand, Torrijos enjoyed considerable support from both domestic and multinational business. Although he expanded the bureaucracy to create more jobs for middle-class supporters, his government avoided interference in the private sector and promoted Panama as an international financial center.

Until 1978 no ruling party was constructed to integrate all of these diverse pro-Torrijos groups. For a time Torrijos did make use of the tiny Communist Panamanian People's party (PPP) because of its disciplined cadres, revolutionary credentials, and student/union connections, but the PPP never represented more than a small part of his coalition. Confronted with growing economic woes and U.S. pressure, Torrijos began to reopen the political system and to prepare for electoral competition in the late 1970s. He recognized the greater need for an official party in this new political environment and set out to construct his Democratic Revolutionary party in the image of Mexico's PRI. Government jobholders were pressured to join the PRD, and an elaborate collection of affiliated groups (labor, peasants, women, youth) were formally incorporated. However, Torrijos's populist coalition, which the PRD was intended to organize, was already eroding as public criticism of the regime mounted after the Panama Canal treaties were signed. Furthermore, since his death, none of the military or civilian leaders associated with the PRD has been able to match the general's popular appeal or his ability to balance contending forces.

By the mid-1980s, Gen. Manuel Antonio Noriega, formerly head of military intelligence, emerged as Panama's new strongman from the complex power struggles that developed after the death of Torrijos. Noriega, now the commander of the Panamanian Defense Forces, clearly demonstrated on several occasions his power to select and to dismiss civilian presidents. After rigging the 1984 elections to produce a victory for PRD presidential candidate

Nicolás Ardito Barletta, for example, Noriega forced him to resign in 1985 in order to prevent an investigation into the murder of Hugo Spadafora, a leading leftist critic of Noriega and the Defense Forces. The new figurehead president, Eric Delvalle, prevented any serious inquiry into this case and otherwise acted in accordance with Noriega's wishes for several years. When in early 1988 Delvalle, with the endorsement of the United States, tried to dismiss Noriega, the Panamanian chief executive was himself deposed and replaced with Noriega loyalist Manuel Solís Palma.

General Noriega, who is a central figure in Panama's extensive narcotics trade and money-laundering operations, apparently has little popular support, hence he is much more dependent on the Defense Forces than was the popular Torrijos. Consequently, the Defense Forces are very well cared for, while the official party is neglected (Ropp, 1986:432). Factionalized by competing ambitions and feuding right and left wings, the PRD has degenerated to the point that it is dominated by opportunists who vie with one another for Noriega's favor. Moreover, in spite of its official status, the party has attracted too little mass support to dominate the party system.

As long as General Noriega or a similar military leader commands Panamanian politics, it is difficult to imagine a significant role for any of Panama's political parties. Even if rising opposition from the middle sectors, much of the urban commercial elite, some unions, and the U.S. government does eventually force Noriega into exile, the corrupt Defense Forces are likely to remain the country's most powerful political institution.

Contemporary Political Parties

Most Panamanian political parties are still little more than ad hoc organizations backing the personal ambitions of a few politicians and their patronage-hungry followers. Lacking coherent ideologies, these weak electoral vehicles continue to be highly vulnerable to factionalization. The PRD, the official party founded by General Torrijos in 1978, is no exception. The Democratic Revolutionary party claims to be a Social Democratic party and pays lip-service to Torrijos's nationalist and populist goals. However, the party actually provides a home to politicians from all across the political spectrum and maintains intimate ties to General Noriega's controversial Defense Forces. The PRD is directed by a secretary-general and a national executive committee, but internal power actually is distributed feudally among competing bosses. Electoral support (officially 27 percent in the 1984 presidential race) tends to come from the remnants of Torrijos's multiclass coalition and from government employees and businessmen favored by the regime. Torrijos also launched the Broad Popular Front (FRAMPO) as a PRD ally composed mainly of professionals and bureaucrats, but this group has never gained any mass constituency.

The PRD's other allies in the five-party, progovernment National Democratic Union (UNADE) coalition were, in order of importance, the Labor party (PALA), the Republican party (PR), the National Liberal party (PLN), and an anti-Arias faction of the *Panameñistas*. The so-called Labor party actually is a conservative group representing urban financial interests and Noriega's brother-in-law has served as its secretary-general. Formed in 1983, PALA was credited with 7 percent of the vote in the 1984 elections and became the second most important element in the cabinet. The Republican party, founded in 1960, is a moderate conservative grouping uniting immigrant whites involved in agroindustrial enterprises with a mass base of Antillean and mestizo workers in the interior (Ropp, 1982:85). The PR garnered just 5 percent of the vote in 1984, but when Ardito Barletta was unseated in 1985, Republican party leader Eric Delvalle was named president (until his ouster in 1988). The Liberal party, Panama's oldest functioning party, still suffers from their divisions of the late 1960s. With the Salmudio faction not participating, the conservative PLN managed to add only 4.5 percent to UNADE's 1984 vote total. The party's leadership continued to come from the urban elite, while its votes are drawn mostly from Panama City and Colón. Lastly, a rump faction of the original Panamanian party (PP) managed to keep the traditional Arias party label, but swung only 1.8 percent of the vote to anti-Arias UNADE.

In the late 1980s Panama's largest opposition party continued to be the Authentic Panamanian party (PPA) led by aged (born 1901) former president Arnulfo Arias until his death in August 1988. Once populist and rabidly nationalistic, the PPA, like its ruling caudillo, became more moderate with age. Despite his growing moderation, Arias still demonstrated an impressive ability to attract lower- and lower-middle-class mestizos in 1984, capturing for the PPA just under 35 percent of the presidential vote. Although the *Panameñistas* were the most important group in the Democratic Opposition Alliance (ADO) and provided the major opposition to the PRD coalition governments during the 1980s, the PPA's future is very much in doubt now that Arias has passed from the scene.

Two parties were allied with the *Panameñistas* in the ADO alliance, the Christian Democrats (PDC) and the Liberal Republican and Nationalist movement (MOLIRENA). Unlike most Panamanian parties, the Christian Democrats, established in 1960, have a genuine program. The PDC is a center party espousing the progressive social doctrine of the Catholic church. Highly critical of the Defense Forces, the political group's greatest base of support lies among the urban middle sectors. The PDC is much better organized than most other parties and maintains an array of affiliated groups, including a labor union, the Isthmian Workers Central (CIT). PDC chief Ricardo Arias Calderón ran as the ADO's vice-presidential candidate in 1984 and is seen by many as the likely successor to Arnulfo Arias as the principal opposition leader. If this comes to pass, the PDC could expand rapidly beyond the modest 7 percent of the electorate it attracted in the last election. MOLIRENA, a right-wing faction of dissident Liberal politicians aligned with the PDC and PPA, has a less promising future. Organized in 1981, the movement added only 4.8 percent to the ADO vote in 1984.

In 1988 the three parties of the ADO electoral coalition endorsed the National Civic Crusade, a broad coalition of more than 150 civic groups (principally middle-class, business, and professional organizations) in its efforts to oust General Noriega. The Defense Forces and the PRD attacked the National Civic Crusade as a tool of U.S. imperialism, and the conservative white commercial elite and staunchly defended Noriega as the legitimate heir to General Torrijos's populist legacy. Despite their dissatisfaction with Noriega, much of the urban and rural working class were hesitant to embrace the private-sector-dominated Civic Crusade.

Five additional small parties, each offering an independent presidential candidate, also competed in the 1984 elections. But none of these minor parties was able to capture more than 2.5 percent of the vote or to win a seat in the Legislative Assembly. The Nationalist People's party (PNP) was created in 1983 to back the presidential ambitions of former National Guard commander, Gen. Rubén Darío Paredes, who ran a dismal third in 1984 (2.5 percent of the vote) after Noriega withdrew the military's promised support. The Popular Action party (PAPO) was organized by a group of urban middle-class social democrats in 1982. Strongly opposed to the Noriega regime, PAPO earned a 2.2 percent following in 1984 and later joined the National Civic Crusade. Each of the other three parties are Marxist organizations that were unable to attract as much as 1 percent of the electorate.

Some analysts believe the Panamanian left has been weakened by the fact that such a large segment of the working class is employed in the Canal Zone and is effectively isolated from domestic politics. The pervasiveness of U.S. influence has also led the right-wing and centrist parties to steal the left's popular anti-imperialist themes. The orthodox Communist party (PPP), in operation since the 1920s, has built up only a very small core of adherents mainly among students and trade unionists. Less numerous still are followers of the two Trotskyist groups, the Socialist Workers party (PST) and the Workers Revolutionary party (PRT).

Electoral Politics

Daniel Goldrich's (1966) classic study of Panamanian students' political opinions focused solely on a small segment of the population and is obviously quite dated. Yet, the deep cynicism and low level of system support he documented also are evident in current national polls (Arias Calderón, 1987–88:332). In light of recent events, it is difficult to imagine how Panamanians could feel otherwise. Although they are highly critical of their political system and not strongly identified with the programless parties, the majority of Panamanians are nevertheless willing to participate in national elections. Unfortunately, military interference and fraud has discredited these channels of mass political involvement. Officially, 75 percent of registered voters turned out for the May 1984 general elections, but after the fraudulent result was imposed by the regime, only 30 percent went to the polls in the municipal elections in June.

Before 1968 Panamanian elections were lively, intense, and sometimes violent affairs. Vote-buying, ballot-box stuffing, and physical intimidation—

particularly by incumbents—were commonplace. In addition, the urban elites saw to it that the legislative seats contested in these elections were distributed so as to overrepresent Panama City and Colón. General Torrijos attempted to reform the electoral system by creating a new rurally biased Assembly of Community Representatives, which was popularly elected in nonpartisan contests. In 1972, with political parties still banned, Torrijos supporters and other nationalists won more than 70 percent of these assembly seats (Priestley, 1986:77). Gradually, a national legislative council became the more important legislative body under Torrijos, and the first elections after parties were restored involved the selection of one-third of its membership in 1980. With the *Panameñistas* boycotting the contest, the recently formed PRD faced significant competition only from Liberals and Christian Democrats. Sixty percent of the electorate did turn out, but the PRD performed poorly, winning just over 40 percent of the vote (Ropp, 1982:82–83). Its status as the largest competing party and a single-member-district electoral system were the only factors that enabled the official party to capture eleven of the nineteen seats at stake.

Panama returned to a unicameral legislative system in 1983 by creating a sixty-seven-member legislative assembly to be elected by proportional representation at five-year intervals beginning in 1984. The presidential election, decided by plurality, is held concurrently. Voting for these offices is obligatory for all citizens over the age of eighteen, but no real penalties are imposed for abstention. An electoral tribunal is in charge of registration, balloting, vote tallying, and investigation of election-law violations. Despite its constitutional autonomy, this institution has little credibility.

Full multiparty competition returned to Panamanian politics in 1984, with fourteen parties participating. The two principal presidential candidates were young, centrist economist Nicolás Ardito Barletta (PRD), backed by the six-party National Democratic Union (PRD, PALA, PR, PLN, PP, FRAMPO), and the perennial populist Arnulfo Arias (PPA), heading the three-party Democratic Opposition Alliance (PPA, PDC, MOLIRENA). Ardito Barletta was supported by the most important urban business sectors and by the Defense Forces, but he failed to arouse much enthusiasm among the mass population during the campaign. In contrast, Arias capitalized on widespread popular discontent with military rule by promising to bring corrupt officers to trial. Voting procedures were orderly, but when vote counting suggested an impending Arias victory, the Defense Forces adjusted the final results to give the PRD's Ardito Barletta a narrow victory. U.S. officials believe that Arias won the election by as many as 30,000 votes (Hersh, 1986:A1).

In spite of the unreliability of the 1984 election returns, it is possible to make some limited observations about the party system on the basis of the official results (Table 15.1). The system clearly revolves around the PRD, founded by Torrijos, and the Arias-founded *Panameñistas*. The latter won the greatest segment of the presidential vote (34.6 percent vs. 27.4 percent), while the former garnered the lion's share of Legislative Assembly seats (thirty-four vs. thirteen). Five other parties act as junior coalition partners

TABLE 15.1
Panamanian Election Results by Party, 1984

	Number of Votes	Percent of Total Votes	Number of Legislative Seats
National Democratic Union			
PRD	175,722	27.4	34
PALA	45,384	7.1	7
PR	34,215	5.3	3
PLN	28,568	4.5	1
PP	11,579	1.8	0
FRAMPO	5,280	0.8	0
Total	300,748	47.0	45
Democratic Opposition Alliance			
PPA	221,335	34.6	13
PDC	46,963	7.3	6
MOLIRENA	30,737	4.8	3
Total	299,035	46.7	22
Other Parties			
PNP	15,976	2.5	0
PAPO	13,782	2.2	0
PPP	4,598	0.7	0
PRT	3,969	0.6	0
PST	2,085	0.3	0
Total	40,410	6.3	0
Total	640,193	100	67

Source: Official Panamanian electoral results compiled by the Tribunal Electoral (May 20, 1984).

of these two principal actors. These minor parties include the Christian Democrats (PDC), the Labor party (PALA), the Republican party (PR), and the two Liberal factions (PLN, MOLIRENA), each of which collected between 4.5 percent and 7.3 percent of the presidential ballots and at least one seat (but not more than seven) in the legislature. The other seven political parties—like the half-dozen or more partisan groups that did not participate in the 1984 race—have too little support to play a significant role in the party system except as possible marginal additions to electoral coalitions.

These patterns are highly unstable, however, because most Panamanian parties are so personalistic and poorly institutionalized, including the two major competitors. The PRD has decayed and become more factionalized since Torrijos's death, and the *Panameñistas* no longer have the personality of their octogenarian leader to unify them. Assuming that the Panamanian Defense Forces allow the multiparty system to continue to exist, great changes in composition and strength are likely.

Long-Term Trends

The highly fragmented and poorly institutionalized character of the Panamanian multiparty system has changed little over time. Throughout Panama's history, its political parties have tended to be personalist, ad hoc organizations lacking in ideological or institutional coherence. The Democratic Revolutionary party (PRD) founded by Torrijos has proved to be no exception to this traditional pattern. Moreover, the PRD, like other parties before it, has failed to establish a genuinely dominant position in the party system. Only the heavy hand of the Defense Forces keeps the PRD and its fractious partners in power.

Elections and party competition have been restored in Panama, but everyone recognizes that party politics and electoral participation count for little under General Noriega. Yet, Noriega's ability to retain control of Panamanian politics in the future is now in doubt. The educated middle class, many business leaders, and much of the broader mass public reject the current regime as wholly illegitimate. In addition, even before his indictment for drug trafficking by a U.S. grand jury in 1988, General Noriega had become a major liability for the U.S. government (despite his past assistance with United States intelligence operations), particularly because of the strategic importance of the Canal and the nearby headquarters of the U.S. Southern Command. The highly conspiratorial Panamanian officer corps also may contain middle-level elements eager to take advantage of the general's present difficulties (Ropp, 1987:434) although Noriega easily squashed an attempted coup in March 1988.

It is difficult to speculate about post-Noriega party politics particularly because both of the major political parties, the PRD and PPA, have such unpredictable futures. Traditional multiparty coalition politics should persist, but the specific parties, coalitions, and power distributions could change radically. The small but unusually well organized Christian Democratic party, which has been very active in the National Civic Crusade, appears well situated to prosper in this changing context. But the continued power of the Defense Forces will make it difficult for any civilian party to gain real control of the government.

References

Arias Calderón, Ricardo. 1987–88. Panama: Disaster or Democracy? *Foreign Affairs* 66:330–347.

Goldrich, Daniel. 1966. *Sons of the Establishment: Elite Youth in Panama and Costa Rica.* Chicago: Rand McNally.

Hersh, Seymour. June 12, 1986. Panama Strongman Said to Trade in Drugs, Arms, and Illicit Money. *New York Times.*

LaFeber, Walter. 1978. *The Panama Canal: The Crisis in Historical Perspective.* New York: Oxford.

Leis, Raúl. 1984. *Radiografía de los Partidos Políticos.* Panama City: Centro de Capitación Social.

Morales, Waltraud Q. 1984. Republic of Panama. In George E. Delury, ed., *World Encyclopedia of Political Systems and Parties.* New York: Facts on File.

Priestley, George. 1986. *Military Government and Popular Participation in Panama.* Boulder, CO: Westview.

Ropp, Steve. 1982. *Panamanian Politics: From Guarded Nation to National Guard.* New York: Praeger.

_____. 1986. General Noriega's Panama. *Current History* 85: 421–424, 431–432.

_____. 1987. Panama's Struggle for Democracy. *Current History* 86:421–424, 434–435.

Rudolph, James. 1981. Government and Politics. In Richard F. Nyrop, ed., *Panama: A Country Study.* Washington, D.C.: U.S. Government Printing Office.

PART FIVE

Emerging Multiparty Systems

16

BRAZIL

Brazil is the largest country in Latin America and the most successful example of economic development in the region, but its party politics has yet to develop permanent or effective institutions. Political parties have existed in Brazil since independence in 1822, and since World War II they have played an important role in the nation's politics. But even then, their influence was interrupted by a long military dictatorship, during which parties were repressed, controlled, and artificially defined. The two decades before the dictatorship and the few years since then have been insufficient to establish a stable or well-defined party system.

The military dictatorship that ruled Brazil from 1964 to 1985 was unusual for Brazil, although military participation in national politics was not. Brazil's military has been monitoring and shaping Brazilian government dating back to the late nineteenth century. It has also identified itself as an institution that can build Brazil into a great economic power, a dream shared by many Brazilians. Economic development was one of the highest priorities of the military leaders, and to a considerable degree it was stimulated by their policies. But the cost to individual Brazilians has also been considerable, creating a legacy of inequality and frustration with which the current civilian regime and political processes must now contend. The dream of a modern and powerful Brazil is still just a dream for most Brazilians.

The pursuit of modernization has, however, transformed Brazilian society in important ways over the past half-century. It has created the basis for mass politics and conditions for the development of strong national political parties. Mass politics is evolving as traditional ways of living have eroded owing to the growth in urban-based industrial and service economies, expanding investments, migration to the urban areas, increased levels of literacy, and the rapid expansion of communications systems. Brazil's vastness and the magnitude and diversity of its population have made political cohesion an elusive goal. National institutions, including political parties, have been difficult to establish and sustain in Brazil and without them the country may remain fragmented and unstable. Brazil's search for cohesion has thus resulted in clearly visible strains: regional fragmentation, competition, and inequalities; personalism substituting for organizations and structures; and unstable and transient political parties symptomatic of a decentralized society.

Brazilian history has six distinct periods, which have tended to define party politics, or the absence of it. Brazil was a monarchy from independence in 1822 to 1889; the First Republic was established in 1889 and lasted until 1930; a civilian dictatorship, controlled by Getúlio Vargas, ruled Brazil from 1930 to 1945; the Second Republic was established in 1945 and endured until 1964; the military ran the country from 1964 to 1985; and today a new "third republic" has been established. The political changes from one period to the next have been fundamental ones, and only marginal influences in the nation's party politics have carried over from one period to another. Almost every conceivable form of party politics and type of party competition can be found within these six periods, including various configurations of multiparty and two-party competitions and government-imposed parties. Likewise, virtually every conceivable type of electoral system has been tried in Brazil at one time or another, usually with the explicit purpose of controlling the outcome of elections.

Brazilian politics nevertheless shows evidence of some consistent trends. The emergence of an increasingly national politics is one such trend. It is characterized by more modern political identifications and expectations, and it demands more from the government. The by-product of rapid economic development and the changes commonly associated with it, Brazil's political evolution has undoubtedly also been affected by the introduction of electronic media in the culture, which has placed a priority on national political campaigning. What has not changed, however, is the comparatively relaxed manner in which Brazilian politics is conducted, even during periods of crisis. This trait has distinguished Brazil from other Latin American nations since its independence, although the potential for confrontation does exist in the society.

The Context of Brazilian Party Politics

Brazil is a large and diffuse nation, characterized by contradictions and potential confrontations. The country's political history has been remarkably placid, and political parties have encouraged little political violence since independence.

Politically, Brazil underwent few changes from independence to 1889. The Brazilian monarchy replaced the Portuguese one, to which it was directly related and remained closely tied. National government and national politics were almost nonexistent. The emperor reigned, but rarely ruled—functioning more as an arbitrator and referee among the stronger, contending regional interests.

By the last decade of the nineteenth century, Brazil was beginning to experience important economic changes, most specifically in the nature of its export economy. Traditional exports had been based on large plantations and relied on the unique Portuguese system of slavery. But by the end of the monarchy in 1889, Brazil's economy was experiencing a new export boom; rubber, a product harvested in the tropical rain forests rather than on traditional plantations, had become Brazil's chief export product. Slavery had become less essential to maintaining exports, and political power was gradually shifting to those who controlled rubber and other new sources of income.

Brazil was also building a military organization in which professionalization was a high priority. Career officers latched onto the then-evolving dream of Brazil as a "great power," a diffuse and imprecise vision that has captivated Brazilian society for more than a century. Toward that end, these officers saw the inevitability of what today would be called "modernization." For them, such a process included ending the old-fashioned monarchy and replacing it with a republic. The military therefore entered into politics, an involvement that would continue and evolve (Stepan, 1971). Their avowed purpose was national development—the pursuit of the dream of modernization. They remained in politics in a distinctively Brazilian way, not so much to rule as to guide their country's evolution, for nationalistic more than personal objectives (Burns, 1968:48–50). The military attempted to intervene in 1910, 1922, and 1924, and they were instrumental in bringing a civilian dictator—Getúlio Vargas—to power in 1930.

By the advent of the First Republic in 1889, Brazil still had only a very small population in an immense territory—less than 20 million inhabitants in an area approximately the size of the continental United States. Yet another change in the nation's export economy—the development of coffee as its principal export—brought still additional changes to Brazilian society. The coffee exports were very profitable and provided revenues for national purposes. Their export generated substantial secondary economic activity, most of which gravitated to southern Brazil generally and to the urban areas of Rio de Janeiro and São Paulo specifically. Brazil's urbanization had begun in earnest, and these two great cities came to dominate the country economically and demographically. Immigration had also begun to increase, as it had elsewhere in the Southern Cone countries. Immigrants from Portugal, Spain, Italy, Germany, and other parts of Europe poured into Brazil, most of them settling in the south, including the southernmost province of Rio Grande do Sul. They injected further economic dynamism into the country and brought middle-class European aspirations. Cultural regionalism—the peculiar blending of European, African, and indigenous peoples in various ratios throughout the country—was being reinforced by economic regionalism. Before coffee exports dominated the economy, the least affluent parts of the country, the northern and northeastern states, had been generating export revenues (sugar, rubber) that were channeled into the burgeoning southern states, the most modern and ultimately most affluent part of the country. A system of "internal colonialism" had been established, whereby the poor subsidized the rich (Soares, 1967). The legacy of this change was the solidification of regional economic and political interests, most notably in the populous, coffee-rich, and dynamic state of São Paulo, which has attracted the overwhelming share of industrial investment over the past half-century (Dean, 1969).

The ultimate expression of political regionalism during the First Republic can be found in the so-called governors' policy, devised by President Campos Salles (1898–1902). This agreement provided for the alternation of the presidency (in effect, control of the national government) between candidates selected by the states of São Paulo and Minas Gerais (which then included the city of Rio) and relinquished control of the northern, northeastern, and western states to the traditional regional elites that dominated them. The issue of regionalism was thus finessed by the allocation of spheres of influence and control and by the alternation of national government between the two powerful states that had the most at stake in national policy. These states in turn were controlled by powerful political machines whose own interests were insulated from national control. São Paulo and Minas Gerais therefore took turns at running the national government, while other state machines were essentially unaffected by central government decisions.

Politics under this arrangement ultimately came to depend largely on personalities, given the absence of national structures that could integrate the political machines. The governors of São Paulo and Minas Gerais, and ultimately the governor of the southernmost state, Rio Grande do Sul, were therefore the most powerful politicians in Brazil. The governors' policy of alternation finally broke down following the international dislocations of the Great Depression and the refusal of São Paulo politicians to relinquish control of the presidency. The military intervened in an effort to stabilize the process of national development and to overcome the self-serving state interests codified by the governors' policy. This time military intervention succeeded. The former governor of Rio Grande do Sul, Getúlio Vargas, was installed as head of state. Rio Grande do Sul came to play an unusually important role in Brazilian politics and government (Cortes, 1974) in part as a balance to the conflicts and competition between São Paulo and Rio de Janeiro. To a considerable extent the conflicts between these two cities were based on personalities and personal political machines. Personalism continues to characterize Brazilian politics, as much as or more than elsewhere in the hemisphere, and has often provided the primary focus for party identifications in a complex, fragmented, and historically unstructured party system.

Another aspect of Brazilian party politics requires consideration. The electoral laws and formulas for representation have been used in Brazil to control parties for explicit, often short-term, political objectives to a degree uncommon even in Latin America. The practice began in 1824 when Pedro I decreed a constitution that established a "constitutional monarchy." Parties were permitted, but they were insulated from mass involvement by highly restrictive regulations that limited enfranchisement and constitutional prerogatives. Complex rules were changed to meet short-term objectives, which led to an extraordinary array of experiences ranging from single- to multimember districts, plurality and proportional representation systems, selective enfranchisement, and a variety of other practices.

Contemporary Brazilian politics remains preoccupied with two fundamental realities: rapid economic growth and modernization, and the correction of persistent imbalances based on region, class, and race. Although such imbalances are common elsewhere, including the United States, they are now politically critical in Brazil. Regional imbalances have been politicized since independence. Class imbalances began to be politicized with the emergence of industrialization, although they had been indigenous to the society since its settlement. Racial imbalances are only now beginning to be politicized. A multiracial and mixed society, Brazil has been known, not always accurately, as a relatively harmonious society, in part because most Brazilians do not identify themselves at one end or another of a racial spectrum. Economic welfare and opportunities are nevertheless correlated with color in Brazil, and these inequalities are fueling the potential for confrontation.

Brazil's fundamental objectives of growth and equality are potentially contradictory. The resolution of some balance therefore requires compromise and constitutes the major task of Brazilian parties and politicians today. Given that growth and equality both require an increasing degree of national cohesion and given that Brazilian society is changing so rapidly, these tasks have taken on an additional urgency and complexity.

The Evolution of Brazilian Party Politics

Brazil's first political parties emerged during the monarchy. They had no base for mass appeal, however, and their importance to Brazilian politics and government was marginal. Following independence, fundamental questions of how to rule Brazil (particularly after the abdication and exile of Pedro I in 1831 in favor of his son, Pedro II) factionalized the parties. Conservatives wanted a strong monarchy, Moderates favored a liberal constitutional monarchy, *Exaltados* favored a provisional republic, and restorationists wanted the return of Pedro I. In 1837 some of these forces formed the Conservative party (PC), consisting primarily of restorationists, *exaltados*, and some moderates. In 1840 the Liberal party (PL) was organized, made up mostly of moderates who wanted "decentralization," a euphemism for regional control. In the 1860s a division occurred within the Liberal party, producing the Progressive party (PP), which advocated a more orthodox, aggressive pursuit of liberal ideals; the organization lasted only a few years, and its members rejoined the Liberal party (Young, 1982:147–150).

In the 1870s the Republican party (PR) emerged. The first of three organizations to use that name, the Republican party had a considerable impact on Brazilian politics. A second one emerged during the First Republic, and a third incarnation appeared during the Second Republic. The original Republican party advocated an end to slavery, the monarchy, and formation of a republican form of government. The organization had its origins in a "radical" club movement in São Paulo, not unlike similar movements to form later in Buenos Aires and Santiago. With the realization of its principal goals in 1889, the party transformed itself into a second, broader organization, subsequently known as the Federal Republican party (PRF), and remained a major influence in Brazil during the First Republic. The party was in fact a "federal" one, a loose affiliation of state-based Republican parties that controlled local machines, which in turn were the principal focus of power in Brazil. With the end of the monarchy, both the Conservative and the Liberal parties disappeared.

The principal opposition to the Federal Republican party during the First Republic was the Liberation party (PL), which was formally organized in 1928 but had existed previously in the form of an alliance in Rio Grande do Sul in opposition to the dominant Republican party organization there. Members of the Liberation party supported Getúlio Vargas as governor of the state beginning in 1928, backing his candidacy for the presidency two years later. When Vargas came to power through the military coup, the organization continued to survive, although it disappeared by decree, along with all the other parties, with the establishment of the Estado Novo in 1938. The Liberation party resumed its activities in the Second Republic as a minor national party; its strength continued to reside primarily in Rio Grande do Sul.

In 1922 the Communist Party of Brazil (PCB) was organized, principally with support in Rio and Porto Alegre. It was almost immediately declared illegal under a state of siege imposed on the country but reappeared briefly again in 1927 when the siege was lifted. Throughout much of its history it was led by Luis Carlos Prestes, and it existed mostly as an underground organization. In the 1930s it promoted the Popular Front and participated in a broader coalition known as the National Liberating Alliance (ANL) just prior to Vargas's imposition of the Estado Novo. Like its counterparts elsewhere in Latin America, the PCB was often divided by personal and ideological questions, particularly by rifts between supporters of Stalin and Trotsky. In 1935 it sponsored a military insurrection in several Brazilian cities, which was effectively crushed by the armed forces. Most of its leaders were either jailed or exiled after this. Prestes himself was given a long prison sentence. The party reappeared as a new organization in the Second Republic.

Just as the Liberation party had emerged in Rio Grande do Sul to oppose the state's entrenched Republican party machine, a similar organization emerged in the 1920s to oppose the dominant machine of São Paulo. The organization was the Democratic party (PD), established in 1926. Its influence and support were almost wholly limited to São Paulo, although like the Liberation party it, too, supported Vargas's candidacy for the presidency in 1930, in addition to the military revolt that brought him to power.

Marxist-oriented leaders in the Brazilian labor movement founded a Socialist party in 1928, calling it the Labor party (PT). It ultimately joined forces with other Marxist parties to form the Brazilian Socialist party (PSB) in 1933, after Vargas had come to power. Although the Labor party gained recognition from the Socialist International, it had only minor support within Brazil.

In general, the First Republic failed to produce parties that could take root as organizations or could attract increasing numbers of voters. The strongest, the Federal Republican party, was little more than a collection of dominant state political machines. The opposition to it, principally from the Liberation and Democratic parties, was confined to single states, Rio Grande do Sul and São Paulo. Marxism failed to establish itself as a significant political force, and indeed none of the parties survived the period as anything more than vestiges of the past.

The Vargas years, 1930–1945, were anathema to political parties. Ruling through the bureaucracy and the military, Vargas failed to build a political party whereby he could consolidate his control or reinforce support for his regime. His assumption of dictatorial powers in 1938 (the Estado Novo) prohibited all party activity and presents a sharp contrast to actions taken by Lázaro Cárdenas in Mexico or Juan Perón in Argentina, both of whom used parties to organize political support for their regimes. Brazil therefore entered the Second Republic in 1945 with no established parties.

The opposition to Vargas coalesced in the Brazilian Democratic Union (UDB) in preparation for the 1930 elections and nominated a presidential candidate. The Vargas-sponsored candidate had no political party to support him. The UDB disappeared along with all other political parties after 1938, but its leadership and supporters formed the nucleus of what was to become the major anti-Vargas political party in the Second Republic, the National Democratic Union (UDN), which remained a source of opposition throughout the Second Republic and in restructured forms during the military period that followed and subsequently in the Third Republic (Skidmore, 1967:100–108).

Shortly after Vargas came to power, an organization known as Integralist Action (AI) was formed by pro-Fascist Brazilians (Levine, 1970:81–99). It adopted the symbols, rituals, and procedures of its Fascist counterparts in Europe and was led by Plínio Salgado. Like all other parties, the Integralist Action party was declared illegal in 1938, and Salgado went into exile. In 1945 he returned to Brazil and reorganized his supporters as the Popular Representation party (PRP), which managed to continue functioning in the Second Republic and gained limited representation in the legislature.

With the end of the Vargas regime in 1945, three principal parties emerged to dominate party politics during the Second Republic. One of these, the National Democratic Union (UDN), was comprised of anti-Vargas politicians who had formed the Brazilian Democratic Union (UDB) a decade earlier. Under pressure, Vargas agreed to hold elections in 1945, throwing his support to two new organizations: the Social Democratic party (PSD), which consisted of Vargas supporters and appointees in the national and state governments and the political bureaucracy; and the Brazilian Labor party (PTB), built around the Vargas-controlled labor unions. Vargas's effort to industrialize

Brazil in the 1930s and the 1940s had succeeded, and the labor movement had grown appreciably during the period. Vargas apparently believed that the labor movement would continue to expand with continued industrialization and that the PTB would benefit from this, eventually developing a mass following that would permit it to dominate other party organizations. At least a dozen other national parties were formed during the Second Republic, although they were dominated by the UDN, the PSD, and the PTB. Parties were weak during the Second Republic, however, and were used primarily as vehicles for the politicians who affiliated with them (Roett, 1978:74).

Brazil after Vargas had a considerably different political context. It was on a steady course of modernization: economic growth, particularly industrialization, was proceeding; literacy was increasing; and large numbers of Brazilians were migrating to the cities. These and other changes increased political awareness and the potential for participation. Vargas had established the first genuinely effective centralized national government in Brazilian history. It was capable of making decisions; of executing them on a national basis; and, least temporarily, of curbing the power of the state machines. In the wings for generations, the military had successfully imposed its will on the country in the 1930 coup and had participated in the modernization of the country under Vargas, playing a key role in both political and economic matters.

By 1945 Vargas had defined the nature of the party competition in the Second Republic by supporting two national parties (the PSD and the PTB) and concentrating his opponents in another one, the UDN. However, he left no established government party on which future leadership could build—none that could consolidate his regime's achievements and support. The implications for Brazilian politics, had he chosen to do so, will be debated forever. Vargas also failed to take into account the rising political importance of Brazil's middle class (Skidmore, 1967:118–121), an oversight that would have important implications in the 1980s. In any event, party politics was largely a new game in 1945.

Vargas had the Social Democratic party organized in early 1945 by his appointed state governors. It embraced individuals at the national and state levels, including members of the upper class who had worked with Vargas during the preceding fifteen years and had benefited from the collaboration. The PSD was in 1945 the most powerful of the new parties, but for the next twenty years, until the 1964 military intervention, its influence and electoral strength steadily declined. It relied on patronage but failed to develop a cohesive or attractive political orientation.

At the same time, Vargas's labor minister organized the Brazilian Labor party at the behest of the dictator, building on labor unions whose leadership was loyal to his regime. Many PTB leaders were government officials, and it is generally believed that the Vargas regime funded the new PTB. Vargas ran for the presidency in 1950 as a candidate for the PTB and won. He appointed João Goulart as minister of labor and assigned him the specific task of expanding and strengthening the PTB. Goulart's influence within the party was controversial, however, and he was forced to resign in early 1954. Vargas committed suicide later that year.

The PTB had many rivals for Brazil's labor vote, and it made electoral alliances that tarnished its image as the champion of the working class. Yet, its representation in the legislature steadily increased over the twenty-year period of the Second Republic, just as the strength of the PSD declined. Never unified or cohesive at the national level, the party failed to mobilize voters in the large and critical state of São Paulo, which had the largest percentage of organized workers. The reality of state and political regionalism continued to haunt even this nominally class-defined party.

The third principal national party during the Second Republic, the National Democratic Union, consisted of opponents to Vargas and his parties; most of the UDN leaders were from São Paulo and Minas Gerais. It also had support from the traditional elites in northeastern Brazil. The UDN appealed largely to the middle classes of the country, whose interests were not met by the other two parties and whose concerns had not been central to the Vargas regime. UDN candidates lost the first three presidential elections after 1945 but achieved a substantial block of legislative representatives and maintained its representation throughout the Second Republic. The party was also more cohesive as an organization than were the two Vargas-inspired parties. In 1960, the UDN reluctantly supported the presidential candidacy of Jânio Quadros of São Paulo, although he was not a member of the UDN, largely for reasons of political expediency. After his election, most UDN leaders abandoned Quadros, who resigned the presidency less than a year later. He was succeeded by his vice president, João Goulart, who was a member of the PTB. Throughout the Second Republic, the UDN found itself in opposition to every regime, a position that brought mixed political consequences.

Many minor parties appeared from 1945 to 1964. Most were a mixture of ideological, personal, and regional orientations. There was, for example, a Trotskyite group—an ideological and regional Revolutionary Socialist party (PSR) centered in São Paulo. It did not submit candidates in the elections, but it was active in the labor movement and tried to organize agricultural workers, a task never before undertaken. Another Marxist party, the Brazilian Socialist party (PSB), drew its leadership from dissident ex-Trotskyites as well as from left-wing opponents of Vargas that had once been affiliated with the UDN. The Brazilian Communist party resurfaced in 1945 and ran candidates in elections that year. Their presidential candidate in 1945 obtained almost 10 percent of the national vote, and they increased their state and municipal influence in the 1947 elections. Under pressure from the United States, the Brazilian Supreme Court declared it illegal in 1947 because of its alleged international connections.

Many other parties participated in the electoral process during the Second Republic, but most had a limited political base and exercised influence only through coalitions with larger parties. The Republican party (PR) in Minas

Gerais (the third Republican incarnation) was conservative but made alliances when necessary with the UDN, the PSD, and even the PTB. The Social Progressive party (PSP) was a personal vehicle for Aldemar de Barros, the governor of São Paulo. He endorsed Vargas for president in 1950 and hoped to receive Vargas's support for his own candidacy in the next presidential election. Vargas's suicide changed those plans, but de Barros ran anyway in 1955, capturing third place and a surprisingly large vote of more than 2 million.

In 1945 a small Christian Democratic party (PDC) was organized, along lines similar to organizations that were emerging elsewhere in Latin America, notably in Chile and Venezuela. It had support scattered throughout several states, and elected a small but stable legislative delegation. The organization, like other Christian Democratic parties, was chronically riven along ideological and doctrinal lines.

A variety of small labor parties were formed during the Second Republic— mostly factions that had broken with PTB—including the National Labor party (PTN), the Renovating Labor movement (MTR), the Republican Labor party (PRT), the Rural Labor party (PRT), and the Social Labor party (PST). None of them was electorally important.

Party politics during the Second Republic constituted a significant break with the past. First, more political parties were competing and they encompassed a much broader political spectrum. Also, mass politics was beginning to define party competition for the first time. Elections therefore became important vehicles for party influence, and the lower socioeconomic classes gained new importance in Brazilian politics. Even after the passing of Vargas, his influence and the controversies of his regime continued to affect Brazilian party politics. The two political parties he initiated remained dominant, the PTB increasing its strength at the expense of the PSD. The anti-Vargas forces in the UDN, while less effective in presidential politics, were strong and the best-organized and most cohesive of the three major parties. But these three groups functioned within a multiparty system. Many of the minor parties had sufficient electoral strength among limited groups and regions to be decisive when in alliance with stronger ones. Alliances and coalitions thus took on increasing importance during this period (Skidmore, 1967:229–233). The impact of alliances on party representation in, for example, the 1962 Brazilian legislature (Table 16.1) is readily apparent. In the lower chamber, 33 percent of the PSD candidates won through alliances, 39 percent of the PTB candidates, and 43 percent of the UDN candidates. Seventy-three percent of the PSP candidates won their seats through cross-endorsement with other parties, and of the remaining sixty-six delegates 80 percent were elected through party alliances.

The military, responding to what they saw as legislative and presidential paralysis and a leftward drift under Goulart, intervened on April 9, 1964, declaring their action to be a "revolution." Although this extraordinary action was uncommon in Brazilian history, it was executed without violence in a characteristically Brazilian way (Palmer, 1979). All party activity was

TABLE 16.1
The 1962 Brazilian Legislature: Representation by Party

	PSD	PTB	UDN	PSD	Other	Total
Senate	21	18	15	2	10	66
Chamber	119	104	97	23	66	409
Percent won by alliances	33	39	43	73	80	48

Source: Adapted from Henry Wells, ed., Brazil: Election Factbook,
September 1965 (Washington, DC: Institute for the Comparative Study
of Political Systems, 1965), pp. 67, 71.

stopped, and the military ruled by decree. On October 3, 1965, elections were held for state governors of eleven states, with the PSD and the PTB winning eight of the eleven. Three weeks later all existing political parties were declared illegal. Wishing to maintain some appearance of legitimacy and civilian participation in the government, the military decreed that two new political parties be formed, one in support of the government and one opposed (Wesson and Fleischer, 1983:103–109).

The pro-government party, the National Renovating Alliance (ARENA), was announced on December 5, 1965; the opposition Brazilian Democratic movement (MDB) was formed shortly thereafter. The ARENA was originally composed of former UDN members and some members of the PSD, in addition to leaders from the smaller parties. The MDB was composed primarily of former PTB leaders, some from the PSD, and some from smaller groups such as the Christian Democratic and Socialist parties.

Notwithstanding its moderate, Social Democratic pronouncements, the ARENA was basically an instrument of the military. It voted, either in congress or through the electoral college, for military candidates for the presidency, and during the period from 1966 to 1979 it controlled the national legislature, normally by substantial margins. It was held together by patronage and access to the military regime and kept in power by the military government's willingness to manipulate the electoral system, discussed below, to such a degree that the ARENA could not lose elections. In 1978, for example, it received 231 deputies and 41 senators with 12 million votes, while the MDB with 16 million votes received only 199 deputies and 21 senators. Representation in the national legislature for the ARENA and the MDB is shown in Table 16.2 for the years 1966–1978. The ARENA was not a cohesive organization. Its members and adherents in the legislature, those civilian politicians who were benefiting from their support of the regime, constituted a civilian political establishment under the military regime. Former party affiliations were at best of secondary importance. When the military decided to liberalize the country's party politics, the ARENA was officially dissolved on November 30, 1979.

TABLE 16.2
Representation by Party in the Brazilian Legislature, 1966-1978

	Chamber of Deputies				Senate			
	ARENA	MBD	Other	Total	ARENA	MBD	Other	Total
1966 (Oct.)	254	149	6	409	43	23	0	66
1966 (Nov.)	277	132	0	409	48	18	0	66
1970	220	90	0	310	59	7	0	66
1974	199	165	0	364	44	20	2	66
1978	231	199	0	430	41	21	4	66

Source: Official Brazilian electoral results compiled by the Tribunal Superior Eleitoral (Brasília), 1966-1978.

Like the ARENA, the MDB was a heterogeneous organization, its members affiliated principally to express opposition to the military regime. It consistently challenged the military governments on legal and constitutional questions, denouncing them with limited results in the legislature. It did make electoral gains in the controlled national elections, particularly after 1970, although the military consistently tried to impede its expansion by changing electoral rules and structures. The MDB went out of existence in 1979 by decree of the military government.

With the liberalization in 1979, new political organizations once again began to form in Brazil. They had antecedents in both the Second Republic and before, but they were all essentially new organizations—new coalitions of Brazilian leaders and, to some extent, a new generation of leaders. Most of the former ARENA politicians affiliated, at least at first, with the new Democratic Social party (PDS), whose name "Partido Democrático Social" was strongly reminiscent of the former PSD, "Partido Social Democrático," which had played a prominent role in the Second Republic. The two groups were alike in another way. The PSD had emerged at the urging of Vargas as the organization of bureaucrats and leaders who had held power during his regime. The PSD thus became a political instrument for maintaining their influence. The PDS likewise was formed on the heels of a dictatorship and was made up of Brazilian politicians who had supported, and prospered from, the military regime. Like the PSD, the PDS was motivated, not so much by ideology or political objectives, but by a desire to remain in power. Strong personal confrontations were thus in store for the PDS.

The adherents of the former MDB formed a new organization that retained their former party name, the new Brazilian Democratic Movement party (PMDB). Unified in their opposition to the military rule and its legacy, the leaders ultimately benefited from their association with that opposition as Brazil returned to civilian politics. But like the PDS, the PMDB was neither ideological nor clear as to its political programs or objectives. But, unlike the PDS leaders, PMDB leaders were more united in their drive to acquire power and to defeat the dominant PDS.

A third group, formed after 1979, was called the Popular party (PP). Led by Tancredo Neves and other well-known politicians from the state of Minas Gerais, the PP was viewed as a moderate party opposed to the military. It did not survive long enough to establish a clear political program, however. One party that had existed in the Second Republic and was reinstated after the military interregnum was the Brazilian Labor party (PTB). An internal struggle among the party leaders, however, resulted in a contest over the right to use the party name and to control the organization. The loser in the struggle, Lionel Brizola, ultimately withdrew from the PTB to form the Democratic Labor party (PDT), taking most former leaders and supporters of the PTB with him. Many who had been in the PTB prior to the military dictatorship had joined the MDB and remained with the PMDB when it was constituted. A fifth party, formed by radical union leaders from São Paulo, was known as the Workers' party (PT), which represented both class and regional interests.

The 1982 national legislative election gave the PDS a plurality in the legislature; the PMDB had the second-largest representation. The 1982 election had functioned under some restraints, however. Many smaller parties had not been legalized, and the PDS victory was thus the result of these controls as well as of a certain degree of inertia in the political system. As the time approached for selecting a new civilian president—to be elected indirectly through an electoral college on January 15, 1985—the newly established parties began to reconstitute themselves further, principally over the issues raised by the presidential ambitions of their leaders. The principal division occurred in the PDS. Several of the party's prominent leaders formed the Liberal Front, originally a faction within the party. Later, in coalition with other groups, it became an independent political group known as the Liberal Front party (PFL). The PMDB, after considerable controversy within its ranks about a presidential candidate, eventually nominated Tancredo Neves, formerly president of the small PP. José Sarney, who had once headed the PDS, was selected as the vice-presidential candidate, although he had to resign from the PDS and join the PMDB for the honor. The PFL endorsed the PMDB candidates in the election, and they provided enough votes for Neves to be elected; he received 480 out of 585 votes in the electoral college. The PMDB and the PFL were together known as the Democratic Alliance, and together they were able to control the legislature. Neves died before taking office, elevating his vice-presidential running mate, José Sarney, to the presidency.

Two months after taking office, the new Sarney government introduced legislation that fully restored the political rights of parties. It also called for the direct election of the next president and, for the first time in Brazilian history, enfranchised all citizens irrespective of literacy. The abolition of the literacy requirement added a potentially large number of new voters, approximately 30 million. Twelve political parties gained representation in the 1986 elections, but the PMDB scored a huge success, winning twenty-two of the twenty-three governorships; the PFL easily gained control of the congress.

The task of redefining national institutions was focused on the issue of a presidential vs. a parliamentary system, and on a four- or five-year term for the president. The question was resolved in mid-1988 in favor of a five-year presidential term and against the parliamentary system. President Sarney was strongly in favor of the outcome, as was the military. His own term as president was extended to five years, until March 1990. New presidential elections were thus scheduled for November 1989. Sarney announced formation of a new progovernment party, the Democratic Transition Bloc (PTD), and broke his formal ties with the PFL and the PMDB. Meanwhile, rumors of a possible military intervention circulated in Brazil. Six generals held ministerial rank in the Sarney cabinet, underlining the continuing involvement of the military in monitoring Brazilian politics.

When the military allowed the political parties to form again without significant restraints, the country more or less had to start all over with new organizations. There was some continuity. The old PTB reappeared, but it soon fractionated and lost most of its strength. The MDB survived in the form of the PMDB. The PDS, notwithstanding the nomenclatural similarity to the PSD, was in effect a reconstituted ARENA. But none of the organizations had any consistent roots in their antecedents nor, for that matter, any consistent leadership. Both the PDS and the PTB were virtually emasculated by internal divisions and disaffections. New political leaders had emerged, and new priorities and objectives were waiting to be discovered—Brazil had changed profoundly during the twenty years of military control. Economic development, particularly industrialization, had resulted in impressive gains for the country. But the living standards for most Brazilians had not undergone the same impressive changes, and the country faced a serious international financial crisis. The Third Republic, like its predecessors, began without an established, institutionalized party system or a genuinely national leadership.

The task of building and institutionalizing effective national parties in Brazil was hampered by the country's size and diversity. Regional interests and identifications, personalism, and an emerging populism presented a challenge to the process of institutionalization. In addition, the ease and regularity with which the regimes manipulated party activity through the electoral systems also obstructed party growth and stabilization. Most regimes in Latin America have used their electoral systems either to ensure tolerable results from elections or to preclude intolerable ones, but none have done so as regularly, effectively, or blatantly as regimes in Brazil.

Electoral Systems

The Brazilian electoral systems have been manipulated historically by regimes for explicit political objectives and short-term advantage, using controls over enfranchisement, voting procedures, and formulas for representation. Electoral processes have expanded to include a greater number of persons and a greater variety of interests, but there have been many deviations from this pattern, particularly during the recent military period. Issues concerning the electoral system have become politicized in Brazil, in ways not characteristic of other Latin American countries.

At the time of independence, enfranchisement was highly restricted and controlled. Women, slaves, illiterates, those who could not meet rigid property requirements, and those under twenty-one years of age were all excluded. Few persons could vote. In 1881 Brazil had a population of approximately 16,000,000 persons, and only 145,000 were eligible to vote. The property requirement was dropped relatively early but was replaced by a minimum income requirement. In 1891 all literate males over the age of twenty-one were enfranchised, leaving women, illiterates, and "beggars" excluded. In 1933 the right to vote was expanded to include women, and the voting age was lowered to eighteen. Illiterate citizens, who at the time composed the majority of the population, were still ineligible. The constitution of the Second Republic in 1945 continued to deny the franchise to illiterate Brazilians, although by that time literacy levels were beginning to rise substantially. The literacy requirement was not dropped until May 1985, allowing all Brazilians who met the age requirement to vote.

The level of those registered to vote since 1945 has risen steadily (Table 16.3), particularly during the past decade. Several factors account for this: increased political awareness and social mobilization; higher levels of literacy; greater urbanization; a somewhat older median age of the population, caused by declining growth rates; and, of course, the enfranchisement of illiterates. Voter turnout has been high for most elections since 1945, even for contests whose outcomes were not in doubt. These participation levels, together with the potentially high levels of political awareness and communications, clearly demonstrate that Brazil has arrived at the point of the genuinely mass politics.

Brazilian politics has long been preoccupied with how to conceptualize and structure national representation and, then, how to manage its political consequences. The Brazilian electoral systems have been subject to explicit controls, efforts to structure the impact of regionalism, and increasing levels of mass participation in elections. Controls have been so extensive and so obvious that electoral results have often seemed unconvincing or illegitimate. The military period was especially characterized by manipulation, which included both the electoral system and the parties. The range of experimentation is impressive. Brazil has tried almost every conceivable type of electoral control at one time or another. David Fleischer (1984) has already explored the subject in great detail, and we can only summarize some of the major experiments here.

Through 1842 Brazil used indirect, multistage elections, with deputies allocated at-large for the states. In 1855 a single-member-district plan was used, which was changed in 1860 to a multimember plan. In 1875, through

TABLE 16.3
Voter Participation in Brazilian National Elections, 1945-1986 (in percentages)

	Population Registered	Registered Voting	Population Voting
1945	16	83	13
1950	22	72	16
1954	27	66	17
1958	22	92	20
1962	25	80	20
1963	24	66	16
1966	27	77	19
1970	31	81	24
1974	34	80	27
1978	40	82	33
1982	48	83	44
1986	54	86	47

Sources: Adapted from Henry Wells, ed., Brazil: Election Factbook, September 1965 (Washington, DC: Institute for the Comparative Study of Political Systems, 1965), p. 19, and official Brazilian electoral results compiled by the Tribunal Superior Eleitoral (Brasília), 1966-1986.

the efforts of the Conservative party, a system of proportional representation was implemented, although it was limited to only two-thirds of those elected; the remaining third was assigned to the party with a plurality in each state. Representation at the time was based not on population but on eligibility, which had regional political implications. The single-member-district plan was reestablished.

When Vargas took power, a new electoral system was devised, using a two-stage system of proportional representation, electoral quotients, and simple majorities. In order to guarantee government control over the outcome of elections, Vargas imposed a form of "functional representation," which reserved one-third of the seats for "election" by organized interest groups, such as professional, labor, employer, and public-employee organizations. After the proclamation of the Estado Novo, no elections were held.

With the advent of the Second Republic in 1945, the electoral system was once again changed, this time to proportional representation. The upper chamber of the legislature was elected by simple majority vote with two senators for each state. The original proportional representation system of 1945 was based on population rather than on eligible voters, but was bracketed to restrain proportionality from one state to another. In 1950 the d'Hondt system of proportional representation was adopted, using an electoral quotient to distribute the "remainder" votes to provide representation for smaller parties. However, a cutoff was employed: below 5 percent no party could receive representation, thereby excluding the smallest of the minor parties from legislative representation.

A "complete" list system was used during the Second Republic in which parties could submit candidates equal to the number of representatives to be elected. Independent lists were not permitted. Prior to 1962 there was no official ballot for the elections; afterward, candidates were grouped by similar numbers (as in the Uruguayan system), which would allow a voter to know by number (if not by name) which party a candidate belonged to. Voters had the option of voting either for a specific candidate (more precisely, a specific "number") or of casting a party-list ballot, in which case the vote counted toward representation in the hierarchy provided by the party list. In theory, this complex procedure combined a "closed" and "open" list ballot, but in practice few, less than 1 percent, of the votes cast were by party.

The military regime tried, mostly in vain, to control civilian influence through electoral laws. They retained the d'Hondt proportional representation system but imposed an artificial two-party system on it. The regime also established a "sub-legenda" device for the majority offices (senators and mayors) similar to Uruguay's sub-lema system: multiple candidates for the major party (ARENA) could sum their votes for the entire group, with the one receiving the largest vote winning the office. As in Uruguay, this meant that the winner might actually have received fewer votes than the candidate of the opposition, depending on how many candidates ran from each of the two parties and on the total vote cast for each.

In the early 1970s the military government changed the basis for calculating representation from total population to the size of the electorate, while reducing the size of the lower house from 409 to 310 deputies. The authorities staggered local, state, and national legislative elections in an effort to separate regional from national political issues. Finally, in an effort to destroy any possibility of coalitions between members of parties that had been abolished in 1966, the regime established a system of "tied balloting," in which voters had to select the same party for state and federal deputies.

By 1974 the military took limited steps to liberalize the electoral system. But when the opposition benefited in the 1974 elections, the military retreated and again tried to distort the system to benefit the ARENA. The government shifted the indirect election of governors from the legislature to an electoral college, which by virtue of its composition could be controlled by ARENA. It decreed that one of the two senators for each state would be elected in 1978 "indirectly" by state electoral colleges; these individuals soon became known as "bionic senators." The sub-legenda device was used for the remaining Senate seats. Finally, state representation, which had previously been keyed to the size of the electorate, was now keyed to the total population size on the assumption that this would increase representation for the northern states, which were voting more strongly for ARENA. For a multitude of reasons, the regime's efforts to manipulate the system failed to achieve the intended results.

By 1979 the military government began another series of liberalization measures, and by the end of the year political parties were again free to organize and the two artificial parties were abolished. In November 1981 a new series of electoral changes were approved. These included straight party voting (*voto vinculado*); the prohibition of alliances and coalitions; postponement of minimum-vote thresholds to encourage smaller parties until after the 1986 elections; an increase in the size of the Chamber of Deputies from 420 to 479; and a mixed electoral system—both single-member plurality and proportional—for the 1986 elections. The military proposal included a provision for dividing each federal district into two state districts. The intention was that about two-thirds of the state legislative deputies would be elected through plurality districts and about one-third through proportional districts.

The military regime's complex and largely counterproductive efforts to manipulate civilian politics by fine-tuning the electoral system to its advantage was based on two principal objectives: (1) to control the surge of populist party politics that had emerged in the 1960s and (2) to maintain the appearance of democratic processes while obtaining favorable electoral results and thus lend legitimacy to the regime (Fleischer, 1986). Neither objective was achieved. All that remained was a complex electoral system that lacked credibility.

Elections and Voting

It is almost impossible to discern long-term trends in Brazilian voting. Party organization and competition have changed profoundly over the past half-century, and regimes have been short lived. Each period was so different and so largely unrelated that any trends are elusive. Soares has suggested in his recent study (1986:281) a decline in "conservatism" in Brazilian party voting, but this is subject to qualification and argument. Perhaps the most that can be concluded about Brazilian voting patterns is that they have been regional, that personalism tends to overwhelm national presidential elections, and that party allegiances are weak and poorly defined.

Only four presidents have come to power in Brazil since 1945 by direct election: Eurico Dutra (PSD) in 1945, Getúlio Vargas (PTB) in 1950, Juscelino Kubitschek (PSD/PTB) in 1955, and Jânio Quadros (UDN) in 1960. During the military period presidents were selected (theoretically, at least) by either an electoral college or the legislature. Tancredo Neves was elected in 1985 by an electoral college (his vice-presidential running mate, José Sarney, succeeded him later that year). Dutra was selected by the Vargas-organized PSD party, Vargas himself ran and was elected, and Kubitschek was regarded at the time as Vargas's successor. In 1955 the two Vargas parties (PSD and PTB) pooled their resources to elect Kubitschek, which they barely did; in 1960 the UDN candidate won. The voting by party for these elections, 1945–1960, is shown in Table 16.4. Vargas's influence was apparently eroding, largely to the benefit of the UDN. But presidential campaigning was based

TABLE 16.4
Brazilian Presidential Voting, 1945-1960 (in percentages)

	1945	1950	1955	1960
PSD	55	22	36^a	33^a
PTB		49		
UDN	35	30	30	48
PSP			26	19
Other	10	0	8	0

^{a}PSD and PTB endorsed same candidate.

Source: Adapted from Henry Wells, ed., Brazil: Election Factbook, September 1965 (Washington, DC: Institute for the Comparative Study of Political Systems, 1965), pp. 56-57.

TABLE 16.5
Brazilian Congressional Elections: Popular Vote by Party, 1945-1962 (in percentages)

	PSD	PTB	UDN	Other	Alliances	Blank	$Total^a$	$Index^b$
1945	42	10	26	20	0	1	99	.635
1950	22	14	14	16	17	18	101	.767
1954	22	15	14	19	26	5	101	.772
1958	18	15	13	13	33	8	100	.778
1962	16	12	11	5	41	15	100	.780

^{a}Percentages do not add to 100 because of rounding.
^{b}Rae fractionalization index.

Source: Adapted from Kenneth Ruddle and Philip Gillette, eds., Latin American Political Statistics (Los Angeles, CA: Latin American Center, 1972), pp. 73-74.

as much on the personalities of the candidates as it was on their party affiliations.

If one looks at the popular vote in elections during the Second Republic, several trends are immediately apparent. The vote for the PSD steadily declined from 42 percent to 16 percent. The vote for the PTB fluctuated (rising modestly), and the vote for the UDN generally declined. During the same period the vote for small parties declined slightly, but voting for party alliances increased dramatically. There was also an increasing tendency for party voting to fragment (Table 16.5), a pattern that could be attributed to (1) the failure of the principal parties to expand their appeals (requiring alliances between them to win) or (2) to voter disaffection with the principal parties in favor of either new, smaller parties or blank voting.

The PDS vote declined significantly in the 1980s, which may be attributed to its close identification with the Brazilian military and the ARENA. But it is also true that the PDS was highly skewed in favor of the more

TABLE 16.6
Age Distribution of Brazilian Legislators Elected in 1986

	Number	Percentage
Under 30	23	4
31–40	102	18
41–50	239	43
51–60	136	24
Over 60	59	11
Total	559	100

Source: Adapted from data published by Folha de São Paulo (São Paulo, January 19, 1987), pp. B5–7.

conservative regions of the country and that those regions exerted a disproportionate influence on the organization. Soares points out (1986:289–290) the unrepresentativeness of the PDS national convention in which it nominated its 1985 presidential candidate. Delegates varied by state from 1 for every 417,000 inhabitants in the industrial state of São Paulo to 1 for every 6,000 inhabitants in the rural, politically traditional state of Roraima; in general, the smaller, more traditional, rural, less economically advanced states were overrepresented. These states in turn were controlled by more conservative political interests. The two candidates selected by the party for the presidential and vice-presidential nominations, Paulo Maluf and Mário Andreazza, were actively disliked by many Brazilians (1986:290), and their victory over more popular candidates such as Aureliano Chaves sealed the party's defeat in the 1985 election.

The decline of the PDS continued to accelerate with the unexpectedly large vote for the PMDB and PFL candidates in the 1986 legislative election, the results of which suggest the possibility of further changes in Brazilian politics: the entrance of a new generation, or at least a new group, of leaders and politicians. Of the 550 candidates elected to the legislature, 320 (57 percent) were candidates who had never before held legislative office. Only 189 (33 percent) were former deputies, and the remainder were either deputies who had been out of office at the time of the election or senators who chose to run for the new assembly. The members of the new legislature (Table 16.6) are remarkably young. Twenty-two percent are younger than forty-one, and 64 percent are under fifty-one years of age; only 10 percent are older than sixty. Most of the legislators have spent much if not all their adult lives living under military rule in Brazil. By age and previous political experience, it would seem a new group of politicians may be coming to power in Brazil—at least based on the results of the 1986 elections.

Given the volatility and the external controls over Brazilian party politics over the past several decades, little if anything generic can be ascertained about the relationships between public opinion and party preferences. Indeed, the difficulties of polling during the military period precluded most serious research in the first place. Polls regarding presidential preferences for the 1985 election, reported by *Jornal do Brazil* and reproduced by Soares (1986:286), suggest the volatility of Brazilian opinion and the importance of personalism. As support for the PDS declined during the 1980s, regional patterns in Brazilian party voting also fell, although it is not clear that this change is permanent.

Brazil's redemocratization took more than a decade. During that time three legislative elections were held (1974, 1978, and 1982), and an indirect election for the presidency took place through an electoral college (1985). The first truly open election was that for the legislature in 1986. Since the imposition of military rule in 1964, Brazil has undergone many changes (Selcher: 1986). New parties have emerged and, in the case of the PFL, have had a major impact very quickly on the nation's politics. The MDB succeeded in transforming itself into the PMDB to become, for the moment at least, the predominant party in the country. In the process, however, as a result of its alliance with the PFL, it underwent continual changes in leadership. The former ARENA leaders and their military supporters seem to have failed to convert the ARENA party into a viable new party, the PDS. The PDS, whose name is so reminiscent of the defunct PSD, lost ground even faster than the latter had following the dictatorship from which it emerged in 1946. At least among the major party participants in the 1980s, Brazilian politics seems no more ideological than before, nor more clearly defined.

The most powerful issue—the one that helped elect Neves and Sarney in 1985 and the PMDB/PFL candidates in 1986—was the redemocratization of Brazil; opposition to any continuing influence by the military was a related issue. Together, they overwhelmed even the traditional regional divisions in the country. Yet, there are unmistakable signs of the continuing interest and involvement of the Brazilian military in politics. The only persistent characteristic of Brazilian party politics that survived the military dictatorship and the process of redemocratization was the transcendant influence of personalities. Voting patterns in the 1980s suggest that public reaction to the parties is in flux, lacking any firm commitments or identifications. Divisions based on states and regions, on class, on local political machines remain, as does the historical legacy of the experiments conducted under Vargas, the Second Republic, and the military regime. Brazil has once again instituted party politics, as it did in 1889, 1930, 1945, and 1964.

After nineteen months of congressional debate, a new constitution for Brazil was promulgated on October 5, 1988. It is a lengthy and complex document, containing 245 articles. Efforts to establish a parliamentary system of government had failed, as had efforts to limit the presidential term to four years. The new constitution permits the direct election of both the congress and the president and establishes a five-year term for the president. The voting age is lowered to sixteen, presidential decree laws have been abolished, and in general greater powers are assigned to the congress.

National elections are scheduled to be held in November 1989, with a new government to be inaugurated in March 1990. Whatever else the new constitution may achieve, its provisions should ensure a vital role for parties in Brazil's political future as long as democratic politics prevails.

Long-Term Trends

Perhaps the most striking quality of Brazilian party politics has been its lack of institutionalization, its weak national organizations, and its ineffective control. Organization has resided primarily at the state level and in the great cities that dominate the country demographically. National parties have therefore often been fragile and transient coalitions of organizations and leaders. National control has also depended on coalitions that, during the Second Republic, brought together at state levels national parties that had no common principles or political objectives, coalitions whose component parties were often at odds from one state to another.

But one can make a more positive interpretation of the Brazilian party experience. The very volatility of its politics—the unreliability of its electoral partisanship and voting dispositions—have made Brazilian party politics flexible, perhaps to a fault. It has not had to contend with intransigent parties sustained by deeply ingrained traditions, as have Colombia and Uruguay. Brazilian politics has also not been traumatized by a single influence, such as Peronism in Argentina or the Mexican revolution—forces that can transfix national politics long after their importance has been eclipsed by new realities. It has not been divided by major ideological confrontations, such as those in Chile, nor has it experienced a long history of self-serving dictatorships. Unfortunately, Brazil has also not experienced a political evolution, nor has it accumulated any democratic traditions over the years. These may eventually evolve, but there is no experience so far to suggest that they will.

If democratic party politics is allowed to continue in Brazil, old tendencies—including regionalism, class divisions, local party machines, and the continuing vacillations of political leaders—may again come to dominate the country. New issues, particularly those related to economic equity, may also surface and serve to restructure party politics in Brazil. It is difficult to imagine how so large and economically dynamic a country can long sustain a commitment to democracy without some considerable evolution in its party politics.

References

Cortes, Carlos. 1974. *Gaucho Politics in Brazil*. Albuquerque: Univ. of New Mexico Press.

Burns, Bradford. 1968. *Nationalism in Brazil*. New York: Praeger.

Dean, Warren. 1969. *The Industrialization of São Paulo, 1880–1945*. Austin: Univ. of Texas Press.

Erickson, Kenneth P. 1985. Brazil: Corporative Authoritarianism, Democratization, and Dependency. In Howard J. Wiarda and Harvey F. Kline, eds., *Latin American Politics and Development*. Boulder, CO: Westview.

Fleischer, David. 1984. Constitutional and Electoral Engineering in Brazil, A Double-Edge Sword. *Inter-American Economic Affairs* 37:3–36.

————. 1986. Brazil at the Crossroads: The Elections of 1982 and 1985. In Paul W. Drake and Eduardo Silva, eds., *Elections and Democratization in Latin America, 1980–1985*. San Diego: Univ. of California, San Diego.

Graham, Richard. 1968. *Britain and the Outset of Modernization in Brazil, 1850–1914*. London: Cambridge Univ. Press.

Levine, Robert M. 1970. *The Vargas Regime: The Critical Years, 1934–1938*. New York: Columbia Univ. Press.

Parker, Phyllis R. 1979. *Brazil and the Quiet Intervention, 1964*. Austin: Univ. of Texas Press.

Roett, Riordan. 1978. *Brazil: Politics in a Patrimonial Society*. New York: Praeger.

Schmitter, Philippe C. 1971. *Interest Conflict and Political Change in Brazil*. Stanford, CA: Stanford Univ. Press.

Selcher, Wayne. 1986. *Political Liberalization in Brazil*. Boulder, CO: Westview.

Skidmore, Thomas E. 1967. *Politics in Brazil, 1930–1964: An Experiment in Democracy*. New York: Oxford Univ. Press.

Soares, Gaucio Ary Dillon. 1967. The Politics of Uneven Development: The Case of Brazil. In Seymour M. Lipset and Stein Rokkan, eds., *Party Systems and Voter Alignments: Cross-National Perspectives*. New York: Free Press.

————. 1986. Elections and the Redemocratization of Brazil. In Paul W. Drake and Eduardo Silva, eds., *Elections and Democratization in Latin America, 1980–1985*. San Diego: Univ. of California, San Diego.

Stepan, Alfred. 1971. *The Military in Politics: Changing Patterns in Brazil*. Princeton, NJ: Princeton Univ. Press.

Wesson, Robert, and David Fleischer, eds. 1983. *Brazil in Transition*. New York: Praeger.

Young, Jordan. 1982. Brazil. In Robert J. Alexander, ed., *Political Parties of the Americas*. Westport, CT: Greenwood.

17

GUATEMALA

Guatemala has been ruled by a succession of military strongmen throughout most of its history. Mass political participation has been discouraged
and democratic elections have been rare. Not surprisingly, political parties
have played only a peripheral role in the nation's political life. During the
late 1940s and early 1950s, reformist president Juan José Arévalo and his
successor, Col. Jacobo Arbenz, broke conservative tradition by mobilizing
the Guatemalan popular sector into new political organizations supportive
of fundamental socioeconomic change. However, after the U.S.-orchestrated
coup in 1954, which ousted Arbenz, the Guatemalan military and private
sector demobilized these political groups and suppressed new threats to
their privileges by violence.

The military officers who have dominated Guatemala since 1954 have
disguised their regime with a facade of regular multiparty elections. A
number of personalist political parties representing rightist and center-right
groups have competed in these contests; leftist parties are excluded. Centrist
parties, such as the Christian Democrats, have been permitted to participate
but have often been defrauded by the authorities. The extreme repression
of the late 1970s and early 1980s, in addition to the unbridled corruption
of the army clique then in office, finally convinced more moderate military
elements to seize power in order to set in motion a transition to civilian
government. In 1985 Christian Democrat Vinicio Cerezo Arévalo became
the first democratically elected civilian president in two decades, although
the armed forces severely restricted his range of action. Whether political
parties and elections can truly become significant factors in Guatemalan
politics still remains to be seen.

The Evolution and Context of
Guatemalan Party Politics

Before 1944 Guatemala's history as an independent nation was dominated
by four dictators, each of whom had at least some connection to a political

party. The first of these autocrats was José Rafael Carrera (1837–1865), who established himself in power after leading the pro-church Conservative party in an uprising against its rival, the Liberal party. Soon after the anticlerical Liberals ousted Carrera's successor in 1871, a new strongman, Justo Rufino Barrios (1873–1885), assumed control. As competition among Guatemalan upper-class factions became concentrated within the loosely structured Liberal party, the Conservative party ceased to be an important political force. After Barrios's death, elite power struggles were sometimes settled by relatively fair electoral contests between Liberals, although few Guatemalans were permitted to vote (Black and Needler, 1983:17). Conflicts within the Liberal party ultimately produced a particularly brutal dictatorship under Manuel Estrada Cabrera (1898–1920).

Opponents of the Cabrera regime and its system of fixed elections organized the Unionist party. Some military officers were involved in this opposition, and after the erratic dictator was deposed, three generals in succession were elected to the presidency. The last of these presidents, upper-class Unionist Jorge Ubico, constructed yet another personalist dictatorship (1931–1944) and suppressed all political dissent. None of the poorly organized and narrowly based Guatemalan parties that figured in pre-1931 politics were able to survive the Ubico era.

With the exception of a small Communist party, the party system that developed after Ubico was overthrown in 1944 was composed of entirely new political parties. Three urban-based parties—the moderate National Renovation party (PRN), the more radical Revolutionary Action party (PAR), in which Communist activists participated, and the student-led Popular Liberation Front (FPL)—joined reformist army officers in backing Social Democrat Juan José Arévalo in the 1945 elections. With this broad base of support, Arévalo succeeded in winning 85 percent of the vote from a vastly expanded electorate. The new president instituted urban-oriented reforms and became the first chief executive in Guatemalan history to encourage unionization and party activity involving the mass population. Arévalo's reformist policies and the more radical opinions of his defense minister, Col. Jacabo Arbenz (whom Arévalo later supported as his successor), generated fierce opposition in both civilian and military circles.

In the 1950 elections, Arbenz was backed by the parties that had endorsed Arévalo in 1945 (PRN, PAR, FPL) as well as by the more openly active Guatemalan Communist party and the newly formed Revolutionary party of National Union (PRUN). He was opposed by Gen. Miguel Ydígoras, a conservative candidate of the Anti-Communist Unification party (PUA), and José García Granados, a moderate who represented a hastily created People's party (PP). Arbenz's victory, with 65 percent of the vote, was marred by government interference in the electoral process, but most analysts believe the colonel was popular enough to win in any case (Woodward, 1976:232; Anderson, 1982:22).

By 1952 Arbenz had merged most of the parties in his electoral coalition into a single official organization, the party of the Guatemalan Revolution

(PRG). The Communist party, now called the Guatemalan Labor party (PGT), remained an independent source of regime support. Concerned that the formation of the broad-based PRG might reduce their influence, however, the Communists sowed dissension in the new government party, which led to the withdrawal of the Revolutionary Action party (PAR) component from the PRG (Sánchez, 1982:427). Yet, in spite of their differences, the three parties (PRG, PAR, PGT) were united behind Arbenz's land-reform program and his efforts to organize the rural population. Each of the progovernment parties also favored the president's concerted action to reduce North American economic and political influence in Guatemala. Understandably, these measures shocked the landed oligarchy and the U.S. government and worried the moderate officers Arbenz had not been able to purge. When a small, CIA-sponsored right-wing exile group invaded the country to depose Arbenz in 1954, the military refused to defend him.

The Guatemalan party system changed dramatically after 1954. Upon taking power, Castillo Armas, who had led the coup, brutally repressed all parties, unions, and peasant organizations that had been associated with the Arbenz regime. In the years following this violent political demobilization, the Guatemalan military and its private-sector allies constructed a "sanitized" party system restricted to political groups that would not threaten the traditional order. The four most important parties in this artificial system (which continue to be active today) were formed during the first dozen years following the ouster of Arbenz.

Castillo Armas organized a right-wing government party in the mid-1950s, which evolved into the National Liberation movement (MLN). In the late 1950s, reformist politicians were permitted to coalesce into a moderate Revolutionary party (PR), which favored the Arévalo era's social and political reforms but opposed communism. Later, during a period of direct military rule (1963–1966), chief of state Col. Enrique Peralta Azurdia created a military-controlled party loosely modeled on Mexico's PRI; it was called the Institutional Democratic party (PID). The PID enlisted much of the government bureaucracy and offered a somewhat less reactionary brand of conservatism than did the MLN. The fourth party in the system was the Christian Democratic party (DCG), founded by conservative Catholic businessmen in 1955. By the time it was legalized in 1966, however, the DCG had developed a center-reformist image.

Confident of the PID's strength, the military conducted the 1966 presidential election without major electoral fraud. It was soundly defeated by Revolutionary party nominee Julio César Méndez Montenegro, the only civilian president to serve during the entire 1955–1985 period. However, in order to take office, Méndez was forced to agree not to interfere in the army's internal affairs or in its extensive counterinsurgency activities. Indeed, during his term (1966–1970) human-rights conditions deteriorated as military forces under Col. Carlos Arana Osorio began to arm the infamous MLN antiguerrilla vigilante groups. The army's counterinsurgency program was highly successful. In 1970 the military-directed PID and right-wing MLN agreed to form an electoral coalition to support Arana for the presidency. Campaigning on a law-and-order platform, the colonel was able to capture a 43 percent plurality over candidates running for the PR and the DCG.

The Guatemalan officer corps continued to rule behind this facade of electoral democracy during the 1970s and early 1980s. Except for the Christian Democrats, all of the parties authorized to participate in elections represented military and private-sector factions. Although animosities among rightist party leaders and political clans sometimes ran deep, they all supported the existing political framework. Even the so-called Revolutionary party (PR) fell under the sway of conservative interests, causing many of its reformist members to defect to form left-of-center splinter parties. These and other leftist parties, however, were excluded from electoral competition. The moderate Christian Democrats were permitted to present candidates opposed to the regime, but the government relied on electoral fraud when necessary to prevent the DCG from winning power. In 1974, for example, the Christian Democratic candidate, retired general Efraín Ríos Montt, apparently won the presidential race, but the military imposed its own choice, Gen. Kjell Laugerud García, who had been endorsed by the PID, MLN, and the outgoing president's newly formed personalist party, the Organized Aranista Center (CAO).

After taking office, Laugerud García attempted briefly to move the PID closer to the political center by distancing the party from its more reactionary electoral ally, the MLN, and by cooperating more closely with the PR. The Laugerud government also tolerated greater organizational activity by opposition parties and unions. However, by 1977 this liberalization experiment was cut short when widening popular organization and a revived guerrilla threat convinced the military that it was losing command of the situation. The 1978 elections, in which only 40 percent of the electorate bothered to vote, were manipulated by the authorities so as to give victory to Gen. Fernando Romeo Lucas García, the candidate backed by the PID, PR, and the Aranistas (whose party was now officially renamed the Authentic Nationalist Center [CAN]). The MLN won the largest number of congressional seats (MLN, 20; PID, 17; PR, 14; DCG, 11; CAN, 3) but remained outside of the military-constructed coalition, claiming that its presidential candidate had been defrauded (Anderson, 1982:32–33). The candidate sponsored by the Christian Democrats and PR dissidents ran a poor third.

Corruption and state-sponsored violence reached new extremes under General Lucas García (1978–1982). The president and his inner circle took gross advantage of national-development projects to enrich themselves, alienating many members of the normally progovernment business community. At the same time, the government launched an all-out attack on opposition groups, including those of the moderate center. The national leaders of the excluded political parties on the center-left, the Democratic Socialist party (PSD) and the United Revolutionary Front (FUR), were assassinated by death squads linked to the security forces; PSD and FUR activists were forced to go underground. Trade unionists, faculty and students of the University of San Carlos, and Christian Democrats were also singled out by death squads. In addition, as the leftist guerrillas began to find increasing support in traditionally passive Indian villages (which account for roughly half the nation's total population), the armed forces unleashed massive assaults on areas suspected of guerrilla sympathies. Conservative estimates put the total death toll from political violence attributable to the Lucas García government at more than fifty thousand.

As conditions worsened, the nation's once lucrative tourist trade dried up and foreign financing became difficult to attract. Angered by the government's corruption and by its incompetence in both the economic and counterinsurgency spheres, a group of younger officers ousted Lucas García shortly after he held a fraudulent presidential election in 1982. Official corruption and political killings in urban areas began to decline under former DCG presidential candidate Efraín Ríos Montt, who was placed in power by the coup leaders. But the rural counterinsurgency campaign continued to accelerate, and little progress toward the restoration of civilian authority was achieved. After the controversial former general (a fervent evangelical Protestant) was removed in another internal coup in 1983 and replaced with defense minister Gen. Oscar Humberto Mejía Victores, a transition to formal civilian control was finally set in motion. The dominant military factions apparently decided to allow the election of a new civilian government in order to (1) secure desperately needed economic assistance and military aid from the United States; (2) restore a measure of legitimacy to the discredited government; and (3) disassociate the army from the nation's severe economic problems.

In 1984 a constituent assembly was elected to draft a new constitution and electoral law. Seventeen political parties participated in the election, with the Christian Democrats, an MLN-CAN coalition, and a new center-right party, the National Center Union (UCN), earning the most votes. The following year, however, the Christian Democrats won both the congressional and the presidential elections by impressive margins. In January 1986, DCG leader Vinicio Cerezo was inaugurated as the first civilian president of Guatemala since Méndez Montenegro.

Upon taking office, the new Christian Democratic president assumed extensive formal governmental powers. He took advantage of the chief executive's broad appointment prerogatives to staff the government with loyal allies. He also used his party's control of the unicameral congress to ensure both the selection of a friendly Supreme Court and favorable treatment of his legislative program. The inexperienced civilian government could generally count on the support of several additional political forces. The Christian Democrats maintained good relations with other moderate political parties, and as labor unions gradually reemerged, they too favored the civilian regime (although the unions increasingly criticized the DCG government in the late 1980s for its failure to enact meaningful socioeconomic reforms). In addition, most analysts regarded the Guatemalan Catholic church and the U.S. government as strong supporters of the Christian Democrats.

Nevertheless, the Christian Democrats's actual ability to change traditional public policy and to respond to the demands of its popular constituency was very limited. The most important players in Guatemalan politics are still the military and private-sector factions that have dominated political life since 1954. Many of these groups maintain ties to right-wing or center-right political parties for the purpose of participating in electoral politics, but their real power is based in financial and/or military strength, not in votes. Although often at odds with one another, these groups are united in their opposition to fundamental socioeconomic reforms, investigations of human rights abuses, and civilian government interference in the armed forces or in business activities. Consequently, Cerezo's government largely avoided controversial programs opposed by the country's traditional power structure and concentrated instead on solidifying the fragile democratic process and pursuing foreign policy initiatives designed to increase economic assistance. Nevertheless, several attempted coups by right-wing military and civilian factions threatened the DCG government in 1987 and 1988.

The Guatemalan army is the most powerful political force in the country. Since the 1950s, the armed forces high command has made or approved all important governmental decisions. However, the army has never been a monolithic institution; its positions on public policy are the products of negotiations among the various factions of the officer corps. Although the military exercises less overt control over public decisionmaking now that the Christian Democrats hold office, its senior officers are able to restrict the range of permissible government action. In addition, the 1985 constitution explicitly recognizes the military's continued authority in rural Guatemala by preserving the counterinsurgency program, including the army-supervised model villages (Trudeau and Schoultz, 1986:41; Handy, 1986:407–408).

The Guatemalan private sector is also critical of the Christian Democratic government, but it has also had increasing frictions with the armed forces in recent years. During the 1970s and 1980s, the military became a major economic force in its own right by acquiring ownership of many business enterprises. The army's encroachment into the economic sphere, in addition to high levels of military corruption, was resented by most Guatemalan business leaders. In addition, private-sector interests were damaged by Guatemala's deteriorating international image. The Guatemalan business community therefore provisionally supported the return to civilian government in hopes of improving the economy and of increasing its influence at the expense of the army.

The diverse Guatemalan private sector encompasses a variety of interest groups that represent different branches of economic activity and powerful competing entrepreneurial "clans" (e.g., Sandoval, García Granados, Arana), which, in turn, are linked to the conservative parties (Anderson, 1982:35–36). The most important voice of Guatemalan business as a whole is the Coordinating Committee of Agricultural, Commercial, Industrial, and Financial Associations (CACIF). The passage by the Cerezo government of a very limited tax reform in 1987 aroused intense opposition from the CACIF.

Guatemala's formal democratic institutions have existed for far too short a time to alter the traditional character of the country's politics. Competitive multiparty elections have put a Christian Democratic civilian government in office, but it has left the army in power. In time, elements in both the private sector and the military may be prepared to let civilian governments have more latitude, but it is too early to speculate on such an outcome now. The obstacles to a successful democratic transition are formidable.

Contemporary Political Parties

The vast majority of Guatemalan political parties are personalist electoral vehicles that possess neither permanent organizational structures nor coherent strategies for governing. Most of the parties that now compose the emerging Guatemalan multiparty system were active during the 1970s, and additional parties have been formed since the transition to civilian government. In this context, the governing Christian Democrats have become Guatemala's most important political party.

In contrast to most of the country's other parties, the centrist DCG offers a fully elaborated reform program based on progressive Catholic social doctrine and possesses a reasonably large grass-roots organization. The party's immediate priority is the establishment of stable liberal democratic institutions and the rule of law. Longer-term goals include land reform and the reduction of military influence. Factional divisions based on policy and/ or personalism have troubled the party since its inception. At present, the dominant party faction is headed by President Cerezo; a small faction of more left-oriented Christian Democrats formed a dissident group with some Social Democrats in 1985 but continued to endorse the DCG presidential candidate. The DCG's mass support is concentrated in the urban middle class and in the rural peasantry. In the 1985 congressional elections, these groups helped the party to win a 39 percent plurality of the valid votes, twice the support that its closest competitor received. Results from the 1988 municipal elections further indicated that the DCG had retained its dominant position in the party system despite the difficulties of the Cerezo administration's initial two years. The party won in 140 of 271 municipalities (51.7 pecent).

The second-largest party (20 percent of the congressional vote) is the National Center Union (UCN), a center-right party formed in the early 1980s to promote the political fortunes of Jorge Carpio Nicolle, the wealthy publisher of Guatemala City's *El Gráfico*. The UCN was the best-financed party in the 1985 elections and employed the most advanced U.S.-style mass-media campaign (Booth et al., 1985:50). The strongly pro–free enterprise party has been able to attract adherents well beyond its initial base in Guatemala City. Since President Cerezo's inauguration, the UCN, through *El Gráfico*, has been the DCG government's most important critic; it has also concentrated on building up its organization. However, it finished a poor second to the DCG in the 1988 municipal elections, winning in 56 of 271 municipalities (20.7 percent).

The DCG and UCN together captured just under 60 percent of the electorate in 1985. At this time, none of the other political parties in the system has a popular following comparable to that of the Christian Democrats or the National Center Union. The Revolutionary party (PR), once led by reformist President Méndez Montenegro, was discredited by its collaboration with the Lucas García regime. More recently, the party has tried to disassociate itself from its rightist image by purging corrupt party boss Jorge García Granados and by forming an electoral alliance with the more progressive Democratic Party of National Cooperation (PDCN). The PDCN was founded in 1983 by Jorge Serrano Elías, a prominent evangelical Protestant who formerly headed President Ríos Montt's advisory Council of State. The small PDCN attempted to integrate the members of a national cooperative movement with Protestant voters, who now represent about a quarter of the Guatemalan population. The PR-PDCN coalition campaigned on a centrist platform with Serrano Elías as its presidential candidate and finished third in the 1985 race with 14 percent of the vote. Not long after the election, however, PDCN leader Serrano Elías withdrew from the party to form a new electoral vehicle for himself, the Solidarity Action movement (MAS).

The three principal parties of the post-1954 Guatemalan right wing—the National Liberation Movement (MLN), the Institutional Democratic party (PID), and the Authentic Nationalist Center (CAN)—have all seen their roles decline in the party system of the 1980s. Led for decades by Mario Sandoval Alarcón (the powerful boss of the Sandoval political clan), the MLN persists in fervent opposition to social reform and continues to advocate the elimination of all "subversives." In foreign policy, the party backs the Nicaraguan *contras* and has called for the invasion of Belize. The National Liberation movement collects its strongest support from the conservative coffee, cotton, and sugar growers, and from traditional middle-class voters in eastern Guatemala (Booth et al., 1985:32). The MLN restored its old electoral alliance with the PID for the 1985 race and cried fraud when the coalition was credited with only 13 percent of the vote. The MLN's partner, the PID, has been weakened by its close ties to the armed forces and its reputation for opportunism. Essentially without a program, the party finds its greatest following among jobholders in the state bureaucracy. Both the MLN and PID have recently lost some militants to new conservative political combinations, such as the Organized Nationalist Unity (UNO). The future of the rightist CAN is also uncertain: the group obtained only 6 percent of the vote in 1985.

The last parties to emerge from the 1985 elections with legal status were the center-left Democratic Socialist party (PSD) and the center-right National Renewal party (PNR). Both parties fell one percentage point short of the 4 percent of the vote required for legalization, managing to maintain legal status only by electing at least one congressman. The Democratic Socialist party was founded in 1978 by PR dissidents, but its leadership has been decimated by the right-wing death squads. Many of the party's activists remain in exile, but one faction, under Mario Solórzano, returned to Guatemala to contest the 1985 election on a platform of thoroughgoing socioeconomic reform and foreign policy nonalignment. The PSD criticizes the Christian Democrats as too timid and stresses the similarities between the DCG and UCN. The Democratic Socialists' greatest following is in the capital, where the party also gained from the endorsement of the center-left United Revolutionary Front (FUR), which did not field candidates in 1985. Should democratic elections become institutionalized, however, the left-of-center PSD and FUN could well expand beyond this urban base.

The future of the National Renewal party, however, appears far less promising. The PNR, legalized in 1978, is a personalist group organized around the ambitions of Alejandro Maldonado Aguirre, a former MLN politician. Projecting a moderate conservative image intended to attract the urban middle and lower-middle classes, the PNR has cooperated at times with the Christian Democrats. The two parties endorsed Maldonado for the presidency in 1982 and ran a few joint candidates in the 1984 constituent assembly races. Previously backed by important industrialists, the PNR lost much of its private-sector funding in 1985 owing in part to its selection of an Indian as a vice-presidential candidate (Maldonado had earlier agreed to join the UCN's Jorge Carpio as his running mate [Booth et al., 1985:35]).

The only other parties to participate in the 1985 elections were three minor personalist groups: the Anti-Communist Unification party (PUA), the National Unity Front (FUN), and the Emergent Movement of Concord (MEC). They formed a right-wing electoral coalition in support of another former MLN politician.

The parties of the Guatemalan left have not participated in an election since the fall of the Arbenz government in 1954. Although Guatemala's new constitution does not prohibit Marxist political parties, none of the left-wing groups had enough faith in the electoral process to present candidates. The most important party on the left is Guatemala's orthodox Communist party—the Guatemalan Labor party (PGT). The Marxist-Leninist, pro-Soviet party appears to have some clandestine union support and maintains a guerrilla arm in the Rebel Armed Forces (FAR). The FAR is one of the smaller components of the four-part guerrilla coalition formed in 1981, the Guatemalan National Revolutionary Union (URNG).

Political Participation and Elections

It is difficult to arrive at any definitive judgments about Guatemalan public opinion. Years of state-sponsored violence have made most Guatemalans afraid of expressing any political views. In spite of the restoration of free elections, human-rights abuses have continued to be an unfortunate fact of life in Guatemala in the late 1980s. Moreover, the feared armed forces remain in full control of rural Guatemala and use civil patrols to "monitor" peasant behavior. Except for a small minority who joined guerrilla groups in the 1970s, the poor and largely illiterate Guatemalan rural Indian population has never really participated in politics.

In this climate of fear, the vast majority of Guatemalans avoid virtually all forms of political participation. Voting was made compulsory, however, by the outgoing military government for all literate citizens between the ages of eighteen and seventy (soldiers are ineligible). Turnout levels of registered voters were thus fairly high in both 1984 and 1985. Nonvoters were threatened with a fine and loss of travel-visa privileges, and the army ran newspaper ads equating abstention with treason. In the three elections held in 1984 and 1985, an average of 71 percent of those registered cast ballots: 78 percent in the constituent assembly elections, 69 percent in the general elections, and 65 percent in the presidential runoff.

Under the new electoral system, which began operation in 1985, Guatemalans concurrently elect a president and members of the unicameral National Congress once every five years. The president must be a civilian and is required to obtain a majority of votes cast. If necessary, a runoff election is held for the two candidates with the most votes; the president is ineligible for reelection. The National Congress is composed of one hundred members. Twenty-five members are chosen nationally at-large according to the d'Hondt proportional-representation formula, using a closed party list system. Seventy-five members are selected by proportional representation in the twenty-three departments. Each department has a minimum of two representatives, plus an additional one for every 100,000 residents (Booth et al., 1985:19). Congressional representatives must be civilians and may be reelected once after a five-year absence.

The electoral process is administered by the Supreme Electoral Tribunal (TSE), a five-member body that constitutes an independent fourth branch of the government. Its members are selected by the Supreme Court from a list of candidates nominated by the San Carlos University faculty. The TSE and its professional staff are responsible for promulgating election regulations, distributing election materials, overseeing balloting, hearing appeals of election-law violations, and tallying the official returns. Impartial observers of recent Guatemalan elections have praised the TSE's scrupulous conduct.

The 1984 constituent assembly elections were held to choose eighty-eight delegates to draft a new Guatemalan constitution. The Christian Democratic party (DCG) won the most votes (21 percent of valid ballots) in a field of seventeen parties; the newly formed National Center Union (UCN) came in second (18 percent). The conservative parties associated with past military regimes did less well than expected: a MLN-CAN coalition garnered 16 percent of the vote while the PR collected a 9.5 percent and the PID less than 7 percent. The moderately conservative National Renewal party (PNR) was the only other party to win an appreciable following (9 percent). Almost one-quarter of the voters cast invalid ballots, some perhaps in protest, others no doubt in confusion. Many Indian voters, most of whom are illiterate, were reported to have had difficulty comprehending the voting process (Booth et al., 1985:74).

In the 1984 elections, no candidate touched on dangerous issues such as military corruption or the need to punish past human-rights abuses

TABLE 17.1
Guatemalan Presidential (First Round) and Congressional Election Results by Party, 1985

	Valid Votes	Total(%)[a]	Seats in Congress[b]	
DCG	648,681	39	51	(11)
UNC	339,522	20	22	(5)
PDCN/PR	231,397	14	11	(4)
MLN/PID	210,806	13	12	(3)
CAN	105,473	6	1	(1)
PSD	57,362	3	2	(1)
PNR	52,941	3	1	(0)
PUA/FUN/MEC	32,118	2	0	(0)
Total	1,678,300	100	100	(25)

[a]Percentage of valid votes in round one of presidential elections; total votes cast equaled 1,906,952, of which 228,652 (12%) were invalid or blank.
[b]Number of seats elected on the national list by proportional representation (25 of 100 seats) shown in parentheses.

Sources: Adapted from Central America Report (November 8, 1985), p. 338, and (November 29, 1985), p. 365.

(Trudeau and Schoultz, 1986:42). The same self-censorship also prevailed in elections the following year, although some candidates became more outspoken during the final week of the campaign. In light of this inhibited political atmosphere, Booth et al. (1985:61–62) conclude that the 1985 contests, although free of fraud, cannot be regarded as wholly free elections. Within their self-imposed limitations, the competing parties carried on active, if old-fashioned, campaigns; e.g., mass rallies in Guatemala City and political caravans through the rest of the country. Television began to play a role: debates were televised, and the better-financed parties, particularly the UCN, conducted expensive mass-media campaigns.

The 1985 elections resulted in an impressive victory for the reformist Christian Democratic party and a clear rejection of the nation's extreme right-wing. In a field narrowed to twelve parties, the DCG greatly improved on its 1984 showing by winning nearly 40 percent of the valid vote and capturing a majority (fifty-one seats) in the National Congress (Table 17.1). Moreover, the Christian Democrats demonstrated great geographical breadth by obtaining congressional seats in every department except Jalapa. The success of the party was attributable to the popularity of Vinicio Cerezo, the strength of the DCG party organization, and the appeal of the party's moderate reformist platform.

Jorge Carpio's National Center Union ran a distant and disappointing second to the DCG with 20 percent of the vote and 22 congressional seats—only a slight improvement over its performance a year earlier. Next to the DCG, the UCN showed the widest geographical base by winning congressional races in fifteen of the country's twenty-three departments. In third place was the newly formed electoral coalition of the Revolutionary party (PR) and the Democratic party of National Cooperation (PDCN), which backed presidential candidate Jorge Serrano Elías. Running together, the two parties improved somewhat on the vote totals they had earned separately in 1984 (11 percent) by garnering 14 percent of the electorate and eleven seats in the National Congress. In contrast, the three most important, extreme right-wing parties lost votes in comparison with 1984. Mario Sandoval headed a coalition ticket of the two dominant parties of the 1970s—the MLN and PID—but he managed to attract only 13 percent of the vote and a paltry twelve congressional seats. The Authentic National Center (CAN) added only another 6 percent of the electorate and a single congressman to the right-wing cause.

In the runoff campaign for the presidency, Jorge Carpio made a frantic effort to win conservative voters by claiming the DCG was Communist-influenced. The UCN's consciously misleading campaign was condemned both by the Catholic church and by the third-place finisher in the first round, the PDCN's Serrano Elías. But, the UCN's ploy failed to attract much right-wing support, in part because Carpio was distrusted as a political opportunist. The MLN, for example, endorsed neither presidential candidate in the runoff. Christian Democrat Vinicio Cerezo, meanwhile, received formal endorsements from the PNR, PR, PSD, and FUR, which helped him to win the December contest by a huge 68.4 percent to 31.6 percent margin. According to Millett (1986:414), Carpio's weakness as a candidate shocked many Guatemalan military officers, who expected him to block a DCG victory. Seeking to protect his electoral victory, Cerezo went to great lengths both before and after the election to assure the armed forces that he would respect their institutional autonomy.

Long-Term Trends

The Christian Democrats' stunning victory in 1985 over the parties of the extreme right raised great hopes for Guatemala's future. The inauguration of civilian president Vinicio Cerezo, once a target for the death squads, was hailed as the beginning of a new democratic era. Political violence declined, the artificial party system gave way to a more authentic one, and the military formally returned to the barracks. Unfortunately, traditional Guatemalan political life has thus far undergone only relatively superficial changes.

In spite of the increasing role of political parties, military and private-sector factions are still the nation's most powerful political actors. It should be recalled that the present civilian government and democratic party competition exist only because—after the excesses of the Lucas García regime (1978–1982)—the dominant military and private-sector groups perceived that democratic institutions could serve their interests. The limits that the armed forces continue to place on political debate and on the government's range of action are recognized by all. In Guatemala, the costs of exceeding those limits have been made very clear in the three decades since Arbenz was overthrown. Indeed, the return of formal democracy and the easing of restraints on party and union activity have not ended the fear and intimidation that still envelop most Guatemalans. Political killings continue and, in fact, began to escalate in 1987–1988.

The development of a truly democratic political system in Guatemala will be extremely difficult. Nothing in the country's violent, dictatorial past suggests such a transition will succeed. The nation's political polarization and deep socioeconomic inequalities still constitute imposing obstacles to a genuine democracy.

References

Anderson, Thomas P. 1982. *Politics in Central America*. New York: Praeger.

Black, Jan K., and Martin C. Needler. 1983. Historical Setting. In Richard Nyrop, ed., *Guatemala: A Country Study*. Washington, DC: U.S. Government Printing Office.

Booth, John A., et al. 1985. *The 1985 Guatemalan Elections: Will the Military Relinquish Power?* Washington, DC: Washington Office on Latin America and International Human Rights Law Group.

Handy, Jim. 1986. Resurgent Democracy and the Guatemalan Military. *Journal of Latin American Studies* 18:383–408.

Millett, Richard. 1986. Guatemala's Painful Progress. *Current History* 85:413–415, 430.

Sánchez, José M. 1982. Guatemala. In Robert J. Alexander, ed., *Political Parties of the Americas*. Westport, CT: Greenwood.

Trudeau, Robert, and Lars Schoultz. 1986. Guatemala. In Morris J. Blachman, William M. LeoGrande, and Kenneth E. Sharpe, eds., *Confronting Revolution: Security Through Diplomacy in Central America*. New York: Pantheon.

Woodward, Ralph L., Jr. 1976. *Central America: A Nation Divided*. New York: Oxford.

18

EL SALVADOR

Political parties and elections played little role in Salvadoran politics until after 1950, when the armed forces attempted to institutionalize their control by creating an official party. In the 1960s, opposition parties were allowed to compete against the ruling National Conciliation party (PCN) in a series of free elections. A centrist Christian Democratic party (PDC) soon mounted a serious challenge. However, when threatened with the possibility of actually losing power, the military resorted to electoral fraud.

After the Christian Democrats and their allies in the National Opposition Union (UNO) were robbed of electoral victories in 1972 and 1977, opposition groups became more militant, and the security forces increased their repressive activities. A reformist civil-military junta took power in 1979 but collapsed soon afterward. By 1980 the country was enveloped in a bloody civil war that divided the UNO coalition. To prevent a revolution led by the Democratic Revolutionary Front (FDR) and Farabundo Martí National Liberation Front (FMLN) alliance from succeeding, the U.S. government became a major player in Salvadoran politics and provided critical assistance to a junta run by an uneasy army-PDC alliance. The United States also pressed for a new series of multiparty elections that, after an initial setback, gave formal control of the government to the Christian Democrats.

In spite of the fact that the PDC controlled both the presidency and Legislative Assembly from 1985 to 1988, the party's range of action was severely restricted. United States officials, the military, and the private sector were all more powerful actors than the country's elected authorities. Moreover, the army was unable to subdue the FDR-FMLN, and the guerrillas continued to disrupt the economy. The weakness and ineffectiveness of the PDC government led to its defeat by the right-wing Nationalist Republican Alliance (ARENA) in the 1988 legislative elections and in the 1989 presidential race.

The Evolution and Context of
Salvadoran Party Politics

After independence, members of El Salvador's landed elite competed for power with one another, usually resolving their conflicts by force of arms. The country's politics did not stabilize until the 1870s, when the leading families, made wealthy by coffee, agreed to settle their disputes nonviolently. Once established, the rule of the coffee aristocracy lasted for the next sixty years.

In 1931 aristocratic President Pío Romero Bosque kept a campaign promise to allow El Salvador's first genuinely competitive election, and a host of ad hoc personalist parties arose to contest it. Much to the displeasure of the coffee elite, the winning candidate was populist Arturo Araujo of the Labor party (PL), backed by an odd combination of forces including students, political opportunists, the new Salvadoran Communist party (PCS), and a segment of the army associated with Araujo's running-mate Gen. Maximiliano Hernández Martínez.

Araujo lasted only a few months in office before he was deposed by military coup in December 1931. General Hernández Martínez became the head of a provisional government intent on stemming the rise of the left, represented by the Regional Federation of Salvadoran Workers (FRTS). A large peasant union founded by Communist Agustín Farabundo Martí, FRTS was based in the opposition to a highly unequal land-tenure system. The new government first suspended voting during the 1932 elections in areas where the FRTS was popular and then crushed an uprising organized by Martí, killing an estimated 10,000 to 30,000 peasants.

General Martínez, as he preferred to be called, established a personalist regime, tolerated no organized opposition, and relied mainly on the military for support. The coffee oligarchy disliked losing control to the enigmatic dictator, but accepted him as the best defense against another peasant rebellion. After ruling El Salvador from 1931 to 1944, Martínez was forced to resign because of U.S. pressure and a general strike for democratic reforms involving the urban middle class and popular sector. The dictator designated a successor who scheduled elections and permitted progressive forces to organize in the Democratic Union party (PUD). A harder-line army faction, however, soon took over and began to suppress these reformist groups. In 1945 a manipulated election assured victory for Col. Salvador Castañeda Castro, the candidate backed by most of the armed forces and the oligarchy. Castañeda Castro imposed a new dictatorship, but when he made plans to run for a second term, he was ousted by a coalition of junior officers in 1948.

With democratic forces still weak, a new junta headed by Col. Oscar Osorio assumed control and laid the foundations for what would become a thirty-year period of institutionalized military rule. Recognizing the armed forces' need for dependable mass support, Osorio founded the Revolutionary party of Democratic Unification (PRUD), consciously modeled on Mexico's

PRI. Running as the PRUD's first presidential candidate on a socially progressive platform, Osorio won the 1950 elections with 57 percent of the vote against opposition from the Renewal Action party (PAR), a reformist group with roots in the civilian anti-Martínez movement. Strengthened by government patronage and control of the electoral apparatus, the PRUD created a hegemonic single-party system. From 1952 to 1961, the PRUD won every seat in the Legislative Assembly in contests with the PAR and other weak, personalist parties.

Following the PRI's example, the PRUD and its post-1961 successor, the National Conciliation party (PCN), attracted popular support with reformist rhetoric and a commitment to economic development. It also adopted a single-term presidency and a five-year administrative turnover cycle reminiscent of the Mexican system, which assured power-sharing among competing military factions (Baloyra, 1982:19). An expanding state bureaucracy provided jobs for middle-class followers; the party also managed to co-opt some union leaders.

Nevertheless, neither the PRUD nor the PCN ever developed the organizational strength or popular legitimacy of Mexico's PRI. The Salvadoran official party, for example, never built a permanent PRI-like civilian organization. Instead, the party relied mostly on the military command structure as its political machine at election time and then lay dormant until the next campaign (Baloyra, 1982:19; Webre, 1979:20). Although it promised socioeconomic reforms—including land redistribution for the crowded and socially volatile rural areas—none ever materialized. Rapid population expansion was placing enormous pressure on scarce resources, and the small country's good transportation and communication networks encouraged social mobilization. Those who directed the official party never appreciated the popular frustration that was growing as a consequence of these changes. The majority of officers were rigid anti-Communists who believed fervently in free enterprise and accepted private-sector claims that fundamental reforms would endanger the country's economic well-being and social stability (Baloyra, 1982:19–20).

Heavy-handed manipulation of the electoral process during the 1950s and the repressive policies of Col. José María Lemus (1956–1960) discredited the PRUD and precipitated a coup by military progressives in 1960. These officers were, in turn, displaced in 1961 by a more conventional military faction headed by Col. Julio Rivera. Recognizing the growing unpopularity of the Lemus-associated PRUD, Colonel Rivera approached both the PAR and the recently registered Christian Democratic party (PDC), offering to make them the army's new official party ally (Montgomery, 1982:74, 205). Rejected by both parties, Rivera combined salvageable PRUD elements with conservative defectors from the PDC to form the National Conciliation party (PCN). In the 1961 constituent assembly elections, the PCN defeated the Union of Democratic parties (UPD), a coalition composed of the PDC, PAR, and a small Social Democratic party (PSD) associated with former president Osorio.

Charges of government-sponsored fraud were again lodged during the 1961 contest. The opposition retaliated by boycotting the 1962 presidential election in which Rivera was chosen president. Confident that the PCN could win a majority without fraud, the military agreed to allow free elections in 1964. In the first honest elections since 1931, the opposition did surprisingly well, electing twenty deputies to the fifty-two-member Legislative Assembly (PDC, fourteen; PAR, six) and the mayor of San Salvador, United States-educated engineer, José Napoleón Duarte (PDC).

In the 1960s, electoral reform and economic prosperity fostered optimism about El Salvador's future. Several new parties formed, although military restrictions caused some to be banned later on as subversive. The Renewal Action party (PAR) divided in 1964 when conservative elements broke away to form the Popular Salvadoran party (PPS). The parent organization was then taken over by a group of radicals, many of whom had been associated with a prohibited pro-Castro group. The new PAR was itself declared illegal in 1968, but most of its activists joined the National Revolutionary movement (MNR), a small democratic socialist party founded in 1965 by intellectual Guillermo Ungo. Representing a dissident PCN personalist faction, the Republican Party of National Evolution (PREN) also participated in the 1960s party system.

The Christian Democratic party constituted the official party's principal opposition. The PDC was formed by urban, middle-class Catholics who wanted to do away with the military regime, yet were opposed to any radical alternatives. The party advocated a centrist program of moderate reform inspired by progressive church doctrines. Led by San Salvador's energetic mayor, the Christian Democrats used their control of the capital and other cities to create a patronage network and to improve services for the urban popular sector. In the 1966 elections, the PDC more than doubled the municipalities under its control and added an additional Legislative Assembly deputy (PCN, thirty-one deputies; PDC, fifteen; leftist PAR, four; PPS, one; PREN, one).

The official party factionalized over how to deal with the PDC's growing electoral potential but still managed to rally around Rivera's interior minister, Fidel Sánchez Hernández, in 1967 and to deal the PDC a temporary setback. The PCN presidential candidate campaigned as a reformer and captured 54 percent of the vote against a divided opposition that included the PDC (22 percent), the leftist PAR (14 percent), and the rightist PPS (10 percent). Nevertheless, in the following year's legislative contest, the PDC, helped by the government's failure to fulfill its promises, increased its legislative delegation to nineteen; the number of PCN deputies fell to twenty-seven. With electoral support based in the growing urban middle class and popular sector (which were concentrated in the country's densely populated and more socially mobilized central departments), the Christian Democrats seemed ready to challenge the ruling party for dominance.

PDC successes placed the military in a quandary. Democratic elections had improved the regime's image but now threatened to dislodge the armed forces from power. In the 1970 elections, the PCN was aided by a wave of patriotism generated by a short war with Honduras yet still felt it necessary to reintroduce electoral fraud in some areas (Webre, 1979:137–138; Anderson, 1982:67). The official returns gave the ruling party thirty-four legislative seats to the PDC's sixteen. Two small parties, the MNR and the newly formed leftist Nationalist Democratic Union (UDN), won one seat each.

Electoral manipulation by the authorities and harassment of the opposition became more blatant two years later. Right-wing dissatisfaction with the PCN's modest reformism produced two conservative presidential contenders in 1972—a PPS candidate and José "Chele" Medrano, founder of the Nationalist Democratic Organization (ORDEN), the PCN's rural vigilante force. The center and left coalesced into the National Opposition Union (UNO)—an electoral alliance of the PDC, the MNR, and the Communist-backed UDN—which nominated José Napoleón Duarte for president and MNR leader Guillermo Ungo as his vice-presidential running-mate. After some highly suspicious vote-counting, the electoral authorities certified PCN candidate Col. Arturo Molina as the winner. To make matters worse, electoral officials disqualified UNO legislative slates in the country's six largest departments on "technicalities." Shortly after these tainted elections, a group of reformist officers attempted a coup that was endorsed by Duarte, but military units loyal to the government suppressed the uprising and exiled the PDC leader.

After 1972, El Salvador's political situation deteriorated rapidly. Obvious frauds against UNO candidates in 1974 and 1976 and in the 1977 presidential race totally discredited the electoral process and the ruling PCN. Opposition parties began to seem irrelevant, and in the mid-1970s many Salvadorans, especially from the lower and lower-middle classes, began to join new, more militant worker and peasant organizations that formed popular coalitions, such as the Popular Revolutionary Bloc (BPR) and the Front of Unified Popular Action (FAPU). President Molina tried to defuse rising discontent with new pledges of land reform, but the private sector again was able to block implementation. After his fraudulent 1977 victory, General Carlos Humberto Romero, Molina's successor, dropped all reformist pretenses and unleashed the security forces against the radicalized opposition (Baloyra, 1982:63). Right-wing violence by military units, ORDEN, and death squads financed by the oligarchy soon raged out of control. Many opponents of the regime allied with Marxist guerrilla organizations, which had become active in the early 1970s.

In 1979 a military coup ousted Romero and instituted a civil-military junta in which UNO as well as the private sector and the army were represented. The MNR's Guillermo Ungo was a junta member, and PDC and UDN adherents both held cabinet positions. Yet, the spiral of violence continued unabated. The first junta collapsed at the end of the year when Ungo and other reformers resigned over their failure to convince the army to stop right-wing killings of both radicals and moderates. Many of the departing reformers forged an alliance with the popular organizations that became formalized as the Democratic Revolutionary Front (FDR).

The military formed a new junta with the Christian Democrats in January 1980, but over the next two months the issue of collaboration with the armed forces split the party—particularly after the assassinations of progressive Archbishop Oscar Romero and a number of PDC activists. Eventually, much of the PDC executive committee and roughly one-fifth of the party's membership left to create the Popular Social Christian movement (MPSC) (Karl, 1986:16). The MPSC joined the FDR, which made a common front with the guerrilla groups united in the Farabundo Martí National Liberation Front (FMLN). PDC stalwarts remained with repatriated José Napoleón Duarte, who had become provisional president with hopes of expanding on recent antioligarchy reforms.

The United States acquired enormous influence in El Salvador in the 1980s. Its military and economic aid was crucial in preventing a victory by the FDR-FMLN. In order to assure continued funding from Congress, U.S. officials forced the army to maintain its tenuous alliance with the Christian Democrats. The United States also orchestrated a series of controversial elections designed to demonstrate the government's legitimacy to the U.S. Congress and to a skeptical international community. Arguing that their candidates would be easy targets for the death squads, the leftist and center-left parties of the FDR did not participate and condemned these contests as propaganda exercises. These races therefore involved only the center and right-wing Salvadoran parties: the PDC, PCN, PPS, and several new parties, including the powerful rightist Nationalist Republican Alliance (ARENA) and the moderate Democratic Action (AD).

With the death toll from political violence exceeding fifty thousand and the population gripped by fear, it was impossible to conduct genuinely free elections even if the ballots were counted accurately. Nonetheless, elections were held for a constituent assembly in 1982, for the presidency in 1984 (two rounds) and 1989 (one round), and for the Legislative Assembly in 1985 and 1988. Contrary to U.S. wishes, the 1982 election resulted in victory for a combination of conservative parties. In response, the United States and the Salvadoran army forced a power-sharing arrangement between the right and the Christian Democrats. The PDC did win the 1984 presidential race—in which Duarte defeated ARENA extremist Roberto D'Aubuisson—and went on to capture a legislative majority in 1985, but in 1988 a resurgent ARENA overpowered the Christian Democrats in the Legislative Assembly elections. In March 1989, ARENA candidate Alfredo Cristiani was elected president.

Traditionally, political parties have been players of secondary importance in Salvadoran politics. The restoration of electoral politics in the 1980s raised their significance but did not alter the basic nature of the system. The Christian Democrats' electoral victories afforded the party temporary formal authority over the executive and legislative branches of the government from 1985 to 1988, but President Duarte's ability to govern the country was still very limited. The conservative parties always had enough votes in the

Legislative Assembly to block any measures requiring a two-thirds majority, and they retained control of the reactionary Supreme Court. The Duarte government also had to contend with the great influence that the U.S. government had acquired in Salvadoran politics. Large-scale U.S. assistance, indispensable to the war effort and the beleaguered economy, bought the United States veto power over government policy.

The strongest domestic political actor in El Salvador is still the armed forces. Although now commanded by pragmatists willing to cooperate with a PDC president in order to keep U.S. funds flowing, the military continues to operate independently of civilian authority and is intent on victory over the guerrillas. President Duarte's ability to obtain military aid gave him some leverage in negotiations with the armed forces, which resulted in the removal of some right-wing officers, the reduction of human-rights abuses (although they began to increase again in late 1987), and the creation of new political space for the center-left union movement (García, 1986:411; Diskin and Sharpe, 1986:73–74). Nevertheless, the armed forces continued to block both serious peace negotiations with the FDR-FMLN and trials of military officers for human-rights abuses.

The coffee oligarchy has been weakened by the partial land reform and by the government's control of export trade, but the private sector as a whole remains a central political actor. The private sector is influential because of its financial support for conservative ARENA, its possession of needed investment funds, its control of the mass media, and its contacts with military officers and probusiness U.S. officials (Diskin and Sharpe, 1986:73–74). Organized in such groups as the National Association of Private Enterprise (ANEP) and the Chamber of Commerce and Industry, most businessmen strongly opposed the Christian Democratic government over economic policy.

With the decline in right-wing violence between 1984 and 1987, organized labor reemerged as a force in Salvadoran politics. Centrist labor unions and peasant organizations provided strong backing to the PDC in 1984 and 1985 but, angered by Duarte's failure to produce promised reforms, sat on the sidelines during the 1988 elections. Leftist labor organizations linked to the FDR, such as the National Federation of Unions of Salvadoran Workers (FENASTRAS), also became more active and joined in the proliferating strikes and demonstrations for higher wages and a political solution to the war. Labor opposition to the government became concentrated in the newly formed National Unity of Salvadoran Workers (UNTS).

The Duarte administration was also opposed by the FMLN guerrillas, who never ceased sabotaging the economy and interfering with the implementation of government programs. Small wonder that the Christian Democrats—faced by powerful adversaries on both left and right and attempting to govern in the midst of civil war—proved ineffective. The party's loss at the polls in 1988, shortly followed by the announcement of President Duarte's terminal illness, ended any hopes that remained for the PDC government.

Contemporary Political Parties

The centrist Christian Democratic party not only endorses private enterprise but also advocates major social reforms such as land redistribution. The party is anti-Communist in ideology and supports the war effort, yet it seeks dialogue with the FDR-FMLN. In the 1980s the PDC became factionalized along ideological and personalist lines: left-oriented Christian Democrats (under José Napoleón Duarte's former protégé Rubén Zamora) formed the Popular Social Christian Movement (MPSC) and defected to the FDR in 1980. By 1987 PDC members who had stayed in the party with Duarte became deeply divided over the competing presidential ambitions of Julio Adolfo Rey Prendes, a longtime party stalwart, and Fidel Chávez Mena, a more popular party leader with closer ties to the private sector. In 1988, after Chávez Mena was declared the PDC's presidential candidate for the 1989 election, Rey Prendes and most of the PDC legislative delegation left the party to form the Authentic Christian movement (MAC), which endorsed Rey Prendes for the presidency.

The PDC is essentially an urban, middle-class party with a strong traditional electoral following among urban professionals, white-collar workers, and smaller entrepreneurs. In addition, by demonstrating concern for the needs of the lower classes, the PDC has attracted popular-sector followers in both urban and rural areas. In 1985, when the Christian Democrats won just over half of the valid votes cast, they ran most strongly in San Salvador and in the eastern departments of San Miguel and La Unión. In contrast, in 1988 the party was defeated by ARENA even in San Salvador (where it had not lost a mayoral race since 1964) and was credited with only about one-third of the vote overall.

The PDC's principal opposition in the 1980s has been the Nationalist Republican Alliance (ARENA), formed in 1981. ARENA is a staunch ideological defender of capitalism and opposes land redistribution and other social reforms. Virulently anti-Communist, ARENA has criticized liberal democracy as prone to left-wing subversion and has portrayed the Christian Democrats as a corrupt front for communism. Not surprisingly, the party advocates an increased war effort free of United States-imposed restrictions. ARENA has been dominated by the personality of Roberto D'Aubuisson since its founding. But D'Aubuisson, former intelligence chief of the National Guard, is a controversial figure disliked by the United States and by army pragmatists. After the 1985 elections, ARENA installed moderate businessman Alfredo Cristiani as the new party leader and adopted a less strident, extremist tone, but D'Aubuisson has remained a key figure. Former army colonel Sigifredo Ochoa, who had clashed with President Duarte, also became an important party spokesman. In the same postelectoral period, D'Aubuisson's 1984 running mate, Hugo Barrera, defected to form the conservative Liberation party (PL), but took few party activists with him. In 1988, Alfredo Cristiani became ARENA's presidential candidate for the 1989 election.

Backed by ANEP and most of the private sector, ARENA has mounted well-financed, well-organized campaigns in each of the recent elections. Before 1988 the Nationalist Republican Alliance generally won about 30 percent of the vote with support based among socially privileged groups and the more conservative (and military-controlled) segments of the peasantry. But in the last two elections, ARENA expanded its appeal to embrace roughly half the electorate. In 1985 ARENA gained its greatest relative share of the vote in the departments of Cuscatlán, Sonsonate, and Cabañas. It ran well in 1988 in each of these departments and also gained seven of the thirteen seats contested in San Salvador and surpassed the PDC in Santa Ana, San Vicente, and La Paz.

During the 1985 election, ARENA ran in coalition with the once-dominant National Conciliation party (PCN), although the parties were listed separately on the ballot. The PCN represents a more moderate brand of conservatism than ARENA, and their alliance ended after the election. The PCN became an occasional ally of the Christian Democrats. The military-founded party even began to term itself "social democratic" in the late 1980s, but its commitment to social change is questionable. The PCN has never been well-organized, and now, without its monopoly on government patronage and with most of the private sector backing ARENA, the party has fallen into decline. The former ruling party has also been disrupted by internal division; the Salvadoran Authentic Institutional party (PAISA), a right-wing splinter, left the PCN in 1982 and won one seat in the 1985 legislative elections.

The National Conciliation party retains support in the armed forces and among some United States officials, but its popular following is eroding; it collected a bare 8 percent of the valid ballots cast in 1985 and did not do significantly better in 1988. The PCN still obtains some votes from conservative, middle-sector elements outside of the capital and central region and a part of its traditional, rural-peasant constituency survives.

Democratic Action, led by René Fortín Magaña, was the only other party participating in the 1985 elections to win representation. But, like PAISA, it failed to keep its seat in 1988. Backed by moderate business interests, the party's mass support (under 4 percent of the vote) is concentrated in San Salvador's urban middle class. Other minor parties that fielded candidates in recent elections, but garnered too few votes to win deputyships, include the conservative Popular Salvadoran party (PPS), active since the 1960s, and the Popular Orientation party (POP), a right-wing, personalist electoral vehicle founded by "Chele" Medrano. In 1988, the PPS, PAISA, and the PL joined in the right-wing Popular Union (UP) to compete in the 1989 election.

Claiming that the threat of right-wing violence against them makes it impossible to campaign, the left and center-left parties allied in the Democratic Revolutionary Front (FDR) did not enter the electoral arena until 1989. Nonetheless, these parties represent an important component of the Salvadoran party system. Estimates of potential FDR electoral support in completely free elections vary widely, but they usually range from 20 percent to 30 percent (Karl, 1986:35). The most important center-left parties in the FDR are Rubén Zamora's MPSC and Guillermo Ungo's small, democratic socialist National Revolutionary Movement (MNR). After the human-rights situation improved and unions once again became active, the two parties began to reestablish their presence in San Salvador, and, in late 1987, both Zamora and Ungo took advantage of the political opening created by the Central American Peace Accord (Esquipulas II) to return to the country. In 1988 the MPSC and the MNR joined with Marco Reni Roldán's newly established center-left Social Democratic party (PSD) in the Democratic Convergence (CD) and announced plans to take part in the 1989 elections.

Nearly all of the other political groups united in the FDR represent the wide array of radical Marxist factions of the Salvadoran left. Many of these groups are splinters of the original Salvadoran Communist party (PCS), the nation's oldest, continuously active party, and/or popular organizations founded in the 1970s. Attempts to form a single revolutionary party have failed thus far because of disputes over ideology and the distribution of power (Garcia, 1986:412). Tensions have also been common between the FDR and its armed partner, the more militant FMLN, itself divided into five separate guerrilla armies.

Recent Elections

The six elections that have been held in El Salvador since 1982 have taken place under extraordinary wartime circumstances. Although not subject to wholesale fraud in the style of the 1970s, these elections cannot be characterized as entirely free and democratic. Conditions are such that it has been unsafe for the left to participate, and years of state-sponsored terrorism have inhibited the freedoms of speech and assembly (Herman and Brodhead, 1984:11).

Under the new Salvadoran constitution and electoral law, elections for president and vice-president are held at five-year intervals. Unless a candidate receives a majority of valid votes cast, a runoff between the two top contenders must be scheduled. Deputies of the sixty-member Legislative Assembly are chosen every three years on the basis of proportional representation using closed party lists. All Salvadorans over the age of eighteen may vote, but beginning with the 1985 race, voting has not been compulsory. Salvadoran elections are supervised by the three-member Central Election Council (CCE), which has been plagued by administrative problems and political controversy.

In the 1982 constituent assembly elections, the government induced voters to go to the polls by mandating compulsory voting, issuing ominous statements that equated nonvoting with treason. Voters had every reason to believe that their absence from the polls could be discovered by interested officials: citizens were informed that their voter-identity cards would be stamped and that their index fingers would be marked with indelible ink

TABLE 18.1
El Salvador: Election Returns by Party, 1982-1988

	Constituent Assembly		Presidential First Round	Legislative Assembly		
	1982 Total(%)[a]	1982 Seats	1984 Total(%)	1985 Total(%)	1985 Seats	1988 Seats[b]
PDC	40.1	24	43.4	52.4	33	23
ARENA	29.5	19	29.8	29.7	13	30
PCN	19.2	14	19.3	8.4	12	7
AD	7.4	2	3.5	3.7	1	0
PPS	2.9	1	1.9	1.7	0	0
POP	0.9	0	0.4	0.1	0	0
PAISA			1.2	3.7	1	0
Other			0.5	0.3	0	0
Total	100.0	60	100.0	100.0	60	60

[a]Percentage of valid votes: invalid or blank votes equaled 11.9 of total votes cast in 1982, 10.8 of votes cast in 1984, and 12.8 of votes in 1985.
[b]Final party vote percentages were not yet available. Also, the award of one PDC seat (La Unión) was disputed by ARENA.

Sources: Segundo Montes, "Las Elecciones del 31 Marzo," Estudios Centroamericanos 40 (April 1985), pp. 221-223, Keesing's Contemporary Archives (November 18, 1982), p. 31810, Latin American Monitor: Central America (March 1984), p. 28, and Central America Report (April 8, 1988), pp. 103-104.

(Herman and Brodhead, 1984:125–128). Salvadorans were pressured by the left to boycott the election, and some guerrilla groups threatened reprisals against those who did not take their advice. In fact, armed guerrilla units disrupted voting in many areas and were able to prevent balloting completely in some localities (Baloyra, 1982:173).

More than one million voters went to the polls in 1982 under these troubled conditions. But the CCE has since admitted that turnout figures were inflated (Karl, 1986:19), so the exact percentage of the eligible population voting cannot be determined. Nonetheless, turnout was high enough to strengthen the Salvadoran government in the eyes of the U.S. Congress and to weaken the claims of the FDR-FMLN that it represented the great majority of the Salvadoran people. In this sense, the election was viewed as a success by U.S. officials, although it resulted in a victory for the right-wing parties.

The PDC won a 40 percent plurality in 1982 and was awarded the largest share of seats in the assembly (Table 18.1), but reactionary ARENA and the conservative PCN together won a larger share of the vote (49 percent) and formed a legislative majority. The right's triumph was based in part on the traditional habit of Salvadorans, especially in rural areas, to vote for the official, pro-army party in order to avoid difficulties (Karl, 1986:18–19). In addition, numbered ballots, transparent ballot boxes, and thin ballot papers may have been a particular inducement to vote for the right. ARENA also organized a far better financed and more aggressive campaign than the Christian Democrats, complete with sophisticated media advertisements designed by the Salvadoran affiliate of a U.S. public relations firm (Baloyra, 1982:168–169). The popular appeal of the right-wing views and charismatic personality of ARENA leader D'Aubuisson in more traditional parts of the country was an added factor in the right's strong showing.

The first round of the 1984 presidential elections was an administrative nightmare. Balloting failed to take place at more than 10 percent of polling places because of tardy voter lists, polling officials, and ballot boxes. Other polling places were disrupted by guerrilla activity, and the new, computerized system that assigned voters to polling stations by identity-card number also turned out to be confusing. In spite of these problems, turnout amounted to an estimated 53 percent of the eligible voters. The results of the presidential first round were not very different from those of the 1982 race, despite heavy U.S. financial assistance to the PDC and, to a lesser extent, to the PCN. Except for the fact that two minor parties, the AD and PPS, both collected a smaller share of the vote, the 1984 returns look remarkably similar to the 1982 results (see Table 18.1). The PDC candidate, Duarte, won a 43 percent plurality, while the two major right-wing candidates, D'Aubuisson (ARENA) and Francisco Guerrero (PCN), collected a combined 49 percent.

The presidential runoff election was less chaotic than the first round, and turnout increased by about 10 percent. D'Aubuisson, who had finished a distant second to Duarte in the first round, campaigned furiously but was handicapped by the PCN's decision to remain neutral. In addition, U.S. officials did everything in their power to prevent a D'Aubuisson victory, including paying for Duarte's mass-media advertising and financing the unions that provided his strongest campaign support (Karl, 1986:25). The Christian Democrat captured the presidency with a fairly comfortable 53.6 percent to 46.4 percent margin.

In the following year, elections were held to select the Legislative Assembly. With voting no longer compulsory, only 41 percent of the eligible electorate went to the polls. Other factors that may have inhibited the turnout include the new requirement that displaced persons cast their ballots where their identity cards were originally registered and the naturally lower interest generated by nonpresidential campaigns (Montes, 1985:222). The guerrillas did not interfere significantly in the balloting.

Although not running for election, President Duarte became the central focus of the 1985 campaign. He asked voters to give him a legislative majority in order to break the deadlock caused by rightist control of the assembly. ARENA and the PCN, in response, attacked Duarte and warned voters that a PDC regime would constitute a left-wing dictatorship. Ultimately, the PDC appeal proved more convincing and produced a resounding victory. With 52 percent of the vote, the PDC won an absolute majority in the Legislative Assembly (thirty-three seats) and in nine of fourteen Salvadoran departments. The Nationalist Republican Alliance (ARENA) and the National

Conciliation party (PCN), running in coalition, attracted only 38 percent of the vote. The steep decline of the once-powerful PCN from 19 percent of the vote in 1984 to 8 percent a year later was the principal reason for the right's reduced vote total. By negotiating with ARENA beforehand, however, the PCN managed to get only one less Legislative Assembly deputy than its stronger ally (i.e., twelve vs. thirteen). Duarte's efforts to promote peace through negotiations with the FDR-FMLN clearly had helped him at the polls, as had the bureaucratic resources won in 1984 and the military's continued neutrality.

But the popularity of President Duarte and the Christian Democrats fell precipitously after 1985. Continuing economic difficulties, exacerbated by the effects of a major earthquake in 1986 and the government's failure to deliver either important social reforms or successful peace negotiations, led to growing disenchantment with the PDC. Salvadorans also became disillusioned by infighting within the often-directionless PDC government and by several well-publicized cases of corruption involving high-ranking Christian Democrats. During the same period, right-wing ARENA labored to develop a more moderate, democratic image while continuing to press for more vigorous prosecution of the war and criticizing the PDC for allowing the United States to dominate El Salvador. Thus, when elections were held for the Legislative Assembly again in 1988, the voting public shocked the Christian Democrats and their U.S. sponsors by stripping the party of its legislative majority and making ARENA the most powerful party in the assembly. With roughly half the vote, ARENA captured 30 seats to the PDC's 23 and the PCN's 7. Shortly after the election, the defection of one PCN deputy to ARENA gave the conservative party a Legislative Assembly majority. In concurrent municipal elections ARENA also won approximately 200 of the 244 mayoralties contested. Elections could not be held in 18 guerrilla-controlled municipalities, and turnout, in general, was reduced by the FMLN's decision to interfere with the elections by enforcing a countrywide transportation ban. Preliminary returns indicated that about 1 million of the 1.9 million registered voters (53 percent) participated in the 1988 elections.

In March 1989, ARENA's Alfredo Cristiani won the presidency on the first round with 53 percent of the vote. In an election marked by a high level of guerrilla interference and low voter turnout, the Christian Democrat Fidel Chávez Meña polled a disappointing 36 percent of the vote.

Long-Term Trends

Political parties have never been actors of primary importance in El Salvador, and elections have seldom determined who will hold power. The armed forces have dominated the country since the 1930s, and their decision to close electoral channels to the opposition in the 1970s ultimately caused a radicalization of Salvadoran politics and a brutal civil war.

Through the influence of the United States, elections were restored in the 1980s, and, by 1985, these contests gave both executive and legislative authority to the Christian Democratic party. Nevertheless, the transition from military rule to civilian democracy was far from completed. The PDC had the constitutional right to govern the nation, but its range of action was constricted by the existence of more powerful forces such as the army, the private sector, and the U.S. government. Moreover, some sections of the country were controlled by the leftist guerrillas, who despite reduced forces, retained the capability to prevent economic recovery. To make matters worse, corruption and dissension within Christian Democratic ranks added to public disapproval of the government and contributed to its loss of legislative control in 1988 and the presidential palace in 1989.

If political parties and elections are ever to become major actors in Salvadoran politics, the civil war must end. The parties allied within the leftist FDR-FMLN must somehow be fully reintegrated into the system, and elections must be held in an atmosphere free from intimidation. Unfortunately, with right-wing ARENA resurgent in the late 1980s, a negotiated settlement between the Salvadoran government and the FDR-FMLN appeared more remote than ever.

References

Anderson, Thomas P. 1982. *Politics in Central America*. New York: Praeger.

Baloyra, Enrique. 1982. *El Salvador in Transition*. Chapel Hill: Univ. of North Carolina Press.

———. 1987. The Seven Plagues of El Salvador. *Current History*, 86:413–416, 433–434.

Diskin, Martin, and Kenneth E. Sharpe. 1986. El Salvador. In Morris J. Blachman, William M. LeoGrande, and Kenneth E. Sharpe, eds., *Confronting Revolution: Security Through Diplomacy in Central America*. New York: Pantheon.

García, José Z. 1986. El Salvador: A Glimmer of Hope. *Current History* 85:409–412.

Herman, Edward S., and Frank Brodhead. 1984. *Demonstration Elections*. Boston: South End.

Karl, Terry. 1986. Imposing Consent? Electoralism vs. Democratization in El Salvador. In Paul W. Drake and Eduardo Silva, eds., *Elections and Democratization in Latin America, 1980–85*. San Diego: Univ. of California, San Diego.

Montes, Segundo. 1985. Las Elecciones del 31 Marzo. *Estudios Centroamericanos* 40:215–228.

Montgomery, Tommie Sue. 1982. *Revolution in El Salvador*. Boulder, CO: Westview.

Sharpe, Kenneth E. 1986. El Salvador Revisited. *World Policy Journal* 3:473–494.

Webre, Stephen. 1979. *José Napoleón Duarte and the Christian Democratic Party in Salvadoran Politics, 1960–1972*. Baton Rouge: Louisiana Univ. Press.

19

ECUADOR

Ecuadoran politics and society are permeated by three dominant realities: the status of the Indian, regional bifurcation, and the persistent influence of personalism in national leadership. Ecuador is also characterized by the common patterns of traditionalism: economic underdevelopment, dependency, and inequality; the strong influence of autonomous military, religious, and socioeconomic elites; and the lack of viable political and governmental institutions. Together, these characteristics have contributed to a long history of political instability, military intervention, and a somewhat incoherent pattern of political-party evolution. Ecuador has nevertheless avoided the extended, traditional dictatorship so common in Latin America, and has thus been able to avoid the political traumas that often accompany such regimes. Elections have been held with some regularity throughout the twentieth century, but military government has been the norm.

Of the three dominant realities mentioned above, two have all but defined Ecuadoran party politics: regionalism and personalism. The third, the status of the Indian, has as yet not played a significant role in the nation's politics, although the importance of the Indian is inescapable, however one defines or measures it. The simple reality is that the overwhelming majority of people in Ecuador are Indian in one way or another, and most of them have not been fundamentally changed by Western influences. Any discussion of Ecuadoran politics must therefore proceed on the assumption that one of the most significant political issues in the country has yet to be embraced within the context of party politics and elections.

The Context of Ecuadoran Party Politics

Ecuador's population historically has been concentrated in two relatively small regions of the country: the highland region dominated by the capital city of Quito, and the lowland, coastal region dominated by the city of Guayaquil. The division of the national population into these two distinct regions has been emphasized historically by the different economic and cultural realities of the two areas and characterized by a political competition between the two cities and their respective interests for hegemony over the national government. The highland region contains the majority of Ecuador's traditional Indian civilization, and its principal city, Quito, has been the center of government and administration from colonial times to the present. It was also home to the country's traditional upper class, whose wealth was defined primarily by the lands it owned in the region. The highland was also the center of influence for the church, whose mission to convert the indigenous peoples was focused there. These and other factors combined to make Quito the center of conservatism in Ecuador, an orientation of both social and political significance (Martz, 1985:384).

Guayaquil, by contrast, evolved as a port city, and with the gradual emergence of the country's export economy in the late nineteenth century, the region became both more dynamic and more influential economically than Quito. It is also more diverse ethnically and racially than the highland region, containing a complex mixture of European, Indian, and African influences. The political interests of Guayaquil have also been distinctive. Historically, it has been the center of liberal thought and politics in the country and, by the turn of the century, the locus for a political party that challenged the traditional dominance of the highland elites. This bipolar regionalism became evident in the development of the country's political parties. The earliest political parties to emerge were the Conservative party (PC), centered in the highland region, and the Radical Liberal party (PLR) (or, as it is more commonly known, the "Liberal party" [PL]) in the coastal region. Guayaquil has historically been the center of the country's reformist politics, as well as the principal area for support of several charismatic leaders who have played an important role in contemporary Ecuadoran politics, particularly José Velasco Ibarra and Assad Bucaram.

As elitist politics slowly became mass politics in Ecuador, the coastal region benefited most. The highland elites could have resisted the coastal incursions on its electoral power by mobilizing the Indian vote, but they were neither disposed to nor able to rely on the Indian for such purposes. By contrast, the mixed population of Guayaquil was mobilized by politicians, and as their numbers increased so, too, did their leaders' ability to prevail in their competition with the elites of Quito, particularly in electoral contests. Guayaquil's more dynamic economic development has also produced a more varied class structure than is found in Quito. It has a middle class, a salaried working class, as well as the clear gradations in affluence commonly associated with economic development. This more complex stratification has injected an element of class conflict into Ecuadoran politics, with the thrust of it coming from the coastal region.

One final demographic influence on Ecuadoran politics should be mentioned. Ecuador has one of the highest population growth rates in the hemisphere—a rate that has been attributed to improved health conditions at a time when population growth rates in most Latin American nations are beginning to decline. Like all nations with high population growth rates, Ecuador has a relatively low median age, with most of its population under the age of eighteen. This demographic reality will have increasing political significance. These younger Ecuadorans tend to be more literate, more educated, and potentially more politically aware. They are also hard-pressed to find employment outside the traditional rural agricultural areas because the rate of economic development and the expansion in jobs cannot possibly keep pace with the demand for employment. Like young people everywhere, they tend to be impatient with change and more sympathetic to radical solutions to their country's manifest problems and their own personal frustrations. They are a great reservoir for political mobilization by party organizations and leaders and have the potential of playing an increasingly significant role in national politics.

Economic realities have also influenced the evolution of party politics in Ecuador, the fundamental one being the traditionalism of its economy. Ecuador remains primarily a preindustrial society, dependent for international trade on primary-product exports. International dependency and the lack of economic development have produced a low standard of living, even by Latin American standards, and a very uneven distribution of income. The very poor, principally the Indian population, have been disinclined to participate politically.

Ecuador's political instability has been stressed by many scholars, who note that the country has had seventeen constitutions since independence and at least twenty-four instances of successful military intervention—indisputable but somewhat misleading facts. Ecuador has had occasional periods of sustained civilian rule and, until the late 1950s, has had more democratic transfers of power than was true in several other Latin American nations, including Venezuela. Moreover, any political instability has yet to be expressed in mass revolutionary violence, although violent acts against specific political leaders have been common. In the early 1960s some tried to initiate a revolutionary movement in the country; indeed, similar efforts have been made more recently. To date, though, revolutionary activity has not threatened the fragile regimes that have controlled the nation.

Ecuador's political or governmental organizations and processes cannot be called institutionalized by any reasonable standard. That is, its political organizations and processes are not broadly perceived as important and legitimate, and large numbers of people do not identify with them—their fate indistinguishable from that of their individual leaders. In fact, one might view the country's preoccupation with writing constitutions as an effort to mandate much-needed institutions. This cannot be done with the stroke of a pen, however. Institutions evolve slowly over generations, and modern governmental and political ones can evolve only within the context of modern values, which even today are still overwhelmed in Ecuador by traditional ones.

The traditional values of what Max Weber termed "patrimonialism" exist in many societies (particularly in Latin America), but they are especially evident in Ecuador. Without modern political institutions, Ecuador has fallen back on personalistic (often charismatic) party politics. There have been many examples of the phenomenon in contemporary Ecuador, but two are of special relevance to party politics: José Velasco Ibarra and Assad Bucaram. Velasco (1893–1979) was a major force in Ecuadoran politics for nearly a half century, and was elected president five times, although he completed only one presidential term, ousted by the military on several occasions. Velasco organized his followers into various parties and movements that cut across ideological, class, and regional divisions in the country, and his performance in office was both unpredictable and inconsistent beyond his preoccupation with remaining in power. Velasco died in 1979 at the age of eighty-six.

Assad Bucaram was a major figure in Ecuadoran politics for more than two decades. Originally the mayor of Guayaquil, Bucaram pursued the presidency without success, provoking resistance and animosity from most military leaders, who were trying to referee national politics. The military's intervention in 1972 was primarily motivated by its fear that Bucaram might be elected president in the election scheduled for 1974. In 1978 the military prevented him from being a presidential candidate on the technicality that his parents had been foreign-born. Bucaram died unexpectedly from a heart attack in November 1981.

Ecuadoran politics is noteworthy not because of personalism, but because there is little beyond personalism to hold parties together. Charismatic leadership has substituted for institutions in a context where the latter are impossible to achieve. Personalistic leadership and the Indians' exclusion from national politics have set the boundaries for Ecuador's party politics, while regionalism in its many and evolving dimensions has been the motive force. Military elites have often exercised influence in the political vacuums created by the vicissitudes of personalistic, multiparty politics. Viewed in this context, the otherwise bewildering proliferation of weak party organizations and the often-futile exercises of national elections and constitution-writing begin to take focus.

The Evolution of Ecuadoran Political Parties

Formal political parties emerged spontaneously in Ecuador out of the country's basic political factions during the nineteenth century. These divisions were ultimately political but were often expressed in philosophical terms and according to regional interests. At just what time these loose affiliations of like-minded politicians became formal political parties is obscure, but it occurred sometime during the last two decades of the nineteenth century.

The earliest parties reflected the familiar Latin American division between Liberals and Conservatives, producing in Ecuador the Conservative party (PC) and the Radical Liberal party (PLR). A third party—the Progressive party (PP)—also participated briefly in national politics during the same period. The first two remained the principal political parties for about half a century; the third disappeared after the 1895 civil war.

The Conservatives emerged specifically out of the dictatorship of Gabriel García Moreno (1860–1875), the first Ecuadoran ruler to establish a degree of central control over the country. García Moreno, seeking some unifying theme for his regime, chose to identify it with catholicism, which to him symbolized unity, structure, and purpose—qualities that paralleled his own temporal objectives. His most visionary plan was the construction of a railway between the cities of Guayaquil and Quito, a project that, upon completion, would permit a degree of national unification for the two regions that had been virtually isolated from each other. While possessing enormous symbolic importance, the project also had immediate economic and political consequences.

The Conservative party, which came to be identified as an advocate of the church, the landowners, and the highland region, exercised power until the civil war of 1895–1896. It never regained control over the national government after the war, although it remained an important opposition party up until the mid-twentieth century.

The Liberal party traces its origin to 1878 and may have been Ecuador's first organized party. Liberals opposed the Conservatives on the issue of the temporal role of the church and advocated the interests of Guayaquil, their principal base of support. They also advocated the interests of the Indians of the Sierra, primarily as an issue to use against the Conservatives, who dominated the highland (Linke, 1960:40). Indians were never really included in the Liberal party, nor did the party ever try to recruit them.

The Progressive party failed to survive more than a few years but did exercise considerable influence for a short period of time. The Progressive party has been all but ignored by most scholars, although it is briefly discussed by Hurtado (1980). The Progressives began as a tendency within the Conservative party and were based originally in the provincial city of Cuenca. They rejected the strict authoritarianism of García Moreno and the dominant Conservatives, criticizing the dictator's political and religious excesses. They also championed the objectives of nineteenth-century European liberalism: democracy, protection of individual rights, and the rule of law. Although the party never created a formal organization, its members saw themselves as a separate group from the Conservatives and Liberals and functioned as such. One of its principal spokesmen, Antonio Flores Jijón, was president from 1888 to 1892. After the civil war, the party disappeared.

All three of these early parties shared one characteristic: they were very limited groups, lacking genuine organizations or mass identification and loyalty. But then again, politics at the time was generally limited to a tiny minority of Ecuador's national population. Liberal dominance began in 1895 and reflected a movement away from the traditional values championed by the Conservatives and an orientation toward more modern ones stressing development and secularism. It also represented a shift in power toward Guayaquil, whose importance was rising along with the development of the Ecuadoran export economy.

The changing balance between Guayaquil and Quito and the growing strength of the Liberals were symbolized by the completion of the rail link between the two cities, accomplished under the administration of Eloy Alfaro. One of the ablest of the liberal leaders, Alfaro served twice as president (1895–1901, 1906–1911). The Liberal party's control of the government endured for several generations, but it was not without opposition. The country's brief period of economic prosperity was quickly superseded by an economic recession lasting almost thirty years (Pike, 1977:187–188). Moreover, the Liberal party presidents became increasingly more arbitrary and authoritarian, and the party failed to modernize itself into a mass-based organization sensitive to the changes occurring in the country.

Until the mid-twentieth century Ecuadoran politics was particularly violent. The Liberals came to power violently in 1895, and throughout their regimes (as well as the preceding Conservative ones) armed insurrection and civil war were ever-present possibilities. Moreover, several prominent Ecuadoran presidents died hideously and violently from politically motivated acts. Juan José Flores, a dictator whose influence spanned fifteen years (1830–1845), was assassinated while in office, his naked body hung from a lamp post in Quito. Gabriel García Moreno was assassinated in 1875—his body was hacked into small pieces. Eloy Alfaro was killed by his political opponents in 1911. His body was mutilated, dragged through the streets of Quito by a drunken mob, and then dismembered and burned in a public square. Velasco Ibarra, perhaps the country's most experienced and long-lived politician, once perceptively observed, "Ecuador is a very difficult country to govern" (Blanksten, 1951:v). He might very well have added the adjective "dangerous."

The dominance of the Liberal party over Ecuadoran politics was challenged by Velasco Ibarra. As mentioned above, he was chosen as president five times and deposed four times by military coups. Four of his five presidencies were achieved by election, one (1945) by insurrection. Velasco embodied the personalistic style of leadership that is so characteristic of Ecuadoran politics. Although he used political parties and, over the years, formed several Velaquista parties and movements, his position was essentially antiparty. Hurtado (1980:200) characterizes *Velasquismo* as a

> political movement directly tied to the personality of its leader and, consequently, absolutely dependent on his will. Since within the movement greater value is ascribed to personal loyalty than to institutional fidelity or party discipline, devotion to the leader has emerged as an indispensable prerequisite for entry into the group of collaborators of Dr. Velasco, and those who lose his confidence fall inevitably into disgrace and are forever ostracized from the exclusive circle of loyal followers and deprived of all opportunity for political advancement.

Blanksten (1951) provides a provocative case study of Velasco Ibarra. His analysis is particularly revealing given that the leader was at that time only midway through his political career. Blanksten describes Velasco as not hesitating to admit that "my destiny is indestructibly tied to the destiny of my country," and that he was "absolutely convinced that the people are with me, they are all with me" (49).

By 1952 Velasco's supporters had been organized into the National Velasquista Federation (FNV), which in 1979 became the Velasquista National party (PNV). Velasco and his party did not hesitate to make alliances with virtually any group that would support his presidential ambitions, and few Ecuadoran parties and politicians did not at one time or another come under his spell (Cueva, 1982:38). While in office, he performed unpredictably, the only constants being the military's opposition to his regime and his desire to remain in power.

In the 1940s new political parties emerged to challenge the dominance of the Liberals. One of these was the Ecuadoran Revolutionary Nationalist Action (ARNE), which appeared in 1942 following, and partly as a result of, Peru's victory over Ecuador in a border war. ARNE drew inspiration from the corporatist (i.e., Fascist) model of Spain's dictator Francisco Franco. In 1952 ARNE briefly supported Velasco Ibarra, but it has never been a successful contender in Ecuadoran elections. It has helped to encourage military coups on several occasions, allegedly once with support from the CIA. It remains a minor political party.

A more important organization that emerged during the 1940s was the Concentration of Popular Forces (CFP). This organization was founded by Carlos Guevara Moreno, once a member of the Communist Party of Ecuador (PCE) and also once a supporter of Velasco Ibarra. Guevara Moreno became mayor of Guayaquil in 1951 and made alliances through the CFP with many parties throughout the 1960s, including the PCE, the Revolutionary Socialist party (PSR), the FNV, as well as the Liberal party. Involved in a scandal, Guevara Moreno went into exile in the early 1960s. The leadership of the CFP was assumed by Assad Bucaram, who supported Jaime Roldós Aguilera in the 1978 presidential election; Roldós was elected. This was the CFP's first major success. After the election, however, Roldós became involved in a bitter conflict with Bucaram over control of the CFP, ultimately breaking with him. Through his control of the congress, Bucaram was able to threaten the Roldós programs. The conflict between the two leaders was extraordinary in part because both Roldós and Bucaram belonged to the same party, but mostly because they were related by marriage: Roldós's wife was Bucaram's niece.

Roldós eventually formed a new political party, People, Change, and Democracy (PCD), with other anti-Bucaram members of the CFP. Shortly after the conflict was thus resolved, however, Roldós was killed in a plane crash. Assad Bucaram died in 1981 after a heart attack. These two deaths left the CFP in disarray—divided over substantive issues, over the general direction and orientation of the party, and by lingering personal conflicts (Martz, 1983). The party's populist aspirations were thus consistently threatened and eventually overwhelmed by the traditionalist nature of its leadership (Levy and Mills, 1983). The frustrations of the CFP were symptomatic of the failure of Ecuadoran parties to break loose from traditional political habits and to create more modern and effective political organizations.

A new strain of party organization was introduced in Ecuador in 1951 with the formation of the Social Christian party (PCS). Formed by former members of the Conservative party, the party sought a broader political base, particularly its leader, Camilio Ponce Enríquez. Conservative in orientation, the PCS has never elected more than a few candidates to congress. It has been more successful in presidential elections. The PCS is not a Christian Democratic party in the sense used in Chile, Guatemala, and elsewhere in Latin America. In 1956 Ponce, with additional support from the Conservative party, was elected president, and in 1984 Febres Cordero won a close election for the presidency as the PCS candidate. The PCS is not a coherent or effective organization, so Febres Cordero relied instead upon business groups to organize and finance his campaign (Schodt, 1987:153).

An authentic Christian Democratic party (PDC), established in Ecuador in 1962, was later known as the Christian Democratic Union (UDC). In 1977 it merged with a Conservative party splinter group, known as the Popular Democracy (DP), to become the DP-UDC. One of the leaders of this organization was Osvaldo Hurtado, who was elected vice president in 1979. Upon the death of Jaime Roldós, he succeeded to the presidency in 1981. Under Hurtado the (renamed) PDC won a plurality of votes in Quito in the 1986 congressional election.

In the past several decades a plethora of new parties has been formed in Ecuador's highly fragmented multiparty system, and many of them continue to compete in elections as minor organizations. Some of these have clearly been personalistic vehicles for promoting the political ambitions of a single leader. Illustrative examples are the Nationalist Revolutionary party (PNR), organized to support Carlos Julio Arosemena Monroy, whose brief presidency (1962–1963) was sabotaged by his alcoholism and a military coup (Needler, 1964); the Institutional Democratic Coalition (CID), formed to promote the career of Otto Arosemena Gómez, another former mayor of Guayaquil and former member of the Liberal party; and the Alfarista Radical Front (FRA), formed to promote Abdón Calderón Muñoz, another former Liberal party member with presidential ambitions. The Ecuadoran Roldosista party (PRE)— led by the nephew of Assad Bucaram, Abdalá Bucaram—won a plurality of the congressional vote in Guayaquil in the 1986 election and was a major contender in the 1988 elections.

One of the most resilient of the newer parties in Ecuador has been the Democratic Left (ID). The ID was organized in 1970 by Rodrigo Borja Cevallos, who had also been a leader of the Liberal party. The new organization was designed primarily to mobilize urban middle-class voters from Quito and Guayaquil, but it also has been successful in recruiting support from the Ecuadoran labor movement and has associated itself with Social Democratic parties that belong to the Socialist International.

The ID nominated Rodrigo Borja for the presidency in the elections of 1978, 1984, and 1988. He did poorly in 1978, and in the presidential runoff election the next year he and his party supported Roldós, who came to depend on ID support following his dispute with Assad Bucaram and his supporters in the CFP. In 1984, Borja received more votes than the other candidates in the presidential election, but he lost the runoff election later that year to Febres Cordero, receiving 48 percent of the vote against Febres Cordero's 52 percent. However, the party did well in the 1984 congressional elections, receiving almost twice as many seats as Febres Cordero's party. The ID then joined a broad coalition opposed to Febres Cordero, the Popular Democratic Bloc (BDP), which controlled a majority of the seats in the congress after 1986. In an effort to counteract the influence of the BDP, Febres Cordero and the PCS formed an alliance of their own, known as the National Reconstruction Front (FRN), which included in addition to the PCS, the Liberal and Conservative parties. Borja won the presidency in the 1988 runoff election.

Marxist parties have had a long if not very successful history in Ecuador, riven by factionalism and ideological quarrels not unlike those found among Marxist parties elsewhere in Latin America. The first Marxist party to emerge was the Ecuadoran Socialist party (PSE) in 1926. That organization divided in 1931 as some party members broke away to form the Ecuadoran Communist party (PCE). The PCE, illegal for much of its history, has been a fairly orthodox, pro-Soviet Communist party. It has initiated several alliances for electoral purposes, none of them very successful.

Besides the division in 1931 that produced the PCE, Socialist party factions have resulted in several new Marxist parties. One division occurred in 1935, producing the Socialist Revolutionary Vanguard (VRS), a reformist group opposed to the Liberals' increasingly authoritarian rule. In 1945 the PSE supported the Velasco regime but soon broke with it. After World War II it had considerable success, however, in the Ecuadoran labor movement. It endorsed the candidacy of Galo Plaza for president in 1960, which caused some of its members to break away to form the Revolutionary Socialist party (PSR); this organization was influenced by and supportive of the Cuban revolution led by Fidel Castro. The PSR ultimately adopted a Marxist-Leninist posture much more radical than the Marxism espoused by the PSE. Other Marxist parties have appeared over the past twenty years but have had little political significance.

The parties mentioned above represent but a small fraction of those that have participated in Ecuadoran multiparty politics. In the mid-1960s it was not uncommon for eighty or ninety parties to be competing for visibility. No party over the past half-century has been able to dominate Ecuadoran politics for more than a brief time, with the arguable exception of the Velasquistas, who constituted more of a personalistic movement than a party. The influence of Velasco and, later, Assad Bucaram illustrates the difficulty involved in creating modern parties that could eventually become institutions. The failures of the Liberal party, the CFP, and other groups (Martz, 1972) are similarly illustrative. The Democratic Left has, since 1978, shown signs of becoming a national party capable of transcending personalism and regionalism. But its political base is tenuous and its relative success inconclusive.

There have been many transient alliances of weak political groups, often not surviving a single election or, at most, a single regime. These alliances are symptomatic of the fundamental difficulty in creating viable party organizations that can survive long enough to become permanent institutions. The result has been a multiparty system without a consistent point of reference, continually shifting and producing no consistent pattern of political evolution. Meanwhile, the country has slowly begun to experience the effects of modernization. The need for viable, modern party organizations is therefore more pressing than ever. The inability of Ecuadoran politicians to escape from traditional practices and to create viable political options that transcend individual leaders suggest that the cycle of civil-military alternation in power is likely to continue and that party politics may remain as unstructured, unstable, and fragile as it has been historically.

Elections and Voting

Until the constitution of 1979 decreed otherwise, Ecuador had a literacy requirement for voting. In a country that historically has had very low literacy rates, this requirement effectively prevented the majority of Ecuadorans from participating in national politics. In Ecuador, literacy was closely related to race: most Indians were illiterate; most Indians, therefore, could not vote. Illiterate citizens were allowed to vote for the first time in the 1984 elections.

Women, by contrast, were granted suffrage in Ecuador before women were enfranchised in the United States. Ecuadoran women were given the right to vote in the constitution of 1883, although they lost that right in the next two constitutions, 1897 and 1906. In 1929 they again were enfranchised and have continued to be in the four constitutions that followed. By Latin American standards of female suffrage, 1929 was an early time.

Obviously the elimination of the literacy requirement was an important development in Ecuador. It has expanded the electorate by a considerable margin, and, more important, has embraced the majority of Ecuadorans hitherto excluded from politics. From 1979 to 1986, the rate of participation doubled in Ecuador. (The levels of participation as a percentage of the total population for elections from 1888 to 1988 are shown in Table 19.1.) Prior to universal enfranchisement, about 15 percent of the national population participated in national elections. In 1984 the level rose to 31 percent, in 1986 to 45 percent, and in 1988 to 49 percent, an astonishingly high level. The 1988 level represents a participation of almost 80 percent of those eligible to vote in Ecuador.

The 1979 constitution also established a unicameral legislature—eliminating the senate, which had existed in Ecuador since 1835. The present legislature is small, containing fifty-nine regional and twelve "national deputies" for a total of seventy-one, the former being elected by provinces and the latter being elected at large. The elected deputies are apportioned to the twenty provinces on the basis of population. There was until 1979

TABLE 19.1
Ecuadoran National Elections: Percent of National Population
Participating, 1888–1988

Percentage		Percentage	
1888	3	1956	15
1924	11	1960	17
1931	3	1968	15
1932	4	1979	19
1933	3	1984	31
1948	9	1986	45
1952	10	1988	49

Source: Ecuadoran electoral results compiled by the Tribunal
Supremo Electoral (Quito), 1888–1988.

a provision in the senate for functional representation that dated from corporatist experiments in the 1920s.

The characteristics of Ecuadoran political parties (discussed above) prompted the formation of a special legislative commission in 1977 to evaluate party regulations. The commission included Jaime Roldós and Osvaldo Hurtado, who were to become the next two presidents of the country. The commission was very explicit in identifying the problems that parties had created in Ecuador; Hurtado specified their vacuous rhetoric, personal conflicts, and ad hoc groupings (Levy and Mills, 1983:21). Accordingly, the Law of the Parties was adopted in 1977 and was later incorporated into the 1979 constitution. It guaranteed all groups the right to organize formal parties but imposed regulations and restrictions on them in regard to party names, membership requirements, organization, and program philosophies. In order to obtain legal recognition, parties also have to provide a membership list comprising at least 0.5 percent of the nation's registered voters, currently about fifteen thousand out of three million. Parties were required to submit proof that they were national in scope, meaning they be formally organized in at least ten of the country's twenty provinces, and that to retain their legal status they participate regularly in elections and receive at least 5 percent of the vote in all congressional, provincial, and municipal elections. Candidates would have to be nominated and endorsed by legal parties to run for national office. The latter provision was subjected to a constitutional referendum in 1986 that would have permitted nonaffiliated candidates to run. The proposed change was supported by President Febres Cordero and, in the wake of considerable opposition to his economic policies, became a referendum on his regime. The proposal was defeated by a 58 percent majority.

Another significant change in the laws regulating parties was the provision in 1977 for state subsidies of the campaigns of legal parties. The objective of this change was to curtail the advantage of charismatic candidates, who, it was argued, stood a better chance of raising campaign funds than most parties did. Two state funds for campaigning were established, and each receives 0.05 percent of total government expenditures. The first fund provides 60 percent of its monies in equal shares to parties that received 10 percent of the vote in the last election; 40 percent goes to parties based on the share of the vote. The second fund provides additional monies distributed according to the number of votes received in the most recent election. The changes did seem to have an impact on party competition, at least on the number of parties. In the mid-1960s (under the old regulations) as many as one hundred parties participated in national elections. In 1984 and 1986 the number had fallen to about seventeen parties. Allocation of seats in the legislature is by proportional representation using the d'Hondt system, and voting is by closed lists established by the parties. Given the relatively small number of legislators elected for each province, the effects of proportional representation are very slight.

Since 1948 there have been eight national presidential elections. The first four represented a cycle of civilian regimes uninterrupted by military intervention. Two of those elections (1952 and 1960) were won by Velasco Ibarra, and it was during his second election that the military intervened. He was elected again in 1968, but before the end of his term the military seized power in an apparent effort to prevent Assad Bucaram from becoming president. The military remained in power through the election of 1978 and the runoff election of 1979, won by Jaime Roldós. Upon his death in 1981, he was succeeded by Osvaldo Hurtado. In 1984 Febres Cordero was elected president, followed in 1988 by Rodrigo Borja Cevallos.

Six presidential candidates competed in the 1978 election, and seven ran in the 1984. In 1978 Roldós and Hurtado won a plurality of 31 percent of the vote, and in the runoff election the next year they received a large majority (69 percent) of the vote. In the 1984 election the ID candidate, Borja Cevallos, won a plurality of the vote and Febres Cordero came in second; however, in the runoff election four months later Febres Cordero defeated Borja Cevallos with a 52 percent majority of the vote.

Ten candidates ran for the presidency in 1988, with a first-round election held in January and the runoff election held in May. The two leading contenders were Rodrigo Borja Cevallos (ID), running for the third time, and Abdalá Bucaram, who had been nominated by the PRE, or Roldosista, party. (Bucaram had organized this party after Jaime Roldós died in 1981 specifically for his successful campaign for mayor of Guayaquil.) Borja won the 1988 presidential election, but Bucaram made a very strong showing. Results of the three presidential elections are shown in Table 19.2.

Abdalá Bucaram carried on the charismatic, unpredictable populist style of his uncle, Assad. He had been forced into exile in Panama before the end of his term as mayor, facing legal charges filed by the Ecuadoran military. Apparently, during a press conference in New York City, he had described the Ecuadoran military as unfit for anything but parades. He

TABLE 19.2
Presidential Vote in Ecuador, 1978, 1984, and 1988 (in percentages)

	Preliminary Election	Runoff Election
1978		
Roldós (CFP)	27.7	68.8[a]
Durán (FNC)	23.8	31.2
Other	48.5	
1984		
Borja (ID)	28.4	47.8
Febres (PSC)	27.5	52.2
Other	44.1	
1988		
Borja (ID)	24.7	52.8[b]
Bucaram (PRE)	17.6	47.2
Other	67.7	

[a]The runoff for the 1978 election was held in 1979.
[b]In 1988, 12.4% of ballots were blank or spoiled.

Source: Adapted from Arthur S. Banks, ed., Political Handbook of the World (Binghamton, NY: CSA Publications, 1988), pp. 167–168, Keesings Record of World Events (August 1988), p. 36097, and El Comercio (Quito), 1978–1988.

returned to campaign for the presidency in August 1987, whereupon he was charged by his niece and nephew, Martha and Santiago Roldós Bucaram, with using the Roldós name to form his party, the PRE. It was commonly believed that were Bucaram to win the presidency in 1988, the military might have intervened and canceled the election. Abdalá Bucaram's sister, Elsa, was elected in 1988 as mayor of Guayaquil by a considerable majority; she became the third Bucaram to be elected to that position, which places her (as it did Assad, Abdalá, and others before them) in a strong position to become a major national political leader.

In an interview in January 1988, published in Madrid's El País newspaper, Abdalá Bucaram expressed his admiration for the "organizational genius" of Adolf Hitler and made outrageous comments about his opponent, Borja, and President Febres Cordero (LAWR, February 18, 1988:6). He claims to hold the Ecuadoran record in the 100-meter dash and characterizes himself politically as "left of center."

In the 1979 congressional election, the CFP (the party of Roldós) won the largest vote, receiving thirty of the sixty-nine legislative seats; the ID received twelve, the second-largest number of seats. In 1984 the largest

TABLE 19.3
Party Representation in the Ecuadoran Congress: Following 1979
Election and After 1981 Realignment

	1979 Vote (%)	1979 Seats	1981 Seats
CFP	27	30	24
ID	14	12	12
PC	7	9	6
PLR	8	4	4
PSC	6	2	2
PNR	5	2	2
MPD	4	1	1
UDP	3	1	1
PNV	2	1	0
CID	5	3	0
PD[a]			1
Independents/			
Others	5	4	9
PD[b]			7

[a]Did not participate in 1979 election.
[b]Former CFP and ID candidates.

Source: Adapted from Arthur S. Banks and William Overstreet, eds.,
Political Handbook of the World (New York: McGraw-Hill, 1983),
p. 137.

number of seats was won by the ID, with twenty-four of seventy-one, while
Febres Cordero's party, the PSC, won only fourteen seats. Party identification
of legislators changed even after 1979, providing a new legislative party
balance by 1981 (Table 19.3). In 1986 the ID won seventeen seats of the
forty-two claimed by the BDP coalition, while Febres Cordero's government
coalition, the FRN, gained a combined total of only nineteen out of the
seventy-one legislative seats. Nine of the seats in 1986 were won by other
groups. In 1988 the ID won twenty-nine seats in the congress, a plurality,
and just short of a majority.

There is some evidence, albeit tenuous, that the traditional pattern of
regionalism in party politics may be breaking down somewhat in Ecuador.
Roldós, for example, did very well in both Quito and Guayaquil in 1978
and 1979. Part of the regional influence in Ecuador proceeds from the
demographic dominance of two provinces—Guayas, which contains the city
of Guayaquil, and Pichincha, which includes the city of Quito. Those two
provinces, along with the province of Manabi (which adjoins Guayas),
contain 56 percent of the national electorate; Guayaquil and Manabi together
constitute almost 45 percent of the national electorate. Several parties are
now more organized by class, particularly the middle class, which may
make them more competitive throughout the country. Control of the political

parties, and perhaps their leaders, may still have a regional dimension, however.

The specter of political violence remains in Ecuadoran politics. A guerrilla movement known as the "Alfaro Vive" was established in 1983, characterizing itself as "nationalist" rather than "Marxist." However, its principal leader, Arturo Jarrín, was killed in late 1986. The movement is thought to have had connections with the M-19 movement in Colombia and the Tupac Amaru movement in Peru. In addition, in 1987, President Febres Cordero was abducted and briefly held prisoner by a group of air force commandos seeking the release from prison of an air force general, Frank Vargas Pazzos. Vargas Pazzos later became a presidential candidate in 1988. There have been both rumors and instances of other attempts by some military officers to intervene, but the civilian regimes have so far thwarted these. However, as yet there is no persuasive reason to believe that the chronic cycle of military intervention is any less likely than it was in the past. In fact, military involvement might be even more likely given the serious economic problems facing the country, the lack of cohesion or stability in the party and electoral processes, and the fragility of the government institutions.

Long-Term Trends

Clearly the military remains a conspicuous factor in Ecuadoran politics, and that reality seems unlikely to change. The military's obsession with eradicating charismatic leaders was at least temporarily assuaged by the deaths of Velasco Ibarra and Assad Bucaram. However, the rise of Abdalá Bucaram threatens to continue the family dynasty and to generate continued military hostility toward him. The temptation to intervene created in 1972 by the sudden abundance of petroleum dollars is also temporarily gone. The country is in a serious financial condition owing to its international indebtedness and the low level of revenues being generated by petroleum exports. The country's economic problems are severe enough to discourage military officers from wanting to take responsibility for solving them. In the past the universal mistrust among officers of Velasco and Assad Bucaram facilitated such a pro-intervention coalition, as did the prospect of vast petroleum dollars that could be spent for national development purposes. Elements within the military may again wish to stage a coup, and indeed, such efforts have already surfaced in Ecuador. But it is not clear that there is a sufficient consensus among the officers to bring off a military coup— at least in the short run.

There is some indication that the traditional regionalism of the country may be breaking down, although the demographic distribution of the population remains favorable to the coastal provinces. Some of the political parties may be able to develop an electoral base capable of transcending regionalism; there is already evidence that this is occurring.

The influence of universal suffrage and, more specifically, of the Indian in Ecuadoran politics remains uncertain. Any political party or leader that can mobilize the Indian communities could become a powerful force in the country. That has yet to happen, but it may. Present demographic trends producing an increasingly younger population—particularly when combined with the existing economic realities—suggest the increasing influence of younger Ecuadorans in national politics. Their vote could be an important strategic consideration for political parties, particularly given greater electoral participation. Their frustrations and political involvement may also suggest a growing possibility of concerted revolutionary activity in the country, as similar realities did a decade ago in El Salvador. There is a heritage of violence in Ecuador that is not inconsistent with revolutionary activity. Although many of the conditions that would support revolutionary activity are present, there are no indications as yet that it will emerge.

There are reasonable arguments to be made on both sides of the question as to whether political parties and elections will play a greater role, or for that matter any role at all, in Ecuadoran politics. Ecuador remains, as Velasco observed, a "difficult country to govern."

References

Blanksten, George I. 1951. *Ecuador: Constitutions and Caudillos.* Berkeley and Los Angeles: Univ. of California Press.

Cueva, Agustín. 1982. *The Process of Political Domination in Ecuador.* New Brunswick, NJ: Transaction.

Fitch, John Samuel. 1977. *The Military Coup d'Etat as a Political Process: Ecuador, 1948–1966.* Baltimore: Johns Hopkins Univ. Press.

Hurtado, Osvaldo. 1980. *Political Power in Ecuador.* Albuquerque: Univ. of New Mexico Press.

Levy, James, and Nick D. Mills, Jr. 1983. The Challenge to Democratic Reformism in Ecuador. *Studies in Comparative International Development* 18(4):3–33.

Linke, Lilo. 1960. *Ecuador: Country of Contrasts.* 3d ed. London: Oxford Univ. Press.

Martz, John D. 1972. *Ecuador: Conflicting Political Culture and the Quest for Progress.* Boston: Allyn and Bacon.

_____. 1983. Populist Leadership and the Party Caudillo: Ecuador and the CFP, 1962–81. *Studies in Comparative International Development* 18(3):22–49.

_____. 1985. Ecuador: Authoritarianism, Personalism, and Dependency. In Howard J. Wiarda and Harvey F. Kline, eds., *Latin American Politics and Development.* Boulder, CO: Westview.

Needler, Martin C. 1964. *Anatomy of a Coup d'Etat: Ecuador, 1963.* Washington, DC: Institute for the Comparative Study of Political Systems.

Pike, Frederick B. 1977. *The United States and the Andean Republics: Peru, Bolivia, and Ecuador.* Cambridge: Harvard Univ. Press.

Robalino Davila, Luis. 1964. *Orígenes del Ecuador de Hoy: Nacimiento y Primeros Años de la República,* vol. 2. Quito: Talleres Gráficos Nacionales.

Schodt, David. 1987. *Ecuador: An Andean Enigma.* Boulder, CO: Westview.

20

DOMINICAN REPUBLIC

Party politics has been important in the Dominican Republic for only about twenty-five years. After independence in 1821 the nation was in almost constant turmoil and beyond the control of political parties and elections. There have been twenty-seven constitutions in the Dominican Republic since independence—approximately one every six years; the current constitution, one of the most long-lived, dates from 1962. Since 1961 political parties have been visible and relevant to national politics. Elections have been held, but neither elections nor parties have strong traditions. Parties are still tied primarily to individual politicians and their careers and have therefore not developed an institutional status of their own nor an identity separate from the leaders who have created and used them.

The country has endured several extended dictatorships, the most recent and longest lasting was that of Rafael Trujillo (1930–1961). The Trujillo dictatorship was one of the most brutal, repressive, self-serving, and authoritarian in recent Latin American history. It was followed by a period of instability in 1965, which included a civil war and foreign intervention—two common experiences for the Dominican Republic. Since then the country has sustained a civilian government with some of the fundamental characteristics of democracy. Political parties and party politicians have played a significant role in this regard with some limited success.

The Evolution and Context of Party Politics in the Dominican Republic

Political parties and elections were not an important characteristic of Dominican politics until the end of the Trujillo dictatorship in 1961. Parties had periodically existed before that time, but they were of little importance and most did not survive very long. Trujillo used a political party to mobilize support for his regime and occasionally even devised "opposition" parties to lend credence to his fraudulent elections.

One clear limitation on the country's politics has been the preponderant influence of foreign countries, often leaving national politics beyond the control of Dominicans. That influence included occupation during the Spanish colonial era, a period of French colonial rule, domination by neighboring Haiti, a second occupation by Spain, and finally intervention and control by the United States. The United States had intervened for economic reasons on several occasions in the Dominican Republic prior to 1914, but in that year U.S. Marines were sent to Santo Domingo for ostensibly political reasons, on the grounds that the United States wanted to "ensure an honest election." Two years later in 1916, President Woodrow Wilson again became concerned about continuing instability on the island and sent the marines in once more. That occupation resulted in a military rule by the United States that lasted until 1924, when U.S. military forces were finally withdrawn, leaving Dominican politics unchanged.

In March 1924 Horacio Vásquez was elected president, and in 1929 there was some unrest when he tried to perpetuate his rule beyond the expiration of his elected term. The next year he was overthrown by a military coup supported by Rafael Trujillo, a brigadier general and the army chief-of-staff. Shortly after the coup Trujillo was elected president of the republic in a fraudulent contest, and his extended dictatorship began. The United States continued to meddle throughout Trujillo's regime. The dictator cultivated close relationships with the United States, and the U.S. government kept a close watch on his regime. In 1961 U.S. officials learned of a conspiracy to assassinate Trujillo and may have encouraged the conspirators. Trujillo was assassinated on May 30, 1961. By the end of his regime, Trujillo was opposed by the leaders of most countries in the Western Hemisphere, including the presidents of Venezuela, Costa Rica, Cuba, and even the United States. The United States intervened again with military force in 1965 on the heels of an unpopular coup and a subsequent rebellion and civil war—the most blatant recent example of overt military intervention by the United States in Latin America (Atkins, 1981).

This long history of foreign intervention made it nearly impossible to establish democratic politics in the Dominican Republic or to develop effective party organizations. But economic problems also inhibited the evolution of parties. One was the lack of economic development and modernization, and another was its economic dependency resulting from an export economy based almost entirely on sugar. These economic conditions sustained the poverty of the masses, which inhibited political participation and generated political alienation. What development and modernization there were occurred under Trujillo, but primarily redounded to his benefit and that of his family, friends, and supporters.

Up to 1961 parties were little more than instruments designed to further the careers of ambitious politicians and to a considerable extent they still are. Political violence has never been far below the surface of Dominican politics. Several presidents have been assassinated while in office, including Ulises Heureaux in 1899, Ramón Cáceres (who had earlier participated in the assassination of Heureaux) in 1911, and, of course, Rafael Trujillo in 1961, who himself had killed several Dominican politicians and attempted to have the president of Venezuela, Rómulo Betancourt, assassinated. Likewise, civil wars, insurrections, protests, and riots have been frequent occurrences, and both the potential and reality of violence continues to this day.

Because the country has a large rural sector and limited educational opportunities, one would normally expect to find low levels of social mobilization and political awareness in the Dominican Republic. But several factors have combined to produce a higher level of social mobilization and political awareness than would otherwise exist. One of these factors is geographical. The island nation has been isolated by its geography from all nations except Haiti. This isolation has produced a strong sense of national awareness and identity among Dominicans, which is further reinforced by its contrast and hostility to Haiti. By culture, language, and history Haiti is very different from the Dominican Republic, and this contrast has further encouraged a sense of national identity in the Dominican Republic. The nation is also densely populated, exceeded in density only by Haiti and El Salvador in Latin America. This density exists within a relatively small territory and mitigates the traditional differences between rural and urban areas. When combined with the nation's isolation, this density encourages informal communication and a sense of closeness, which reinforces the country's national identity and political awareness. The relatively high level of political awareness and identity helps explain why Dominican politics has been and still is so potentially turbulent. The legacy of political violence, economic deprivation, inequalities, and the sensitivity to international penetration and exploitation as well as domestic oppression reinforces the potential for political instability.

There is another, more subtle, factor that has been politically significant in the Dominican Republic: the existence of a social caste system deeply rooted in the country's history and culture. Wiarda and Krysanek (1982:16) suggest that race and class are closely related in the country. White Dominicans tend to be wealthier and have historically constituted the dominant elites. The middle classes have been primarily mulatto, and the urban and rural working classes have tended to be black or dark mulatto. Race has separated social classes and reinforced barriers to upward mobility in the society. These divisions have not produced open hostility or conflict but underlie many of the assumptions of Dominican society and politics. Trujillo's appeal, at least in the earlier days of his regime, was based in part on his open hostility as a mulatto to the caste system and those who had benefited from it.

The Trujillo regime was a major dividing point in Dominican history, and parties can be categorized in regard to that experience: (1) those that existed prior to Trujillo and ceased to exist with his dictatorship, (2) those created by Trujillo to reinforce his regime and by others to destroy it, and (3) those that emerged and competed following the Trujillo regime. Almost all of the parties in each period were personalistic and limited to the period in which they emerged. A few of the parties that opposed Trujillo survived into the post-Trujillo period, but the others disappeared and had no lasting impact on the nation's politics.

The parties that predate Trujillo exhibit traditional personalistic and transient qualities. The oldest ones date from the 1880s and were clusters of politicians known as "reds" and "blues," designations that simply distinguished those seeking power from those holding it. They had no programs, organizations, or permanent loyalties. One of the first parties to emerge was the National party (PN), formed in the 1890s to further the political ambitions of Gen. Horacio Vásquez, who eventually became president of the republic in 1924. The PN was originally established to oppose the repressive dictatorship of Ulises Heureaux, which had initiated economic development in the country by leasing or selling its resources to foreign interests. Vásquez led the opposition to Heureaux and helped organize his assassination. The weakness of the party as an organization may be illustrated by the fact that its congressional vote in the 1918 and 1924 elections was officially recorded by the government as *Horacista* rather than by the legal party name (Campillo Pérez, 1982:431). Just as Vásquez was responsible for the formation of a party to support his political ambitions, he was indirectly responsible for the formation of a party that opposed his ambitions—the Progressive party (PP), founded in the 1920s.

As Vásquez's career continued, a second opposition group—the Republican party (PR)—formed to oppose his candidacy in the 1924 election. Vásquez was elected in spite of the efforts of the PP and the PR to defeat him. Prior to the scheduled 1930 election the PR and its principal leader, Rafael Estrella Urena, staged a successful coup against Vásquez, and Estrella Urena temporarily became president. Trujillo did nothing to discourage the coup and may have been involved with planning it. Afterward, he ran for president in a very fraudulent election with Estrella Urena as his vice-presidential running mate, suggesting the possibility that they struck a political deal to eliminate Vásquez. Neither the PR nor Urena survived politically after Trujillo was elected. His political ambitions prompted the formation of an opposition political alliance in 1930 known as the National Progressive Alliance (ANP), a coalition comprising vestiges of the PN, the Vásquez supporters, and the PP, and its leader, Federico Velásquez. Aware that Trujillo had no intention of allowing a free or honest election, the ANP withdrew from the contest a few weeks before the election. Vásquez left the country after Trujillo's election, and from that point on there was no effective opposition in the country.

The thirty-one-year Trujillo reign was one of the most thoroughly controlled and repressive dictatorships of any previously known in Latin America. Its history has been well documented and analyzed elsewhere (Wiarda, 1970).

Essentially authoritarian, the Trujillo dictatorship is also an example of what Max Weber termed a "patrimonial" rule, whereby the state is run virtually as though it were the private property of the ruler, and those who derived their living or welfare from this "private estate" were subject to his rule and dependent on his beneficence for survival. Trujillo eventually acquired enormous control over the wealth of the country and used much of it for his own benefit and that of his immediate relatives and associates. He owned or controlled much of the good land, business, and industry in the country. Like the Somozas in Nicaragua, he ran the Dominican Republic to a large extent as though it were his property. He even renamed Santo Domingo, the capital and oldest city in Latin America, Ciudad Trujillo (Trujillo City) and designated himself "Generalissimo" and "The Great Benefactor." The Dominican Republic became a police state, whose opponents were arbitrarily arrested, imprisoned, and tortured. The lucky ones made it into exile, the less fortunate were killed.

As sometimes happens in such dictatorships, Trujillo was careful to go through the ritual of holding elections at the constitutionally prescribed intervals, from 1930 to 1942 every four years, and from 1942 to 1957 every five years. He was unopposed in all but one election, 1947, and his "opponents" in that election were no more than agents chosen by him to go through the motions of an "honest" election. He received 781,000 votes, and his two opponents each received 29,000 votes in the 1947 election— a balance in the vote no doubt decided beforehand by Trujillo. In all the other presidential elections the official Dominican records show that no votes were cast against candidate Trujillo. In fact, in the 1930 election more votes were reported for Trujillo than there were voters in the country.

The dictator utilized an official party to further his control over the country, a party that defended his rule and his role as the country's "benefactor." Trujillo called it the Dominican party (PD), and it was often the only party organization permitted in the single-party system. A mechanism for political control, the PD was a political machine that dispensed patronage, enforced discipline among the Dominican elites, and solicited contributions from those who wanted a favorable relationship with the regime—a form of "legal extortion."

The PD also was the principal source of propaganda for Trujillo, giving personal credit to him for development projects initiated by the government. There were a great many such projects, most designed to stimulate economic development that would benefit primarily the Trujillo family. Membership campaigns were held regularly by the PD, coercing Dominicans to join and contribute to the party. It is estimated that as many as 80 percent of all Dominicans at one time or another were forced to join the PD (Sánchez, 1982:360). The party performed many nonpolitical functions. Wiarda (1969:77) observes that it was involved "with raising the standard of living of the rural peasants; the construction of parks, clinics, hospitals, churches, streets, hotels, libraries and schools; the printing of books and newspapers; and the showing of movies." Trujillo was given credit for all these benefits, and on his frequent trips to the rural areas he would reiterate his accomplishments and listen to complaints and aspirations of the peasants, while handing out bundles of money to them. Millions of dollars passed through the PD during the Trujillo period, much of it skimmed off by the dictator for his own use. The party was also an intelligence network for the regime, gathering information on possible dissidents and maintaining dossiers on individuals and groups.

Trujillo organized other political parties when it was useful to do so. In 1942 there appeared the Trujillo party (PT), created at Trujillo's request by his dentist, José Enrique Aybar. It officially endorsed candidates of the PD, including, of course, Trujillo, but its principal purpose was to assist Trujillo in a purge of uncooperative members of the PD. In 1947 he ordered two "opposition" political parties organized, the Labor party (PL) and the National Democratic party (PND). The PND nominated Francisco Prats Ramírez for the presidency, who was also running at the same time for congress on the PD party list. During the campaign Prats in an absent-minded moment signed a petition along with other members of congress urging Trujillo's reelection as president, apparently forgetting that Trujillo had also assigned him the role of running as an opposition presidential candidate who would be defeated. The PL also nominated a presidential candidate, Rafael Espaillat, as well as candidates for the congress at Trujillo's request. In 1957 Trujillo decided to have a vice-presidential running mate for the first time since 1938. He was Joaquín Balaguer, who was to reemerge after Trujillo's death as a major political leader. Balaguer eventually served four terms as president, a time in office equal to about half that of his mentor. With the end of the Trujillo dictatorship, Balaguer founded the Reformist party (PR) to advance his own ambitions and objectives; it participated in the 1963 elections.

During the dictatorship, exiles created organizations committed to overthrowing Trujillo, some of which were subsequently converted into political parties. The earliest of the anti-Trujillo exile organizations was the Dominican Revolutionary party (PRD), which was founded in 1939 by Juan Bosch. The PRD was committed both to the overthrow of Trujillo and the implementation of extensive economic and social reforms. It was one of several political parties in Latin America at the time influenced by the Peruvian APRA and Haya de la Torre's call for an indigenous ideological movement to promote hemispheric reform. Bosch and his colleagues in the PRD also established close relationships with Democratic Action (AD) in Venezuela and enjoyed the support of Venezuela's president Rómulo Betancourt. Betancourt's opposition to Trujillo and his support of the PRD provoked Trujillo into an abortive attempt to have Betancourt assassinated, following which Betancourt, the AD, and Venezuela generally became even more hostile to Trujillo.

With Trujillo's death in 1961, the PRD was officially constituted as a political party. Juan Bosch became its presidential candidate, and the PRD swept the 1962 national elections. However, it remained in power only seven months, falling victim to a military coup and subsequent instability that ultimately provoked an invasion by U.S. military forces. Bosch had impeccable credentials as a longtime opponent of Trujillo and his family, as well as being an advocate for basic structural changes in Dominican society. But his election coincided with U.S. alarm over Cuba and Fidel Castro—specifically, the disastrous Bay of Pigs invasion. Many in the new Johnson administration apparently came to view Bosch specifically and events in the Dominican Republic generally as parallel to their problems with Fidel Castro and events in Cuba, and they wanted to eliminate Bosch from the scene (Szulc, 1965). Thereafter, leadership in the Dominican Republic gravitated through elections to Joaquín Balaguer, Trujillo's former vice president. The PRD failed to achieve its original objectives, and its weak organization and strategies proved to be ineffective instruments for reform in the short period it was in power (Kryzanek, 1977).

The Dominican Communist party (PCD) was established clandestinely in 1942 and was originally known as the Popular Socialist party (PSP). Trujillo used the PSP for his own purposes, alternating between a policy of persecuting it as a threat to Dominican security and one of apparent conciliation to elicit U.S. attention and foreign assistance. The leadership of the PCD has been relatively orthodox and pro-Soviet in its orientation. Under pressure from the United States following the 1965 events, it was outlawed and remained illegal until 1974.

Another opposition exile group was the Dominican Popular movement (MPD), organized in 1956 in prerevolutionary Cuba. After Trujillo's death, it became increasingly radicalized, eventually adopting a Marxist political orientation. It was never recognized legally as a party, and its influence declined after the mid-1960s. The Fourteenth of June movement was another exile group with a Marxist orientation, its name coming from an attempted invasion of the Dominican Republic by exiles supported by Castro on June 14, 1959. Like the MPD, the organization never participated in elections and also became radicalized, advocating a Fidelista program of armed insurrection.

A final group that formed just at the time of Trujillo's assassination was the Social Christian Revolutionary party (PRSC), which received support from Venezuela's COPEI party, with which it shared many ideological and political orientations. It cooperated with Balaguer following the 1966 election and opposed the PRD. In 1984 the PR and the PRSC merged into one party, a move long advocated by Balaguer. The organization retained the PRSC name while Balaguer assumed leadership and control. The new PRSC became the vehicle for Balaguer in the 1986 election, winning a substantial victory over the PRD in both the presidential and the congressional contests.

The instability that occurred in the aftermath of Trujillo's assassination— the 1963 military coup, the civil war, and the 1965 occupation by U.S. Marines—profoundly affected Dominican politics. By the time of the 1966 elections the country's political forces had undergone major changes, the most important being the increased influence of Joaquín Balaguer and his Reformist party. By comparison to the PRD and Bosch, the PR and Balaguer had a more moderate and pragmatic political orientation. Balaguer did not seem to be politically damaged by his association with Trujillo, and he may even have been helped by it. He was known as an honest and well-intentioned leader, and he and the PR won three elections (1966, 1970, and 1974), capturing in the process nearly total dominance of the two legislative chambers in each election. Balaguer continued to use the PR as an instrument for his political ambitions, but in 1982 he was narrowly defeated for the presidency. He ran again for the presidency in 1986 and was elected, after merging his party with the PRSC (Black, 1986:84–85).

In the 1962 election the principal opposition to Bosch came from a newly formed coalition known as the National Civic Union (UCN), composed largely of business and professional leaders in the country. With the formation of the PR, the UCN disappeared. It was, like so many Dominican parties, a personalistic one, in this case anti-Bosch. It was established for a short-term political objective and disappeared after that was achieved.

A similar party was formed in 1970 to oppose the reelection of Balaguer. Known as the Movement for Democratic Integration Against Reelection (MIDA), the group was led by Vice President Francisco Augusto Lora, who himself had presidential ambitions. The party never had any organization or clear objectives other than opposition to Balaguer and support for Lora's candidacy. But after failing in 1972, it resurfaced and participated in the campaigns of 1974 and 1978. In the latter election Lora combined the forces of MIDA with those of a small party known as the Quisqueyan Democratic party (PQD), which had been established as a vehicle for Gen. Elias Wessin y Wessin, one of the major actors in the 1965 civil war. Joining in that coalition was a small party, the Movement for National Conciliation (MCN), which had been founded to advance the presidential ambitions of yet another Dominican politician, Héctor García Godoy, who had served as provisional president between the 1965 civil war and the 1966 election.

In 1973 personal conflicts between Bosch and members of his own political party prompted him to leave the PRD and to establish the Democratic Liberation party (PLD). It won a few legislative seats in the 1984 and 1986 elections, but Bosch's subsequent presidential efforts were ineffective. He was, however, a key political figure in the Dominican Republic. He established two significant political parties, the PRD and the PLD, prompted at least two opposition parties to form (UCN and PR), and by his election in 1962 presided over a period of instability, civil war, and foreign military intervention that all profoundly influenced the subsequent evolution of party politics. He was also one of the first and most effective critics of the Trujillo regime, a colorful, charismatic, but also enigmatic and controversial, figure in Dominican politics.

One final political group of the post-Trujillo period should also be mentioned, the National Action party (PAN), formed in 1980 to support the candidacy of retired Gen. Neid Rafael Nivar Seíjas, who had served earlier as chief of the national police under Balaguer. The party had no success in the 1982 election and subsequently disappeared.

The Dominican party system has had a substantial number of political parties in recent years, although none has yet established viable roots in the political experience of the country. Even the two strongest have been overwhelmed by personal considerations of their leaders. Bosch left the PRD and formed another party, and Balaguer merged the PR with the PRSC. The PRD, at least after Bosch's resignation in 1973, seemed to be proving capable of transcending a specific leader, encouraged in part by President Antonio Guzmán's decision not to seek reelection in 1982 and the success of its candidate, Salvador Jorge Blanco, in defeating Balaguer in that election. But Guzmán was implicated personally in several scandals while he was president. He committed suicide just before the end of his term, and the PRD lost the 1986 election in a close race with Balaguer. It is not clear whether the PRD can regain its strength and renew its organization under different leadership. None of the other parties has yet demonstrated an ability to survive the fate of their founders, and they continue to exist solely for electoral purposes, without organizations, strong loyalty or identification from the voters, and normally without any clear political or ideological direction.

Electoral Politics

Elections in the Dominican Republic can be divided into the same three periods as parties: those prior to the Trujillo regime, those held under the Trujillo dictatorship, and those held after the fall of Trujillo, beginning in 1962. The electoral system currently in effect dates from 1962. Voter participation levels prior to 1930 were relatively low, and given the country's political conditions, the elections did not directly affect very many Dominicans. Moreover, most presidential elections prior to 1930 were indirect—specifically from 1848 to 1859 and from 1888 to 1924. Presidents were elected directly by the voters only from 1866 to 1888. Only a few congressmen were elected, making the elections more on the scale of a small city or county in the United States than like national elections in larger countries. The results of two congressional elections prior to the Trujillo dictatorship illustrate the limited nature of national politics in the country. The combined number of congressional seats for both chambers of the national legislature in 1914 was only thirty-six, and in 1924 was only forty-two (Table 20.1). The groups that sponsored legislators in 1914 were ad hoc organizations, and those in 1924 were no more than loose coalitions.

Data on electoral participation levels since 1930 (shown in Table 20.2) are inconclusive, largely because of the fraudulent records kept during the Trujillo period. There would appear to have been a steady, even dramatic, rise in participation levels from 1930 to 1957—at least as a percentage of the total population—reaching higher levels in 1957 than in most other Latin American nations. Two explanations are possible: either Trujillo mobilized increasingly large numbers of Dominicans to vote for him and his candidates during the period, or the data are simply false. The likelihood of the latter is suggested by the substantial drop in participation reported for the 1962 election, the first after the fall of Trujillo. One would have

TABLE 20.1
Congressional Party Representation in the Dominican Republic, 1914 and 1924

	Senate	Chamber of Deputies
1914		
Jimenes-Velásquez		
coalition	7	14
Horacista	4	8
Legalista	1	2
Total	12	24
1924		
ANP	10	24
CPC	2	7
Total	12	31

Source: Adapted from Julio G. Campillo Pérez, Elecciones Dominicanas (Santo Domingo: Academia Dominicana de la Historia, 1982), p. 431.

TABLE 20.2
Participation Levels in the Dominican Republic as a Percentage of the National Population, 1930–1986

	Percentage		Percentage
1930	13	1962	29
1934	15	1966	35
1938	16	1970	30
1942	29	1974	22
1947	36	1978	27
1952	43	1982	30
1957	46	1986	28

Sources: Adapted from Julio G. Campillo Pérez, Elecciones Dominicanas (Santo Domingo: Academia Dominicana de la Historia, 1982), pp. 388, 487, and El Nacional (Santo Domingo), 1982, 1986.

expected the participation rate to have been at least as high in 1962 as it had been in 1957. Since 1962 the level of participation has remained about the same, except for 1974 and 1978 when it was substantially lower.

Participation is regulated in the Dominican Republic by laws proclaimed in 1962. Citizens eighteen years of age and older are eligible to vote (married citizens who are younger than eighteen may also vote); there is no literacy requirement. Voters are required by law to register either with local authorities or with a political party, which can act as an agent for their registration. Voting is mandatory in the Dominican Republic, and fines may be imposed on those who do not vote. Voting is by closed-list ballots; each party lists all its national and local candidates on separate ballots in a hierarchy determined by its leadership.

TABLE 20.3
Presidential Elections in the Dominican Republic, 1930-1986

		Elected			Principal Opposition	
Party	Candidate		Number of Votes in 1,000s	Party	Candidate	Number of Votes in 1,000s
1930	PD	Trujillo	224	AND	Urena	2
1934	PD	Trujillo	256			
1938	PD	Peynado	320			
1942	PD	Trujillo	582			
1947	PD	Trujillo	781	PND	Espaillat	30
1952	PD	Trujillo	1,039			
1957	PD	Trujillo	1,265			
1962	PRD	Bosch	629	UCN	Fiallo	317
1966	PR	Balaguer	769	PRD	Bosch	525
1970	PR	Balaguer	653	MIDA	Lora	252
1974	PR	Balaguer	942	PDP	Lajava	171
1978	PRD	Guzmán	856	PR	Balaguer	689
1982	PRD	Blanco	855	PR	Balaguer	825
1986	PRSC	Balaguer	857	PRD	Majluta	814

Sources: Adapted from Julio G. Campillo Pérez, Elecciones Dominicanas (Santo Domingo: Academia Dominicana de la Historia, 1982), pp. 388, 488, and El Nacional (Santo Domingo), 1982, 1986.

Representation for the Senate and the Chamber of Deputies was allocated until 1986 on the basis of 26 provinces and the National District. Each district received 1 senator, for a total of 27; in 1986 the number of Senate districts was increased to 30. Senators are elected by simple plurality. Deputies are allocated on the basis of 1 for every 50,000 inhabitants or fraction over 25,000. Currently, the number of deputies is 120. Local officials are also elected, but the elections are unimportant because the local officials have very limited powers in the Dominican Republic. The president and vice president are elected to four-year terms and may be reelected under the present law.

Representation in the Chamber is determined by proportional representation, specifically the d'Hondt system adopted in 1962. Given the small number of deputies elected and the relatively weak and transient opposition parties, the system has not encouraged a proliferation of parties in the lower chamber. Support for the smaller parties is fairly evenly divided among the provinces, and there is no evidence of significant regionalism in the voting patterns beyond a slight difference between the National District and the rural provinces.

The presidential vote for the period since 1930 is summarized in Table 20.3. In most of the elections since 1962, the presidential contests have proved to be relatively uneven. The two exceptions are the elections of 1982 and 1986, which were close contests, with Balaguer narrowly losing the first and winning the second.

TABLE 20.4
Party Representation in the Dominican Congress, 1962-1986

	Senate					Chamber of Deputies					
	PRD	PR/ PRSC	UCN	Other	Total	PRD	PR/ PRSC	UCN	PLD	Other	Total
1962	22	0	4	1	27	49	0	20	0	5	74
1966	5	22	0	0	27	26	48	0	0	0	74
1970	0	21	0	6	27	0	45	0	0	29	74
1974	0	27	0	0	27	0	86	0	0	5	91
1978	11	16	0	0	27	48	43	0	0	0	91
1982	17	10	0	0	27	62	50	0	7	1	120
1986	7	21	0	2	30	48	56	0	16	0	120

Sources: Adapted from Julio G. Campillo Pérez, Elecciones Dominicanas (Santo
Domingo: Academia Dominicana de la Historia, 1982), pp. 445, 488, and
El Nacional (Santo Domingo), 1982, 1986.

Party representation in the congress has also been uneven, with one
party or another winning a substantial majority in both houses since 1962
(Table 20.4). In the case of the Senate, this imbalance in party representation
persisted from 1962 to 1986. In the lower chamber one party achieved an
absolute majority from 1962 until 1978, but since that time no party has
been able to obtain an absolute majority, which has effectively increased
the influence of third parties in legislation. After the 1986 election Juan
Bosch and the PLD received eighteen deputies, enough to determine whether
the government party (PRSC) or the opposition (PRD) would prevail in
legislative confrontations in the lower chamber.

Elections prior to Trujillo were of limited importance. Since 1962 elections
have been regular and competitive, but they have yet to evolve beyond the
traditional personalism and ad hoc alliances that have characterized the
nation's politics. In the relatively short period since Trujillo, it would be
reasonable to describe the Dominican Republic as having a multiparty system
dominated at any moment in time by two stronger groups, but not necessarily
the same ones. There is no reason to assume that even this is a particularly
stable or permanent configuration. It could change very rapidly depending
on political developments and personal ambitions. Because parties are loose
alliances maintained by strong leaders by virtue of their personalities and
their political appeal, they are dependent upon those leaders for their
survival. Since 1962 two strong personalities have emerged, Juan Bosch and
Joaquín Balaguer. Without such leadership, political parties in the country
have little to sustain them.

Long-Term Trends

It would be foolish to anticipate long-term trends in the Dominican
Republic based on the experience of the past quarter-century. However,

there are several important factors that will affect the future of party politics in the country. First is the impact of chronic economic problems on political parties and their candidates. The country was in a state of severe economic crisis during the 1980s, precipitated by low prices and low demand for its principal export, sugar, and a dangerously high international debt. The country is almost wholly dependent on the United States for trade, and more specifically for its sugar quota; continuing U.S. influence in the country may be inevitable. The opportunities for economic development are limited, and the task of improving the country's economy therefore promises to be vexing.

A second factor is particularly provocative—namely the possibly high levels of social mobilization in the country that are not suggested by traditional indicators. The Dominican Republic still has a large rural sector, with relatively low levels of educational attainment and a large peasant class barely at the subsistence level. Yet, because of its geographic realities, social mobilization may be higher than one would expect. The country is small and very densely populated, conditions that mitigate the usual political distinctions between rural and urban. These conditions effectively increase the levels of political communication and information in the country. Against a background of poorly institutionalized parties, elections, and democratic structures and processes, there is a significant potential for political alienation and instability during times of acute economic stress or deprivation. Such conditions contributed to the instability of the country in the mid-1960s, and could precipitate a similar eruption in the future. Many of the same conditions have existed in El Salvador—the only Hispanic country in the Western Hemisphere that is more densely populated than the Dominican Republic—and have contributed to El Salvador's instability over the past two decades.

Party politics in the Dominican Republic has been dominated by Joaquín Balaguer for twenty-five years and he has served four terms as president. It was generally assumed that the 1986 election would be his last because of his age and poor health. However, Balaguer let it be known in late 1988 that he intended to run for reelection. His eventual withdrawal from party politics, whenever it comes, may create another political vacuum at a vulnerable time for the country. What future political role Bosch will have is unclear and unpredictable. The issue of leadership compounds an already long list of political uncertainties and economic anxieties in the Dominican Republic and does not augur well for the future stability of the country.

On a more positive note, there has been a period of relative stability since 1966, although sporadic violence and rioting began to erupt in the mid-1980s. Democratic elections have been held, viable options have been presented to the voters, and participation in elections has been reasonably high. Politicians have refrained from excessive demagogy, and some seem to be genuinely committed to finding solutions to the many problems the nation faces. The military so far has largely stayed out of politics, and extremist groups, while present, so far have not constituted a serious challenge to the fragile political system; they easily could in the near future, however. The difficult task of sustaining a period of relative stability is complicated by the urgent necessity to relieve, to some extent, the worsening economic conditions and deprivations in the country. Only by doing so are political parties, elections, and democratic processes likely to have a chance to institutionalize and to take root in Dominican culture. The specter of renewed turmoil and foreign intervention remains a real one in the country. The odds are not favorable and the challenges are formidable, but for Dominicans the stakes are very high.

References

Atkins, G. Pope. 1981. *Arms and Politics in the Dominican Republic*. Boulder, CO: Westview.

Black, Jan Knippers. 1986. *The Dominican Republic: Politics and Development in an Unsovereign State*. Winchester, MA: Allen & Unwin.

Campillo Pérez, Julio G. 1982. *Electiones Dominicanas*. Santo Domingo: Academía Dominicana de la Historia.

Kryzanek, Michael J. 1977. Political Party Decline and the Failure of Liberal Democracy: The PRD in Dominican Politics. *Journal of Latin American Studies* 9:115–143.

Rodman, Selden. 1964. *Quisqueya: A History of the Dominican Republic*. Seattle: Univ. of Washington Press.

Sánchez, José M. 1982. Dominican Republic. In Robert J. Alexander, ed., *Political Parties of the Americas*. Westport, CT: Greenwood.

Szulc, Tad. 1965. *Dominican Diary*. New York: Dell.

Wiarda, Howard J. 1969. *The Dominican Republic: Nation in Transition*. New York: Praeger.

———. 1970. *Dictatorship and Development: The Methods of Control in Trujillo's Dominican Republic*. Gainesville: Univ. of Florida Press.

Wiarda, Howard J., and Michael J. Kryzanek. 1982. *The Dominican Republic: Caribbean Crucible*. Boulder, CO: Westview.

21

CONCLUSION

Political Behavior and
Party Evolution in Latin America

The study of party politics and elections in Latin America is still a relatively new area of research and analysis in political science. Although significant contributions have been made over the past two decades, important questions remain. There are also some countries for which little research has been accumulated. Our task has been to present a comprehensive introduction to the subject that draws upon and illustrates the present state of research in the field.

It is premature to propose any general theory or integration of the existing research, both because of its incompleteness and, in some areas, its contradictory and controversial implications. What we can do is present a summary of the common experiences, general patterns, and themes that have emerged from this review of political behavior and the evolution of parties in Latin America. We do not intend these as general theories or scientific propositions but, rather, as conclusions emerging from our analysis.

It is our assumption that the causes of political behavior generally and the evolution of political parties specifically are universal, that they are not exclusively characteristic of one country or one region, and that these universal causes are apparent only when carefully identified, specified, and compared in cross-cultural contexts. In our survey of Latin America we have found general, or common, patterns—particularly the changing conditions produced as countries have pursued modernization—and parochial patterns, the idiosyncratic experiences and conditions that have affected political behavior and the evolution of parties in specific countries.

Too often studies of Latin American politics have employed either universal or parochial explanations, stressing one to the exclusion of the other and creating thereby a false dichotomy. Those who stress universal forces often identify economic ones as paramount. Such orientations are diverse, ranging from Marxists who fail to make contextual distinctions between Latin American countries and the experiences of the USSR or China, to others who believe that all Latin American politics, particularly the dysfunctions, can be explained by economic underdevelopment or the absence of a large middle class. There are some who stress the military as a universal but pernicious influence, whose actions determine rather than interact in Latin American politics.

At the other extreme are contextualists who stress parochial factors to the exclusion of universal ones, those who believe that the political experience of each Latin American nation is totally unique and not comparable to the experiences of other countries—often including even Latin American ones—and that only a preoccupation with historical chronologies and personalities can explain a country's politics. It is our feeling that parochial influences qualify universal ones, that the two must be considered simultaneously, and that an appropriate balance between them must be established for each country.

The important parochial influences have already been identified for each of the countries. They include historical events—the Mexican revolution; the U.S. occupations of Cuba, Nicaragua, Panama, and other nations; and *la Violencia* in Colombia to mention only three. Unusual geographical influences have also been at work—Mexico's proximity to the United States, large petroleum deposits in Mexico and Venezuela, and Uruguay's two large neighbors. Indigenous populations in Mexico, Guatemala, Ecuador, Peru, and Bolivia have also played an important role. And there have been extraordinary personalities historically who have distinctively influenced and shaped politics—including, among others, Vargas in Brazil, Batlle in Uruguay, Perón in Argentina, Castro in Cuba, the Somozas in Nicaragua, Trujillo in the Dominican Republic, Stroessner in Paraguay, Cárdenas in Mexico, and Velasco Ibarra in Ecuador. These experiences, conditions, and personalities are specific to the countries involved and help to explain the evolution of party politics in each of the countries.

What we wish to identify here are some of the more general, or common, patterns that have also been important in the evolution of Latin American party politics. Specifically, we are concerned with the influence of social mobilization and other patterns of modernization on party politics, elections, and political behavior, and the responses of party politics to them. We present these observations as tentative propositions, based on our survey, that seem reasonable at this juncture but that clearly require more analysis and greater specification.

The cumulative, or aggregate, impact of modernization on individuals tends to be felt in the rising levels of social mobilization, as citizens are influenced and changed by modern values, aspirations, and identifications through education, communications, urban living, and new employment patterns. These changes inject increasing numbers of persons into political processes at different levels and in varied ways. Social mobilization ultimately affects party politics and elections and can be seen through rising levels of electoral participation and the emergence of mass-based party movements. Social mobilization has been rising steadily and often rapidly throughout Latin America over the past century, determined by the level and rate of increase of modernizing influences. In those countries where the process began relatively early—Argentina, Uruguay, and Chile—it has reached high levels, and mass politics and high levels of electoral participation have existed in those countries for several generations. Social mobilization redefines the political system, expanding it to include more, and a greater variety of, individuals. And with the emergence of middle and lower classes—an inevitable by-product of modernization—politically significant new sectors are created. Political parties breed on this process, adapting to it in their pursuit of supporters, creating new organizations, and reorienting existing ones.

Greater political awareness within the often troublesome and uncertain context of modernization tends to generate discontent, because modernization not only creates new expectations and demands that are normally unsatisfied and frustrated, but also new social inequities through class stratification and conflict. Social mobilization is a selective process, it does not proceed evenly through all classes or regions of a country. Those affected most by it tend to become more politically aware and, we find, often politically alienated and disenchanted. Social mobilization is a risky experience, for it may precipitate military governments that suppress political party activity and elections, or revolutionary movements that wish to change party politics radically.

What follows is a summary of the tentative propositions derived from this study.

1. As levels of social mobilization rise, opposition to existing regimes tends to increase irrespective of the type of regime or its policies. At the same time, social mobilization does not necessarily increase the role of ideology in party politics or render parties less reliant on patronage networks and personalism.

Social mobilization changes both the level and the focus of political activity, and encourages political parties to use the voters' disenchantment prompted by regional and class divisions. An implicitly high potential for opposition to any regime thus exists among the most highly mobilized sectors. This is most clearly seen in Latin America in the higher levels of opposition in both voting and party activity, particularly in urban areas. Urban areas, which tend to be affected by modernization first, have a more diverse selection of parties and are more likely to exhibit greater opposition to ruling elites in elections. The phenomena were observed by Dix (1984) in his discussion of the high tendency for electoral turnover of incumbent regimes.

At the same time, however, social mobilization does not necessarily translate into parties that are more ideological or less dependent on traditional networks of patronage or personalism. Argentina and Brazil illustrate both these points. Party politics in both countries over the past generation has been highly personalistic and patronage-based. The same is true in most other Latin American nations as well.

2. Marxist parties normally have a class base, but their leaders and adherents both tend to be based in urban classes, ranging from the salaried working class to the upper-middle class. When permitted to compete freely in electoral contexts, Marxist parties have not tended to gain a larger share of the national vote or to attract increasing numbers of peasants.

There is a common belief among Marxists and anti-Marxists that the changes and inequities brought on by modernization will benefit Marxist organizations, and that, if allowed to participate freely in elections, they may ultimately prevail. Marxist parties, particularly Communist ones, have been repressed in many Latin American nations. But when they have been relatively free to compete—in Chile before 1973, in Uruguay except during the military dictatorship, and in Venezuela, Colombia, and Costa Rica among others—there is little evidence to support these assumptions. Research in both Chile and Uruguay up to the time of the military takeovers suggests that Marxist organizations did not appreciably increase their support, and persuasive evidence elsewhere suggests their following has been restricted to the urban classes, particularly those regularly employed and unionized, and that their leadership (and, at least in Uruguay, their adherents) have been predominantly from the upper-middle classes. Even in Chile, where a Marxist regime took power through elections in 1970, Marxist voting underwent few changes. Following the presidential election Marxist voting rose in subsequent municipal and congressional elections, but it was slight compared to the increases experienced by the Chilean Christian Democrats in the two elections subsequent to their 1964 presidential victory. For whatever reason, Marxist electoral movements have not been particularly effective in mobilizing the poorest sectors of the societies, the peasants.

What this suggests is that the fate of Marxist parties seems to have been more affected by the successes, failures, divisions, and leadership of traditional or moderate parties than by their ability to mobilize new supporters. Their support has also been limited by the chronic factionalization of Marxist organizations in virtually all Latin American nations. Although the level of Marxist voting has remained remarkably stable over long periods of time, it has been divided differently according to how many and what Marxist parties were competing. When they have been permitted to compete openly with other political parties, Marxist parties have succeeded in absorbing some of those who have been affected by, but benefited least from, modernization, but only among those urban groups where modernization has had its most profound influence. Some Marxist parties have also benefited from close relationships and support from organized labor, but this support has not generated significant growth.

3. Generational conflicts are often critical in party politics and are most likely to occur during and following periods of high population growth.

There is some evidence of important generational divisions in Latin American party politics. These divisions are partly the result of rapid demographic changes and partly the result of social mobilization. Higher levels of education affect the younger generations more than older ones as new strata are mobilized. Generational conflict is also linked to high population growth rates, which skew the population balance in societies toward the young. These two phenomena, expanding education and an increased proportion of youth, are commonly found together and create a situation in which the total proportion of youth in societies is growing, while their rate of social mobilization is increasing faster than that for other age groups. Youth generally tend to be more idealistic, impatient, and, in Latin America, more unemployed than other age groups, and these realities can result in their being more politically radical and active as well.

Generational divisions often divide parties. The factionalization of AD in Venezuela during the early 1960s was partly a result of generational divisions. A brief period of rapid population growth occurred in Chile in the late 1940s, and that generation came of age in the late 1960s. The high level of political participation in Chile at that time was partly the result of this demographic phenomenon—young Chileans were the principal activists both supporting and opposing President Allende and Popular Unity. In some instances, generational barriers and divisions have produced alienation from the political processes along generational lines. The inability of a younger generation to progress in El Salvador, Uruguay, Nicaragua, and Brazil produced revolutionary movements opposed to established parties and political processes; in the case of Nicaragua, a successful one. Evidence of generational divisions exists in other party systems as well. For several generations of Cubans prior to the revolution, young political leaders attempted to work for reform within Cuba's established party structures, but to no avail; in the late 1940s Fidel Castro was one of these young leaders.

4. The entry of the middle class into party leadership, and its ability to gain national power through parties and elections, is a critical threshold in the evolution of political parties. The exclusion of the middle class from, or its frustration with regard to, party politics encourages weak parties and political instability as countries modernize.

One of the earliest by-products of economic development as countries modernize is the emergence of a middle class. It is the first class to benefit from expanded education and employment and initially appears in the urban areas, where modernization first occurs. The middle class is also most affected by the vagaries of modernization, suffering from periods of economic recession, inflation and from expectations that tend to rise faster than standards of living. The success or failure of its political absorption has important implications for party politics. One of the most striking differences in this regard may be seen in a comparison of Chile and Argentina. The middle class gained entrance into party politics in Chile but in Argentina encountered chronic frustration in its attempt to do so. In El Salvador, the middle class's inability to gain influence in the 1960s through the Christian Democratic party was a critical factor contributing to the instability that subsequently developed. When the middle class succeeds in gaining entrance to a party system by finding parties to advocate its interests or by gaining control over party leadership, it becomes a conservative force. When it is frustrated or fails, it tends to become destabilizing, alienated from the existing system and hostile to the dominant political groups. Chronic frustration increases the hostility of the middle class as it finds itself constrained by the upper class and increasingly threatened by lower classes as they become politically relevant. Portions of the middle class of Mexico have been excluded from the PRI and national political influence, and that sector accounts for the leadership and principal support of the country's largest opposition party, the PAN. The middle classes were also critical in the success of the Peronist movement in Argentina despite its strongly working-class image.

There is a natural tendency for parties to expand their appeals as modernization occurs and as social mobilization swells the reservoir of potential voters and activists. This logically entails absorbing less-affluent sectors of the society. If the middle classes as they are socially mobilized cannot gain access to the party system or compete effectively in elections, their resulting frustration can radicalize these classes, weaken existing traditional parties, and ultimately destabilize the political system. The absorption of the middle classes into party politics has occurred by now in most Latin American nations, but with varying degrees of success and diverse implications. As social mobilization proceeds, absorption continues down through the socioeconomic strata of the society with the same challenges and consequences there as for the middle classes.

5. Sustained modernization increases levels of voter participation and party activity; party identification, however, may weaken, particularly for traditional parties as modernization proceeds. As countries modernize, new parties must emerge or existing ones must expand in order to absorb a larger proportion of the population and a more complex set of political interests if party politics is to remain stable. Traditional parties that build a mass base are likely to remain strong as modernization proceeds.

Strong evidence suggests that levels of voter participation have increased as economic development and other changes resulting from modernization have occurred. Voting is not the only barometer of political participation nor even necessarily the most important, but it is an easily observed and understood one. There has been a steady increase in voter participation in most Latin American countries over the past century, and its rate of increase seems closely correlated with the rate of modernization. In Argentina participation increased rapidly in the early part of the twentieth century and has remained at a high level since. In Chile it increased slowly but steadily throughout the century, reaching by the late 1960s extraordinarily high levels. Similar increases are visible elsewhere, and in general voter participation is associated with the level of modernization of the countries, as are demands for expansion of the voting franchise.

Likewise, the intensity and range of party activity seems to increase as countries modernize, partly because of the expansion in the number of politically aware and relevant citizens, the expansion of opportunities for communication, and the growing diversity of interests. Party politics in controlled or constrained environments may not become more relevant to national decisionmaking, but it becomes a more conspicuous and potentially influential part of national politics.

However, sustained modernization can also increase alienation in societies and decrease mass identification with traditional parties. There is evidence, for example, to suggest that partisan identification with the traditional parties of Colombia and Honduras has declined. Historically, the traditional parties of Chile failed to expand their appeals and to renovate their programs. Partisan identification with them therefore declined until they reversed their strategies in the 1960s. A similar pattern has occurred in Uruguay and elsewhere. Unless new organizations can mobilize these alienated interests, citizens may become "floating voters" without strong partisan identification, an unpredictable if not necessarily destabilizing influence in elections.

As Latin American countries have modernized, either new political parties have emerged to reflect new interests and groups in society, or existing ones have expanded their political base to include such interests and groups. In Chile and Argentina the emergence of new parties from the 1880s on reflected the emergence of new class interests. In Uruguay the two traditional parties differed in their ability to absorb a larger proportion of the population. The Colorado party succeeded to a much greater extent than the Blanco party and therefore dominated the country's politics for all but a few years of the twentieth century. Social Democratic and Christian Democratic parties have emerged in many countries during the past two generations primarily as an instrument for the middle class, much as the radical parties did earlier in Chile and Argentina. The expansion has continued with Marxist parties as they have tried to mobilize the lower urban classes and the peasants.

Relatively few of the nineteenth-century parties succeeded in expanding their political base. A notable exception occurred with the Liberal and Conservative parties in Colombia, which have drawn on their traditional loyalties but at the same time have tried with some success to broaden their appeals, particularly during the past generation. Conservative and Liberal parties have disappeared in Mexico, Venezuela, Peru, Brazil, and elsewhere. Chile's Liberal and Conservative parties eventually merged into a new organization and waged a vigorous campaign to broaden their appeal in the growing ideological polarization of the 1960s.

The emergence of new parties would seem a "natural" response to the fundamental social changes, especially in nations where traditional party loyalties or electoral traditicAs are relatively weak or where existing parties are unwilling or unable to modernize their appeals.

6. Strong traditional values persist in Latin American party politics and coexist with modern ones; namely, personalism, patrimonialism, clientelism, kinship and community networks, orthodoxy among female voters, and nostalgia for earlier times and former leaders.

Traditional values and habits do not disappear even in the face of rapid change and modernization, particularly, it would seem, in Latin America.

The resilience of traditional values in national politics is reinforced by their support from social and religious institutions, a reinforcement that is particularly strong when these institutions are relatively uniform and deeply rooted in the societies. To some extent, each of the traditional values identified above is evident in the party politics of all Latin American nations. In a few cases, they have been institutionally incorporated into party politics. Mexico's PRI has succeeded in part because of its clever incorporation of some of these traditional values, and Uruguay's otherwise modern party system embodies many of them in its organizations and electoral rules.

The result is a varied and evolving mixture of modern and traditional party politics. Modern techniques of campaigning and mobilization are superimposed on traditional systems of patronage, clientelism, and kinship and local-community networks. Female voting is generally strongly "orthodox" and tends to support established leaders and organizations rather than new or radical ones. This tendency is often, but not necessarily, more conservative than male voting. Personalism, which is found in all political systems, takes on often characteristically traditional forms in Latin America, including nostalgic support for former dictators and leaders such as Perón in Argentina, Arnulfo Arias in Panama, Rojas Pinilla in Colombia, Pérez Jiménez in Venezuela, Velasco Ibarra in Ecuador, Paz Estenssoro in Bolivia, Jorge Alessandri in Chile, and countless others.

We are struck by the expression in party politics of what others have characterized as the "corporatist tradition" in Latin America. This tradition assumes that there is a natural order in societies, one hierarchy of authority and values that is preferable to others. It is a tradition that stands in sharp contrast with pluralistic traditions, which assume that no single hierarchy is inherently justified beyond the purposes it serves. The authoritarian implications of this traditional Latin American corporatism are obvious, and there have been innumerable military and party leaders advocating such values.

Less obvious is that corporatist values prevail in many democratic societies in Latin America, and in party politics they have led to the practice and expectation of "coparticipation," that is, the incorporation of minority interests and leaders into a unified, governing hierarchy. The major purpose of Uruguayan party politics has historically been coparticipation; the country was able to stabilize and democratic party politics was possible only after this question was resolved. Colombia used coparticipation under the National Front for the same purpose—to permit political stabilization by incorporating minority interests and leaders into the governing hierarchy. The integration of regional interests in Brazil also presumed coparticipation, and Brazilian party politics failed when that was not achieved. The issue exists in Mexico, as portions of the middle class seek inclusion in that country's authoritarian, hierarchical system that now largely excludes them. The ferocious party conflicts during the 1960s in Chile were based on irreconcilable corporatist orientations of the right, the Christian Democrats, and the Marxists, each of whom held equally specific and intransigent notions of a natural hierarchy of authority and values. Chilean party politics was dominated by corporatist, not pluralist, political values. These traditional corporatist values in Latin America have affected attitudes toward party politics as commonly as they have reinforced authoritarian tendencies in the region.

7. The level of party dominance, measured by fractionalization, is unrelated to the likelihood of political stability in a country.

There is an old debate in political science, noted in Chapter 1, concerning the relationship between the number of political parties and the stability of a country. Several scholars believe that a proliferation of parties, the extreme instances of multiparty systems, was inherently destabilizing and that two-party systems were inherently stabilizing. The experience of Latin American party politics should lay this debate to rest once and for all. We find no relationship between the number of political parties, or the level of party fractionalization, and the likelihood for political stability. Two-party systems, such as those in Colombia, Honduras, and Uruguay, have not only experienced significant periods of political instability and military intervention, they have also, it can be argued, directly contributed to the instability. Single-party systems historically have also been unstable, particularly when the party hegemony was created artificially through electoral controls and coercion, as in the case of Somoza's Nicaragua, and in Argentina and the Dominican Republic, while some multiparty systems have achieved political stability, such as those in Venezuela and Costa Rica.

More important is the viability of the parties that do exist and the ability of their leaders to function politically in a way that can produce an effective consensus about national policy and establish credibility for the parties themselves.

8. Personalism and charismatic leadership are a functional substitute for institutions. Extreme or persistent levels of personalism and charismatic leadership impede institutionalization of parties.

As countries modernize and become more complex, political parties as organizations must respond in kind or face the likelihood of decreasing viability and relevance. In Latin America political leadership has often been highly personalistic and charismatic leaders have been common, not only in less modern nations but also in the more modern ones.

It is our belief that personalism and charismatic leadership are functional substitutes for party institutions. That is, they perform the same functions as institutions, albeit in different ways, and for short periods of time they can perform them relatively well. Many political parties have been built around strong personalities and charismatic leaders. The illustrations are numerous: Perón in Argentina, Vargas (after 1946) in Brazil, Batlle in Uruguay, Haya de la Torre in Peru, Velasco Ibarra in Ecuador. In a few cases political parties as institutions have survived charismatic leaders that dominated them in their initial stages, particularly those that have had a strong ideological or programmatic orientation. AD in Venezuela has survived Rómulo Bétancourt, the Peronists have withstood the death of Perón, the PLN has outlived José Figueres, and the APRA in Peru has survived Haya de la Torre.

Personalism exists in all nations, and charismatic leaders are not uncommon. What is distinctive in Latin America is the tendency for this kind of leadership to persist in a modernizing context that would otherwise necessarily require institutional growth of parties. Charisma and personalism not only serve as functional substitutes for institutions, but they also impede the growth of institutional parties.

Max Weber, who coined the term "charismatic," believed charismatic leadership to be a transitional stage from traditional to what he called "bureaucratic" leadership and organizations. Charisma is a means of creating broader loyalties and control then what would normally emerge in traditional societies, but it lacks the persistence and renovating capabilities possessed by modern bureaucratic organizations. Because Latin America is in a transitional stage, charismatic leadership is not surprising. It may be the only effective option to military rule in contexts where viable political parties have not emerged. But it risks impeding the emergence of such organizations as long as it persists.

9. All elections in Latin America are to some extent politically destabilizing. Other things being equal, the likelihood of military intervention increases prior to and following an election.

Elections are complex political rituals or processes that require substantial organization and imply considerable political risk. They are highly structured political games that require clear rules that are accepted by participating leaders and parties. Elections are risky because they heighten political awareness to abnormally high levels, focus it on very specific outcomes, and establish very clear rewards for those who win. Not all Latin American nations can easily accommodate the organizational and political demands that elections make, with results that are uncertain at best and potentially destabilizing at worst. Regulating elections so that they appear to be fair is a challenging task for governments even with the best of intentions. First, they are only nominally controlling their countries, and, second, the best of intentions do not always exist. Opportunities for party leaders to manipulate large sectors of the population through campaign appeals are expanding through the increasing availability and use of mass media, and the skills and resources for manipulation are never equally distributed among the participants.

Political instability is not the only reason for military intervention, but in combination with other concerns, it is often sufficient cause for intervention. If there is one preoccupation that seems to transcend political, personal, and ideological differences among military leaders it is their shared fear of massive political instability and the coming to power of leaders whom they find for whatever reasons unacceptable. The subject has not been one of our specific concerns, but clearly military intervention has been common in Latin America during the periods immediately preceding and following elections as military elites anticipate and consider the consequences of elections.

What makes elections potentially destabilizing in Latin America is the lack of viable political and governmental institutions or a strong consensus about the "rules of the game" for elections. Some countries are clearly exceptions to this tendency, such as Venezuela, Colombia, Costa Rica, and, for many years, Chile and Uruguay. Elections are risky even in authoritarian regimes and are usually held because the risk of holding them is perceived to be less than the risk of not holding them. In Latin America many regimes fail to complete their term in office, and even more fail to renew their mandate through elections. Elections can be somewhat destabilizing even in modern countries, but in Latin America the potential for instability is greater because the regimes are not able to accommodate it as effectively.

10. The specific conditions surrounding the development of or rapid increase in a country's export economy have a significant influence on the evolution of party politics by (a) defining elite structures, (b) determining the extent and kind of foreign influence, (c) shaping mass expectations and demands, and (d) stimulating public investment and services. The ease with which traditional rural elites are replaced or absorbed by modernizing urban elites is critical to the stable evolution of political parties.

The development of or rapid increase in a country's export economy usually initiates or stimulates other patterns of modernization, and the specific conditions surrounding that development strongly affect the evolution of party politics. It may force a redefinition of the balance between rural and urban political elites, depending on which are principally in control of the export economy. Exports based on raw materials, such as petroleum or minerals, very often require large capital investments, which in turn encourage, and may require, foreign investors. Some agricultural products, sugar and bananas for example, may also encourage foreign investment. The presence of such investments encourages foreign political intervention and creates the potential for conflict between domestic and foreign elites, which is difficult if not impossible for party politics to resolve.

The ease with which traditional rural elites are replaced or absorbed by modernizing elites is also critical to the stable evolution of political parties. The traditional rural landowners in Chile were overwhelmed by and eventually absorbed into new elites created by the development of nontraditional mineral exports. Much of the Chilean export economy was owned by foreigners, which both restrained the influence of Chilean elites and restrained rivalries between elites by giving them a common foe.

In Argentina the rural landowning elites participated in the development of the export economy and profited directly from it, which reinforced their control over Argentine politics and made them a difficult force to control or counterbalance. A similar situation existed in El Salvador. The control or absorption of rural elites by modernizing ones reduces one of the earliest and most fundamental conflicts commonly expressed through party politics, allowing party competition to focus on newer and more salient conflicts.

The competition between the traditional and modernizing elites of Colombia—expressed through the struggle between the Liberals and Conservatives—brought the country to the edge of anarchy during *la Violencia*. The success of these elites in merging their political and economic interests since then has been an important factor in sustaining their control and maintaining the relative viability of their party and electoral systems.

More recent efforts to challenge and control the traditional rural elites have often created disruptive political situations. In Bolivia, the task was pursued through revolution, in Peru it was pursued by a reformist military dictatorship, and in El Salvador it has led to an extended period of civil strife and revolutionary confrontation. Land reform, quite apart from its popularity for those who are landless, is also an important way to limit or control the influence of landowners over national politics. The longer traditional rural elites remain in control of national party politics in the face of modernization the more precarious the system may become. Their control or absorption is therefore a critical task in the evolution of party politics.

Concurrent with the development of export economies, public investment and spending normally increase and fundamental changes are set in motion. Public expenditures increase for education, health, communications, and public projects, expanding the size of the bureaucracy and the number of salaried workers. Social mobilization increases, creating new demands and expectations and injecting new issues into party politics.

11. The evolution of political parties is strongly affected by decisions concerning the electoral system, and that evolution can be subsidized, manipulated, or repressed as a result of those decisions.

The electoral systems—rules established that define recognition and status of parties, enfranchisement, and representation—are infinitely malleable and strongly influence party competition. Requiring literacy in a largely illiterate nation, for example (as was historically the case in Peru, Ecuador, and Brazil), selectively restricts the political debate and the base for party appeals. Plurality electoral systems used in Mexico, Paraguay, and Somoza's Nicaragua have benefited the ruling parties and made competition difficult for small or new party organizations.

Because all elections must be structured in some manner and the status of political parties defined, party politics depends on the rules that regulate it. There is no such thing as a "neutral" electoral system; whatever decisions are made will encourage some groups and restrain others. The opportunities for manipulation of the systems toward specific objectives are almost endless.

The ability of parties to compete and to stand a chance of gaining some formal recognition and influence through legislative representation are particularly critical questions in rapidly changing societies. Proportional representation is more permissive than its alternatives, but some PR formulas are more generous to smaller parties than others. After 1958 Venezuela went further than any other Latin American country in supporting access to the political system through elections to new organizations by providing special legislative deputies based on party vote.

Except on rare occasions when questions about the electoral system are politicized, electoral controls are largely invisible to the general public. They are known, however, to party leaders, whose willingness to remain within the established system rather than trying to subvert it may be partly determined by their perception of the fairness of these rules.

12. Elections often have nonpolitical as well as political implications, ritualistic as well as decisionmaking functions. Elections and party activity do not necessarily indicate that parties are important political actors or that genuine democracy exists. In authoritarian or dictatorial regimes elections can perform important political, non-decisionmaking functions. In such contexts, regime parties are most durable and effective when they are permitted to develop some institutional autonomy.

Outside observers sometimes mistakenly assume that Latin American elections are strictly political events. Sometimes they are, but not always. They often have nonpolitical implications and function as much as rituals as decisionmaking exercises. The misinterpretation stems from an assumption drawn from modern political cultures, where elections are more functionally specialized. Elections, like so many other realities in Latin America, often combine traditional ritual with modern function.

One of the rituals is the celebration of nationhood and allegiance to a leader, party, or regime, in which many who participate see no particular cause-and-effect relationship between their participation in the event and what occurs afterward. As in the rituals of the church and other institutions, elections are a time for celebration and affirmation. Voting connects the individual to a broader community in more of a cultural than a political way. This characteristic is a result of mixing traditional values and rituals with modern ones.

But even vigorously staged elections may be controlled to such an extent that decisionmaking functions are effectively obviated. Elections in authoritarian regimes illustrate this, including those in the Dominican Republic under Trujillo, Venezuela under Pérez Jiménez, Nicaragua under Somoza, Paraguay under Stroessner, and arguably most of those in Mexico. While elections without opposition are the most conspicuous example, even elections with party opposition may be largely irrelevant to decisionmaking. Opposition political parties have participated in Mexican elections since the revolution. An opposition party in Nicaragua functioned during elections under the Somoza regime. And opposition parties have competed in Paraguay and revolutionary Nicaragua. But in each case the opposition has no possibility of winning, and the electoral exercise, while political, has little if anything to do with democratic politics as it is commonly conceived.

Although elections in authoritarian nations may not perform decision-making functions, they commonly do perform political ones, including mobilizing support for a regime and lending a degree of legitimacy to it domestically and internationally. There have been few instances of dictatorships where elections have never been held. Military regimes such as those in Chile and Uruguay avoided general elections during the 1970s, but even those regimes felt obliged to hold referendums. Both the Brazilian and Argentine military dictatorships experimented with elections, in Brazil regularly throughout its extended period of military rule. Elections in such contexts are controlled and are not designed to produce decisions, but they are clearly important enough politically for regimes to go through the often arduous and risky task of holding them anyway.

Official parties with some institutional autonomy can transcend the influence of individual leaders and permit new leaders to take power. This has occurred in Mexico. Those parties that are wholly the instrument of a single dictator, such as the Dominican party under Trujillo, cannot survive without the dictator. In a somewhat different pattern, Stroessner in Paraguay and Somoza in Nicaragua co-opted existing, traditional parties as their own official ones, thereby drawing a limited degree of perceived autonomy to their party organizations.

13. Distinctions between traditional and modern voting patterns conform to urban/rural divisions in Latin America. Rural voting patterns tend to be more favorable to established regimes and/or parties than do urban ones.

The influence of modernization and modern values is strongest in urban areas, and this influence can be seen in voting patterns characteristic of urban and rural areas in Latin America. As we have already noted, urban areas tend to spawn a greater variety and often a greater intensity of party opposition, but it is also true that participation levels tend to be much higher in urban areas than in rural areas. In modern nations such as the United States there is little difference between urban and rural participation levels. Because of the ritualistic element in traditional rural voting (as well as the greater opportunity for control by the regime and the decreased likelihood of organized party opposition), rural voting tends to be more supportive of existing regimes than urban voting. The difference is largely the result of the persistence of traditional values in rural areas and the often accurate perception that elections have little or no consequences in the countryside.

It also seems to be the case that fraud is both more possible and more likely in rural areas than in urban ones, and election results from rural areas must be interpreted with that in mind. There is less scrutiny over electoral processes in rural areas and fraudulent practices are less visible there. The absence of well-organized opposition parties contributes to this. Local or regional bosses or leaders normally by definition owe their position to the central government and the regime party. It is therefore in their personal interest to "bring in the vote" for the regime to demonstrate their ability to guarantee strong support for those who can protect their position in the community. The relationship is a traditional, patrimonial one. It is not uncommon to see an astonishingly high progovernment vote in rural areas in Latin America, sometimes more votes than there are voters.

14. Transcending regional divisions sufficiently to permit national parties and voting patterns to evolve is often a critical threshold in party evolution in Latin America. Cultural or geographic regionalism, however, does not necessarily translate into party conflict.

Regionalism has played an important role in Latin American politics since independence, and the task of creating viable nations out of often disparate, hostile, and isolated regions has been a continuing preoccupation. We noted the importance of regionalism in party activity and voting in many countries, including Brazil, Argentina, Colombia, Honduras, Ecuador, and, to a lesser extent, Mexico and Bolivia. It is critical for viable national party politics that the effects of regionalism be sufficiently controlled to permit truly national party politics. Regional parties have historically created dilemmas in Brazil, particularly parties associated with the states of São Paulo and Rio Grande do Sul.

There is some evidence that regionalism may be declining as a political factor in most countries. The profound regional divisions once characteristic of Colombia have been contained to a large extent through its two-party system, which has forced regional leaders and political machines into alliances with each other in ways not dissimilar to practices in the United States. To some extent, the same is happening now in Brazil and Argentina.

We also note that cultural or geographic regionialism does not necessarily translate into party politics. Chile, perhaps the most geographically compartmentalized country in Latin America, has never seen its geographical regionalism reflected in party politics. Regionalism becomes particularly important when geographical identifications correlate with cultural, ethnic, and racial differences and with economic disadvantage. Such a situation has existed in northeastern Brazil, which is geographically identifiable, ethnically distinctive, and economically disadvantaged. On a small scale it exists today in Nicaragua for the Atlantic coast. Regionalism has combined with economic antagonisms and cultural differences in modern Mexico to acquire political significance. But, on balance, the general pattern in Latin America is for regionalism to be a declining factor in party politics as nations modernize and become more homogeneous. Regionally defined conflicts also exist in many modern nations (England, Canada, Belgium, Italy, Spain, as well as the United States) and where geographic, ethnic, and economic distinctions correlate (as in Québec, Scotland, or the Basque provinces), their political implications increase.

15. Problems created by ethnic and racial divisions are not easily resolved by party politics. Establishing a critical level of consensus about national identity is a prerequisite for stable party politics.

The experience in Latin America of dealing with major ethnic and racial divisions through party politics has not been a very successful one. National identity has been a lingering political issue in many countries with large Indian populations, particularly Bolivia, Peru, Ecuador, and Guatemala, and, in earlier times, Mexico. One of the important results, if not causes, of the Mexican and Bolivian revolutions was the effort to redefine the countries as "indigenous" or Indian ones. In the case of Mexico, this proved to be a critical step toward establishing a sense of national identity and permitting a greater degree of central control over the country. The Bolivian experience has also been significant if for no other reason than eliminating one very divisive issue from a political system already overloaded with divisive issues. The issue of national identity has been raised in Peru—primarily by the

APRA and to some extent by the 1968 military regime—but it has yet to be fully resolved. Party politics has not resolved the issue in Peru, nor has it contributed much to the process of resolving it in Ecuador or Guatemala. In those countries, political parties still tend to ignore the question of the Indian, who constitutes a significant proportion, if not majority, of their population. Paraguay, another country with a strong Indian heritage, created a sense of national identity through that heritage, but the task was relatively easy because virtually all Paraguayans were descendants of one Indian culture (Guaraní), spoke the same indigenous language, and historically were less affected by European culture and rule than other Latin American nations.

Like regional and class divisions, ethnic and racial ones impede national unity and national identity, and except for postrevolutionary Mexico and Bolivia, party politics has not effectively resolved the dilemma or even confronted it directly.

16. Extreme economic change, either rapid development or decline, may be destabilizing to party politics.

In Latin America as elsewhere it is fairly obvious that extreme or persistent economic decline that is beyond the ability of governments to control creates political dilemmas that cannot be resolved by party politics or elections; it thus tends to be destabilizing. Unfortunately, there are many such examples in Latin America. To recall only one, the extended if gradual pattern of economic decline in Uruguay following World War II ultimately corroded the party system to the point of paralysis, creating conditions for a revolutionary movement and ultimately a military dictatorship that destroyed the country's heritage of democratic politics.

But it is also true that rapid economic growth may also be destabilizing. Economic development, unless closely monitored and controlled by regimes, tends to accentuate class differences, and the benefits of economic development are distributed in highly unequal ways. In other words, it heightens class antagonisms and conflicts. The very success of Brazil in economic development over the past generation has produced these results, and the backlash is perhaps the most fundamental issue currently facing Brazilian leaders. The very sudden increase in public revenues resulting from the increasing export and rising price of petroleum in the early 1970s in Ecuador was a strong factor in prompting the military to intervene. The Peruvian military coup against President Belaunde in 1968 was rationalized as discontent over his policy toward petroleum exports. Mexico's current economic plight and many of its serious political problems can be traced to the sudden increase and subsequent decline in revenues brought by petroleum exports in the 1970s. The stage is set in Paraguay for a similar set of problems, owing to a strong pattern of economic growth shown over the past decade based somewhat precariously on the export development of its hydroelectric resources.

Extreme economic change creates problems that commonly seem beyond the ability of regimes or parties to resolve. If they are persistent, they can be destabilizing. Economic growth has been managed with reasonable effectiveness in some countries. Venezuela—through nationalization of foreign petroleum investments and a plan for investing petroleum revenues for long-term economic growth and diversification—has experienced considerable success; however, declining revenues from petroleum exports have created problems in recent years even in Venezuela.

The study of party politics and elections in Latin America reveals much about both the parochial and the universal influences in the region. Party politics and elections are universal phenomena, but their meaning is infinitely variable. The region has one of the longest histories and experiences with party politics and elections in the world. There are political parties currently participating in Latin America that are as old as those in the United States. Many Latin American traditions of party politics, elections, and democratic heritages predate those of most of Europe, and distinguish Latin America from other developing areas. Yet, opportunities for comparing Latin American party politics and elections, and learning from them, are only beginning to be realized and systematically explored.

References

Dix, Robert H. 1984. Incumbency and Electoral Turnover in Latin America. *Journal of Interamerican Studies and World Affairs* 25:435–447.

Glossary of Political Parties

AD Democratic Action (Acción Democrática), El Salvador, Venezuela

ADN Nationalist Democratic Action (Acción Democrática Nacionalista), Bolivia

ADO Democratic Opposition Alliance (Alianza Demócratica de Oposición), Panama

AE Electoral Action (Acción Electoral), Venezuela

AI Integralist Action (Ação Integralista), Brazil

ALIPO Popular Liberal Alliance (Alianza Liberal Popular), Honduras

AN National Accord (Acuerdo Nacional), Paraguay

AN National Action (Acción Nacional), Venezuela

ANAPO National Popular Alliance (Alianza Nacional Popular), Colombia

ANL National Liberating Alliance (Alianca Nacional Libertador), Brazil

ANP Progressive National Alliance (Alianza Nacional Progresista), Dominican Republic

AP Popular Action (Acción Popular), Peru

AP Popular Alliance (Alianza Popular), Costa Rica

APF Federal Popular Alliance (Alianza Popular Federal), Argentina

APRA American Popular Revolutionary Alliance (Alianza Popular Revolucionaria Americana), Peru

ARDI Revolutionary Action of the Left (Acción Revolucionario de la Izquierda), Venezuela

ARENA Nationalist Republican Alliance (Alianza Republicana Nacionalista), El Salvador

ARENA National Renovating Alliance (Alianca Renovadora Nacional), Brazil

ARF Federal Republican Alliance (Alianza Republicano Federal), Argentina

ARNE Ecuadoran Nationalist Revolutionary Action (Acción Revolucionario Nacionalista Ecuadoriana), Ecuador

BDN National Democratic bloc (Bloque Democrático Nacional), Venezuela
BDP Popular Democratic bloc (Bloque Democrático Popular), Ecuador
BTD Democratic Transition bloc (Bloque Transicão Democrático), Brazil

CAN Authentic Nationalist Center (Central Auténtica Nacionalista), Guatemala
CAO Organized Aranista Center (Central Aranista Organizada), Guatemala
CCN National Civic Crusade (Cruzada Cívica Nacional), Venezuela
CD Democratic Convergence (Convergencia Democrática), El Salvador
CDN Nicaraguan Democratic Coordinating Committee (Coordinadora Democrática Nicaragüense), Nicaragua
CFP Concentration of Popular Forces (Concentración de Fuerzas Populares), Ecuador
CID Democratic Institutional Coalition (Coalición Institucional Democrático), Ecuador
CODE Democratic Convergence (Convergencia Democrática), Peru
COPEI Committee of Independent Electoral Political Organization (Comité de Organización Política Electoral Independiente), Venezuela
CPN National Patriotic Coalition (Coalición Patriótica Nacional), Panama

DCG Guatemalan Christian Democratic party (Democracia Cristiana Guatemalteca), Guatemala
DER Revolutionary Student Directorate (Directorio Estudiantil Revolucionario), Cuba
DP Popular Democracy (Democracia Popular), Ecuador
DPBB White Flag Provincial Defense (Defensa Provincial Bandera Blanca), Argentina
DR Radical Democracy (Democracia Radical), Chile

FA Broad Front (Frente Amplio) Uruguay, Venezuela
FDN National Democratic Front (Frente Democrático Nacional), Mexico
FDP Democratic Popular Front (Frente Democrático Popular), Peru
FDP Popular Democratic Force (Fuerza Democrática Popular), Venezuela
FDR Democratic Revolutionary Front (Frente Democrático Revolucionario), El Salvador
FIDEL Leftist Front of Liberation (Frente Izquierda de Libertad), Uruguay
FJ Justicialist Front (Frente Justicialista), Argentina
FNC National Constitutionalist Front (Frente Nacional Constitucionalista), Ecuador
FNV National Velasquista Federation (Federación Nacional Velasquista), Ecuador
FOCEP Popular Front of Workers, Peasants, and Students (Frente Obrero Campesino Estudiantil y Popular), Peru
FPL Popular Liberation Front (Frente Popular de Liberación), Guatemala
FPR Revolutionary Patriotic Front (Frente Patriótico de la Revolución), Nicaragua
FPU United People's Front (Frente del Pueblo Unido), Bolivia
FRA Alfarista Radical Front (Frente Radical Alfarista), Ecuador
FRAMPO Broad Popular Front (Frente Amplio Popular), Panama
FRAP Popular Action Front (Frente de Acción Popular), Chile
FREDEMO Democratic Front (Frente Democrático), Peru
FRN National Reconstruction Front (Frente de Reconstrucción Nacional), Ecuador
FSB Bolivian Socialist Falange (Falange Socialista Boliviana), Bolivia

FSLN   Sandinista National Liberation Front (Frente Sandinista de Liberación Nacional), Nicaragua
FUN   National Unity Front (Frente de Unidad Nacional), Guatemala
FUR   United Revolutionary Front (Frente Unido Revolucionario), Guatemala

ID   Democratic Left (Izquierda Democrática), Ecuador
IU   United Left (Izquierda Unida), Chile, Peru

MAC   Authentic Christian movement (Movimiento Auténtico Cristiano), El Salvador
MAP-ML   Marxist-Leninist Popular Action movement (Movimiento Acción Popular Marxist-Leninista), Nicaragua
MAPU   Movement of Popular Action (Movimiento de Acción Popular), Chile
MAS   Movement to Socialism (Movimiento al Socialismo), Venezuela
MAS   Solidarity Action movement (Movimiento de Acción Solidaria), Guatemala
MBH   Hayista Bases movement (Movimiento de Bases Hayistas), Peru
MCN   National Coalition movement (Movimiento de Coalición Nacional), Dominican Republic
MDB   Brazilian Democratic movement (Movimiento Democrático Brasileiro), Brazil
MDP   Peruvian Democratic movement (Movimiento Democrático Peruano), Peru
MEC   Emergent Movement of Concord (Movimiento Emergente de Concordia), Guatemala
MENI   Independent National Electoral movement (Movimiento Electoral Nacional Independiente), Venezuela
MEP   Electoral Movement of the People (Movimiento Electoral del Pueblo), Argentina
MFD   Democratic Federal movement (Movimiento Federal Democrático), Argentina
MID   Development and Integration movement (Movimiento de Integración y Desarrollo), Argentina
MIDA   Movement for Democratic Integration Against Reelection (Movimiento de Integración Democrática Anti-Reeleccionista), Dominican Republic
MIR   Movement of the Revolutionary Left (Movimiento Izquierda Revolucionario), Bolivia
MIR   Movement of the Revolutionary Left (Movimiento Izquierdista Revolucionario), Venezuela
M-LIDER   Liberal Democratic Revolutionary movement (Movimiento Liberal Democrático Revolucionario), Honduras
MLN   National Liberation movement (Movimiento de Liberación Nacional), Guatemala, Uruguay
MLR   Rodista Liberal movement (Movimiento Liberal Rodista), Honduras
MNB   Barrientista National movement (Movimiento Nacional Barrentista), Bolivia
MNR   National Reformist movement (Movimiento Nacional Reformista), Honduras
MNR   National Revolutionary movement (Movimiento Nacionalista Revolucionario), El Salvador
MNR   Revolutionary Nationalist movement (Movimiento Nacionalista Revolucionario), Bolivia
MNRH   Historical Revolutionary Nationalist movement (Movimiento Nacionalista Revolucionario Histórico), Bolivia
MNRI   Revolutionary National movement of the Left (Movimiento Nacionalista Revolucionario Izquierdista), Bolivia

MOLIRENA Liberal Republican and Nationalist movement (Movimiento Liberal Republicano Nacionalista), Panama

MONARCA Nationalist Rafael Callejas movement (Movimiento Nacionalista Rafael Callejas), Honduras

MPC Popular Christian movement (Movimiento Popular Cristiano), Bolivia

MPC Colorado Popular movement (Movimiento Popular Colorado), Paraguay

MPD Dominican Popular movement (Movimiento Popular Dominicana), Dominican Republic

MPD Popular Democratic movement (Movimiento Popular Democrático), Ecuador

MPN Neuquén Popular movement (Movimiento Popular Neuquén), Argentina

MPSC Popular Social Christian movement (Movimiento Popular Social Cristiano), El Salvador

MRL Liberal Renovation movement (Movimiento de Renovación Liberal), Paraguay

MRL Liberal Revolutionary movement (Movimiento Revolucionario Liberal), Colombia

MRP Peronist Revolutionary movement (Movimiento Revolucionaria Peronista), Argentina

MRP Popular Radical movement (Movimiento Radical Popular), Argentina

MRP Progressive Republican movement (Movimiento Republicano Progresista), Venezuela

MRR Radical Recuperation movement (Movimiento Radical de Recuperación), Argentina

MRTK-L Tupaj Katari Revolutionary movement—Liberation (Movimiento Revolucionario Tupaj Katari—Liberación), Bolivia

MTR Renovating Labor movement (Movimiento Trabalhista Renovar), Brazil

M-26-7 July 26th movement (Movimiento de Julio 26), Cuba

ORI Integrated Revolutionary organizations (Organizaciones Revolucionarias Integradas), Cuba

ORVE Movement of Venezuelan Organization (Movimiento de Organización Venezolano), Venezuela

PA Anti-Reelectionist party (Partido Anti-Reeleccionista), Mexico

PA Autonomist party (Partido Autonomista), Argentina

PADENA National Democratic party (Partido Demócrata Nacional), Chile

PAISA Salvadoran Authentic Institutional party (Partido Auténtico Institucional Salvadoreño), El Salvador

PALA Labor party (Partido Laborista), Panama

PAN National Action party (Partido de Acción Nacional), Dominican Republic, Mexico

PAN National Autonomist party (Partido Autonomista Nacional), Argentina

PAP Peruvian Aprista party (Partido Aprista Peruana), Peru

PAPO Popular Action party (Partido de Acción Popular), Panama

PAR Renewal Action party (Partido Acción Renovadora), El Salvador

PAR Revolutionary Action party (Partido de Acción Revolucionaria), Guatemala

PARM Authentic Party of the Mexican Revolution (Partido Auténtico de la Revolución Mexicana), Mexico

PAU United Action party (Partido de Acción Unitario), Cuba

PB White party (Partido Blanco), Argentina

PC Civil party (Partido Civil), Peru

PC   Colorado party (Partido Colorado), Paraguay, Uruguay
PC   Conservative party (Partido Conservador), Argentina, Bolivia, Brazil, Chile, Colombia, Ecuador, Venezuela
PCA   Communist party (Partido Comunista), Argentina
PCB   Bolivian Communist party (Partido Comunista Boliviano), Bolivia
PCB   Communist Party of Brazil (Partido Comunista do Brazil), Brazil
PCC   Colombian Communist party (Partido Comunista Colombiano), Colombia
PCC   Cuban Communist party (Partido Comunista de Cuba), Cuba
PCCh   Communist Party of Chile (Partido Comunista de Chile), Chile
PCCS   Social Christian Conservative party (Partido Conservador Cristiano Social), Chile
PCD   Democratic Conservative party (Partido Conservador Democrática), Nicaragua
PCD   Dominican Communist party (Partido Comunista Dominicana), Dominican Republic
PCD   People, Change, and Democracy (Pueblo, Cambio, y Democracia), Ecuador
PC de N   Communist Party of Nicaragua (Partido Comunista de Nicaragua), Nicaragua
PCE   Communist Party of Ecuador (Partido Comunista del Ecuador), Ecuador
PCH   Honduran Communist party (Partido Comunista de Honduras), Honduras
PCM   Mexican Communist party (Partido Comunista de México), Mexico
PCML   Marxist-Leninist Communist party (Partido Comunista Marxista-Leninista), Bolivia
PCN   National Christian party (Partido Cristiano Nacional), Chile
PCN   National Conciliation party (Partido de Conciliación Nacional), El Salvador
PCN   Nicaraguan Conservative party (Partido Conservador Nicaragüense), Nicaragua
PCP   Peruvian Communist party (Partido Comunista Peruana), Peru
PCR   Revolutionary Communist party (Partido Comunista Revolucionaria), Peru
PCS   Salvadoran Communist party (Partido Comunista Salvadoreño), El Salvador
PCS   Social Christian party (Partido Cristiano Social), Bolivia, Ecuador
PCU   Uruguayan Communist party (Partido Comunista Uruguayo), Uruguay
PCV   Venezuelan Communist party (Partido Comunista Venezolano), Venezuela
PD   Democratic party (Partido Demócrata), Brazil, Chile, Costa Rica
PD   Democratic party (Partido Democrático), Ecuador
PD   Dominican party (Partido Dominicana), Dominican Republic
PDC   Christian Democratic party (Partido Demócrata Cristão), Brazil
PDC   Christian Democratic party (Partido Demócrata Cristiano), Argentina, Bolivia, Chile, Costa Rica, Ecuador, El Salvador, Peru, Venezuela
PDC   Christian Democratic party (Partido Democrática Cristiano), Panama
PDCH   Honduran Christian Democratic party (Partido Democrática Cristiano de Honduras), Honduras
PDCN   Democratic Party of National Cooperation (Partido Democrático de Cooperación Nacional), Guatemala
PDCP   Popular Conservative Democratic party (Partido Demócrata Conservador Popular), Argentina
PDL   Liberal Democratic party (Partido Demócrata Liberal), Argentina
PDM   Mexican Democratic party (Partido Democrático Mexicano), Mexico
PDN   National Democratic party (Partido Demócrata Nacional), Dominican Republic, Venezuela
PDS   Democratic Social party (Partido Democrático Social), Brazil

PDT   Democratic Labor party (Partido Democrático Trabalhista), Brazil
PFCRN   Cardenist Front for National Reconstruction (Partido Frente Cardenista de Reconstrucción Nacional), Mexico
PFL   Liberal Front party (Partido Frente Liberal), Brazil
PFR   Revolutionary Febrerista Party (Partido Febrerista Revolucionario), Paraguay
PGT   Guatemalan Labor party (Partido Guatemalteco del Trabajo), Guatemala
PI   Independent party (Partido Independiente), Argentina
PI   Intransigent party (Partido Intransigente), Argentina
PIC   Independent Colored party (Partido Independiente de Color), Cuba
PID   Institutional Democratic party (Partido Institucional Democrático), Guatemala
PIN   Nationalist Left party (Partido de Izquierda Nacionalista), Peru
PINU   National Innovation party (Partido de Innovación Nacional), Honduras
PIR   Party of the Revolutionary Left (Partido de la Izquierda Revolucionario), Bolivia
PJ   Justicialist party (Partido Justicialista), Argentina
PL   Labor party (Partido Laborista), Argentina, Dominican Republic, El Salvador
PL   Liberal party (Partido Liberal), Argentina, Bolivia, Brazil, Chile, Colombia, Ecuador, Paraguay, Venezuela
PL   Liberation party (Partido Liberación), El Salvador
PL   Liberation party (Partido Libertador), Brazil
PLC   Constitutionalist Liberal party (Partido Liberal Constitucionalista), Nicaragua
PLD   Democratic Liberation party (Partido de Liberación Democrático), Dominican Republic
PLH   Honduran Liberal party (Partido Liberal de Honduras), Honduras
PLI   Independent Liberal party (Partido Liberal Independiente), Nicaragua
PLN   Nationalist Liberal party (Partido Liberal Nacionalista), Nicaragua
PLN   National Labor party (Partido Laborista Nacional), Argentina
PLN   National Liberal party (Partido Liberal Nacional), Panama
PLN   National Liberation party (Partido Liberación Nacional), Costa Rica
PLR   Radical Liberal party (Partido Liberal Radical), Ecuador, Paraguay
PLRA   Authentic Radical Liberal party (Partido Liberal Radical Auténtico), Paraguay
PLU   United Liberal party (Partido Liberal Unido), Paraguay
PMDB   Brazilian Democratic Movement party (Partido Movimiento Democrático Brasileiro), Brazil
PMS   Mexican Socialist party (Partido Mexicano Socialista), Mexico
PMT   Mexican Workers party (Partido Mexicano de los Trabajadores), Mexico
PN   Nationalist party (Partido Nacionalista), Bolivia
PN   National party (Partido Nacional), Chile, Dominican Republic, Uruguay
PNA   National Agrarian party (Partido Nacional Agrarista), Mexico
PNC   National Cooperatist party (Partido Nacional Cooperatista), Mexico
PND   National Democratic party (Partido Democrático Nacional), Dominican Republic
PNH   Honduran National party (Partido Nacional de Honduras), Honduras
PNI   National Independent party (Partido Nacional Independiente), Costa Rica
PNL   National Labor party (Partido Nacional Laborista), Mexico
PNP   Nationalist People's party (Partido Nacionalista Popular), Panama
PNR   National Renewal party (Partido Nacional Renovador), Guatemala
PNR   National Revolutionary party (Partido Nacional Revolucionario), Mexico, Panama
PNR   Revolutionary Nationalist party (Partido Nacional Revolucionario), Ecuador

PNV Velasquista National party (Partido Nacional Velasquista), Ecuador
POP Popular Orientation party (Partido de Orientación Popular), El Salvador
POR Revolutionary Workers party (Partido de Obreros Revolucionarios), Bolivia
PP Panamanian party (Partido Panameñista), Panama
PP People's party (Partido del Pueblo), Guatemala, Peru
PP Peronist party (Partido Peronista), Argentina
PP Popular party (Partido Popular), Brazil, Cuba
PP Populist party (Partido Populista), Argentina
PP Progressive party (Partido Progresista), Brazil, Dominican Republic, Ecuador
PPA Authentic Panamanian party (Partido Panameñista Auténtico), Panama
PPC Costa Rican People's party (Partido del Pueblo Costarricense), Costa Rica
PPC Popular Christian party (Partido Popular Cristiano), Peru
PPC Popular Corporative party (Partido Popular Coporativo), Chile
PPCO Orthodox Cuban People's party (Partido del Pueblo Cubano-Ortodoxo), Cuba
PPD Party for Democracy (Partido Para Democracia), Chile
PPF Feminist Peronist party (Partido Peronista Feminino), Argentina
PPP Panamanian People's party (Partido del Pueblo de Panamá), Panama
PPS Popular Socialist party (Partido Popular Socialista), Mexico
PPS Popular Salvadoran party (Partido Popular Salvadoreño), El Salvador
PPSC Popular Social Christian party (Partido Popular Social Cristiano), Nicaragua
PQD Quisqueyán Democratic party (Partido Quisqueyano Democrático), Dominican Republic
PR Radical party (Partido Radical), Chile
PR Reformist party (Partido Reformista), Costa Rica, Dominican Republic
PR Republican party (Partido Republicano), Argentina, Bolivia, Brazil, Costa Rica, Cuba, Dominican Republic, Panama
PR Revolutionary party (Partido Revolucionario), Guatemala
PRA Authentic Revolutionary party (Partido Revolucionario Auténtico), Bolivia
PRC Calderonist Republican party (Partido Republicano Calderonista), Costa Rica
PRC Cuban Revolutionary party (Partido Revolucionario Cubano), Cuba
PRCA Authentic Cuban Revolutionary party (Partido Revolucionario Cubano Auténtico), Cuba
PRD Democratic Renewal party (Partido Renovación Democrática), Costa Rica
PRD Democratic Revolutionary party (Partido Revolucionario Democrática), Panama
PRD Doctrinal Radical party (Partido Radical Doctrinario), Chile
PRD Dominican Revolutionary party (Partido Revolucionario Dominicana), Dominican Republic
PRE Ecuadoran Roldosista party (Partido Roldosista Ecuadoreano), Ecuador
PREN Republican Party of National Evolution (Partido Republicano de Evolución Nacional), El Salvador
PRF Federal Republican party (Partido Republicano Federal), Brazil
PRG Genuine Republican party (Partido Republicano Genuino), Bolivia
PRG Party of the Guatemalan Revolution (Partido de la Revolución Guatemalteca), Guatemala
PRI Institutional Revolutionary party (Partido Revolucionario Institucional), Mexico
PRIN Revolutionary Party of National Integration (Partido Revolucionario de Integración Nacionalista), Venezuela

PRIN   Revolutionary Party of the Nationalist Left (Partido Revolucionario de Izquierda Nacionalista), Bolivia

PRM   Party of the Mexican Revolution (Partido de la Revolución Mexicana), Mexico

PRN   National Renovation party (Partido de Renovación Nacional), Chile, Guatemala

PRN   National Republican party (Partido Republicano Nacional), Costa Rica

PRN   National Revolutionary party (Partido Revolucionario Nacional), Venezuela

PRO   Workers Revolutionary party (Partido Revolucionario Obrero), Argentina

PRP   Popular Representation party (Partido de Representacão Popular), Brazil

PRP   Progressive Republican party (Partido Republicano Progresivo), Venezuela

PRS   Socialist Republican party (Partido Republicano Socialista), Bolivia

PRSC   Christian Social Revolutionary party (Partido Revolucionario Social Cristiano), Dominican Republic

PRT   Rural Labor party (Partido Rural Trabalhista), Brazil

PRT   Workers Revolutionary party (Partido Revolucionario de los Trabajadores), Argentina, Mexico, Panama, Peru

PRUD   Revolutionary Party of Democratic Unification (Partido Revolucionario de Unificación Democrática), El Salvador

PRUN   Revolutionary Party of National Union (Partido Revolucionario de Unión Nacional), Guatemala

PS   Socialist party (Partido Socialista), Bolivia, Brazil, Chile, Uruguay

PSA   Agrarian Socialist party (Partido Socialista Agraria), Venezuela

PSA   Argentine Socialist party (Partido Socialista Argentino), Argentina

PSB   Brazilian Socialist party (Partido Socialista Brasileiro)

PSC   Social Christian party (Partido Social Cristiano), Bolivia, Ecuador

PSCN   Nicaraguan Social Christian party (Partido Social Cristiano Nicaragüense), Nicaragua

PSD   Democratic Socialist party (Partido Socialista Democrático), Argentina, Guatemala, Venezuela

PSD   Social Democratic party (Partido Social Demócrata), El Salvador

PSD   Social Democratic party (Partido Social Democrática), Bolivia, Brazil, El Salvador, Nicaragua

PSDC   Christian Democratic Social party (Partido Social Demócrata Cristiano), Paraguay

PSE   Ecuadoran Socialist party (Partido Socialista Ecuadoreano), Ecuador

PSE   State Socialist party (Partido Socialista del Estado), Bolivia

PSI   Independent Socialist party (Partido Socialista Independiente), Bolivia

PSI   International Socialist party (Partido Socialista Internacional), Argentina

PSN   Nicaraguan Socialist party (Partido Socialista Nicaragüense), Nicaragua

PSO   Socialist Labor party (Partido Socialista Obrero), Argentina

PSOB   Bolivian Socialist Labor party (Partido Socialista de Obreros Bolivianos), Bolivia

PS-1, -2   Socialist party—One, —Two (Partido Socialista—Uno, —Dos), Bolivia

PSP   Popular Socialist party (Partido Socialista Popular), Chile, Cuba, Dominican Republic

PSP   Social Progressive party (Partido Social Progresista), Brazil

PSR   Revolutionary Socialist party (Partido Socialista Revolucionario), Brazil, Ecuador, Peru

PST   Socialist Workers party (Partido Socialista de los Trabajadores), Mexico, Panama

PST   Social Labor party (Partido Social Trabalhista), Brazil
PST   Socialist Workers party (Partido Socialista Trabajadora), Venezuela
PSU   United Socialist party (Partido Socialista Unido), Bolivia
PSUM   Unified Socialist Party of Mexico (Partido Socialista Unificado de México), Mexico
PSV   Venezuelan Socialist party (Partido Socialista Venezolano), Venezuela
PT   Labor party (Partido Trabalhista), Brazil
PT   Trujillo party (Partido Trujillista), Dominican Republic
PT   Workers' party (Partido dos Trabalhadores), Brazil
PTB   Brazilian Labor party (Partido Trabalhista Brasileiro), Brazil
PTN   National Labor party (Partido Trabalhista Nacional), Brazil
PTP   Progress and Work party (Partido del Trabajo y Progeso), Argentina
PTR   Renovating Labor party (Partido Trabalhista Renovador), Brazil
PTR   Republican Labor party (Partido Trabalhista Republicano), Brazil
PTR   Rural Labor party (Partido Trabalhista Rural), Brazil
PTS   Social Labor party (Partido Trabalhista Social), Brazil
PU   United People (Pueblo Unido), Costa Rica
PUA   Anti-Communist Unification party (Partido de Unificación Anticomunista), Guatemala
PUC   Catholic Union party (Partido Unión Católica), Costa Rica
PUC   Civic Union party (Partido Unión Cívica), Uruguay
PUCR   Radical Civic Union party (Partido Unión Cívica Radical), Argentina
PUD   Democratic Union party (Partido Unión Democrática), El Salvador
PUM   Unified Mariateguista party (Partido Unificado Mariatequista), Peru
PUN   National Union party (Partido de Unión Nacional), Costa Rica
PUN   National Unity party (Partido de Unidad Nacional), Honduras
PUP   Popular Union party (Partido Unión Popular), Costa Rica
PUP   Provincial Union party (Partido Unión Provincial), Argentina
PURA   Authentic Republican Union party (Partido Unión Republicana Auténtica), Costa Rica
PURS   Republican Socialist Union party (Partido de Unión Republicano Socialista), Bolivia
PURS   United Party of the Socialist Revolution (Partido Unido de la Revolución Socialista), Cuba
PUSC   Social Christian Unity party (Partido Unidad Social Cristiana), Costa Rica
PVP   Popular Vanguard party (Partido Vanguardia Popular), Costa Rica

SINAMOS   National System to Support Social Mobilization (Sistema Nacional de Apoyo a la Movilización Social), Peru

TB   Three Flags (Tres Banderas), Argentina

UC   Civic Union (Unión Cívica), Argentina
UC   Conservative Union (Unión Conservadora), Argentina
UCD   Center Democratic Union (Unión del Centro Democrático), Argentina
UCJ   Youth Civic Union (Unión Cívica de Juventud), Argentina
UCN   National Center Union (Unión del Centro Nacional), Guatemala
UCN   National Civic Union (Unión Cívica Nacional), Dominican Republic
UCR   Radical Civic Union (Unión Cívica Radical), Argentina
UCRB   Blocking Radical Civic Union (Unión Cívica Radical Bloquista), Argentina

UCR-CR   Renovating Cross of the Radical Civic Union (Unión Cívica Radical— Cruzada Renovadora), Argentina

UCRI   Intransigent Radical Civic Union (Unión Cívica Radical Intransigente), Argentina

UCRP   Popular Radical Civic Union (Unión Cívica Radical Popular), Argentina

UCRR   Renovating Radical Civic Union (Unión Cívica Radical Renaovadora), Argentina

UDB   Brazilian Democratic Union (União Democrática Brasileira), Brazil

UDC   Christian Democratic Union (Unión Democrático Cristiano), Ecuador

UDELPA   Union of the Argentine People (Unión del Pueblo Argentino), Argentina

UDN   National Democratic Union (União Democrática Nacional), Brazil

UDN   Nationalist Democratic Union (Unión Democrática Nacionalista), El Salvador

UDP   Democratic Popular Union (Unión Democrático Popular), Ecuador

UN   National Unification (Unificación Nacional), Costa Rica

UNADE   National Democratic Union (Unión Nacional Democrática), Panama

UNE   National Student Union (Unión Nacional Estudiantil), Venezuela

Unidad   Unity (Unidad), Costa Rica

UNIR   Union of the Revolutionary Left (Unión de Izquierda Revolucionaria), Peru

UNO   National Odriist Union (Unión Nacional Odriista), Peru

UNO   National Opposition Union (Unión Nacional Opositora), Colombia, El Salvador

UNO   Organized Nationalist Unity (Unidad Nacionalista Organizada), Guatemala

UNR   Republican National Union (Unión Nacional Republicano), Venezuela

UNS   National Union Against Anarchy (Unión Nacional Sinarquista), Mexico

UP   Patriotic Union (Unión Patriótica), Colombia

UP   Popular Union (Unión Popular), Argentina, El Salvador

UP   Popular Unity (Unidad Popular), Chile

UP   Provincial Union (Unión Provincial), Argentina

UPD   Union of Democratic parties (Unión de Partidos Democráticos), El Salvador

UR   Revolutionary Union (Unión Revolucionaria), Peru

URD   Democratic Republican Union (Unión Republicano Democrático), Venezuela

URNG   Guatemalan National Revolutionary Union (Unión Revolucionaria National Guatemalteca), Guatemala

VPN   National Popular Vanguard (Vanguardia Popular Nacional), Venezuela

VRS   Socialist Revolutionary Vanguard (Vanguardia Revolucionario Socialista), Ecuador

Index